SCEPTRE

Gielgud on Gielgud

John Gielgud

SCEPTRE

Copyright © 1972, 1974, 1987, 1989 The Estate of John Gielgud

Early Stages first published in Great Britain in 1939 by Macmillan and Co. Ltd.
First published in a revised edition in 1987 by Hodder and Stoughton Ltd.

Backward Glances first published in Great Britain in 1989 by Hodder and Stoughton Ltd.
Parts of the book were first published in Great Britain in 1972
as *Distinguished Company* by Heinemann Educational Books Ltd.

This edition first published in Great Britain in 2000
by Hodder and Stoughton
A division of Hodder Headline

The right of John Gielgud to be identified as the
Author of the Work has been asserted by him in accordance
with the Copyright, Designs and Patents Act 1988.

10 9 8 7 6 5 4 3 2 1

A CIP catalogue record for this title
is available from the British Library.

ISBN 0 340 77089 9

Typeset by Hewer Text Ltd, Edinburgh
Printed and bound in Great Britain by
Mackays of Chatham PLC, Chatham, Kent

Hodder and Stoughton
A division of Hodder Headline
338 Euston Road
London NW1 3BH

Richard II, Old Vic, 1929
Lino-cut by Pauline Logan

Contents

BACKWARD GLANCES

List of Illustrations

Early Stages

My experiences convinced me that the actor must imagine first and observe afterwards. It is no good observing life and bringing the result to the stage without a definite idea. The idea must come first, the realism afterwards.

ELLEN TERRY
The Story of my Life

An actor hearing an author read a play in which he is to impersonate a character ought never to be told in advance the part which is to be assigned to him, as otherwise he only pays languid attention to everything that is not his part, and the ideas of the author escape him. He forgets too often that he is not himself the keyboard but that he forms part of the general harmony.

SARAH BERNHARDT
The Art of the Theatre

Foreword

This book was first published by Macmillan as long ago as 1939. It was republished by the Falcon Press in 1948, but has been out of print for many years. Since then I have written three further books, *Stage Directions, Distinguished Company*, and *An Actor and his Time* and a biography of me by Ronald Hayman was published in 1971. A further biography by Gyles Brandreth, *A Celebration* was published three years ago, in 1984.

This new edition of *Early Stages* is ostensibly the same as the 1939 edition except for a few minor cuts and revisions. The impetus which originally gave me the idea of writing this book was my wish to describe the Terry family (my relations on my mother's side) while the impact of their remarkable personalities was still comparatively fresh in my memory, though none of them were still alive by 1936, the year in which I started work on the book. These passages, I hope, may still stand as something of my own individual record of their remarkable charm and talents.

In this new edition I have added four short excerpts of mine which I wrote for another book: Hallam Fordham's 'Photobiography' of me, published by John Lehmann in 1952 and now out of print. The first of these excerpts I have included as a Preface — and the others as a Coda. These bring my story another thirteen years forward and seem to me to follow smoothly on the original narrative.

1987   JOHN GIELGUD

Acknowledgments

I am greatly indebted to Phyllis Hartnoll and Alan Dent who gave me such invaluable help with the first edition of this book. I am also grateful to Alan Dent for compiling the index. [1987 edition]

Preface

The expression 'Let's go to a show' is currently used nowadays to refer to all forms of entertainment including the living theatre. This expression would have horrified my relations, the players of a former generation, who always spoke of the theatre as their 'work', and of the 'play' or the 'piece' in which they were appearing. They also liked to mention that they had been offered (or had accepted) an 'engagement'. Yet it is the 'show' that has always appealed to me in the theatre, and I have never been able to look at a play from a purely literary point of view, or care very greatly for its intellectual or philosophical contribution, unless its theatrical effectiveness has appealed to me first.

I was born into the purple of the Terry family (though my parents were neither of them at any time upon the stage), so it was natural, I suppose, that the theatre should have attracted me at an early age. It appealed to my eyes first, soon it caught at my heart, and lastly its magic reached my ear. Colour, romance, and passion – suspense, action, splendour and emotional self-indulgence – all these I longed for and revelled in from my youngest days of theatregoing. The writing of a play meant little to me, and the art of acting I took for granted.

Consequently it was many years before I began to understand anything of the selective control and technical skill needed by an actor. I thought acting was an imitation of life, that emotion had only to be felt in order to be expressed upon the stage. The art of diction, timing, rapport with other actors, pace, clarity, style, the means of reproducing a part continually over a number of performances – of all this I was entirely ignorant. I found it very hard, as a beginner, to concentrate on my own small part and work at it doggedly in order to perfect it. I was often more interested in the other characters than in the role I played myself. As soon as I began to think how *I* must walk and speak and act I was paralysed by self-consciousness and affectation.

I did not know then that my real ambition was not to act but to direct. I think I began to suspect it a little when I worked with Komisarjevsky, after I had been an actor for three or four fumbling years. It was his influence that set my feet, for the first time, on the right track in my attitude towards my work. Acting in Chekhov under his direction, I began to realize how a part should be lived from within, and how certain significant characteristics from that life should be selected in order to illuminate the character in the particular situations demanded by the author. From him I learnt, too, the essence of musical form with which all good acting and direction must be concerned – the pace and rhythm, tune and shape of scenes and speeches, as well as the art and force of pause, crescendo, and climax.

Ambitious as I was from the first to see my name outside a West End theatre, I was, as it turned out later, fortunate in being considered, as a young actor, to be highbrow and precociously unreliable. I was not sufficiently handsome to be immediately eligible for the juvenile leads who decorated many of the fashionable plays of the twenties, swinging their tennis racquets in open-necked shirts and immaculate white flannels. My only experiment of this kind (in the immortal *Charley's Aunt*) was a conspicuous failure, and I was not to attempt a similar part (Inigo Jollifant in *The Good Companions*) until nine years later, when I was a comparatively seasoned veteran and had played both Hamlet and King Lear.

J. B. Faggan, Nigel Playfair, Barry Jackson and Komisarjevsky were the first to show an interest in my early amateurish efforts at self-expression. They developed my taste by engaging me to act in fine plays with many gifted players. I was observant and industrious, though also vain and affected.

It was a good time for experimental work, done modestly and cheaply. Classical revivals were out of fashion. The actor managers' reign was over. The London theatre was recovering slowly from the confusion of the 1914–18 war. Nöel Coward was writing his first play. Basil Dean's productions at the St. Martin's were the most ambitious contribution to the new era. The other West End theatres were mostly filled with light comedies, farces and melodramas, many of them, even in those far-off days, imported from America.

Barrie, Galsworthy and Pinero were almost at the end of their long and successful careers, though Maugham and Shaw were still to write several of their best plays.

The most popular stars of the period were probably Gerald du Maurier, Henry Ainely, Marie Tempest, Gladys Cooper and Matheson Lang, the last-named (with his costume and melo-dramas) carrying on the romantic tradition of Fred Terry and Martin Harvey, both of whom only appeared occasionally in London but still toured the provinces successfully. Ellen Terry had made her last professional appearance at the Lyric as the Nurse in Doris Keane's *Romeo and Juliet* in 1919, and Bernhardt and Duse were about to make their farewell visits to London under the banner of C. B. Cochran (who also presented the Guitrys – with Yvonne Printemps, and Reinhardt's great spec-tacles *The Miracle* and *Sumurûn* at Olympia and the Coliseum). Karsavina was still appearing with the Russian Ballet of Diaghilev at the old Alhambra. Sybil Thorndike was acting in Grand Guignol, and was not to play *Saint Joan* until 1924.

Players still took curtain calls after every act of a play (even if they had just performed a death scene), and understudies seemed to appear with great frequency in leading parts, especially at matinées. This was lucky for the understudies (and I have always boasted that I never understudied a leading part in my young days without getting an opportunity to play it), but it was less agreeable for the public: I well remember my baffled rage as a boy, when, after three or four hours' queueing for the pit during my holidays from school, the slip fluttering from the programme told of the absence of the star whom I most desired to see.

As a beginner my career was uneven and seemed to lead in no particularly definite direction. I was tall, mannered, highly strung. I spoke and moved jerkily, my emotions were sincere but undisciplined, I had some gift for character, some feeling for poetry, some idea of timing in comedy, yet my sense of humour was strictly limited by a youthful self-importance and terror of being ridiculed. I longed for encouragement and popularity, and count myself fortunate now (though at the time I resented it bitterly) that I had candid friends who laughed at my obsession with myself and the theatre, and made fun of my mannerisms and vanities at a time when a crowd of sycophantic admirers might have encouraged me to a fatal indulgence in my worst faults. Several times in these early years I seemed to be bound for a certain success in London – each time some chance intervened to disappoint me and I was forced to make another start on a slightly less ambitious scale. When I finally decided to go to the Old Vic in 1929 I had already been a leading man (of a sort) in the West End for three years, but the haphazard mixture of parts which had come my way made me feel that I was chosen at random and that no manager or director cared particularly whether or not he engaged me, and it depressed me, even then, to be drawn out of a hat, as it were, from a crowd of other competing players, for a juvenile part of no particular quality, even though the living this offered me was a fairly good one. The special performances in which I had appeared for the Sunday societies, my work at Barnes with Komisarjevsky and at the Regent with Playfair, had given me greater artistic satisfaction than my run of over a year in Basil Dean's *Constant Nymph* with a star cast in the West End, and I vaguely felt that in Shakespeare I might somehow satisfy some of my ambitions, and develop such latent abilities as I believed were lurking in me, if only I could find a way of expressing them successfully.

Chapter 1

1904–12

Shortly before I was born my parents moved into a new house.

Mother, with her usual care as a housewife, insisted on sitting in the hall to watch the furniture being unloaded from the vans. Somebody suggested that the cradle ought to be brought in first, as it was obvious that it might be needed at any moment. I suppose this was my first attempt at working up an entrance, as we say on the stage.

The new house was tall and thin and semi-detached. The square in which it stood was most confusingly numbered and the houses all looked alike, so we were grateful for the one original feature ours possessed. We used to shout to the cabdrivers who tried to take us the wrong way, 'No, no. Number 7. In the Main road. The house with the blue window-boxes'.

There was stained-glass in the hall, and an enormous basement below, to which we sometimes penetrated, clattering down the wooden stairs to stir the Christmas puddings in the kitchen or watch Mother sorting large piles of linen in the servants' hall.

Our nurseries were upstairs on the third floor, with a gate on the landing and wire-netting to prevent us from tumbling over the banisters – one of my recurring nightmares when I was little.

The house was very draughty, and there was never enough hot water for baths, but I loved every inch of it, and, perhaps because *The Cherry Orchard* had in the meantime become one of my favourite plays, I felt quite a Chekhovian regret when I came to leave it for ever, some twenty-five years later. (It has since been converted into flats.)

I have two elder brothers, and one sister, three years younger than myself. I can remember seeing her in one of those wooden pens where very young children are put just before they can walk, and solemnly shaking hands with her over the top. I can also dimly recall my nurse washing herself as she got up in the night nursery, before we were supposed to be awake, and wondering at her many petticoats and the elaborate way she did her hair. She used to wear filigree silver belts, lace blouses with ribs in the neck and a watch on a silver bow. I remember the pain of having appendicitis, and being operated on in the day nursery in a great hurry, and walking to my first kindergarten school with my father. He used to madden me by crossing the streets at exactly the same kerbstone every morning. I did not greatly care for the kindergarten, it appears. On the first day I sat down in the middle of the room and burst into tears. 'But, darling, this isn't school. It is only play', someone said, at which I cried all the more and proclaimed loudly, 'I want to go to a real school, like my brothers'.

Our name is Lithuanian — not Scottish, as many people imagine. It lends itself to an amazing variety of mispronunciations and strange spellings. (Mother once had a letter addressed to Mrs Gradgrind.) Everyone told me I ought to change it when I first went on the stage but I was very obstinate on the subject. My father's grandfather, another John Gielgud, who had fought with the Polish cavalry, left his native country after the insurrection of 1831, when his brother, General Anthony Gielgud, was killed and the family estates were confiscated. Father's parents were both Polish, but my grandfather was born in England. He worked at the War Office for some years, and was Foreign Correspondent to a number of newspapers.

I feel that I ought to apologize for this rather scrappy information about my Polish ancestors. I have never been able to follow the various ramifications of father's family, and my mother's theatrical relations, the Terrys, always had the stronger hold upon my interest. I gather that the Gielguds were patriots, with more enthusiasm than competence; but I was very much interested to hear that my father's grandmother had been a very well-known Polish actress, Madame Aszperger. I believe that a bust of her still stands in the foyer of the Opera House at Lvov. My father, when he was a little boy, was sometimes sent to stay with her in her flat, which was over the theatre, and on one occasion, when he had been naughty, she took him out of bed and put him into one of the boxes to watch the performance. I was not surprised to hear that this treatment restored him to good behaviour immediately.

Father's parents were not well-off, but they were charming and cultured and knew many of the artistic and literary celebrities of the day. Among these were the Arthur Lewises and their four daughters, of whom my mother was the eldest. Arthur Lewis was a rich man who loved entertaining. He was one of the directors of Lewis and Allenby, a well-known and fashionable haberdasher's shop in Conduit Street. He was also an enthusiastic amateur painter and often exhibited at the Royal Academy. He owned a beautiful house on Campden Hill, called Moray Lodge, where he gave parties and organized a mildly Bohemian Glee Club called 'the Moray Minstrels'. At Moray Lodge you could wander in the garden, sniff the hay, and perhaps meet a cow which the Lewises kept for fresh milk for the children. Such was the blessed rusticity of Kensington in the eighties. You might also see Arthur Lewis at his easel, and his wife and daughters, wearing bustles, playing lawn-tennis or sitting under the trees. There were horses and grooms, dog-carts and a conservatory, and a Highland cottage called *Divach* near Inverness, where the family went for summer holidays.

At Moray Lodge, and in Scotland too, there were parties, picnics, governesses, children, distinguished visitors, and all the leisured comfort of late Victorian family life, made more exciting in this particular family by a (strictly proper) link with the arts and the theatre, for Kate Terry, the eldest sister of the family to which Ellen, Marion, and Fred belonged, had married Arthur Lewis in 1867.

Her four daughters, though they adored their father, were all proud to use their mother's name as well, and the two who did not marry, and the third, who kept her maiden name for the stage, called themselves Terry-Lewis. Grandmother Kate had made the name of Terry famous long before Ellen first appeared. In the short time that she was on the stage she was the rage of London and Manchester, leading lady to Henry Neville, Ophelia to Fechter. She played Juliet, Beatrice, Cordelia, Portia and other Shakespearean heroines, besides the heroines of many plays by authors of her own day. As a child she had been praised by no less a person than Charles Dickens, in a letter that is still treasured by the family, for her performance as Prince Arthur in *King John* with the Charles Keans, and had appeared in most of their famous Shakespearean productions at the Princess's Theatre in Oxford Street. While little Ellen was making her début in the children's parts, acting Mamilius and Puck, Kate was playing leading parts as Ariel and Cordelia. The sisters must have studied together a great deal during these early years, and Kate's salary paid for the education of most of her younger brothers and sisters.

When she married Arthur Lewis, Grandmother was still in her early twenties, but in 1867 she decided to leave the stage. Her farewell performances as Juliet, first in Manchester, then in London at the Adelphi, were great nights in theatrical history. After her wedding she was strong-minded enough to put the thought of acting completely from her, in order to concentrate on the duties of a wife and mother. Kate Terry retired, but many years later in the 1890s, when her youngest daughter, Mabel Terry-Lewis, was to make her début as an actress, her return to the stage was announced. The play was *The Master* and it was produced under the management of John Hare. It was not a success, and I believe my grandmother had a very poor part, but Bernard Shaw, in one of his brilliant notices in the *Saturday Review*, describes her performance vividly. He writes of her coming on as a modest, middle-aged lady, determined to show the audience that she was only there to encourage and help her daughter's first appearance. Then suddenly she seemed unable to help herself, twenty years fell from her in a flash, and she was revealed as the accomplished actress who had forgotten nothing of the mysteries of her craft.

Kate Terry was something of a martinet where her household and children were concerned. The interview between her and my father, when he called at Moray Lodge to ask the hand of her eldest daughter, was an alarming occasion, slightly mitigated by the gentle charm of Arthur Lewis. But all was well in the end, and stately approval was given to the marriage. This was in 1893. Not many years afterwards Arthur Lewis lost his money and had to give up his beautiful houses. He died while I was a child, to the great regret of everyone who loved him, and by the time I was aware of my grandmother, she was a gay but slightly formidable old lady with a beautiful voice, a fine expressive face, and the Terry nose and mouth. She lived at the far end of the Cromwell Road, which I detested for its dreariness as we walked along it to visit her. Fortunately, we were sure of finding considerable amusement and fascinating company when we arrived. Grandmother's house was small and slightly sinister. There were masses of pictures on the walls, photographs and sculpture everywhere, and an ostrich egg hung in a net in the library window. Grandmother demanded that her many possessions should be scrupulously dusted and kept in order, and the servants were always giving notice. On the ground floor, the sitting-room had sliding doors which led into the dining-room, and when I saw the set for the fourth act of *The Seagull* at the New Theatre in 1935, that room suddenly came back to me, with Grandmother playing Miss Milligan and laughing good-naturedly at the gossip of a very loud-voiced old American lady who was her paying guest. I have always regretted that I was too young to talk much about the theatre to Kate Terry. What thrilling stories she might have told me of the Charles Kean days, with their processions and tableaux and flying ballets and sumptuous archaeological scenic effects. I cannot remember now what I did talk to Grandmother about, but she used to take me to many of my early theatres.

The first play I ever saw was *Peter Pan*, when I was seven. My parents caused me agonies by arriving late. Even now, I cannot bear to miss the beginning of a play. I still love to see the curtain glow as the footlights come up, and to hear the first notes of the orchestra – always provided there is an orchestra. Once, during the First World War, when I was about thirteen years old, my brother came home on leave, and we had a big party at the Gobelins Restaurant, which was fashionable then, for lunch and a matinée of *The Bing Boys on Broadway*. I dismayed the party by making a scene when I saw from the clock that we were twenty minutes late for the performance. When I went to the theatre with Grandmother we nearly always sat in a box, and I would see the principals specially bowing to her when they took their calls. The management would send us tea in the interval, and often we would go round behind and meet the leading actors in their dressing-rooms. Grandmother was a wonderful audience. She laughed and cried whole-heartedly in the theatre, and I naturally did the same. Even today I still weep so easily at a play that I am sometimes ashamed of myself. The Terrys all have the same weakness, on and off the stage. 'Weak lachrymal glands, my dear', said a famous specialist to my mother, who was parti-cularly afflicted in this way. This capacity for crying easily is sometimes useful to me as an actor, and the sight of real tears always impresses those in an audience who are sitting close enough to see them. But on some nights the tears refuse to come, and then I feel I am not giving my best at that particular performance. Fortunately, however, the effect is more impor-tant than the tears themselves, which actually convince the actor more than the audience. I remember being much impressed by hearing my cousin, Phyllis Neilson-Terry, say one night, standing in the wings before she went on for an emotional scene, 'Shall I give them real tears to-night?' Although the impulse may be a natural one, crying on the stage is quite a technical feat. One learns to cry with one's eyes, but not, as in real life, to choke or run at the nose. Ellen Terry says in her book 'My real tears on the stage astonished some people, and have been the envy of others, but they have often been a hindrance to me. I have had to *work* to restrain them.'

Sometimes Grandmother would take me to see Fred, Marion and Ellen act. How excited I used to be when I was taken to a theatre where one of them was appearing! I saw Marion in a play called *Wonderful James*. She played the wife of a penniless adventurer who posed as a wealthy man, and in the first act they came together to some business-office. Marion swept in, very dignified, in a grey velvet cloak with ospreys in her hat. Biscuits and port were brought and she went on talking grandly, furtively dropping biscuits into her hand-bag all the time. Later in the play she had a very funny scene in which she sat working a sewing-machine, with an overall over her smart dress, murmuring sadly, 'Nothing in the larder but half a chicken and a bit of tinned tongue!' I saw her play Mrs Higgins in Shaw's *Pygmalion* with Mrs Patrick Campbell, in *Reparation* at the St. James's with Henry Ainley, and, last of all, at the Globe in Somerset Maugham's *Our Betters*. In private life she was regal and kind, with a low voice and very beautiful diction. She had a most charming figure when she was younger, and waltzed with infinite grace. She always spoke of a job as 'an engagement' and told me two things I have never forgotten: 'Never say your salary is so-and-so; let them make you an offer first and then tell them, if necessary, what you had in your last engagement', and 'You must never say it is a bad audience. It is your business to make it a good one.' She was an odd woman in many ways. She had an amazing gift for enslaving people, friends or servants, making them happy to fetch and carry for her, in spite of the fact that she was rather autocratic and exacting in her demands; and she was extremely secretive about her personal life and the state of her finances. On one occasion, I believe, she walked out of Moray Lodge in a rage because Arthur Lewis had looked at her pass-book.

It is sad that Marion has been so soon forgotten. Many people of her time thought her a better actress than her more famous sister. This generation seems scarcely to have heard of her, but there is little doubt that she shared with Mrs Kendal the distinction of being one of the finest comédiennes of her time. Also, like Dame Madge, she was equally good in emotional or sentimental parts. She seldom appeared in Shakespeare but she played occasionally for Ellen at the Lyceum when the latter was ill, and acted some of her parts in provincial tours. My father remembered a wonderful performance she once gave of Rosalind at Stratford-on-Avon. In *Lady Windermere's Fan* she created a precedent by playing an adventuress, a daring departure from her usual run of parts, and it was one of her greatest successes. Years later, something of the same kind was to happen when Lilian Braithwaite played in *The Vortex*. It is always interesting for an audience to see an actress of sympathetic parts playing a 'woman with a past'. As Mrs Erlynne, Marion, with her brown hair powdered with bronze dust, made an enormous success and delighted Wilde, the author of the play, as well as the public. She played with Wyndham and Alexander, created many of the leading parts in the plays of W.S. Gilbert, and was the original Susan Throssel in Barrie's *Quality Street*, in which she appeared with Seymour Hicks and Ellaline Terriss.

When I saw her towards the end of her career in *Reparation* she had only two short scenes, but her performance was immensely distinguished, and Henry Ainley, with his usual courtesy, would bring her out at the end of the play and kiss her hand before the audience. I remember another example of Ainley's tact and fine manners. The occasion was a not very successful opening performance of *Much Ado about Nothing* in which he had played Benedick, very finely I thought, to Madge Titheradge's Beatrice. When the play was over, he stepped forward, and bowing towards the stage box where Ellen Terry was sitting, half hidden by the curtains, he said, 'We have had the honour of playing before the greatest Beatrice of all time'.

Like Ellen and Fred, Marion had great difficulty with her memory in later years, and her devoted nieces would spend hours helping her to memorize her lines. She was very reluctant to admit her weakness in this direction, and developed a brilliant technique for covering her lapses or mistakes, gazing majestically at the other actors until the prompter came to her rescue.

Florence Terry, another sister, died at an early age. I never knew her. Edith Craig has told me that Florence had had little recognition from biographers, though her talent was also considerable. She played Nerissa to Ellen's Portia, both at the Lyceum and on tour, and the sisters loved acting together in their charming scenes. Florence and Marion were very devoted and were often photographed together.

Though Kate and Marion Terry were sisters, they were actresses too, and I had an amusing glimpse of this when I went one evening in 1919, with my mother this time, to the first night of *Romeo and Juliet* at the Lyric Theatre, when Ellen Terry played the Nurse to Doris Keane's Juliet. Kate and Marion were standing together in the foyer as we passed. They chatted together, and people going in bowed to them, thinking no doubt that the scene was a pretty expression of family affection. But no! It was the Terry blood and not the Terry charm which was at work. They were to enter the auditorium of a theatre. I did not understand why they parted, Kate to enter the stalls by one door and Marion by another. Kate must have hurried, for she entered the right-hand door first. As I walked down the opposite passage to the stalls with my mother I could hear the applause, and we saw Grandmother smiling and bowing as we went to our seats. Then Marion entered, close behind us, and received an ovation from the audience. But I made the mistake of saying to her proudly in the interval, 'Grandmother had a wonderful reception'. Aunt Marion's voice was very gentle as she answered, 'Did she, darling? I expect they thought it was me.'

Fred Terry and his lovely wife, Julia Neilson, were my idols of course. I saw them first together on the stage in *Sweet Nell of Old Drury* and I remember how Julia saw us and threw a dazzling smile in the direction of our box. On another afternoon I was taken down to the Boro' Theatre, Stratford, now, alas, no more, to see *The Scarlet Pimpernel*. After the play I went round to the stage-door. It was a dark foggy evening. Uncle Fred came out on to the step in all the glory of his white satin and lace, and pressed a sovereign into my hand, like some dandified deity from Olympus.

By this time I was deep in dressing up, charades and acting games of all kinds. I was about eight or nine years old. I was not yet stage-struck in the sense of wanting to go on the stage, and I am not conscious of any moment when I suddenly sat up and said 'I am going to be an actor'. But I see now that my Terry instinct to act was pretty strong from the beginning, though I did not recognize it at the time. I was supposed to be delicate when I was a child, and I enjoyed and exaggerated my illnesses, with the special food and added attentions. My mother used to read aloud to me. Scott rather bored me, and I used to be horribly embarrassed by the passages which she rendered in a rather good Scotch accent. But Dickens I loved. We would both be quite overcome with emotion in the sentimental scenes, and by the time we had killed Dora or Sydney Carton we would both be choking and 'too full of woe to speak'!

When I was recovering from some disease or other (jaundice or chicken-pox, I forget which) I developed a passion for painting backcloths and designs in pastel for my toy theatre. The colours, in spite of liberal applications of 'Fixatif', which smelt like peardrops, would blow about all over the room and make chalky smears everywhere. I used to prop my cardboard scenery on the mantelpiece and get up in the middle of the night and turn on the light to look at it. (Already I had the stage illusion that everything looks twice as good by artificial light.) I was furious next morning because the doctor seemed too busy to congratulate me when I drew his attention to my efforts. I was very fond of an audience. I found that I could play the Merry Widow Waltz by ear, and was deeply hurt when, after a triumphant rendering of it for my nurse's benefit she said drily, 'Your bass is wrong, and it isn't written in that key', and sat down and played it correctly herself.

My eldest brother Lewis was a scholar at Eton, and there were three of us upstairs in the nursery, my sister Eleanor, my brother

Val and myself. We began our stage enterprises with a model theatre – an inspiring affair of cream and gold with a red velvet curtain, given me as a birthday present by Mother. We all made up plays and took turns in performing them, standing behind the theatre and moving the leaden figures about with our hands which were plainly seen by the audience. Cardboard figures with wires were too flimsy and difficult to manage, we decided, and in the strangely unquestioning manner of children we accepted the giant's hands moving about in every scene, and simply ignored their existence. Val was responsible for most of the plots and dialogue, and I used to paint the scenery. I had a very strong feeling for space and colour on the stage from the first, and the fascination of scenery, costume and pictorial illusion has never left me. As a child I had no real talent in this direction or I should certainly have become a scenic designer and not an actor at all, but in those early days it was the scenery first and the play afterwards so far as I was concerned.

We were very mercenary in the management of our theatre. Val and I were partners in management, in the manner of Uncle Fred. My sister was 'Lady Jones', a fabulously rich patron of the theatre who financed our brave productions. As a family the Terrys have not a great sense of humour (Ellen always excepted), and we played the theatre game all day long with dreadful seriousness. 'Lady Jones' financed us in a series of alarming plays dealing with our grand Terry relations. In one of these we put Grandmother Kate Terry on the stage, and most of our aunts as well. There was a ship scene, with Grandmother in the throes of seasickness shouting for her deaf maid. We thought this Family Play extremely funny, but unlike our more serious performances – mystery plays, costume melodramas and society triangles, to which we tried to inveigle an audience of parents or servants – it could only be performed in guilty secret.

On the top floor of the house was an attic in which Val and I laid down an intricate model railway system. Here also were Val's toy soldiers. He must have had nearly a thousand of them, and amused himself ceaselessly with battles and manœuvres. We came to a working agreement by which Val helped me with my theatre on condition that I took part in his campaigns upstairs. I fancy that he got the best of the bargain, for he entered into my form of make-believe with enthusiasm, while I was rather bored by his. The most practical use his soldiers had, so far as I could see, was to serve as puppets in my theatre. I used to steal them when he was not looking and convert them to my own use by judicious applications of gold paint. I also used the passengers of a toy station that I had been given. Two ladies in motor veils and red Edwardian dresses did duty for almost every female character and I spent hours transforming them with plasticine into Elizabethans, a sticky and unconvincing process. I used also to invent opportunities for firework displays, and compile scenarios which involved magic thunderstorms or naval reviews with showers of electric sparklers and magnesium flares. Where the requirements of my theatre were concerned I was quite shameless. I robbed the canary of its seed and sand for a convincing 'set' representing a stormy desert, and stole the miniature grand piano out of Eleanor's doll's house for a drawing-room scene.

Not only did we play the soldier game and the theatre game continually, but we kept wonderful notebooks in which we recorded every detail of both games with a wealth of lavish journalistic style. My mother has preserved one of the volumes in which some of our magnificent productions are recorded. The title-page announces grandiloquently, 'The New Mars Theatre, in Trafalgar Square, W1. Erected between April 1912 and March 1913. A list of plays produced between 1913 and 1919. Under the joint management of V. H. and A. J. Gielgud.'[1] It should be noticed that 'Lady Jones', though she certainly did her duty as the principal and frequently the only member of our audience, receives no kind of recognition. The plays have imposing titles: *Lady Fawcett's Ruby* — this has a pleasing ring of Pinero or Wilde — *Kill That Spy*, a war play, of course — and

1 I was christened Arthur John.

Plots in the Harem, probably inspired by *Kismet* and *Chu-Chin-Chow*. The volume is embellished by a photograph of the Mars Theatre, with Val, Eleanor and myself posed in front of it. Val is sitting stiffly in a chair, wearing a straw hat. I am on the ground in less formal headgear, and Eleanor has the uneasy air and ingratiating smile of someone who is there on sufferance – which she probably was.

When we became older, Val was given the nursery for his study and I was allowed to install my paints, books, gramophone and records, and of course the theatre, in the attic. This was to be my own special room until I left home to take a flat for myself. I spent hours up there designing and constructing stage scenery, years after we had outgrown the theatre game. We no longer fought campaigns or made up plays, and I built my sets more solidly with bricks and plasticine, and balanced electric bulbs hanging at the end of wires above the stage, on piles of books, boxes and magazines. Sometimes in the middle of the night, jumping out of bed and creeping upstairs to look again at some marvel I had created earlier in the day, I would trip over the wires in the dark, and everything would collapse with a loud crash and wake the entire household. I felt sure that I was destined to be a stage designer if only I could manage to draw correctly, but my father kept telling me that I would first have to study architecture, and, with my utter incapacity for maths, this prospect filled me with dismay.

One afternoon Uncle Fred had treated me to a terrific luncheon at the Eccentric Club. The lunch had been delicious, but not an unqualified success so far as I was concerned. Over the soup I had rashly enthused over my second cousin, Gordon Craig, the son of Ellen Terry. Fred was somewhat sceptical and I did not then know that he had recently suffered an expensive failure with *Sword and Song*, a play which Craig had decorated (very beautifully) for him. Later, as I ate my pudding, I remarked how much I had admired Moscovitch's[1] performance in *The Great*

1 Maurice Moscovitch had previously had a great success at the Royal Court, under Fagan's direction and management, as Shylock – a vivid performance which I well remember.

Lover. Fred went quite red in the face and told me with some wealth of language what he thought of an actor who made love to a woman on the stage leering up at her suggestively as he kissed her hand. I did not dare to say that this behaviour had seemed to me quite in the spirit of the character in the play. I felt it was time to change the subject, and wondered if I could persuade Uncle Fred to appreciate my talents as a stage designer. I succeeded in taking him home with me, and dragged him up the many flights of stairs to my workroom. Proudly I showed him two of my latest efforts, a sand-strewn desert, and a street for *Twelfth Night* (both inspired by *Chu-Chin-Chow*). The street went up to the back of the stage in rows of uneven steps, with arches and perspectives, shutters, balconies and so on. Uncle Fred gazed in silence, then solemnly shook his head. 'Much too expensive for touring', he said reflectively. 'Too many rostrums, my boy.'

The nicest room in our South Kensington house was the large white drawing-room on the ground floor, which was seldom used except for parties and celebrations. There was a grand piano (on which father's playing sounded much finer than on the upright in the nursery), gold wallpaper and a large painted Chinese screen which I still possess. I was deeply embarrassed when Father pointed out to me that one of the ladies painted on it was 'in the family way'. I think I had never heard that pregnant phrase before. The screen hid the door from the people sitting in the main part of the room, and kept out some of the draught as well. On Christmas Day my various Terry relatives used to come to lunch or tea, and then my stage-struck heart would beat and I was in a state of unmitigated rapture. First, Grandmother, stout and jolly, with a special armchair at table and special pickings from the turkey (the Terry appetite was as unfailing as the Terry charm). Then my mother's three sisters, Janet, Lucy and Mabel. Next to appear would be Marion, making a superb entrance with her gracious smile and beautiful sweeping carriage. After lunch we would hear someone else arriving with a jolly laugh and jingling of coins, and Fred's head and shoulders would loom up over the screen, with Julia behind him in lovely clothes, her arms laden with beautiful and expensive presents.

All of a sudden there would be a hush in the room. An old lady had come in and was finding her way from one group to another, settling at last in a low chair. It was Ellen Terry, bowed and mysterious, under the shadow of a big black straw hat, covered in scarves and shawls, with a large bag holding two or three pairs of spectacles, like a godmother in a fairy tale. She wore a black and grey gown, very cleverly draped on her slim body, too long in front (as she always wore her stage dresses), and bunched up over one arm with wonderful instinctive grace. When her hat and shawls had been taken from her, there were coral combs in her short grey hair and coral beads round her neck. With her lovely turned-up nose and wide mouth, and that husky voice – a 'veiled voice' somebody called it once – and her enchanting smile, no wonder everyone adored her. We children, of course, found her far the most thrilling and lovable of all our exciting aunts and uncles. Even though she was vague and we felt she was not quite sure where she was or who we were, her magic was irresistible. 'Who is this? Who? Jack? Oh, of course, I remember. Well, do you read your Shakespeare? My Ted[1] has written a wonderful book on the theatre. I'll send it to you.' So she did. I have it still – her own copy, scribbled all over with notes and comments. 'You know, I fell down this morning in Charing-Cross Road and I was laughing so much that I could hardly move when the policeman came to help me up. Hullo, old Kate. Hullo, Polly.[2] Who's this? Fred? Where's my bag? My other spectacles are in it. Oh, I have to go on somewhere. I can't remember. Oh yes, Edy Gwynne's. I must be off. I have a nice new flat in St. Martin's Lane, near all the theatres and do you know, the other day who should come in but Jim' (James Carew, her husband). 'Imagine, he is living in the same building. Wasn't it sweet of him to come and see how I was getting along?' And so with much fluttering and kissing and bundling she was gone.

1 Gordon Craig.
2 Marion Terry – a pet name.

Chapter 2

1913–19

Ellen Terry had said, 'Do you read your Shakespeare?' In those days I certainly did not. I read Henty, *The Jungle Books*, most of Harrison Ainsworth, all E. Nesbit, and Clement Scott's notices of the Lyceum productions, Ellen Terry's Memoirs and everything else about the theatre that I could find on the library bookshelves. Also I saved up to buy, or begged people to give me as presents, books with pictures by Beardsley, Kay Nielsen or Dulac. These artists inspired me at different times to make masses of indifferent drawings and stage designs. I was always talking about Gordon Craig too, but I am sure I did not really understand in those days what his books and drawings meant, and was chiefly impressed by the fact that he was my second cousin.

Val used to read history, especially anything about Napoleon and his campaigns, *Raffles, Arsène Lupin* and John Buchan. We both of us discovered Compton Mackenzie and Hugh Walpole about the same time, and devoured all their early books with terrific enthusiasm – but not Shakespeare.

The first Shakespeare play I ever saw was *As You Like It* at the Coronet Theatre, Notting Hill Gate, with Benson and Dorothy Green. This must have been in 1912 or 1913. Of course I only took in the plot and the scenery. There was solid ivy for Orlando to nail on to a very shaky canvas wall in the opening scene, and the terraces of Duke Frederick's garden were ingeniously transformed into forest glades by covering them with autumn leaves, which the actors had to plough through for the rest of the performance. The Doris Keane *Romeo and Juliet* of 1919 was the next Shakespeare play I went to see. I was much older by then and, as if I knew that this play was to be a very important one for me when I grew up, I remember the whole production very vividly. Edith Craig had arranged the thrilling fights. The ball was lovely too, staged very simply in tall curtains, with big Della Robbia swags hanging between the pillars and in a great circular wreath above the centre of the stage. Juliet was in silver lamé. This was not perhaps quite the correct thing, but it looked very grand to me, and Ellen Terry as the Nurse wore a big hat tied under her chin, and a gay yellow and black checked cloak in the street scene. When she forgot her lines she pretended to be deaf, and one of the other characters whispered them in her ear.

Léon Quartermaine, as Mercutio, made an enormous success on the first night. With his usual modesty, he left the theatre after his death scene, and was not to be found when the audience clamoured for him at the end. I thought he gave a beautiful performance, though Fred Terry, who had once been a fine Mercutio himself, disagreed with me. I always seemed to say the wrong thing to Uncle Fred. 'My dear fellow', he said, 'he jeers at Tybalt for being a lisping affected fantastico, but that is exactly the way he himself plays Mercutio!'

There was a very unfortunate arrangement in the bedroom scene in this production. The curtain rose to reveal Juliet lying asleep in a very narrow bed, with Romeo dressing himself on the other side of the room. It was not until he had buckled on his sword that Juliet awoke with a start and leapt out of bed with 'Wilt thou be gone? It is not yet near day'. People in the stalls were shaking their heads, and even I had an inkling that the scene had not begun in a very poetic atmosphere. During the interval I kept remarking in a loud voice, 'Isn't Aunt Nell wonderful?' and my relatives hushed me saying, 'You must never discuss actors aloud in the stalls on a first night', a warning which I have often tried to remember since. In the scene when the Nurse comes to waken Juliet, Ellen Terry played exquisitely, though the audience held its breath when she stumbled on the darkened stage, feeling her way up the steps to draw the curtains at the window.

After the mourners had left the scene she stood by Juliet's bed, folded the girl's hands, and knelt down beside her body as the curtain fell. I shall never forget the absolute simplicity with which she did this.

I suppose it was not a great performance of the Nurse. There was too much of Ellen Terry's own sweetness and personal charm, but now and again there were superb hints of character. 'He that can lay hold of her shall have the chinks' was one, and 'No, truly, sir, not a penny' was another. And in the scene with Romeo and Friar Laurence how perfectly she conveyed the tiredness of the poor old lady, yawning very discreetly when she said, 'O Lord, I could have stayed here all the night, to hear good counsel'. Like all great players she listened beautifully, making the scenes alive for the other characters by the unselfish way she 'gave' to them.

The 'cords' scene, as I remember, was cut altogether. Perhaps Ellen Terry could not learn it, and even without that scene the evening was far too long. In the last act, poor Basil Sydney began to beat on the tomb doors, and the stage hands, supposing the signal had been given to 'strike', began to lift the front cloth, displaying large scurrying boots and bright lights. The curtain hastily descended, but the atmosphere was ruined and the play ended tamely. It was embarrassing to feel that Mercutio and the Nurse had stolen the success of the evening, but Ellen Terry brought Romeo and Juliet before the curtain, linked her arms in theirs, and said with infinite tact and charm, 'I do so hope you will love these young people as much as I do'.

When it was all over we went round behind, and there was a tiny room with masses of flowers, and Aunt Nell, tucked up on a sofa, tired out but still adorably greeting crowds of people, none of whom, I am sure, she recognized at all.

I am a born Cockney, and as soon as I was given a latch-key and allowed to go out alone I used to walk about the London streets all day long, discovering Chelsea and the City churches and Chiswick Mall and Hampton Court. As children we all felt more at home in London than anywhere else. At any rate, we never looked forward half so much to our Easter and summer holidays as we did to the weeks at Christmas, when we stayed at home in London and theatres were the order of the day. For one thing, our parents had no outdoor hobbies. They were rather unusual in not liking games or sports of any kind. They did not play cards or go racing or swim or ride, and so we were never forced to learn to play games ourselves, nor were we ridiculed at home when we were bad at them, as most children are when they are little. When we were older we still invented our own games, which we found easier to excel in, and went on playing these until we were almost grown-up. We could none of us ride or swim, and we were dreadfully bad at cricket and football. I was conceited too, and hating to make a fool of myself. I tried to avoid learning anything that did not come easily to me. We used to go to the seaside at Easter and to the country in August – furnished houses at Littlehampton and Selsey, at Beaconsfield, Chipstead, Berkhamsted and Uckfield. I expect we were extremely lazy, and that other children found us very maddening and superior. Of course, we were also self-conscious about our shortcomings, and hated being shown up. We therefore avoided making friends so far as we could until we went to school. There we had a pretty bad time at first, and no doubt we richly deserved it.

Mother was inclined to spoil me, particularly as I was supposed to be delicate and 'artistic', and Father was a somewhat distant figure who had to be met at the station every evening when we were in the country and accompanied on long walks at week-ends, or to museums, picture galleries and concerts on Sundays when we were in London. He was very alarming when he was angry and very charming at other times. I owe to him such grounding as I possess in music, painting and history, and he never tried to crush my mania for the theatre, which he loved himself but within more modest bounds.

He deplored the extravagance which seemed to be natural to all his children, though I cannot imagine whence we all inherited it, for my mother was ever a most economical and unostentatious person. Father gave us all allowances and latch-keys at an early age, but frowned severely on taxis, theatre seats and expensive restaurants. He always travelled by bus himself (as he did almost until his death, at the age of 88), went to the theatre in the pit, and chose the hard seats above the organ at the Albert Hall, because you could hear there better than anywhere else. After a while Val and I began to look forward to concerts with real enthusiasm, though Eleanor never cared for them very much. All the same, our parents decided for some reason or other that she was to be the musician of the family, and she endured several years' training with various teachers. She has never touched a piano since, while I, who played quite well by ear (which made me lazy in learning from music), was not forced to study as I should have been, and gave up my music lessons as soon as I went to school.

My education began at Hillside, a preparatory school at Godalming, and continued at Westminster School in London. My brothers were both at Hillside before me, and both were head boys. Lewis left for Eton with a scholarship, and afterwards took a Demyship at Magdalen, Oxford. Val and I were rather dejected by his brilliant success, as our parents were constantly reminding us that they hoped we should follow his example at the earliest opportunity.

Val was head boy at Hillside when I arrived there, and I was Gielgud Minor. I took in my surroundings with my usual passion for detail. I believe I could still draw an accurate plan of the house, and the big playing field, with the corrugated iron gymnasium in a corner of it, the cricket pavilion, and the six poplar trees which used to rustle and toss in stormy weather. When Lewis was at the front during the First World War he wrote a poem about some poplar trees, and I was much impressed when it was published in the old green *Westminster Gazette* which Father used to bring home from the City every evening. I always imagined the trees of the poem were those of Hillside, but Mother has assured me since that Lewis was thinking of the poplar trees in France.

Hillside was a ramshackle house, built on a very steep incline. Changing rooms and classrooms had been added to the original structure, and to reach them we had to toil up and down endless flights of wooden stairs, round unexpected corners, and through dark stone passages. The most terrifying corridor led, round several winding turns, to the squash court and the school lavatories. I disliked walking here alone on murky winter afternoons, when the light came fitfully through the corrugated iron roof, casting enormous and appalling shadows, and the cisterns dripped and gurgled in the distance but, it was alarming to meet someone unexpectedly, or to hear footsteps close behind me — worst of all if some humorist jumped out on me as I passed.

In the library I could read the papers. I would rush through my breakfast and dash there to snatch the *Daily Sketch* on the morning following the Theatrical Garden Party, when the centre page would be filled with photographs of the stars — (I can see one now — Nelson Keys as Katharine of Aragon and Arthur Playfair as Henry VIII in a skit on the Tree production in *The Grand Giggle*). On these I would gaze enraptured. The library was a favourite retreat of mine. The only alarming feature of the room was the window seat, which had cupboards running all round it underneath, making a sort of tunnel in which I was sometimes imprisoned by my enemies. Here I would lie, bent double, and half suffocated, while my captors sat on the window seat above me, drumming with their boots on the cupboard doors which barred all chances of escape.

I took pleasure in the poetic melancholy of the winter, which I had never spent in the country before — the foggy, mysterious playing-field, with the high goal-posts wreathed in mist and the ground churned up and caked with frost, echoing to the dull thud of the footballs and the squeal of the referee's whistle as we grunted and panted up and down in our red and black striped jerseys, with our breaths streaming out in white jets in front of us. I reached the extreme pitch of nostalgia on Sunday afternoons, when we walked, two and two, for five miles over the muddy fields, to Compton or Puttenham or the Hog's Back, trudging slowly home again in the twilight past the gates of Charterhouse, with the lights twinkling in the shadowy houses, trees and hedges looming up in the darkness along the steep lanes on either side of us, and church bells ringing sadly in the distance.

Food seems very important in my memories of Hillside – the noisy meals, which the masters carved, the joint which was 'roast on Monday, cold on Tuesday, and hashed on Wednesday',[1] and the rude jokes about the 'skivvies' who served us. Sunday morning with sausages, and the days when there were loathsome parsnips. Then there was 'fruit' in the matron's room in the afternoons, which we were allowed to order once a week ourselves out of our pocket-money – almonds and raisins and tangerines and brazil nuts in the winter, and baskets of raspberries and cherries in the summer. These we would take outdoors and eat slowly, luxuriously, lying out on our rugs under the trees, with grey felt hats pulled over our eyes, gossiping and whispering smutty jokes while we watched a cricket match through a long sunny afternoon. And at the beginning of term there would be a great smuggling of plum cakes and sweets and dates and figs, and 'feasts' in the dormitory after lights out.

I enjoyed my years at Hillside, although I cannot claim to have distinguished myself when I was there. My best school subjects were Divinity and English. I scrambled through Latin and Greek after a fashion, but mathematics defeated me altogether. I tried my hand at carpentry for a little while, and my mother probably cherished a hideous carved box which I proudly presented to her, though I omitted to explain that most of the work had been done by the Carpentry Master, who realized after many weeks of toil that I should never complete my work without some help from him.

I thought I sang rather well. At Sunday services my shrill treble would soar above the other voices during the hymns, as I stood with my head thrown back, hoping to be seen as well as heard.

1 As Lewis Dodd was to say later in *The Constant Nymph*.

My histrionic cravings found another more legitimate outlet. We were encouraged to act in the winter and spring terms, and it was then that I appeared for the first time before an audience. My performance of the Mock Turtle in *Alice* was duly tearful, and I sang 'Soup of the Evening, Beautiful Soup', with increasing volume and shrillness in every verse. I was a bland Humpty-Dumpty and an impassioned Shylock. Another term I played Mark Antony. I remember waiting for my entrance standing on an icy stone conservatory floor shivering in my toga. I warmed up, however, as soon as I began to act, and as my courage grew I must have played with all my might, for I succeeded in reducing the only titled parent to tears and was presented to her afterwards in the headmaster's drawing-room.

Another boy who was with me at Hillside was Ronald Mackenzie, afterwards the brilliant author of *Musical Chairs* and *The Maitlands*. I was not particularly friendly with him when we were at school, but, years afterwards, a line in *The Maitlands* brought Hillside vividly to my mind, when the backward son admitted that all he had learned at school was 'a little Latin and how to swing across the dormitory on the iron girders'. I must explain that at Hillside there were iron girders running across the dormitory which was called 'Cubicles' (though the wooden partitions which had given it its name had disappeared by my time). There were two rows of beds with red rugs on them, and newcomers each term were always initiated by the same ceremony. They had to cross the room, from one row of beds to the other, swinging hand-over-hand on these girders, an alarming ordeal frequently accompanied by the flicking of wet towels and the hurling of sponges.

My talent for games remained at zero, but I somehow managed to get into the Second XI at football. When a notice was put up at the end of the term assessing the merits of each individual member of the team, my name was at the bottom with the remark: 'Gielgud. An opportunist merely.' I have always tried to live up to this.

When I became head of the school, I was, as a matter of

prestige I suppose, appointed scorer for the First XI at cricket. There were enviable privileges attached to this position. On the occasion of 'away' matches, I would be let off morning school and drive by brake to the opposing camp, where I ate an enormous tea and enjoyed the satisfaction of making entries in the scoring book in my small neat handwriting, of which I was inordinately vain.

The First World War began while I was on holiday from Hillside. I was going by train with my mother, Val and Eleanor, to a house my parents had taken at Crowborough for the summer, and I vaguely remember buying newspapers at some junction, and Mother's face as she read the news. Soon after this the headmaster's brother, in whose form I had been a pupil only a term before, was killed, and even in our small school the casualty lists used to be read out every few days.

Lewis went to France with a commission and was badly wounded. He was not expected to live, and my parents were rushed over to see him in hospital. Their reactions were unexpected. My father was very much knocked-out by the strain, and came home exhausted as soon as Lewis was off the danger-list, whereas Mother, whose nerves were usually her greatest weakness, rose to the occasion with amazing calm, and made herself so useful writing letters and doing jobs for the nurses and men that she was allowed, contrary to all precedent, to stay at Le Touquet for eleven weeks, which gave her enormous pride and satisfaction.

Our headmaster went to the front, leaving the school in charge of a Mr Taylor, who wore a W. G. Grace beard, and played in staff matches in a minute cricket cap which looked extremely odd in conjunction with his otherwise dignified appearance. He used to interview us, sitting in a very low creaking basket-chair and wearing ancient leather bedroom slippers, in a funny little study reeking of tobacco and Harris tweed. The walls were hung with scores of photographs of former pupils in little elaborately carved picture-frames, with pipe racks and University shields hanging on the wall above their heads. The later chapters of *Goodbye Mr Chips* reminded me of him forcibly.

On the whole, I was sorry to leave my preparatory school when the time came, and I even regretted the places I had always disliked most, the Charterhouse swimming bath (which I had always hated, with its dreary sort of watery echo), and the stone-cold passages of Hillside, with the steep steps leading from the long dreary corridor where we kept our play-boxes.

I looked at the landmarks on the journey between Godalming and Waterloo for the last time – Guildford station, Brooklands, Carter's seed ground, and the big building near Clapham Junction with the words 'Shakespeare Theatre' painted on it in enormous letters. The sight of that theatre had always cheered me as I went back to school, and I used to wonder excitedly what delights lay concealed behind that grim brick wall.

I had failed to get a scholarship at Eton as Lewis had done. My mother went down with me to Windsor for the examination, but I felt sure that it would be a wasted journey. I suppose I knew that I had not done enough work. I had a bad attack of conscience at the hotel, and sat up half the night searching the dictionary for words I thought I should be asked next day. I cribbed the only correct answer to my maths paper, but even so I was awarded only four marks out of a hundred!

A few months later I tried to get a scholarship at Rugby, where Val was, but failed again, to my secret satisfaction, as the atmosphere of the place sounded, from my brother's description, a great deal too uncomfortable for my luxurious tastes. In the end I went to Westminster.

I managed to win a non-resident scholarship, but I was extremely idle. Drawing was still my obsession, and I spent hours in the Abbey, trying to copy the banners and fanvaulting in a pastel drawing of Henry VII Chapel. But I think that even my love of the Abbey was very much mixed up with my love of the theatre. Only the other day I found a black-edged card which I had persuaded a friendly verger to give me when the wreaths were thrown away after an anniversary commemoration of

Irving's death. On it was written, 'Rosemary for remembrance. E.T.'

When I first went to Westminster I was a boarder. Our nights were frequently disturbed by air raids. When the alarm sounded, we would put overcoats on over our pyjamas, and go down through the cloisters into the Norman Undercroft, one of the oldest vaults in the Abbey. There all the canons and deans would be collected, with their wives and families and servants. The three beautiful daughters of Canon Carnegie, in evening dresses and cloaks, sat on a bench with a white bulldog at their feet, looking for all the world like a conversation-piece by Sargent. One night the buttresses of the Abbey were covered with snow. They sparkled in the brilliant moonlight, while the bursting shells overhead and the search-lights swinging to and fro made an extraordinary picture in the sky. But air raids soon lost their exciting novelty, and some of us would seek an added thrill by creeping out of the Undercroft to see if one of the statues in the cloisters really turned over the pages of its book at midnight, as legend said it did.

We were allowed home for week-ends, and this seemed to prevent my settling down at school. At last I begged my parents to make me a day boy, using the raids and my subsequent loss of sleep as an excuse. My stratagem was successful, and I was allowed to go home in the evenings, work at my preparation in the library, and then go to bed. My father was not so fortunate. He was a Special Constable, and had to patrol the Chelsea Embankment, near Lot's Road Power House. When there was a bad raid he used to say that the spectacle over the river was so magnificent that it quite made up for his long hours of dreariness, but I imagine those nights must have been something of an ordeal for him after a long day's work in the City, and a great strain for my mother, who used to sit up half the night waiting for him, with a spirit lamp and sandwiches, trying to read, and listening for the 'all clear' signal which would herald his return.

How we loathed our clothes at Westminster! — the top-hats, which looked like sealskin after a few days, and the hideous allround stiff collars which we had to wear. Ivor Montagu, who was in the same house as I was, brought special food to school, which he used to carry, for convenience' sake, in his hat. He was considerably discomfited, though the rest of us thought it a great joke, when somebody knocked it off in Dean's Yard with a snowball. On O.T.C. days we looked better (and felt more comfortable) in our uniforms, though our puttees were always a sore trial. On wet Saturday afternoons I used to climb, top-hat and all, to the galleries of theatres, undaunted by the sniggers which my appearance usually provoked. My father had taken me for the first time to see the Russian Ballet at the Alhambra, and I saved all my pocket-money (which I suppose I called an 'allowance' by now) to go again and again, enchanted by the brilliant décors and passionate dancing. Arnold Haskell, the ballet critic, was at Westminster. He became one of my greatest friends of those days, and we used to stand in queues for hours together. That first production of *Boutique Fantasque*, the exquisite blue back-cloth and the little sofas in *Carnaval, Thamar's* enchanted tower and the glories of Bakst's rococo places in *The Sleeping Princess*, these were early ecstasies – though my youthful admiration was also extended quite indiscriminately to *The Bing Boys, Yes, Uncle*, and finally *The Beggar's Opera*.

I was still a boy, but I was lucky to have been born just in time to touch the fringe of the great century of the theatre. I saw Sarah Bernhardt in a one-act play in which she appeared as a wounded *poilu* of eighteen, dying on the battlefield. She looked unbelievably young and her voice rang through the theatre. Though her leg had been amputated, she stood up to take her call, leaning on the shoulder of one of the other actors. I saw Adeline Genée dance, and heard Albert Chevalier singing 'My old Dutch', and I saw Vesta Tilley once, and Marie Lloyd, too, in her last days.

In 1923 I stood in a packed audience at the Oxford Theatre to see Duse in *Ghosts*. It was the very last time she was to act in London. She seemed to me like some romantic Spanish empress, with her shawl draped wonderfully about her, and her fluttering hands. Her expression when she listened was marvellous, but I was not familiar with the play and could not follow it with any pleasure. There was certainly nothing Nordic about this Mrs Alving. What impressed me most was the tremendous reception the audience gave her, their breathless silence during the performance, and the air of majestic weariness with which Duse seemed to accept it all. There was something poignant and ascetic about her when she was old and ill, quite different from the indomitable gallantry of the crippled Bernhardt, and the ageless beauty and fun that Ellen Terry still brought with her upon the stage.

Sometimes, when we were not at school or at the theatre, Val and I used to roller-skate at Holland Park Rink. I was fascinated by the little model stages, with scenes from all the current plays, which were grouped in dark booths in the promenade. I have always loved aquariums, grottoes and waxworks, because they remind me of the peepshow side of the theatre. The effigies in the Abbey used to fascinate me for the same reason.

I longed for a great ceremony to be performed while I was at Westminster. I am sure I pictured myself singing 'Vivat Rex' at a coronation. As a matter of fact we were privileged, as Westminster boys, to be present on several exciting occasions before I left the school. I saw the procession at each opening of Parliament, and I was much impressed by the beautiful voice and faultless diction of Mr Bonar Law in the House of Commons, where we were allowed to sit in one of the Stranger's Galleries. When the Unknown Soldier was buried, we stood, dressed in our O.T.C. uniforms, lining the path from the street to the door of the Abbey. It was extraordinary to stand there, with arms reversed and faces lowered, and to know that the greatest men of our time were passing within a few feet of us. We were in the Abbey, too, at the wedding of the Princess Royal, and had a very close glimpse of the Royal Family as they passed. This was the last time I saw Queen Alexandra, still slim and elegant, walking beside the more opulent figure of Queen Mary. She had always been one of my heroines. I was taken to the Mansion House when I was quite small to present a purse to her for the Treloar

Hospital, and took away with me the memory of a lovely bowing lady, as well as a real signed picture of her which hung over my bed for many years afterwards.

It was about this time that I made my first shy hints that I wished to renounce the idea of going to Oxford and try my fortune on the stage. I made the suggestion that, if I did not succeed before I was twenty-five, I would follow my parents' wishes and work to become an architect. Mother and Father were not very enthusiastic. They had just arranged for me to specialize in History at Westminster with the idea of trying for a scholarship at Oxford, but I felt how useless it would be to waste another four to five years before I began training for the stage. If I were to become an actor I must start at once.

Finally, after a good deal of discussion, I was allowed to enter for a scholarship at the dramatic school of which Lady Benson was the principal.

Here I arrived one morning, trembling with nerves, to find Lady Benson and Helen Haye confronting me in a tiny office. I recited 'Bredon Hill' from the *Shropshire Lad*, which I had heard Henry Ainley (dressed in uniform, with jingling spurs), give magnificently a few weeks before at a charity concert at the Grafton Galleries. I thought I had shouted the roof off, and was overcome with emotion when I was told I had won the scholarship. I was free to leave Westminster, and begin to study acting.

Chapter 3

1920–21

I stayed with Lady Benson for a year, and found her a delightful woman and a splendid teacher. She worked in a funny ramshackle little drill-hall only a few yards away from my grandmother's house in the detested Cromwell Road. There was a minute stage and auditorium, with a glass conservatory leading out into a yard. The place was pulled down many years ago, but I always think of it when I pass the corner where it stood.

The war had come to an end shortly before I left Westminster. The rumour that the Armistice had been signed spread round the classrooms early in the morning, and no one was paying much attention to work when eleven o'clock came at last and bells began to ring. We streamed into Little Dean's Yard, and up the steps to Big School, where the headmaster dismissed us for the day. Some of us joined the enormous crowd of people in Whitehall, and were swept along up the Mall to the steps of the Victoria Memorial, where we stood for hours, waving our limp top-hats and shouting for the King and Queen. Lewis was demobilized soon afterwards. He had been working at the War Office since his wounds invalided him out of the army, and now he was able to go back to Oxford for another year. I went to lunch with him at Magdalen. He had beautiful white-panelled rooms in New Buildings, and we fed the deer out of the windows. He showed me Addison's Walk and the sweep of the High, the Shelley Memorial and Tom Quad. At the time I was mad about *Sinister Street* and *Guy and Pauline* and *Zuleika Dobson*, and Oxford seemed to me, next to London, the most glamorous place I had ever seen. We punted up the Cherwell for a moonlight picnic, and floated down again late at night with Chinese lanterns, and I stayed awake for hours when I got back to the hotel, listening to the bells and clocks striking in the darkness. I thought myself very noble to have given up the chance of becoming an undergraduate. What if I should make a failure of the stage? I don't believe the possibility had ever occurred to me before.

Naomi Mitchison and Aldous Huxley were great friends of Lewis's while he was at Oxford. Aldous had been with him at Eton too, and often came to our house in London. He looked then very much as he did in later life, with his thick glasses and long stooping body. He, Lewis and Naomi used to speak very slowly and drawl the ends of their words affectedly. This was the real 'Oxford accent' so much ridiculed and imitated since that time.

Naomi Haldane, as she then was, had an extraordinary personality. She was incredibly shy and clumsy, wore amazing clothes of strange cut and shape, and knew everything there was to know about Greek and Roman history and the archaeology of Egypt and Byzantium. At the age of eleven she wrote a play about Ancient Greece, which was acted on the lawn of the Haldanes' house at Oxford. Lewis produced it and also appeared in the same programme as Dionysos in *The Frogs* of Aristophanes. He looked very handsome, dressed in a leopard-skin and blue and gold buskins, with a vine-wreath round his head. Aldous played Charon, and rowed him over the Styx in a little boat with rockers set down upon the grass. Naomi had written another play, very elaborate and ambitious, with an archaic setting and modern dialogue. Val and I were both invited to appear in it, and the Margaret Morris Theatre in King's Road, Chelsea, was hired for the performance. The cast included Julian Huxley, the scientist, and Helen Simpson, the authoress. I only remember that I played a young Greek officer who befriended a British prisoner of war who was in my charge, and that Nigel Playfair's two sons, Giles and Lyon, aged eight and six respectively, acted far better than anyone else.

I had already made several amateur appearances since my days at Hillside. Some years before, at Beaconsfield, Val, Eleanor and I had got up a play with some friends with whom we were staying for the summer holidays. The performance was given in a charming studio belonging to G.K. Chesterton, and the great man himself came to see it, and delighted us by laughing uproariously. Val had written the scenario, and we all invented the dialogue as we went along – quite in the Commedia dell' Arte tradition! Eleanor played a maid in a very large cap, and I was a sinister adventuress in a big hat and evening dress, smoking a cigarette through a long black holder. I had appeared in Shakespeare too; I was asked to play Orlando in some performances of *As You Like It* which were to be given in the garden of a rectory at St. Leonards, and later in the grounds of Battle Abbey. I was sixteen by now and very vain. I affected very light grey flannels braced much too high, silk socks, broad-brimmed black soft hats, and even, I blush to admit, an eye-glass upon occasion, and I wore my hair very long and washed it a great deal to make it look fluffy and romantic. For Orlando, I slipped off to a hairdresser in St. Leonards and asked the man to wave it – 'For a play,' I added hastily. 'Certainly, sir,' he said. 'I suppose you'd be in the Variety Company that's opening on the Pier this week.' Undaunted, I strode on to the lawn at the first performance, drew my sword fiercely, and declaimed, 'Forbear, and eat no more!' but unfortunately I tripped over a large log and fell flat on my face. This was only the beginning of my troubles, for in the last act, when I pointed to the path where I was expecting Rosalind, with 'Ah, here comes my Ganymede' – no Ganymede was to be seen. I said the line again, with a little less confidence this time; still no one appeared. I looked helplessly round, to find the prompter, his hands to his mouth, whispering as loudly as he dared across the hundred yards that separated us, 'She's changed back into her girl's clothes a scene too soon!'

I had also replaced a student who was ill in a couple of performances at Rosina Filippi's school in Whitehead's Grove, near Sloane Square, in an adaptation of a novel by Rhoda

Broughton, and as Mercutio in three scenes from *Romeo and Juliet*. Miss Filippi had a broad, motherly face, grey hair and a rich, jolly laugh. She walked with an ebony cane, and wore black taffeta that rustled a great deal and a gold watch on a long chain round her neck. She conducted rehearsals with much authority and humour, but I was rather put out at the actual performance, when she sat down at a piano at the side of the stage and played twiddly bits all through my delivery of the Queen Mab speech!

With such a wealth of amateur experience behind me, I naturally started at Lady Benson's full of hope and self-assurance, once the terror of the scholarship examination was safely passed. Grandmother must have been in the country, for I received the following letter from her which I proudly pasted into the new scrapbook which I had bought that morning:

DEAR OLD JACK,

I am delighted to hear of your intended real start in a profession you love, and wish you every success. You must not anticipate a bed of roses, for on the stage as in every other profession there are 'rubs and arrows' to contend with. 'Be kind and affable to all your co-mates, but if possible be intimate with none of them.' This is a quotation of my parents' advice to me and I pass it on as I have proved it to be very sound. Theatrical intimacy breeds jealousy of a petty kind which is very disturbing. I hope you may have many chances with your various studies and prove yourself worthy.

I am returning on Monday and shall, I hope, have an opportunity to have a good old talk with you.

Meanwhile my love and congratulations.

Your affectionate grandmother,

KATE LEWIS

There were about thirty students at Lady Benson's, and only four of them were men. This of course led to great competition amongst us, so Lady Benson used to split up the good parts (such as Hamlet or Sir Peter Teazle), so that none of us should be made to feel important or indispensable, and made each of us play the same part in different scenes. When there were too many male characters in a play the slim girls played the young men's parts and the fat ones would appear in 'character' as Crabtree or Moses. I loved the rehearsal classes, but was less keen on the fencing, dancing, and elocution which completed the curriculum. There was also a 'gesture' class once a week, which Lady Benson took herself. One of her exercises was to make us rush in and express different emotions with the same line of dialogue. It must have been distinctly comic to see twenty-five young women and four self-conscious young men rushing through a door one after the other, uttering with hate, fear, disgust or joy the remark 'Baby's burning'.

Still I had not taken Ellen Terry's advice and read my Shakespeare. I cheerfully rushed at the purple patches set for us by the elocution master, and, having a good memory and a quick eye, polished off St. Crispin and Clarence's dream, Wolsey's farewell and Othello's speech to the Senate, in a very short space of time. I rehearsed some of Benedick, which I found very difficult to understand; and, as a crowning glory, I was allowed to study half a dozen scenes of *Hamlet*. When the day of the performance came, however, and my costume arrived, I was so delighted with the long black cloak I had to wear that I spent most of the first scene draping it over my arm and looking over my shoulder to see if it were trailing on the floor to my satisfaction. Shakespeare seemed easy to learn, at any rate, and I liked it because it was full of tradition and effective 'business'. There were plenty of good parts and strong situations, and I could make myself weep when I said certain lines, and listen to my voice as it soared in interesting cadences from one register to another.

I suddenly became aware of my legs. This was a terrible moment, for, until I realized that I was handicapped by a strange way of standing and a still stranger way of walking, I really thought acting might be a comparatively simple matter. I was not embarrassed at using my hands and arms, in fact at first I used them a bit too freely, but the moment I tried to move my legs they refused to carry out the simplest instructions. Only a few days after my arrival at the school Lady Benson had burst out laughing in the middle of a rehearsal and pointed at me with dismay. 'Good heavens', she cried, 'you walk exactly like a cat with rickets!'

I became acutely self-conscious, knowing that my laziness and my dislike of games had prevented me from learning, when I was a boy, to move freely and naturally. I walked from the knees instead of from the hips, and bent my legs when I was standing still instead of holding them straight. I am sure if I had been forced to run and swim when I was a child I should not have developed these mannerisms so badly, but it was too late to think of that now. Such a discovery in my first term at Lady Benson's was extremely depressing. However, it dealt a severe blow to my conceit, which was a good thing. Vainly I pored over books on Irving, describing his dragging leg and odd movements – vainly I imagined myself triumphing, like Sarah Bernhardt, in a part where I was lying in bed, or sitting in an invalid chair. (I had just been to see Claude Rains as Dubedat in *The Doctor's Dilemma* at the Everyman Theatre.) It was no use. My 'rickets' were to remain my principal bugbear on the stage for many years to come.

Somebody told me that theatrical students were able to walk on (without payment) in the crowds at the Old Vic, and as soon as term was over at Lady Benson's, I rushed off to the Waterloo Road to try my luck. I was taken on without an audition – perhaps some kind person had recommended me. I only remember climbing the stairs to the old saloon bar at the back of the dress-circle to my first professional rehearsal. The room was rather like a shabby version of the old Café Royal – fly-blown mirrors, plush benches, gilded plaster figures, and dust everywhere. The play in rehearsal was *Henry V*, with Robert Atkins as producer and Rupert Harvey playing the part of the King, Andrew Leigh as Fluellen, Hay Petrie as the Boy, and

Florence Buckton as Chorus, dressed in black topboots and Elizabethan man's costume. Through the glass doors I could see the rounded backs of the dress-circle seats, and the gilt decorations on top of the proscenium. All around me actors were sitting, crouching, muttering their lines to themselves, hearing one another from tattered little green books, slipping in and out for drinks or newspapers. Lilian Baylis occasionally hovered in the distance, but I never spoke to her. Sometimes I would timidly offer to hold the book for one of the actors, and sometimes Atkins would call out to 'that boy in the brown suit' to 'take his hands out of his pockets', as I shifted from one foot to another while a long scene, in which I held a spear, was repeated over and over again.

The first night drew nearer and nearer, and at last we were dressing, making up – six of us supers in one of the top boxes next to the proscenium. There was no dressing-room space in those days at the Vic. The leading lady dressed in Miss Baylis's office, and the rest of the women in the saloon bar. They could be seen during the performance scurrying round the back of the circle dressed as Court Ladies, and scurrying back again dressed as Nuns a few moments later. There was no call-boy of course, so we used to peep through the felt curtains of our box to see if our cue was getting near, taking care to open the side closest to the stage so that no one in the audience should notice us. One night somebody dragged the curtain roughly aside, and down it came, revealing us all, half naked, to the astonished and delighted gallery!

Well, even if my first engagement was neither luxurious nor profitable, I was in a real theatre at last, working in a professional company, playing Shakespeare, and it was with high hopes and a beating heart, my knees pressed firmly back (for by this time they were knocking together as well as bending in their usual fashion), that I walked for the first time on to a professional stage, looked out across the footlights towards the exits glimmering like beacons in the darkness, and boldly uttered the only line of my first speaking part, 'Here is the number of the slaughter'd French'.

I was enormously impressed by some of the acting at the Vic. Andrew Leigh as the Fool in *Lear*; Ernest Milton as Richard II and Shylock; Hay Petrie as Shallow and Verges; Russell Thorndike and Florence Buckton in Ase's death scene in *Peer Gynt*. The Ibsen play was amazingly well put on, though I am sure it cost little enough. Russell was fine, especially in the ironic passages – in the African scenes he looked like Mr Fogg in Jules Verne's *Around the World in Eighty Days* – and he had some immensely funny business. In one scene he took off his trousers meditatively during one of his speeches and put up a large white umbrella. Later on, when he was leaving Anitra, he suddenly turned over a large cushion, produced the trousers from underneath, where they were being carefully pressed, and gravely put them on again. No one was supposed to watch the dress rehearsal of the play, but I climbed into the gallery and sat there for hours, all through a long Sunday, crouching under a large dust-sheet and hardly daring to breathe, determined not to miss a moment of the performance.

It was lucky for me that the actors at the Old Vic were all so busy that they had little time to spare for giving advice to young beginners. Some of them have told me since that I was so dreadfully bad as a super that they would have liked to have warned me against becoming an actor. Fortunately, I was quite unconscious of the bad impression I had created, and was only a little dashed when I was given no line to speak either in *King Lear*, Halcott Glover's *Wat Tyler*, or *Peer Gynt*, in all of which I 'walked on' in quick succession. Term was beginning again at Lady Benson's, and I left the Vic. Certainly nobody pressed me to stay on; and it was nine years before I passed through the stage-door in the Waterloo Road again.

Chapter 4

1921–22

I am always embarrassed when people ask me how they should set about looking for an opening on the stage, for I gained my first engagement entirely through influence. I had just completed three terms at Lady Benson's. Grandmother had been to see one of the performances, but otherwise I imagined that the family were not particularly interested in the new recruit. But I was wrong – for out of the blue one morning came a letter from Phyllis Neilson-Terry. Again I rushed to paste into my book the second important document in my stage career. The letter offered me four pounds a week to play a few lines, understudy, and make myself generally useful on a tour of *The Wheel*, under Phyllis's management, in the autumn of 1921.

I had met Phyllis, of course, and admired her very much. I knew of her spectacular success at His Majesty's under Tree, when she had played Desdemona and Viola at seventeen. Later she had acted in *Priscilla Runs Away* at the Haymarket, as Trilby and Lady Teazle at His Majesty's, and as Juliet at the New under her father, Fred Terry's, management. Then she had married Cecil King and gone away to America. Grandmother had once taken me on the stage to meet her after a performance of *Drake* – the only time, by the way, I ever went to His Majesty's as a boy – and I was bewildered at my efforts to talk to her while such exciting things were going on all round us. White horses were being led away in one direction, the porch of St. Paul's Cathedral was being rolled off in another, there were cloths being raised and borders dropped. I stood gaping with wonder and bewilderment, and there was Phyllis towering over me, looking even taller than she really was in her magnificent robes and crown, smiling and telling me to feel the weight of the wonderful necklaces she wore. She came once or twice to our house at Christmas, but I hardly saw her again until she offered me my first engagement. Her reappearance in London, on her return from America, in *The Wheel*, by J.B. Fagan (which she presented herself), was a great success. Now she had booked a long tour of fourteen or fifteen weeks in the provinces, and I was to be in her company. It was not a big cast, and rehearsals were not very alarming, as most of the company knew the play already and there were only a few changes to be made. I appeared for two minutes right at the end of the last act with a few lines to speak, but found I was given plenty of other things to do, holding the book, checking the actors' entrances, giving cues, helping to work the effects, and so on. Cecil King, Phyllis's husband, was charming to me and joked a great deal with everyone, and there was no question of my being singled out for favouritism. If anyone resented the fact that I was only there because I had the luck to be Phyllis's second cousin they were far too nice to show it.

We opened at Bradford, a romantic city in my imagination because Irving died there. There was not much romance about it in reality. I had a back 'combined' room, where I stood the first afternoon, looking very glum, gazing out of the window at a vista of smoke-stacks, factory chimneys and grubby back gardens. On the table, with its thick plush cloth edged with bobbles, lay strewn the contents of the tuck-box packed by my thoughtful mother – tinned tongue, sardines and pots of jam. I was very home-sick, but slightly embarrassed when the landlady, in a large hat with feathers, took pity on me and cheerfully bade me join her in the kitchen for a drink, introducing me to several of the 'turns' from the local music-hall. What a snob they must have thought me!

I was very inexperienced as a toper. After a few weeks, I began to go 'pub-crawling' with three or four men from the company, and one morning I ordered Guinness and Gin and Italian in quick succession (I had picked up the names of these drinks from the others), turned green and fainted dead away.

I found the assistant stage management work harder than I expected. I had to dress in my uniform and be made up some time before the curtain went up every night so as to see that everything was ready on the stage. The two men with whom I shared a dressing-room helped me as much as they could, but I was an absolute duffer with greasepaints for many weeks. After half an hour's work I used to look either as red as a Cherokee Indian or else yellow and streaky, and I used far too much grease and not enough powder, so that my face shone like a full moon. On Saturday nights I had to see the scenery out of the theatre, which was rather alarming – especially if the staff had got a little drunk by one in the morning – and I would drag myself wearily home to my digs as the last big waggon rumbled away to the station in the darkness. Then all day Monday there would be the business of unpacking and 'hanging' the play in the new theatre, rehearsing the lighting and the orchestra, arranging the cue-lights, the call-sheets, and the thousand and one other details on which the smooth running of a play depends.

It was good for me to find out from the very first something of the complicated routine of a theatrical production. Playing a small part eight times a week takes up little of the day, and on tour there was nothing to do but read or go for walks or to the cinema. So I was quite glad of a full night's work and two full days a week in the theatre, though, of course I grumbled when matinée days and understudy rehearsals interfered with my spare time. I had the usual kind of touring adventures. Once I arrived in Leeds with two other members of the company, with whom I had arranged to share that week, and the door of the digs was opened by a Chinese gentleman. 'My son', said the Yorkshire landlady, and then, as we looked startled – 'You should see my girl – she's in hospital now, unfortunately, burnt herself badly. Fair as a lily she is.' The bath upstairs was full of coal, and strange sounds came from the basement. After an uncomfortable week, we rashly paid our bill on Saturday night, although our train did not leave until the following evening. So we were a little dismayed when we woke late on Sunday morning to find an empty house, and a little burnt porridge in a bowl in the sitting-room grate, apparently the only food available. The landlady had decamped, taking her Oriental family with her. We were firmly convinced that we had spent a week in an opium den!

Sheffield was deadly, Hanley, Preston and Leeds not much more cheerful, and the digs varied from extreme discomfort to comparative luxury ('Lav. in Pub opp.' as a theatrical paper once advertised laconically). At Aberdeen I was asleep in a strange kind of box bed let into the wall – the rooms were very tiny but spotlessly clean, and the porridge was delicious – when someone arrived from the theatre to tell me I had to play one of the leading parts that night, as the principal was ill. It was an important moment for me to appear for the first time in a big part under Phyllis's critical eye, but apparently I rose to the occasion. Everyone seemed agreeably surprised, and I was delighted at the congratulations I received. But Nemesis was to follow. Phyllis wrote to my parents of my success, and, as they were coming to visit me at Oxford a few weeks later, she most kindly suggested that I should play the part again for the performance at which they would be present. The principal was asked to stand down, and again I dressed and made up with a trembling hand. Alas! my acting was dreadful. Nothing that I had done well before seemed to be right a second time; half-way through the play I knew that I had failed. I was deeply ashamed when I had to go out to tea with Phyllis and my parents afterwards, and imagined that the chauffeur shot me a look of unutterable disdain as I stepped into the grand car belonging to the management.

I lived, for the week we were at Oxford, in theatrical lodgings in Paradise Square. It was strange to be playing there as an actor, and to wander round Magdalen, where I had lunched with Lewis, and Trinity, where I had stayed with Val. In two years' time my contemporaries from Westminster would be coming up to Oxford as undergraduates. I wondered how far I should have progressed in my profession in those two years and whether I should regret my choice. I shared my lodgings that week with a charming actor in Phyllis's company, and he talked to me very kindly about my work. He had guessed, when I had gone on as understudy, that I had some instinct for the stage, but he also realized that I needed to learn control and to gain some technical knowledge for my work. I told him I had studied with Lady Benson, but he urged me to spend at least another year at a dramatic school when the tour came to an end. He suggested the Royal Academy of Dramatic Art, in Gower Street, where he had been trained himself. I took his advice, and managed to win a scholarship there on my return to London.

The school was much larger than Lady Benson's, though the classes were similarly arranged. Kenneth Barnes was the Principal. Claude Rains and Helen Haye were two of the teachers – also Miss Elsie Chester, a formidable old actress with a crutch, which she was reputed to hurl at people when she was displeased with their behaviour. The old house in Gower Street has been quite rebuilt since my time. In those days there used to be a labyrinth of stone steps leading to a basement canteen, presided over by a large lady called 'Henney', where we all used to gather for 'elevenses'. Another flight of stairs led up to the little theatre, which had just been opened with the all-star professional matinée for which Barrie wrote *Shall We Join the Ladies?*

Claude Rains was an enormous favourite with us all – his vitality and enthusiasm made him a delightful teacher, and most of the girls were in love with him.

I worked as hard as I could, and imitated Rains's acting until I became extremely mannered. I felt sure I had some sort of instinct for impersonation, but the imaginative part of my playing came too easily, and the technical side was non-existent. I strained every fibre in my efforts to appear violent or emotional, and only succeeded in forcing my voice and striking strange attitudes with my body. Rehearsing every day in a small room, with rows of girls sitting round on chairs staring at me, made me acutely self-conscious, and it was not until the performances at the end of the term that I was able to let myself go with any degree of confidence. But I was very lucky. At the end of the first term, Nigel Playfair, who knew my mother (more influence, I fear), came to a performance given by my class. The play was *The Admirable Crichton*, and I played the silly ass, Woolley, in the first two acts and Crichton himself in the last two. We gave the performance, not in the theatre, but in the Rehearsal Room, which was a glorified classroom with a small rickety stage at one end of it. After the performance I was sent for, and found Playfair sitting alone among a litter of empty chairs. He offered me the part of Felix, the Poet Butterfly in *The Insect Play* which he was putting on at the Regent Theatre, King's Cross, in a few weeks' time. I was told that after the play was produced, I might continue my classes at the Academy in the daytime except on matinée days.

The rehearsals at the Regent were very exciting. It was thrilling to play a part that had never been played by anyone before, and to see the production taking shape. Claude Rains was in the cast, to my great delight, and also Angela Baddeley, Maire O'Neill, Elsa Lanchester, and Bromley Davenport. Playfair had just discovered at Liverpool Doris Zinkeisen, who was to make her first success in London with her brilliant scenery and dresses for this play. Miss Zinkeisen was very good-looking and wore exotic clothes. She was at that time engaged to James Whale, a tall young man with side-whiskers and suède shoes, who was stage-managing for Playfair at the time. (He was later to direct the first production of *Journey's End* and ended his life and career as a very successful Hollywood director.) These two made a striking pair at the dances to which Playfair, with his charming hospitality, used to invite the company at Thurloe Lodge, a beautiful little house off the Brompton Road which he had just rebuilt, and which Zinkeisen had decorated for him in a very modern style. There was an attractive square hall with a tessellated pavement, a charming staircase, and a white-panelled drawing-room with chandeliers. As a devotee of *The Beggar's Opera* I was of course enraptured to be asked to the Playfairs, to see the Lovat Fraser drawings which decorated the rooms, and to meet, amongst others Violet Marquesita, who had been my special favourite among the Lyric cast.

The Insect Play was a failure, and I created a very bad impression in it. The first act (The Butterflies) was not good, and the weakness of the opening was the more regrettable since the rest of the play was extremely interesting. In the original Czech, I believe, the Butterfly episode had been very improper but very amusing; however, Clifford Bax and Playfair, who translated the play together, removed the indecency but found little material to replace it. The two girls and I, who played the principal parts, were all quite inexperienced, and in spite of our efforts, the act proved ineffective. I wore white flannels, black pumps, a silk shirt, a green laurel-wreath, fair hair, and a golden battledore and shuttlecock – I am surprised that the audience did not throw things at me.

The play ran for six weeks. On the last night, Playfair sat in a box with his back turned to the stage all through the first act. It was a bitter disappointment to him that the play had failed, but my indifferent performance in it did not prevent him from being kind enough to offer me a part in Drinkwater's *Robert E. Lee* which was to follow. In fact, he re-engaged as many of the cast of *The Insect Play* as he possibly could. Zinkeisen was again engaged to design the scenery, but at the dress rehearsal it was found to be far too impressionistic for a straightforward biographical play. Most of it was discarded accordingly, and real trees and bushes planted about the stage. These, placed against a cyclorama, served for the outdoor scenes of the play, most of which took place in woods and on battlefields. Unfortunately, the foliage withered and died after a short space of time, and the stage looked very woebegone as the play dragged on, to increasingly sparse audiences, during the summer months.

The notices were extremely good and the play was full of well-written effective scenes. It was beautifully acted, especially by Claude Rains, but it was never a success and I am sure that Playfair continued to run it chiefly to keep the company in work.

He must have lost money every week. One afternoon Claude Rains was taken ill, and I appeared in his place for several performances. As in *The Wheel*, I made a surprising success the first time I played, but lost confidence on subsequent occasions; but I think everybody was agreeably impressed with my ability in the emotional scenes. The 'feeling' of them came to me without much difficulty, and the sincerity of that feeling 'got over' to the audience, despite my lack of technical accomplishment, whereas in the 'walking' part of the orderly, which I usually played, my clumsiness and slovenly movements were conspicuous, and there were no moments of emotion or drama in which I could atone for them.

During the summer my parents went away, and I borrowed a little flat in Mecklenburgh Square, near the Regent Theatre, where I was appearing. I felt very independent with a home of my own, and the flat was charming, with curved corners to the panelled rooms, and a delightful Irish landlady, like Lee White,[1] who wore mob-caps in the morning.

Meanwhile, I was still working at the Academy with Rains. He directed me in Tolstoy's *Reparation*, in which he himself had recently played with Ainley, I had seen it and was wildly excited at the chance of playing the part of Fédya, and we all worked madly at the gypsy scenes, learning songs and collecting 'properties' from home to dress the stage on the day of the performance.

I also played the opening scene of Hotspur, from *Henry IV, Part I*, for a diploma competition, and was complimented by the judges. Next day, one of them sent me a charming letter of congratulation, and summoned me to his office, where he spent half an hour sipping a glass of milk and begging me to change my name for the stage, as no one would ever be able to spell or pronounce it properly. I answered obstinately that if anyone did notice it they would not easily forget it, and so we parted.

I completed my year's tuition at the RADA shortly

1 A delightful Australian revue actress, who, with her husband Clay Smith, charmed London audiences during the First World War.

afterwards. I appeared in *Les Caprices de Marianne*, and in a scene from *L'Aiglon*, endeavouring to act in French. The producer, Mlle Alice Gachet, was one of the most brilliant professors at the Academy. But my French vocabulary is not equal to my accent, and I did her little credit, I'm afraid. It was left to Charles Laughton to become Mlle Gachet's star pupil, and act as brilliantly in French as he did in English. Some years later he was invited to appear, playing in French, at the Comédie Française, and on that memorable occasion Mlle Gachet accompanied him as a guest of honour.

Chapter 5

1922–23

I remember well the interviews preceding my next two engagements, but I have no idea how my new employers heard of me or why they should have thought me likely to be promising material. My first visit, just before Christmas, after *Robert E. Lee* had come to an end, was to Mrs Brandon-Thomas in Gordon Square; my second, a month or so later, to J. B. Fagan in a charming house in St. John's Wood, just behind Lord's Cricket Ground. Both interviews proved satisfactory, and I went into *Charley's Aunt* for the Christmas season at the Comedy Theatre, and, in the following spring, to Fagan's Repertory Company at the Oxford Playhouse.

Charley's Aunt was rather a disappointment to me. I played Charley, the 'feed' part of the two tiresome undergraduates who provide the juvenile love interest in the play. Finding, when I read the part, that I had few opportunities for distinguishing myself, I arrived at rehearsal fully determined to wear horn-rimmed spectacles and adopt a silly-ass manner, copying as far as I could the methods of an actor whom I had recently admired in a musical comedy called *Battling Butler*. My hopes were rudely shattered by Amy Brandon-Thomas, the producer and daughter of the author, who arrived in a large grey squirrel coat and strode on to the stage bristling with authority. She very soon informed me that the play was a classic – every move, nay, every garment worn by the actors was sacrosanct, and no deviation of any kind was to be tolerated for a moment. It seemed to me a great pity that, in spite of this, the play had been brought up to date. It is full of references to chaperons and carriages (changed in later years rather lamely to 'cars'), and a revival in the original trappings of the nineties would, I am sure, be an enormous success today. The romantic and sentimental scenes alone would be hailed by a modern audience with shouts of joy. Many of the lines have stayed with me ever since; such gems as these:

> 'Oh, to live for ever among these dreaming spires and sculptured nooks – like silent music – a scholar's fairyland!'

and

> 'He never called me 'the angel of the watch'; but he did get as far as a stammering compliment and a blush and then—'
> 'And then—?'
> 'Then he was ordered off with his regiment.'
> 'Without ever—?'
> 'Without *ever*.'
> 'Oh! Auntie!'

We played twice daily for six weeks, and I had to dash up and down stairs an innumerable number of times changing my clothes. It was fun at first hearing people laugh so much, but after a few performances it was agony to me to keep a straight face myself, especially as the old actor who had played Mr Spettigue hundreds of times took a particular delight in making us giggle on the stage and then reporting us to the stage management, when Miss Brandon-Thomas would descend upon us again and lecture us severely. Laughing on the stage is a disgraceful habit, and she was perfectly right to make a fuss about it. It is particularly fatal to succumb in farce (the most tempting kind of play to giggle in) for the absolute seriousness of the actors is usually the very thing which makes the situations funny to the audience. My most disgraceful exhibition occurred years afterwards in *The Importance of Being Earnest*, when, at a very hot matinée rather poorly attended, I suddenly noticed four old ladies, in different parts of the stalls, not only fast asleep, but hanging down over the edges of their seats like discarded marionettes in a Punch-and-Judy show. I became so hysterical that the muffins I was eating refused to go down my throat, and by the end of the scene the audience were roaring with laughter, not at the play, but at my hopeless efforts to keep myself under control. I was so ashamed that I hardly knew how to finish the performance.

I had refused the chance of becoming a real undergraduate, and now I had acted one on the stage in *Charley's Aunt*. My engagement with Fagan took me to Oxford after all, with a very nice little salary to live on, and there I stayed for three terms at a time when many of the schoolboys with whom I had been at Westminster were members of the University.

Fagan was an Irishman of great personal charm. Also he was extremely talented as author, producer, and impresario. His death in Hollywood in 1933 was a real loss to the theatre. He and Playfair (whose life also was cut short) were both Oxford men, both Bensonians, and both ardent devotees of Granville-Barker. The productions given by Playfair at the Lyric, Hammersmith and by Fagan at the Court were among the most distinguished and individual of their time, and as a boy I had seen many of them — *The Merchant of Venice* (with Moscovitch as Shylock), *Abraham Lincoln, Henry IV, Part II* (with Frank Cellier as the King), the Lovat Fraser *As You Like It*, and *Othello* with Godfrey Tearle. I had never read the last play — I only knew that Desdemona was strangled in the last act — and my terror and excitement as the jealousy scenes drew to a climax were almost more than I could bear.

The Playfair-Lovat Fraser *As You Like It* was a commercial failure, but it broke entirely fresh ground in the easy natural way in which the scenes were played, without cuts or traditional business, and in the originality and simplicity of the *décor*. Athene Seyler was a delicious Rosalind, and Herbert Marshall a fine Jacques — his first appearance after the War, in which he had lost a leg. There were unforgettable beauties in the scenery and costumes – a wood scene like a children's fairy tale, with straight white-and-grey silver birch trees and conventionalized curved borders, and a Court Lady in the wrestling scene (which took place in a kind of cloister) with a particoloured black-and-grey fuzzy wig, and a dress belted high up with the skirt billowing out in front in that charming 'pregnant' manner which is typical of the fourteenth-century missals.

The whole production was strikingly simple and bold in its conception, but it was before its time, and at Stratford-on-Avon, where it was tried out, the Press was outraged and the company almost mobbed in the streets. Yet one remembers the success of far more 'advanced' productions by Komisarjevsky in later years at Stratford, and cannot help wishing Playfair had been spared to rival them. Both he and Fagan understood actors very well, and though neither of them seemed to display much authority at rehearsals, their influence on a production was extraordinarily individual and characteristic. Both men really understood Shakespeare and had a wide knowledge of plays of all periods. Besides, they had excellent taste in music and painting, and a flair for discovering unknown talent.

The company at Oxford was a delightful one. Tyrone Guthrie was an actor in those days, and Veronica Turleigh, Flora Robson, James Whale, Richard Golden, Reginald Denham, Alan Napier, and Glen Byam Shaw were among our number. Mary Grey was the leading lady, and Dorothy Green, Doris Lytton, Minnie Rayner and Raymond Massey were others who joined the company for various productions. We acted on a tiny stage, which Fagan had cleverly built out in an 'apron' several feet in width, with side doors leading on to it. There was no front curtain, except to the inner stage, and any properties needed on the forestage used to be 'set' in view of the audience by a stage hand, dressed in a white coat like a cricket umpire, at the beginning of each scene. In *Monna Vanna*, when the furniture set in this way consisted of a voluptuous-looking couch, with cushions and a leopard-skin, the under-graduate section of the audience could not resist bursting into ironic applause! The prompter was a further difficulty, as there was nowhere in the front part of the stage where he could be effectively concealed. Since we presented a new play every Monday his services were apt to be greatly in demand, particularly at the beginning of the week, and, for fear of not finding him within our reach, we resorted to the old trick of writing out our lines and pinning them about the stage. Disaster came on two occasions – once in *Oedipus*, when a local super stood with both feet and a spear firmly planted on the all-important piece of paper, and Jocasta had to shove him aside with her elbow and then stoop to the ground apparently overcome by a sudden onrush of emotion; and another time, in *Captain Brassbound's Conversion*, when Massey, who played the American Captain, upset an entire bottle of ink over the table on which had been carefully pinned three pages of the dialogue for the final scene between Sir Howard and Lady Cecily.

We had to be very careful in our diction at the Playhouse. The hall, for it was little more, was situated near the junction of the Banbury and Woodstock Roads, and any lorry or bus which passed outside during the play drowned our lines with its vibrations, while inside the cane chairs placed in rows, with slats of wood running underneath them to keep them in position, groaned and squeaked in a running commentary whenever anyone sat down or got up or moved their legs into a more comfortable position. There was no foyer, and smoking was not allowed, so it is little wonder that our audiences varied in number and that we relied principally on the faithful few who patronized us regularly with season tickets. On the other hand we presented a very interesting programme and the company acted increasingly well together. Reginald Denham and James Whale helped Fagan with the producing, and Fagan and Whale took turns in designing the scenery, which we all used to help paint and construct between Saturday night and Monday afternoon. Some of the effects were quite ambitious. Whale did a wood for *Deirdre of the Sorrows* consisting almost entirely of a few light tree-trunks cut in three-ply, and we had a most regal tent scene in *Monna Vanna*, contrived from the rose-coloured curtains used by Fagan at the Court Theatre for the Moscovitch *Merchant of Venice* Trial Scene.

We acted plays by Congreve, Sheridan, Wilde, Pinero, Milne, Shaw, Ibsen, Chekhov, Pirandello, Synge, Sierra and Benavente during the two eight-week seasons when I was in the company, and the biggest success of the first season was *Love for Love*, which shocked North Oxford and a lot of our regular patrons, but delighted a large section of the University and drew many people to the Playhouse for the first time, chiefly, I am afraid, on account of its scandalous dialogue and improper situations.

It was very pleasant to live in Oxford, to have meals with people in College, and drinks at the OUDS.[1] We actors used to march home together along St. Giles' with linked arms after the play at night, singing army marching songs at the top of our voices, in the hope of being mistaken for undergraduates, pursued by the bull-dogs, and brought before the proctors. 'Your name and college, sir?' 'Not a member of the University!'

Gyles Isham was the 'star' of the OUDS. that year. Fagan produced twice for the Society at this time, first *Henry IV, Part I* in which Gyles played Hotspur, and then Hamlet. Gyles was greatly helped in both performances by 'J.B.', who set the *Hamlet* in Dürer scenery and costumes, and lit his scenes most beautifully. There was a dawn, faintly pink and pearl grey, in the scene of the swearing after the exit of the ghost, that was unforgettably lovely – and the last scene was splendidly arranged and unusually moving and poetic.

Gyles had beautiful rooms at Magdalen, once occupied by Oscar Wilde. I lunched with him there one day towards the end of the first season, and he was full of a plan to play Romeo during the vacation for a special performance in London, at the RADA. theatre in Gower Street. The Juliet was to be a well-to-do young woman, who was in love with Gyles and had theatrical ambitions and a rich mama.

1 Oxford University Dramatic Society.

The day after our lunch my face and neck began to swell, and the doctor told me I had mumps. There was nothing to be done but resign myself to going home. Fagan read my part at the Playhouse that night (and developed mumps himself a few days later), and Mother, always prompt in an emergency, arrived at my rooms in St. John's Street and took me home in a hired car, with large pillows on which to rest my face, which looked by this time so like Humpty Dumpty's that I wanted to laugh every time I caught sight of myself in a glass, though it was much too painful to do so.

I recovered in a few weeks, but my luncheon at Magdalen had been a fatal mistake. Gyles went down with mumps just as his *Romeo and Juliet* rehearsals were due to begin. He immediately suggested that I should learn the part and rehearse for him until he was well enough to work himself, and of course I readily consented. The part appealed to me tremendously, and secretly I hoped that he might not recover in time to appear, but a week before the date of production he returned to the cast, and, as I was on good terms with most of the company by this time, I was asked to stay on and appear as Paris at the performance.

I had put down my name at one or two theatrical agents after my *Charley's Aunt* engagement, and all of a sudden one morning I received the following charmingly worded communication from Akerman May:

2nd April 1924

DEAR MR. GIELGUD,

If you would like to play the finest lead among the plays by the late William Shakespeare, will you please call upon Mr. Peacock and Mr. Ayliff at the Regent Theatre on Friday at 2.30 p.m. Here is an opportunity to become a London Star in a night.

Please confirm.

Yours very truly,
AKERMAN MAY.

I rang up everyone I knew who might give me further information on the subject and discovered at length that Barry Jackson was putting on *Romeo and Juliet* shortly at the Regent Theatre with Gwen Ffrangcon Davies, and was searching for a Romeo to act with her. As I had studied and rehearsed the part so recently and was word-perfect in it, I took my courage in both hands and went to King's Cross to apply for the engagement. Another letter followed a few days later:

April 11, 1924

DEAR MR. GIELGUD,

I am feeling quite excited (as an old Actor) to hear this morning that it is most likely we have fixed you to play in 'Romeo' in London.

Best hopes and congratulations.

AKERMAN MAY.

So it was largely owing to Gyles Isham and the epidemic of mumps at Oxford that I was lucky enough to play my first big Shakespearean part in London at the age of nineteen.

I had to endure the agony of three auditions and a great deal of uncertainty before I was finally engaged. Walter Peacock was advising Jackson at the time and seemed inclined to believe in me from the first, but I was so young and inexperienced that there was every reason to doubt my capacity to sustain such an important part. Jackson was kind and non-committal – his very pale blue eyes twinkled, and he smoked countless cigarettes through white cardboard holders during our interview. H. K. Ayliff, his producer, was rather terrifying, immensely tall and thin like a Franciscan Friar, with brown boots and very long-waisted green tweeds. These three were to decide my fate. Several other young actors besides myself were under considera-tion, I knew, and I was determined to defeat them all. I gave one audition at the Kingsway and another, more hopefully, at the Regent, where I felt a little more at home as I had acted there so recently. There I stood, with a working-light casting its hard cold beam on to the empty stage, trying to give some sort of reading of the passionate farewell scene with Juliet, whose lines Ayliff read from the wings in hollow tones. In the shrouded stalls Jackson and Peacock were sitting in hats and overcoats. My voice echoed bleakly in the cold theatre, and I felt that in the circumstances I could have done better justice to the sentiments of Juliet in the Potion scene:

'I have a faint cold fear thrills through my veins,
That almost freezes up the heat of life—.'

At last the committee seemed to be satisfied, and I was engaged. I was wildly excited, of course. Rehearsals were not to begin until the following week, and meanwhile I took my father to the Regent, where *The Immortal Hour*[1] was being played at night, to see Gwen as Etain. It was my second visit. Now that I was to work with Gwen I was impatient to see her performance again, and the beauties of her acting and singing enchanted me even more than before – her silver dress, her braided black hair, and those lovely stylized movements of her hands! Her high, clear voice seemed to belong to another world as she glided through the forest in the first act and up the steps in the final scene, hardly seeming to touch the ground. I could not believe that in a few days' time I should be holding her in my arms as Juliet.

The Gwen that appeared at the first rehearsal was a very different person. She wore an old dress and carried a business-like overall on her arm. Her face was no longer pale, and she was brisk and impulsive in her movements. We were introduced. I thought she looked strangely at me for a moment. Then she began rather nervously to talk. After a few minutes she suddenly gasped and said, 'Thank God'. Then she explained that she had seen me in *The Insect Play* as that wretched butterfly-poet. I had made a most unfortunate impression on her, and when she had

---

1 An opera by Rutland Boughton, which had a rather highbrow vogue for a time.

heard that I was under consideration for Romeo she had been appalled at the idea. She told me all this in the most sincere and charming way, and I was relieved to find that she seemed to like me after all, though at the same time it was a nasty shock to my vanity to find that my performance had affected her so unpleasantly. We started to rehearse. Both of us were word-perfect from the beginning (for Gwen had played Juliet at Birmingham some time before) and we plunged into the work at once. There is usually some excuse for restraint at early rehearsals while one still holds the book in one's hand, but here there was no chance of postponing the moment when I must let myself go. I had to attack my scenes at once with power and confidence, and try and convince everybody that I was worthy of my big chance.

When I had understudied in *The Wheel*, Phyllis had come down once or twice to rehearsals and shown me how to hold her in a love scene. I had been amazed to find how skilled a business it was to handle a woman effectively on the stage, to avoid cramping her movements, disarranging her hair, or turning her awkwardly away from the audience at some important moment of the dialogue. Of course I had played love scenes at Lady Benson's and at the Academy too, and very embarrassing they were. Clinging self-consciously to a girl as shy as oneself in front of a classroom full of sniggering students at half past ten in the morning is a cold-blooded business; but it is probably just as well for the beginner to realize as early as possible how difficult (and how unromantic) the craft of stage love-making can be.

Gwen was wonderfully helpful. She herself was so extraordinarily keen and unselfconscious. From the very first rehearsal she threw herself wholeheartedly into every moment of her part, running the whole gamut of emotions, experimenting, simplifying, but never losing for an instant the style or the pictorial aspect of the character she had so vividly imagined for herself. She told me not to be frightened of our 'clinches', and when the moment came to embrace her passionately, I was amazed to find how naturally she slipped into my arms, sweeping her draperies in the most natural and yet artful way so that they should neither lose their line nor impede her movements, and arranging her head and arms in a position in which we could both speak and breathe in comfort, and extricate ourselves easily when the action demanded.

I know *Romeo and Juliet* by heart, and I have played Romeo three times, yet I cannot say that I ever pleased myself in the part. I always felt I knew exactly how the part should be played, but I had neither the looks, the dash, nor the virility to make a real success of it, however well I spoke the verse and felt the emotion. My Romeo was always 'careful', and I loved the lines and revelled in them too obviously. My big nose and sliding movements were accentuated by the costume and wig, however carefully designed, and in this early Romeo I looked a sight. I was given white tights with soles attached to them underneath and no shoes. My feet looked enormous, and it was most uncomfortable to fight or run about. My wig was coal-black, and parted in the middle. Wearing an orange make-up and a very low-necked doublet, I look, in the photographs, a mixture of Rameses of Egypt and a Victorian matron.

Romeo has only three scenes in the play with Juliet, and I think I was best in those scenes, thanks to the help Gwen had given me at rehearsal and her unfailing co-operation throughout the performance. Most of the others in the cast were not good, and the small parts were really badly played. Paul Shelving's scenery was hard and rather crude, though it solved the problem of speed very satisfactorily, and the production was commendably free from cuts or extraneous business. I lost confidence badly a few days before the first performance. It was a trying time. The clothes, made in the theatre wardrobe, were only half finished. They smelt abominably of the gold paint with which they were lavishly stencilled and fitted very badly. Gwen's dresses alone were most successful. She sat up in the wardrobe and finished sewing them herself in the few hours she could spare, and when the dress-rehearsal came she looked a vision. She wore a red-gold wig with small sausage curls at the neck, a wreath on her head, and high-waisted Botticelli dresses with flowing skirts, each one more becoming than the last. The stage was still in chaos, and the whole production so unfinished that Ayliff cleared the theatre, which was full of invited guests, and conducted the dress-rehearsal with the safety curtain down, a proceeding which did not increase our confidence, especially when I found in the ball scene that Gwen and I could not kiss for the pins which were still holding my costume together and pricking me in various parts of my anatomy.

The notices were very mixed, though Gwen was tremendously and deservingly praised. A. B. Walkley was very encouraging to me in *The Times*, and some of the other critics were amiable about my performance, but on the whole I was not a great success. Ivor Brown said I was 'Niminy-Piminy – Castle Bunthorne'. A weekly paper had a notice which I have always cherished. It said, 'Mr Gielgud from the waist downwards means absolutely nothing. He has the most meaningless legs imaginable . . . At times he reminded me of that much better actor, Philip Yale Drew [then playing Young Buffalo in a melodrama at the Lyceum]. He has the same sort of hysterical laugh, which is almost a giggle, and quite meaningless!' Some people thought that I was promising, spoke the verse well, and understood the character. Considering my lack of experience, I think it is remarkable that I was let off so lightly. It was too soon for me to dare to play Romeo in London – even at King's Cross.

The people who liked *Romeo and Juliet* liked it very much. Although the theatre was not often full, the production created a good deal of interest. Small bands of faithful admirers came again and again to see it and I met some interesting people.

We were asked out to smart parties once or twice. A rich lady who lived a little way out of London invited us to play the balcony scene on her lawn one Sunday night. We were too shy to ask for a cheque, which no doubt she would have been delighted to give us, but we were pleased to accept her invitation. Mrs Gordon Woodhouse, dressed in purple scarves and a turban, was playing Bach and Mozart on a clavichord when we arrived, and the drawing-room was crammed to suffocation and looked like a scene from one of Aldous Huxley's novels. Ernest Thesiger was sitting about on the lawn, and Lopokova[1] was eating cherries out of a big straw hat. After supper we went up to dress, and then the outdoor performance began. I ran across a flower-bed to my place below the window from which Gwen was leaning (her wig looking strangely orange in the moonlight), and found that I had to risk life and limb on a very rickety espalier before I could touch her hand with mine. I looked round desperately to invoke the moon, but realized at last that it was shining on the wrong side of the house. Our lines were punctuated by our hostess's voice murmuring in a rich Dutch accent, 'Oh! it's so r-r-romantic!' and the wrigglings and slappings of the other guests who were vainly battling with mosquitoes.

One day at the matinée I felt extremely ill. The balcony scene is always a very tiring one to play. It is not easy to produce one's voice correctly while standing and gazing upwards in a strained position. That afternoon I found it particularly exhausting. Suddenly in the middle of it, everything went black. There was a long pause, and the curtain slowly fell. Poor Gwen was left in her balcony with a crumpled Romeo on the floor below. The house applauded, thinking, I suppose, that I had swooned with ecstasy. I came to after a few minutes and finished the two performances somehow. But I had pneumonia, and could not play for a fortnight. I had two understudies, neither of whom was competent to appear (one of them, being sent for to rehearse with Gwen, became stone deaf from sheer terror), and Ion Swinley stepped into the breach and played the part with the book in his hand for a few performances. Then Ernest Milton played for a week till I was well enough to act again. A month later the production came to an end after being played for six weeks altogether, but I was away for two of them. My baptism of fire was over.

---

[1] Ballerina in Diaghilev's company. Afterwards married to Maynard Keynes, the great economist.

Chapter 6

1924–25

I went back to the Oxford Playhouse for another season. I was tired of living in 'digs', and I had taken a two-roomed flat on the second floor of a house in the High, opposite the 'Mitre'. It was simply furnished and had sloping wooden floors and a charming view. I was very proud of it as it satisfied all my instincts for tidiness and space. I used to get my own breakfast, boiling an egg and making tea on a gas-ring by my bed, and eat it while I studied my next week's part propped against the looking-glass. While I was putting on my clothes I would wander about between the two rooms reciting my lines, shouting above the noise of the gramophone, which, for some unknown reason, I always played after my bath. Sometimes on Sunday evenings following our dress rehearsals, I gave small parties, and we drank a great deal of beer and shouted out of the windows.

Fagan allowed more rehearsals than usual for *The Cherry Orchard*, which he had determined should be the most interesting production of our new season. He talked to us at some length about the play, but at the first reading it mystified us all considerably. There was little time for discussion, however, and we set to work as best we could. The work was utterly different from anything I had attempted before, but, even though I understood so little of the style and construction of the play, I saw at once how effectively my part was placed to make the greatest possible effect in the simplest way – the first entrance of Trofimov, peering in to the nursery through his spectacles, and Madame Ranevsky's emotion at seeing him again, because he was the tutor of her little boy who was drowned – his idealistic scene in the country with Anya – his clumsy efforts to comfort Madame Ranevsky at the party when she hears that the orchard has been sold, and his exit when he rushes from the room in confusion and tumbles downstairs – finally the scene where he burrows among the luggage for his goloshes, and leaves the deserted house with Anya, hallooing through the empty rooms.

Making up for Trofimov, I put on a black wig, very thin on the top and in front, a little beard and steel glasses, and found myself looking like a shabby bleary-eyed caricature of my brother Val. I was very pleased with my make-up. It acted as a kind of protection from my usual self-consciousness and I felt easy and confident when my turn came to make my appearance on the stage. For once I need not worry whether I was moving gracefully or looking handsome; I had not to declaim or die or express violent emotion in fine language. Instead, I must try to create a character utterly different from myself, and behave as I imagined the creature would behave whose odd appearance I saw in my looking-glass.

Of course, all acting should be character-acting, but in those days I did not realize this. When I played a part of my own age I was acutely aware of my own graces and defects. I could not imagine a young man unless he was like myself. My own personality kept interfering, and I began to consider how I was looking, whether my walk was bad, how I was standing; my attention was continually distracted and I could not keep inside the character I was trying to represent. As Trofimov, for the first time I looked in the glass and thought, 'I know how this man would speak and move and behave', and to my great surprise I found I was able to keep that picture in my mind throughout the action without my imagination deserting me for a moment, and to lose myself completely as my appearance and the circumstances of the play seemed to demand. I suppose the truth of the matter was that I was relaxed for the first time. The finest producers I have worked with since have told me that this relaxation is the secret of all good acting but we were never taught it at the dramatic schools. One's instinct in trying to work oneself into an emotional state is to tighten up. When one is young and nervous one tightens the moment one attempts to act at all, and this violent tension, if it is passionately sincere, can sometimes be effective on the stage. But it is utterly exhausting to the actor and only impresses the audience for a very short space of time.

In playing Shakespeare one is bound to be conscious of the audience. The compromise between a declamatory and a naturalistic style is extremely subtle, and needs tremendous technical skill in its achievement. In Chekhov, provided one can be heard and seen distinctly, it is possible, even advisable, to ignore the audience altogether, and this was another reason why I suddenly felt so much more at ease in playing Trofimov than I had as Romeo.

I have extremely good eyesight and I am very observant. From the stage, if I am not careful, I can recognize people I know eight or ten rows back in the stalls, even on a first night when I am shaking with nervousness: late-comers, people who whisper or rustle chocolates or fall asleep, I have an eye for every one of them, and my performance suffers accordingly. I once asked Marion Terry about this difficulty and she said, 'Hold your eyes level with the front of the dress-circle when you are looking out into the front'. It has taken me years to learn to follow her advice. But in Chekhov, whose plays are written to be acted, as Komisarjevsky used to say, 'with the fourth wall down', I have always been able to shut out the faces in front even when I look in their direction and am conscious of no one but the other characters round me on the stage.

The Cherry Orchard made a stir at Oxford, and Playfair, who came to see it, offered to transfer the whole production to the Lyric, Hammersmith,[1] at the end of the Oxford season. The prospects of success were not very hopeful, however. People

1 The Lyric was managed at this time by Playfair and he produced a number of brilliant successes there until his death. This charming old theatre was pulled down in 1971, and I gave a television interview from the empty stage there just before it was destroyed. It has of course been recently rebuilt and reopened with success.

remembered how the audience had walked out at the original Stage Society performance some years before, and at the dress-rehearsal at Hammersmith the backers smoked many cigarettes and shook their heads over the booking sheets. But Arnold Bennett[1] and Playfair were still hopeful and enthusiastic, and the play went very well on the first night even though the theatre was not as full as it might have been. There was a mixed press and several very empty houses afterwards, and Playfair hastily arranged for a revival of *The Beggar's Opera* and engaged his cast. All of a sudden the business began to improve. James Agate wrote a most helpful and illuminating notice in the *Sunday Times* and also spoke enthusiastically about the play over the radio. Basil Macdonald Hastings, on the other hand, wrote a violently denunciatory notice, saying *The Cherry Orchard* was the worst play in London. Fagan and Playfair printed Hastings' and Agate's notices together on the same posters and in the advertisements in the newspapers, and the curiosity of the public was aroused. We began to play to really good audiences at last and, though a few people walked out at every performance, the general verdict was enthusiastic. We could not remain at the Lyric, of course, as *The Beggar's Opera* was already in rehearsal, but moved to the Royalty[2] where the play ran through the summer.

The committee of the Phoenix Society had lately been very successful with their Sunday night and Monday afternoon per-formances of Elizabethan and Restoration plays. Isabel Jeans had made one of her first big successes for the Phoenix in *The Country Wife*. Now Norman Wilkinson[3] asked me to play Castalio in Otway's *The Orphan* for the Society and I jumped at the opportunity. I had a very good declamatory part, and there was a curious plot, in which the heroine, Monimia, came in mad like Ophelia and everybody died in the last act. I remember nothing else about the play, except that Melville Cooper (who afterwards made such a success as Trotter in *Journey's End*) played

1 Bennett and Duff Taylor were partners with Playfair in the management of the theatre.
2 In Dean Street, Soho. The theatre was bombed in the Second World War.
3 A brilliant designer for Granville-Barker in his Savoy Shakespeare seasons, 1912–13, was one of the promoters of the Phoenix Society.

somebody's old father and had a line beginning very dramatically 'Ruin like a vulture' which he delivered at the dress-rehearsal 'Run like a vulture' and paralysed us all with laughter. At the Monday afternoon performance I saw two figures outlined in the stage-box, and at one moment during the play I distinctly heard a voice which I recognized at once, saying in a loud stage-whisper, 'Now I know how he must have looked as Romeo'. It was Ellen Terry.

I had seen her four or five times on the stage as I was growing up, but one of my most vivid memories is of an evening when I went to hear her read Beatrice in a private house in Grosvenor Square. I had never seen *Much Ado About Nothing* acted on the stage, and here there were only gilt chairs placed in a semicircle, a hushed, respectful audience, and a company of nervous amateurs in evening dress reading their parts from little books. In an armchair in the middle sat Ellen Terry, provided with a large book with very big print. Off she started, spectacles on nose, eyes on the text – no showing off to frighten the others. Just a sweet old lady with a lovely voice – but not for long. The words of the play seemed to catch her by the throat, she rose from her chair and she began to act. A few more lines and she had mastered her forgetfulness completely. She was old no longer. She needed no lights or scenery or costume to show us how divinely she could play Beatrice. 'No, sure, my lord, my mother cried; but then there was a star danced, and under that was I born', and then with such a tender change of tone, 'Cousins, God give you joy'. There was nothing frail about her now, no hesitation in her sweeping generous movements and the strong expressive movements of her hands,[1] now at her lips, now darting to her lap to bunch up her skirts as if she were poised for flight:

> 'For look where Beatrice, like a lapwing, runs
> Close by the ground, to hear our conference.'

---

1 Her hands were not beautiful, but she used them with marvellous fluency.

One could see how she must have glided across the stage. Then, in the Church scene, when Hero swoons, Ellen Terry rushed across the platform, upsetting several of the little gilt chairs on the way, and clasped her 'cousin' in her arms to that young lady's considerable embarrassment.

I saw her act another time in a theatre on one of the piers at Brighton. She gave the Trial Scene from *The Merchant of Venice* and two scenes from *The Merry Wives of Windsor*. The orchestra played a gay little tune and Ellen Terry came dancing on, dressed in the wimple and head-dress and flowing gown of Collier's famous picture.[1] Among the company who appeared with her and had the privilege of learning from her was Edith Evans, who played Nerissa and Mistress Ford on this occasion. 'A girl after my own heart' Ellen wrote once in a book she gave her, and Edith's own lusty performance of Mistress Page a few years afterwards (for Playfair at the Lyric, Hammersmith) showed what an apt pupil she had been.

It was very cold at Brighton when I saw the performance, and I was told that Ellen Terry, well wrapped up against the wind, had been wheeled down the pier in a bath-chair, past the empty benches and penny-in-the-slot machines, to the stage-door. But when she swept in to the court as Portia half an hour later, the elderly lady of the bath-chair was forgotten, though her hair was unashamedly white under the scarlet lawyer's cap. Like Duse, whom she loved and admired so much, she needed no artificial aids to bring the spirit of youth with her on to the stage. The Trial Scene was her favourite in her last years, and in that one scene her memory seldom seemed to fail her. But I have heard that one night, when she was playing it at the Coliseum during the First World War there was a Zeppelin raid. No one could keep Ellen Terry from seeing everything that was going on, and she insisted on being taken up on to the roof to watch the raid until the time came for her to appear. She made her entrance towards the end of the programme and was received tumul-

1 With Sir Herbert Tree and Dame Madge Kendal in the 1902 Coronation Performance of the *Merry Wives of Windsor* at His Majesty's Theatre. The picture is now in the Garrick Club.

tuously by the excited audience, but the bangings and poppings outside the theatre were not helpful to her concentration. When she came to the line, 'This bond doth give thee here no jot of –' she stopped dead. The actor standing nearest to her on the stage, realizing what had happened, was preparing to whisper the missing word into her ear, when the voice of Edith Craig, her daughter, shattered the silence from the prompt corner with the words 'Blood, Mother, blood!'

The newspapers were full of Noël Coward's triumph in *The Vortex* at the Everyman Theatre in Hampstead, and off I went to see it with my parents. In that tiny auditorium the atmosphere was extraordinarily tense, and the curtain of the second act, with Noël sitting in profile to the audience, his white face lifted, chin jutting forward, head thrown back, playing that infuriating little tune over and over, louder and louder, till the curtain fell, was one of the most effective things I ever saw in a theatre. The night we were there Noël was not at the door when the moment came for his entrance in the last act – the call-boy had missed his cue, or perhaps there was no call-boy at the Everyman – and there was an agonizing stage 'wait' while Miss Braithwaite trod the stage like a baulked tigress, holding the excitement as best she could until he arrived some moments later. We in the audience were so engrossed by this time, however, that the unfortunate hitch seemed hardly to affect us, and after the performance, clattering back in the half empty tube on the long journey home to South Kensington, we all sat silent, in that state of flushed exhaustion that only a really exciting evening in the theatre can produce.

When *The Vortex* was transferred to the Royalty (and later to the Comedy and the Little), someone must have suggested that I might be suitable to understudy Coward, as it was essential to have an actor who could play the piano. Fagan released me for the second time. I hope I thanked him properly – looking back on that time I realize what an extraordinarily kind and thoughtful manager he was. I was introduced to Noël one evening as he was making up. In those days I was used to seeing a few sticks of

Leichner greasepaint in an old cigarette-box and a shabby tin of talcum powder on actors' dressing-tables, and Noël's room looked very glittering, with large bottles of eau-de-Cologne on the wash-stand and an array of dressing-gowns hanging in the wardrobe. Noël was charming to me. He said it was a great relief to him to have someone reliable in the theatre, and that he would help me in any way he could. I shared a room with three other understudies with whom I played games and did crossword puzzles, and I went into the pit every night to see the last act from the front and watch as carefully as I could the way Noël and Lilian worked up the very long difficult duologue which made the last act so exciting to the audience.

Noël Coward used to arrive late at the theatre for *The Vortex*, as his entrance in the play did not occur until forty minutes after the rise of the curtain. He was rehearsing his revue *On with the Dance* all day long, and enjoyed sitting over his dinner as long as he possibly could. I used to stand at the stage-door looking down the street with a stick of greasepaint in my hand, ready to rush off to his dressing-room and make up if he should fail to appear. At last my patience was rewarded. Noël wanted to go to Manchester to see the opening of his revue, and told me I was to play his part on the night he was away. He gave me two rehearsals beforehand with Lilian Braithwaite and all the principals. I was naturally very nervous. Some of Noël's lines are so extraordinarily characteristic that, when once you have heard him deliver them himself, it is almost impossible to speak them without giving a poor imitation of him. Lines like:

'The last time I saw you you were at Sandhurst.'
'Such a pretty place.'
'You know, the very nicest type of Englishman.'
'I hate the very nicest type of Englishman.'

I thought I had studied minutely, during the many performances of the play I had watched, all the gradations of voice and inflection that the actors used in their big scenes, but I found that technically I had a very poor idea of how to reproduce them. The only moment I managed well at the rehearsal was the boy's final outburst against his mother, when he sweeps the glass off her dressing-table and flings himself into her arms. Even then I was so excited that I cut myself with the bottles, but in spite of my clumsiness Noël and Lilian seemed very pleased at my obvious sincerity, and their good opinion encouraged me to play my very best when the important night arrived.

There are few occasions more nerve-racking than playing a leading part in the absence of a principal. Before I went on that evening some kind person knocked at my door to tell me that several people had asked for their money back because they saw the notice posted at the box-office announcing that Noël was not appearing. But audiences are extraordinarily fair and well-disposed towards young understudies, especially if the play is an interesting one. At the end of the evening the applause was just as warm as it had been on other nights, and Lilian Braithwaite, who had helped me so generously all though the performance, sent for me to her room to meet Mr and Mrs George Arliss who had happened to be in the audience. Violet Loraine[1] also wrote to Noël, saying how much she had regretted finding him out of the bill, but how well she thought I had filled the breach. Altogether I felt that I had made a good impression.

The play was moved again, first to the Comedy and then to the Little Theatre.[2] The last weeks were announced, as the production was to be done in New York in the autumn and Noël needed a six weeks' holiday. But the management asked Miss Braithwaite whether she would consent to continue the run for another four weeks after Noël had left the cast, with me replacing him as Nicky. It was characteristic of her to think of my chances and the company's salaries instead of her own much-needed holiday – for, of course, she was to appear in the play in America too.

1 A great and popular revue artiste, who created with George Robey the immortal popular song of both World Wars, 'If you were the only girl in the world', written by Nat D. Ayer for 'The Bing Boys'.
2 The Adelphi in John Street, destroyed by bombs in the Second World War.

Chapter 7

1925–26

Chekhov's *The Seagull* provided me with my next part. The manager of this venture, Philip Ridgeway, was a curious man. The success of Fagan's production of *The Cherry Orchard* had led him to consider putting on several of Chekhov's plays, and after *The Seagull* he proposed to do productions of *Three Sisters, Ivanov* and *Uncle Vanya*. He had taken a lease of a tiny theatre at Barnes, across the bridge by the gates of Ranelagh Club, and for the first production there he had presented a rather indifferent stage version of *Tess of the D'Urbervilles*. This occasion was the signal for a good deal of publicity. Thomas Hardy was too old to come to London, and Gwen Ffrangcon Davies and Ion Swinley, who were in the play at Barnes, went down to Max Gate one afternoon and acted a scene for the great man on the hearthrug of his drawing-room. Photographs and descriptions followed and the play opened with a good deal of éclat. The acting was good enough to make the version seem a good deal better than it was, and the critics were kind to Ridgeway's enterprising scheme of running a theatre so far from the West End. *Tess* played for many weeks, and *The Seagull*, which had been planned to follow at Barnes, was produced instead at the Little. Then *Tess* moved to the Garrick, and *Three Sisters* followed it at Barnes.

The Seagull seemed to me to be written in a more conventional manner than *The Cherry Orchard*. There are 'big scenes' in every act, and the four principal characters carry the interest in a far simpler method of exposition than in the later Chekhov plays. Konstantin is a very romantic character, a sort of miniature

Hamlet, and a very exciting part for an ambitious young actor. I was given very good notices on the whole and thought at first that I was very well suited to the part. I resented the laughter of the audience when I came on in the second act holding the dead seagull, but on a very small stage it did look rather like a stuffed Christmas goose, however carefully I arranged its wings and legs beforehand. The last act used to go magnificently, thanks to the really beautiful acting of Valerie Taylor, whose performance of Nina made her reputation overnight. It was largely owing to her success that the play was a good deal talked about, and people came to see it for quite an unexpected number of weeks.

In contrast to the praise I received in some quarters for my performances, I received a good deal of personal criticism from a few discriminating friends, who told me that my mannerisms were becoming extremely pronounced, my walk as bad as ever, and my diction slovenly and affected. In one scene I had to quote Hamlet's 'Words, words, words'. My critics were perfectly right when they said I pronounced the line to sound like 'Wirds, wirds, wirds', but I found it surprisingly difficult to rid myself of this habit of closed vowels. I had begun to learn something of pace and the way to build up to a climax, my emotional outbursts were sincere, and I found I could make a great effect at times with pauses carefully timed and spaced, or with a suddenly simple delivery of a line at a pathetic moment. But as soon as I made one of these momentous discoveries I could not resist showing off what a clever technician I had become. The audience was quick to notice my self-satisfaction, and my acting became alternately shamefaced and 'tricky', according to the way I felt I was failing or succeeding in that particular part of the play.

At the end of the run of *The Seagull*, Philip Ridgeway sent for me to meet Theodore Komisarjevsky.

What prompted Ridgeway to engage Komis to produce the other three Chekhov plays for him I cannot imagine, except perhaps the fact that he was, like Chekhov, supposed to be a highbrow with a Russian name. He had, of course, done a number of interesting productions in London before this and he was a friend of the Fagans, for whose productions he had designed costumes. But I doubt if Ridgeway knew much about his work.

Komis was one of the most contradictory and fascinating characters I have ever met in a theatre. He was bitter and cynical about the English stage and the English public, destructive, pessimistic, and at the same time a real artist, a wise and brilliant teacher, and often an inspired director. He had an odd sense of humour quite unlike anyone else's, and would often spend thousands of pounds with less perfect results than he could achieve (as he did at Barnes when I was working under him) with a hundred or two as the outside limit of his expenditure. He loved to work with young people, adored enthusiasm, and inspired the greatest devotion from his actors and staff. His knowledge of painting, music and languages was considerable, and he had produced plays and operas in Berlin, Paris, Rome and Vienna, as well as in London and New York. He nearly always designed his own scenery and dresses, and his lighting was brilliantly clever. He was an architect as well as a painter, and designed all the decorations for the Phoenix Theatre and for a number of big cinemas in the suburbs of London. He was also the author of several fascinating books about the theatre.

Komis's sister, Vera Komisarjevskaia, had been one of the finest actresses of the Moscow Art Theatre, and had created the part of Nina for Stanislavsky. After a brilliant career she died of consumption at an early age. Komis had been to see our *Seagull*, and he had thought the production 'very funny'. But in spite of the fact that he was amazed to find us all playing in such a welter of gloom and Russian blouses and boots (and I dare say we should have been equally astounded at a Russian production of *The Importance of Being Earnest*), he decided that Margaret Swallow, who played Masha, and I were both conceivably promising material, and offered to engage us both for *Three Sisters*, in the parts of Masha and Tusenbach respectively.

Rehearsals started in a flat in Bloomsbury where Komis was living at the time, having rented it from the actor, Franklin

Dyall. There we all sat, crowded round a table at first, reading the play for many days on end, then laboriously trying to 'set' our complicated movements by keeping to chalk marks carefully drawn all over the floor to mark the exits, entrances, etc. Some five weeks later, when we reached a more advanced stage of rehearsals and arrived at the Barnes Theatre, we realized why so much care had been taken in dealing with the limited space at our disposal. Komis's ingenuity in making use of a tiny stage on a restricted budget was quite extraordinary. He arranged the first and last acts on a sort of terrace. Through big open windows, stretching right across the stage, one could see the room within – the dining-table (to seat thirteen) angled off-stage into the wings. In front, a clothesline on one side and the shadow of a tree on the other (a branch tied with a piece of string to the front of a strong lamp in the wings was responsible for this effect) gave the feeling of outdoors. For the two middle acts the windows were removed, and the same back walls suggested the interiors, hung with different lamps and pictures and arranged at a different angle. In the sisters' bedroom the beds were not seen, but a chintz-covered partition some four feet high stretched across the stage, dividing it in two. At the end of the act the girls retired behind this partition with their candles, and one saw, on the wall above, their huge shadows as Irina sat up in bed crying and Olga came across the room and leaned over to comfort her.

Three Sisters can be produced and played with many different interpretations, just as a play of Shakespeare's might be quite differently conceived by, say, William Poel and Granville-Barker, Komis's production certainly emphasized the romantic quality of the play, and he made some curious cuts and alterations in the text. He dressed the play twenty years earlier than the author intended, and the sisters wore the bustles and chignons of the eighties, which looked very attractive and certainly heightened their picturesque appearance. But his principal change affected me particularly, as he cut all references to the Baron being an ugly man – which is Chekhov's reason why Irina cannot love him – and made me play the part in a juvenile make-up, with a smart uniform and side-whiskers, looking as handsome as possible. I have never been able to discover why he did this – but I have a suspicion that he felt that a juvenile love-interest was essential in any play that was to appeal to an English audience. He persisted in casting the part in this way in every subsequent revival of the play, and it was extraordinary to me that not one of the critics, who went into ecstasies over the beauty of the production, noticed this very marked divergence from the express stage-directions and dialogue of the author. Of course I much preferred playing the part as a handsome young Lothario, and it did not then occur to me for a moment to question Komis's validity on any point in such a brilliant ensemble as he had achieved in his beautiful production.

Actors loved working for Komisarjevsky. He let them find their own way, watched, kept silent, then placed the phrasing of a scene in a series of pauses, the timing of which he rehearsed minutely. Very occasionally he would make some short but intensely illuminating comment, immensely significant and easy to remember. Martita Hunt once rehearsed for him a scene of Charlotta, the German governess in *The Cherry Orchard*. When she had finished Komis patted her on the shoulder and murmured the one word 'Irony'.

There were some wonderfully good performances in the Barnes *Three Sisters*. We played twice daily for eight weeks, and the road from Hammersmith was crowded with cars every night. Chekhov was a hit. Komis was very pleased with the tremendous appreciation both of the press and the public, and I think he was pleased, too, at our delight in working with him. When the scenery and effects were revealed for the first time at the dress rehearsal there was a spontaneous burst of applause from the whole company.

The next production at Barnes was a play called *Katerina* by Andreyev. It was a sensational play, and nearly a very good one. I played Katerina's husband, a sort of Slavonic Othello. At first when Komis showed me the play I was amazed that he should dream of entrusting this strong character-part to me, but, as it turned out, it seemed to be one of the best performances I gave in my early years. There were some magnificent moments of 'theatre' in the play, and Komis arranged them superbly. The curtain rose in the first act upon a darkened stage, faintly lit under the door of a room on the right, where the husband and wife could be heard quarrelling. Their voices, muffled at first, grew louder and louder, till after nearly a minute they reached a climax. Then two shots rang out, and Katerina threw open the door and rushed across the stage. I followed her and fired again, missing her, and from this exciting opening the act proceeded. This first scene was difficult to get right, as the quarrel off-stage was not written in the text, and Frances Carson and I used to make up our lines every night, following the rough outline of a quarrel which we had carefully rehearsed for volume and climax. Punch had a delightful cartoon the following week, representing me with my forehead pressed against the wall, with the smoking revolver in my hand, and the caption 'O, how I miss my wife!'

The theme of the play was interesting. A madly jealous husband suspects his innocent wife of infidelity. She leaves him, and, her mind infected by his suspicions, commits adultery with a very insignificant man, a friend of her husband. The husband comes to beg her to return to him, and she confesses what has happened. In his shame he takes her back, but her mind is completely poisoned, and she begins having affairs with a number of other men, until in the last act, we see her dancing half naked at a studio party, while the husband sits helplessly looking on. At the end of the play she goes out for a drive in the sledge of a drunken artist who makes advances to her, and the husband is left on the stage, amid the débris of the party, mechanically accepting a cigarette from the insignificant little man who was his wife's first lover.

My part began on the very highest note of violent emotion – which then became lower and lower in tone as the play proceeded. There was a beautiful scene of reconciliation in the second act, when Katerina confesses her guilt. Afterwards she goes into the house and plays Debussy on the piano, leaving her husband and her first lover sitting in the garden outside. As the curtain falls the lover offers his cigarette case, but on this first occasion the husband ignores it. There was a fine duologue between the husband and an artist friend (who, later in the play, has also become Katerina's lover) when the husband tries to find courage to kill himself – the whole play was Slav and intense. Ernest Milton played the artist, and we both used to find it hard to keep a straight face in this very dramatic scene if the house was not sympathetic. The dialogue ran:

'There's a fine view from that window. Is it high?'
'The sixth storey. A precipice.' (*Long pause.*)
'Could you kill yourself, Charles? I'm just interested to know.'

Komis cut up the floor of the tiny stage for this production, so that in the garden of the second act people seemed to come up from below on to a terrace, and in the studio scene of the third and fourth acts there were steep stairs ascending to the stage, giving the effect of a very lofty attic. But, as usual, I was rather too conscious of the good effect Komis had created for me, and James Agate remarked: 'Mr Gielgud is becoming one of our most admirable actors; there is mind behind everything he does. Only, he must avoid the snag of portentousness, of being intense about nothing in particular. Twice in this play he has to make an entry upstairs from below stage. The first time is an occasion of great solemnity, but on the second he is merely paying a friendly call, to do which it is unnecessary to put on the manner of one rising from the grave.'

About this time I had the honour of meeting Mrs Patrick Campbell. She had been to see *Katerina*, and when I was introduced to her she was very complimentary and said: 'You acted beautifully. And you should always wear a goatee.' I was introduced to her at the late Lord Lathom's beautiful flat in Mount Street, where I used sometimes to be asked to luncheon parties. Ned Lathom was a tremendous enthusiast about everything to do with the theatre, and he was always putting money into plays as well as writing them himself. If he had not been so rich (and so delicate in health), he might have become a very successful playwright, for he was inventive and had a real flair for good stage-situations and caustic, witty dialogue. I was quite bewildered by the elegance of his flat, with the Romney portraits, the library filled with lovely hand-bound books, the thick carpets, the burning sandalwood which scented the rooms, the exquisite food and fascinating company. Here I met Marie Tempest and Gladys Cooper for the first time, and Ned also introduced me to H. M. Harwood, the playwright, through whose kind offices I acted shortly afterwards, for a special Sunday night performance, in a version he had made of *L'École des Cocottes*, in which I appeared with Gladys Cooper and Leslie Faber.

It was exciting to meet some famous West End stars, and still more exciting to act with them. Ned Lathom used to laugh at my 'highbrow' tendencies, and my enthusiasm for Chekhov and Shakespeare — and indeed my career seemed to have been curiously diverted towards intellectual plays since the days of *Charley's Aunt*. I was longing now to earn a bigger salary and to see my name painted on the boards of a theatre in Shaftesbury Avenue, but at the same time I realized how profitably I had spent my time at Barnes and with the Fagans. Komis's interest and help had encouraged me tremendously, and I began to feel that I could study a part from the inside, as he had taught me, not seizing at once on the obvious showy effects and histrionics, but trying to absorb the atmosphere of the play and the background of the character, and then to build it outwards so that it came to life naturally, developing in proper relationship to the other actors under the control of the director.

The boy in *L'École des Cocottes* was not a big part, but there was a lot of boyish horseplay with the heroine in the first act which embarrassed me acutely (though Miss Cooper did her best to put me at my ease) and two rather charming sentimental scenes towards the end. I was paralysed with nerves at the performance and acted indifferently. The play proved rather disappointing, though Gladys Cooper gave an extraordinary exhibition of virtuosity, and looked absolutely dazzling in a black velvet dress in the third act, and Faber was immense as the Professor of Etiquette, demonstrating to the heroine and her very unsophisticated friend (played inimitably by Dorothy Hamilton) the proper way for ladies to behave on a visit to the Opera. Ned Lathom arranged the scenery for the third act – one of the first 'white' rooms ever done in the theatre. Although the play had been banned at first, it was passed by the Censor after the Sunday performance. When it was done later by Miss Cooper (under the title of *Excelsior*) at the Playhouse, without Faber or Dorothy Hamilton, I thought it not nearly so amusing, though Denys Blakelock was very much better than I had been in the part of the boy.

I appeared for The Three Hundred Club in a play called *Confession* with Cathleen Nesbitt at the Court one Sunday night. After the performance I received a message that Basil Dean was outside waiting to see me. I dressed as quickly as I could and when I came out of the stage-door, there, sure enough, was Dean, standing under a lamp-post by the Sloane Square Underground Station. He murmured something about having liked my performance, thrust a manuscript into my hand, told me to read it and call on him next day, and hurried away into the darkness.

Dean had sent for me once before and asked me to play the effeminate young man in Lonsdale's *Spring Cleaning*. I had always wanted to work at the St. Martin's, which had been the scene of so many of my early thrills as a playgoer – *A Bill of Divorcement, The Skin Game, Loyalties* – and the prospect of acting with a star cast at that theatre had tempted me greatly. But after reading the part I decided to ask twice the salary I had ever dared to ask before, and was not unduly disappointed when it was refused. I had not forgotten *The Insect Play*, and the bad impression I seemed to have made in it on actors and managers alike, and I was glad that the temptation to play an equally unpleasant character had been summarily removed.

The manuscript which I took home from the Court that night, however, was a very different matter. When I had finished reading *The Constant Nymph*, adapted by Margaret Kennedy, with the help of Basil Dean, from her best-selling novel, I could hardly believe it possible that such an opportunity should have fallen to me out of the blue. The part of Lewis Dodd was a tremendously long and difficult one, but it gave wonderful opportunities to the actor; it had comedy, pathos, drama, temperament, scenes at the piano, love scenes. Besides all this, the story was delightful, the atmosphere original and convincing, and the play seemed to demand, and would obviously receive, all the advantages of a first-class West End production.

I arrived next morning at the St. Martin's long before the time for my appointment with Dean, and suffered agonies of apprehension while many other actors and actresses were passed into the inner sanctum ahead of me. The room kept filling up and emptying all the morning, and there were continual comings and goings in the passage through the frosted-glass door. Still my name was not called. I should have been even more dismayed had I known what was going on in Dean's office, for I heard afterwards that Miss Kennedy was violently championing my cause in opposition to that of Ivor Novello, whom Dean had also approached with a view to playing Dodd. At last, when it was nearly lunch-time, I was ushered in, clutching my manuscript to my chest as if I defied the world to take it from me. Dean and Miss Kennedy were very amiable. Dates and salary were mentioned, but somehow I had a feeling that it was all too good to be true. At length I plucked up my courage and said, 'You are quite sure you really want *me* for this part?' Dean was very bland and reassuring. He said I should have a contract as soon as the play was passed by the Censor, and that rehearsals would begin in a few weeks' time. I left the office treading on air, took a fortnight's holiday in the country and, on my return, asked a friend to lunch with me at the Ivy to celebrate my good fortune. Noël Coward was at a table by the door and I nodded to him as I passed. After I had finished my lunch, I noticed that Noël was looking across at me with rather a serious face, and I felt suddenly frightened when he beckoned me to go over to his table. Then he said, very gently and kindly 'I think I ought to tell you before Dean does. I am going to play Lewis Dodd for the first month of the run of *The Constant Nymph*.'

I was bitterly disappointed. I felt Dean had been unfair in not telling me frankly that if he could get a star he would not risk me in the part. Noël had been so kind to me in *The Vortex* that I could not resent his playing Lewis, but I knew how difficult it would be to follow him, and that anyway all the joys of original creation would be snatched from my grasp. I was summoned to Dean's office that afternoon. He offered me half salary to understudy Noël for a month and then the salary he had originally mentioned to play the part afterwards. I swallowed this added insult and then saw that I had been foolish not to have made a bit of a scene, for Dean looked quite relieved and said, 'You are taking this very well'. I smiled sheepishly and retired (wearing a martyr's crown) to seek consolation from my friends.

I sat through all the rehearsals of the play, and very interesting they were, though I was too discontented and depressed to enjoy my first experience of a big new production to the full. There were stormy scenes almost every day. The cast had been brilliantly chosen, but there were complicated ensemble effects, the charades and breakfast scene in the first act, the musical party in the second, and the Queen's Hall scene in the third. In all of these episodes Dean demanded a most complicated perfection of detail to be carried out as if by clockwork. Edna Best had been cast for Tessa (after a great deal of argument during which the part had nearly been given to Tallulah Bankhead) and Cathleen Nesbitt said to me bitterly: 'I am always Basil's last choice. When he can't get anyone else to play a part he sends for me.' Noël disagreed with Dean and Margaret Kennedy on several occasions, and one morning he left the rehearsal at a standstill and retired with them to the bar, whence their voices could be heard in violent argument. Noël came in to the Ivy for lunch with a set face half an hour afterwards telling me he was going to throw up the part, and my heart leapt as I thought my chance was coming after all. Dean asked me that afternoon whether I knew the lines, and I went home and studied them all night – but next morning the row had been patched up, and the rehearsals went on as if nothing at all had happened.

Every day the stage management arrived with piles of 'props'. If the rehearsal was moved to another theatre, everything had to be taken there – siphons, sandwiches, beer-mugs, soup-plates. Over and over again Dean rehearsed the musical party, until the guests went nearly mad, making bright conversation in high-pitched voices, and stopping short with abrupt resignation every few minutes when the same person made the same mistake for the eighth time and the whole scene had to be done all over again.

Dean's efficiency was certainly remarkable and *The Constant Nymph* was one of his most accomplished achievements. He got good results from the actors in the end, but usually after a great deal of heartburning. He would not allow people to think for themselves or develop their characters freely, and his meticulous method of giving them every inflection and tone before they had experimented themselves made them feel helpless and inefficient. As part author of the play as well as director, he was naturally intensely anxious, but his enthusiasm carried the final rehearsals to a remarkable level of perfection.

On the first night I could not bear to watch the play. I slipped off to see Florence Mills in *Blackbirds* at the Pavilion, and only came back between the acts to the stage-door of the New, where they told me that the play was being enormously well received. The Press was unanimous next morning. Edna Best had made the greatest success of her career, Noël had splendid notices, Mary Clare, Keneth Kent, Cathleen Nesbitt, Helen Spencer were all much praised. George Harris's *décor* and Dean's production won superlatives, and the theatre was packed at every performance.

Noël was to have played for a month and I had been promised newspaper announcements and a certain amount of publicity when he left. Ten days before the month was up, however, he sent for me and said he felt terribly ill. He left in the middle of the third week and I opened at a matinée the following day. As I had rehearsed with the understudies, as well as once with Dean and with the principals and once with Noël, I hoped that I should not disgrace myself. At first everything seemed to go well. The houses were still packed in spite of the fact that Coward had left the cast. But I was made to feel rather small. I was billed, after a few days, in the newspapers, but otherwise I was baulked of my hopes for publicity. Noël's photographs remained outside the theatre for the whole year's run which followed, a fact that annoyed me whenever I passed the doors. He had tried to pave my way with the company before he left, but unfortunately I did not seem to be able to live up to the good character he had given me. Dean had gone to America, and there was no one really in control. It was a most unhappy time for me. I acted as well as I could, but at first I was terribly hampered, just as I had been in *The Vortex*, by Noël's reading of the lines, which were so indelibly printed on my mind that I could not easily discover how to play the part in my own way.

It was a very unfortunate thing that, with such a big success and a certainty of a long run, everyone in the company seemed to be at loggerheads with everyone else. At least three of the cast were 'not speaking' to me, and at least three more were 'not speaking' to several others. People accused one another of spoiling their best effects, of cheating on laughs or letting down some important moment. I used to wonder every night how much the general dissatisfaction behind the scenes affected our playing from the point of view of the audience.

My own acting became increasingly self-conscious. Dean returned some twelve weeks after I had opened, saw a performance, and came to my room with 'Very nice for an understudy. You know we want more than that.' The next day he called an intensive rehearsal at which he reduced me to pulp and Edna Best to tears. The rows and complaints continued unceasingly for many months, until at last I got really ill and had to leave the cast for ten days. When I returned, the atmosphere seemed a little more friendly and, to my surprise, several of the company came up to me and asked me why I was not going on tour with the play. I replied rather grandly that nobody had asked me. Next day I was sent for to the office, where I was officially invited to play Lewis in the provinces, upon which I demanded double my salary and star billing. To my amazement, both were conceded without a murmur.

It was extraordinary how often in those early years I seemed to be on the fringe of real achievement. If I had been hailed as a leading juvenile after Romeo in 1922, I might never have played in *The Cherry Orchard* or at Barnes. Again, if I had created the part of Lewis Dodd in 1926 and made a success of it, my subsequent career would probably not have followed the devious route which led me to the Old Vic in 1929. Although my work was extraordinarily varied and I gained a great deal of experience of different kinds, I was always prevented by a series of chances from achieving any spectacular personal success.

Chapter 8

1927–28

The Constant Nymph gave me my first experience of a long run. To play the same part eight times a week for more than a year is a severe test for any actor. The routine is nerve-racking, and it is agonizing work trying to keep one's performance fresh without either slackening or over-acting. I am usually guilty of the latter fault, and my tendency to exaggerate every effect becomes more and more marked as the weeks go by. After a long run in London, touring is at first a pleasant change, even in the same play, as one is forced to change the tone and breadth of one's performance to suit the different sizes of the provincial theatres; but by the end of a year's run in London with a six weeks' tour of the provinces to follow, acting becomes a real nightmare, and it seems hard to believe one is ever going to enjoy it again.

Long runs have their advantages, however. To begin with, they are necessary for an actor if he is to attract the notice of a large public. Many people can only afford to go to the theatre two or three times a year, and naturally they are inclined to choose for their visits the plays which are big hits of several months' standing. Young actors can often make personal successes in a series of short runs or even in failures. The critics may indeed notice them with more attention if they distinguish themselves several times running in a series of indifferent plays, as Laurence Olivier did so markedly in the early part of his career. But, though they may be well spoken of in the Press, and 'fancied' in the small world of the theatre, the general public will never have heard of them until their names have once been connected with a big commercial success.

There is also the question of discipline. A long run, with continual good houses, gives the actor confidence and sureness in his technique. He is able to try many different ways of timing, to study the details of tone and inflection, to watch his mannerisms, and to develop his capacity for give-and-take in acting with his partners. He is forced to control his boredom, to discover a means of producing effects of emotion of which the spontaneous feeling has long since deserted him, to resist the temptation to giggle and play the fool, to find a way of rousing a lethargic house, and to remind himself continually that there are many people in every audience who are seeing and judging his acting for the first time.

Long runs are also very useful for making money. As soon as *The Constant Nymph* had settled down to a certain success, I persuaded my parents to let me leave home. Frank Vosper was shortly to move from a little flat in Seven Dials, where he had been living for some time. I greatly admired this flat and arranged to take over from him the rest of his lease.

The flat was full of character and I stayed there for eight years. There was no proper kitchen, and the bathroom, with a rather erratic geyser, was down a very draughty flight of stairs. But otherwise the place was charming. The sitting-room walls had been covered with brown hessian by Vosper, and there was a ceiling in one of the bedrooms painted by an artist friend of his (under the influence, I imagine, of Braque), with large nude figures sprawling about. This I thought very modern and original. Later, when I became a little more affluent, I took over a large attic belonging to the landlord. It had a huge cistern in one corner, windows black with the dust of ages, and an incredible conglomeration of rubbish which had to be taken away by relays of dustmen. When it was cleaned, I painted the floor, silenced the gurglings of the cistern, built in some cupboards, and turned it into a spare room and studio. I acquired a charming Irish cook, and gave small lunch parties at which her Irish stew was the principal attraction.

It was exciting to be in a success in the West End and to be able to afford to take a flat on my own, and I had an exceedingly good time when I was away from the theatre. But I used to get very depressed about my unpopularity at the New, and the strain of the long emotional part of Lewis Dodd was very exhausting. I opened the play, had six changes of clothes, and was hardly ever off the stage except when I was making these changes. Occasionally I saw something of my brother Val. He had been unlucky ever since the War, and had tried a number of schoolmastering and tutoring jobs without much success. Later, he had taken to the stage, and had even understudied me in *The Cherry Orchard* at the Royalty. Fagan had given him work at the Oxford Playhouse for a time and now he was appearing (as a policeman!) and understudying in *The Ringer*, Edgar Wallace's first big success, which was running at Wyndham's, just across the court from the New where we were playing *The Constant Nymph*.

Naomi Jacob, the authoress, was also acting in *The Ringer*, and very good she was. She left the stage a year or two after this time owing to ill-health which forced her to live abroad. Val and I used sometimes to go to parties at her flat near Baker Street, which were delightful, as she knew a lot of music-hall people as well as 'legitimates'. 'Micky' Jacob was also a great friend of Leslie Faber and his wife.

Faber was playing the Scotch doctor in *The Ringer*, and playing it magnificently. I was already one of his most ardent admirers, having worked with him in *L'École des Cocottes*, in which he was very kind to me. But even before that, I had thought his acting of Henry, the drunken, good-for-nothing husband in St. John Ervine's *Jane Clegg*, which he played with Sybil Thorndike and Clare Greet, one of the finest pieces of character acting I had ever seen. Today I still doubt if I shall ever see a better. So I was in the seventh heaven of delight when, after a gruelling matinée of *The Constant Nymph*, Leslie Faber walked into my dressing-room, said a few immensely gratifying words about my acting, slipped away again, and then wrote me a long letter which he sent across by his dresser during the evening performance.

A week or two after this, Faber took me to supper at the Garrick Club, where I admired the lovely theatrical pictures, the Zoffanys and Hogarths, met Allan Aynesworth, and listened with wonder to some of the older actors reminiscing about Irving. One story, which deeply impressed me but which may be quite apocryphal, described 'the old man' sitting in front of the fire at the Garrick very late one night, crouching apathetically in his armchair with the night's return for *Peter the Great* clutched in his hand, and murmuring bitterly, half-aloud, 'Henry Irving. Ellen Terry. Lyceum Theatre. Twenty-five pounds'.

Leslie Faber's belief in my possibilities carried me through a very difficult time in my career, and I was deeply flattered to have the honour of his friendship. But soon he showed his kindness in a more practical way than by coming to see me act or taking me out to supper. I was summoned to the Gilbert Miller Offices, where 'Tommy' Vaughan, Miller's famous business manager, told me that I was offered the part of the Tsarevitch Alexander in Alfred Neumann's *The Patriot*[1] in America. Leslie Faber, Madge Titheradge and Lyn Harding had already left for New York to rehearse the play. The actor engaged for the young Prince had proved inadequate, and Leslie had put forward my name. If I was to accept the engagement, I must sail in forty-eight hours, learn my short part on the boat, and arrive just in time for the dress-rehearsal. I demanded a good salary and a six weeks' guarantee, packed my trunks, and sailed on a small German boat, the *Berlin*, with only two other English-speaking passengers on board.

I had planned a big New Year party at my flat, but it had to be given without me. The guests sent me a wire to the boat wishing me good luck, and I hoped I should not be very homesick and seasick. I detest uprooting myself and imagine a million disasters and miseries whenever I have to go to a strange place, especially if I am alone. It was just as well, therefore, that on this occasion I had had to make up my mind at once. In New York I was met by

1 Translated by Ashley Dukes.

a very tall coloured gentleman called John (from the Gilbert Miller offices) and was driven straight to the theatre, where the final dress rehearsal was already in progress.

The very striking scenery and dresses for the play had been designed by Norman Bel-Geddes. The scenes were set on three trucks mounted on castors – one placed at the back of the scene dock and one on each side of the stage. These were 'set' separately, each with a full scene, and then rolled on and off alternately, as they were needed, by stage hands pulling ropes attached to the corners of the trucks. A loud roll of drums in the orchestra covered the noise as they were being moved, and the changes were accomplished in a few seconds. The device is common nowadays in a big production, but in those days it seemed a marvel to me.

When I arrived the theatre was in a state of pandemonium. Milier was rushing about in his shirt-sleeves, with two or three secretaries and stenographers behind him. Bel-Geddes, who looked as if he ought to be playing Lewis Dodd, was gesticulating and shouting through a megaphone, also attended by a retinue of assistants. The stage was covered with scenery and strewn with débris, and Faber was walking up and down, in costume, calling angrily for his dresser.

I did not know how to announce my humble presence and slipped through the pass door to the corridor where the dressing-rooms were, nervously clutching my manuscript in my hand. I knocked at the door marked 'Lyn Harding' and a rich voice bade me enter. Mr Harding, dressed in a very tight but magnificent uniform and made up as the Tsar of All the Russias, was eating a plate of huge oysters from a tray balanced on his knee. I said rather timidly: 'I've come from England to play the Tsarevitch. Shall we go through our lines?' This we proceeded to do.

I had only two or three short scenes in *The Patriot*, but Faber and Lyn Harding gave me every kind of help and generously yielded me the stage in the few effective moments provided for me in the part. It was an alarming prospect to appear after only one rehearsal, but my costume was a great help. My uniform was superb; I wore a beautiful wig, which looked like natural chestnut hair powdered, and a magnificent cloak with an ermine cape, so that one way and another I hoped to cut a dash.

On the first night the play appeared to go very well, though there seemed to be less enthusiasm than at a successful London *première*. I thought this was accounted for by the fact that there was neither pit nor gallery. Miller gave a big party afterwards at his father-in-law's house, and on our way home, in the small hours, Leslie and I sat in Childs' Restaurant drinking coffee and composing hopeful cablegrams to send off to England.

The Press next day was not enthusiastic. The notices ranged from expressions of mild approval to complete boredom. It seemed that a great many people had walked out on the first night – the New Yorkers' polite method of expressing disapproval. Certainly very few walked in to see the eight performances that followed. Then the play was withdrawn. The film rights had been sold beforehand for a large sum, so that the management's losses were covered; all the same, a huge amount of money had been wasted. Some months later the play was done in London under the title of *Such Men are Dangerous*. Matheson Lang appeared in Faber's part, Robert Farquharson in Lyn Harding's, and Isobel Elsom followed Madge Titheradge. Gyles Isham played my part. Aubrey Hammond's *décor* and the production generally were less effective, in my opinion, than ours had been in America. Yet the play was a great success with English audiences and ran for many months.

Faber and I stayed in New York for a day or two in icy weather. The Fagans were playing *And So To Bed* in the theatre next door to the Majestic, where we had been in *The Patriot*. I went with Yvonne Arnaud and young Emlyn Williams to parties, and we had drinks in 'speak-easies', descending steep flights of slippery area steps to little doors, where there would be countersigns and passwords, and faces peering through gratings, before we could be admitted.

I was interviewed during the next few days by one or two managements, the Theatre Guild among others, and promised work later in the season if I would remain in New York. But I could not afford to stay on indefinitely and decided I had better return to try my luck again in London.

Leslie Faber was very much depressed by the failure of the play. The critics had said he looked like George Washington – he did, in fact, resemble him slightly with his powdered hair – and completely failed to appreciate the skill with which he had conceived and executed his performance. I had watched him rehearsing one scene in which he entered a boudoir in his dressing-gown, and forced his mistress to write a letter at his dictation. All the time he was speaking he had to move in and out of the room, tying a complicated neckerchief and completing his toilet in elaborate detail. The scene could have been commonplace enough. As Faber played it, it was a miracle of timing and dexterity.

I saw a great deal of Leslie during the following year in London. He found the play *By Candle Light*, which had been adapted from the German by Harry Graham, produced it brilliantly and played it with Yvonne Arnaud (whom he adored) and Ronald Squire.

While it was running, I acted in a Sunday night performance of *Hunter's Moon*, an adaptation from the Danish. Leslie was very enthusiastic about this play. He directed it superbly, and spent a lot of his own money on accessories, costumes, etc., which otherwise could not have been afforded for one night by the society under whose auspices the play was given. I had a very effective part as a neurotic young coward, and Phyllis Neilson-Terry looked and played radiantly as the heroine. But there was something wrong with the play. I told Leslie I thought he did not take the stage with sufficient *bravura*. He played a kind of Sydney Carton part, all villainy at first with love-scenes and sacrifice to follow, and he was too retiring and generous in the way he acted it. Uncle Fred came to the performance, and I thought how he would have – quite rightly – acted us all off the stage if he had been playing the part instead of Leslie. At the end of the play I was in my dressing-room with a crowd of friends, when there was a knock at the door, and Fred came in. We all stood up, and I said, 'How very kind of you to come round to see me!' I think mine was the best kind of pride when he answered grandly, 'My dear boy, you are one of the Family now'.

I was not long without a regular engagement. Anmer Hall asked me to play two parts in some Spanish plays which he was presenting at the Court Theatre – *Fortunato* and *The Lady from Alfaqueque*, by the brothers Quintero, translated by Helen and Harley Granville-Barker. James Whale was to be the producer. James had had an increasingly interesting career since those first days when I had met him at Oxford. He had worked for Playfair and for Fagan, designed scenery, acted, stage-managed and produced plays; but one could not have foreseen that only a few years later he would go to Hollywood, make the film of *Journey's End, Frankenstein*, and then direct *The Invisible Man* and other pictures.

Anmer Hall had cast James Whale for Fortunato, and we were hard at work when we heard one morning that the Granville-Barkers were coming to a rehearsal. When the day arrived and Barker appeared in the stalls, we were all extremely nervous. Everyone whispered, people smoothed their hair and walked about, and Miriam Lewes sat, dressed in her best frock, beating a tattoo with her fingers on the arm of her chair. Barker was certainly a revelation. He rehearsed us for about two hours, changed nearly every move and arrangement of the stage, acted, criticized, advised, in an easy flow of practical efficiency, never stopping for a moment. We all sat spellbound, trying to drink in his words of wisdom and at the same time to remember all the hints he was giving us, none of which we had time to write down or memorize. Everything he said was obviously and irrefutably right. Even when he announced that James could not possibly play Fortunato and that O. B. Clarence must be engaged, everyone gasped but nobody ventured to disagree.[1] Finally

1 By this I do not mean to disparage the admirable acting of Clarence in the part. But the decision was naturally a sweeping change for us all, and Whale, who had cast and started to direct both plays, as well as designing the scenery, was deeply disappointed of course.

we came to my last and best scene in *Alfaqueque*. The young poet who has been found fainting on the door-step has been looked after by the kind lady of the house, and is then discovered by the other characters to be a frightful humbug. But in the last act he brings off another coup and the play ends as he sits in the middle of the stage reading a poem aloud to an admiring circle.

Barker showed me exactly how to play this scene – the business, the timing, everything which would make it effective in performance. I implored him to wait a moment and let me rehearse it two or three times running, but he looked at his watch, signed to Mrs Barker, who was concealed somewhere in the dress-circle, bade us all good-morning, and disappeared through the front of the house never to return.

Shortly after the Court season came to an end, Leon M. Lion decided to contribute to the celebrations that were being arranged for Ibsen's Centenary with some special performances of *Ghosts*. Mrs Patrick Campbell was to appear for the first time in the part of Mrs Alving, and I was asked to play Oswald.

Peter Godfrey, who was running the Gate Theatre at the time, was to be the director, and our first rehearsals took place on the minute stage in Villiers Street.[1] Mrs Campbell arrived and sat in our midst, enthroned in a low wicker armchair which creaked, with her Pekinese on her lap, reading her part from an exercise-book in which some devoted handmaid had copied it out in a large distinct hand. When anybody else was reading she lowered the exercise-book and stared mournfully and intently at the speaker.

We soon found that she knew far more about the play, and every part in it, than any of the rest of us. Mrs Campbell could have been as fine a director as she was an actress. She helped me enormously with the emotional effects of my difficult part, couching her advice in graphic terms. In the scene where Oswald tells his mother of his terrible disease, she said: 'Keep still. Gaze at me. Now, you must speak in a Channel-steamer voice. Empty

---

1 In the arches underneath Charing Cross Station. Now Ridgeways Late Joys.

your voice of meaning and speak as if you were going to be sick. Pinero once told me this and I have never forgotten it.'

Mrs Campbell herself gave a very uneven performance as Mrs Alving. For several days she appeared not to know a line of her part, yet at the dress-rehearsal, when we expected her to be temperamental and inaccurate, she astonished us by arriving punctual to the minute, word-perfect, and in full control of her brilliant talents.

We played eight matinées of the play at Wyndham's Theatre following the special Sunday night performance. But the play did not seem to interest the public and the houses were very indifferent. Mrs Campbell used to say to me in her best party voice as she turned away from the audience, 'The Marquis and Marchioness of Empty are in front again'. To add to our difficulties, Charing Cross Road was being repaired with pneumatic drills and the noise in the theatre nearly drove us mad.

I used to take Mrs Campbell to lunch at the Escargot Restaurant in Greek Street, where she taught me to eat snails and discoursed to me on all kinds of topics. I think she was almost the best company in the world, particularly if one was alone with her. The famous stories of her temperament, her 'impossibility' in the theatre, and her brilliant wit, are not at all exaggerated, but, in speaking about these idiosyncrasies to someone who never met her, one is liable to miss giving any impression of her greatness as a woman. It is not often that beauty and success in the world of the theatre are allied to genius. Few people would deny that Mrs Patrick Campbell was one of the really great figures of her theatrical generation. Everything she said or did has been repeated and publicized. She never suffered fools gladly and she was immensely temperamental. But so are all first-class artists. One must remember that Irving and Sarah Bernhardt had their own theatres and could make their own rules of conduct and break them if they felt so inclined. Authors, managers, producers and actors naturally resented being overridden by a personality more powerful than their own, and refused, in her later years, to shoulder the responsibility which the engagement of such an artist as Mrs Campbell involved.

In 1928 Ellen Terry died. St. Paul's Church, Covent Garden, where a service was held in her honour, was a memorable sight. The floor was strewn with sweet-smelling herbs, and in the middle of the aisle was a catafalque covered by a golden pall, with candles burning round it, but there was no coffin and nobody was wearing mourning. At the close of the service the organist played 'The Londonderry Air', and then the huge congregation in its light suits and gay summer dresses streamed out into the sunshine . . .

I thought of the Christmas parties at Gledhow Gardens, and the fairy-Godmother who said 'Read your Shakespeare', and I remembered how once she had read Shakespeare for·me herself, not many years before her death. There was a matinée at the Haymarket Theatre and when the curtain rose there were only tall grey curtains and masses of flowers on a table and a lectern with a big book. I still loved scenery and I was rather disappointed. Then Ellen Terry came with her white clubbed hair parted in the middle and her beautifully-lined generous face, bunching up her long white dress with her graceful restless hands. First she talked rather seriously, like a professor, reading out the lecture she had prepared so carefully, but every now and then she slipped her eyes from her book and made some delightfully ordinary comment or improvised some little joke to keep us all happy and amused. Then, cunningly distributed amidst the talk, came the scenes from Shakespeare. There were speeches from many of her great parts, from Juliet, Portia and Beatrice, and there were a few lines from *As You Like It*, in the scene when Rosalind is banished by the Duke. When Ellen Terry came to this, she snatched the big book down from the lectern and walked up and down the stage hugging it in her arms. Of course, she was acting all the parts herself, Frederick and Celia as well as Rosalind.

'Mistress, dispatch you with your safest haste, and get you from our court.'

'Me, uncle?'

'You, cousin.'

'Oh, my poor Rosalind, whither wilt thou go? . . .'

'. . . To seek my father in the forest of Arden'—

Down she plumped on the table, the book in her arms, swinging her foot in the air. Over went the vases, the tall lilies, the masses of carnations, and the water fell dripping down over the velvet tablecloth, across the stage, down into the footlights, while Ellen Terry sat there, peering over her spectacles and laughing like a schoolgirl.

I saw her appearing once again before the public. She was announced to recite at a charity matinée at the Palladium one afternoon and I went up into the gallery to see the performance. She seemed to be blinded by the lights when she came on, and held her hands behind her, touching the curtains with her fingers to make sure she had not stepped too far forward on the stage. She spoke the title of a poem that every child in the audience knew by heart, 'The Burial of Sir John Moore', but almost as soon as she began the first verse she started to look round wildly for the prompter. She fumbled, muddled two more lines and then stopped dead. It was agonizing to watch her struggling with her memory. One felt sure she did not remember what she was doing or even where she was. Suddenly she lifted her hands towards the audience and smiled. 'Oh, dear,' she said, 'I can't remember it.' Then she threw back her head and began, 'The quality of mercy is not strain'd' – her face lit up, her voice grew strong and beautiful as of old, and on she went triumphantly to the end of the speech.

I have only one more picture of her, and in some ways it is the most vivid of all. I had never in my life been alone with Ellen Terry. Always I had met her at parties, in crowded rooms or theatre boxes or in public. This time, which was the last time that I should ever see her, there was no one by to distract her or to disturb my vision of her.

I was driving one summer day near her lovely Elizabethan cottage at Smallhythe in Kent, where the garden looks across the marsh. It was very hot. I wondered if I dared to call on Ellen Terry all by myself. At last I stopped the car, plucked up my courage and knocked at the door. They told me yes, she was getting up and would be down in a moment.

I went into the farm-kitchen that had been made into a sitting-room. There was a poster of Irving as Becket on the wall. The house was furnished very simply. I like empty, simple rooms myself, but I was rather surprised to find that Ellen Terry did too. Fred and Marion were great hoarders, and towards the end of their lives it was difficult to move in their crowded quarters. Here was a brick floor with rough mats and rugs, a few simple chairs, and a table by the window. Everything was spotlessly clean and airy, and on the table there were big bunches of flowers from the garden, which smelt delicious. There was a steep staircase leading to the rooms above, and I could hear someone moving about, speaking to a servant in a gruff voice, husky but frank and distinct: 'Who is it? Where's my bag?'

Her companion came in and whispered to me quickly: 'Please don't stay for lunch. She is sure to ask you to, but don't, because there's not enough.' Then Ellen Terry came slowly down the staircase. She wore a grey dress like a pilgrim's gown, with long sleeves and something white at her neck. She carried the big worn leather handbag with the padlock that I remembered from my childhood, and there were still red coral combs in her white hair.

She asked me who I was and I told her. She seemed to remember for a while and asked if I was acting now and whether my parents were well. I had on a bright-blue shirt, and she said how gay it was and that bright colours always cheered her up. She asked me to stay to lunch but I pretended I had to go on somewhere else. She seemed suddenly to grow inattentive and I knew I must not tire her any longer. As I turned to go she said: 'Oh, it's so exciting. They have promised to drive me out tomorrow night. I'm going to see the swans at Bodiam Castle. They look so beautiful by moonlight.' I kissed her, and she came with me down the path as far as the gate. As I got into the car she was still standing there, shading her eyes with her hand against the sun. Then she smiled and lifted the other hand to wave goodbye. I looked back from the car for a last sight of her before I turned the corner, but she had disappeared.

Chapter 9

1928–29

I seemed to be getting on well in my profession. I had doubled my salary since the days of *The Constant Nymph* and several managers appeared to know of my existence. I began to be asked to Lady Wyndham's[1] *thés-dansants* in York Terrace on Sunday afternoons, where many well-known stage people were to be seen. I was much flattered by these invitations, for I had never met Lady Wyndham except to say how-do-you-do, and could not imagine that she knew anything about my work, as she very seldom went to the theatre. It was not till after her death, some years later, that I was told that she had 'spotted' me when I was acting in *The Constant Nymph* at the New Theatre, of which she was the owner.

I played in a revival of *The Seagull* for a few performances at the Arts Theatre. The cast and production were almost exactly the same as they had been at the Little in 1925, and Miriam Lewes was very angry with me when I said, over a cup of coffee between the acts at the dress rehearsal: 'It's very boring not to have got any further with this play after all these years. We ought to have found out far more about it this second time.' When I said to the producer: 'I've never played this scene right. Do let me try it some other way', he merely shrugged his shoulders and replied, 'What a pity you always want to gild the lily', which was meant, I believe, as a compliment, but infuriated me none the less.

1 Mary Moore, well-known comedienne, wife of James Albery, the playwright, who wrote *Two Roses*. Afterwards she married Sir Charles Wyndham, the actor. She was the mother of Irving Albery, and of Bronson Albery and Howard Wyndham, to whom she bequeathed the three theatres built by Wyndham, The New (now the Albery). The Criterion and Wyndham's.

I acted for several other clubs and private societies which flourished about this time. For the Stage Society I played in O'Neill's *The Great God Brown* with Hugh Williams, Mary Clare and Moyna Macgill.[1] We held masks to cover our faces in certain scenes and speeches which seemed to me rather a pretentious and unsatisfactory convention.

At the Arts Theatre, too, I acted in a play called *Prejudice*, by Mercedes d'Acosta. This was a rather effective melodrama about the persecution of a Polish Jew living in a small town in the Middle West of America. I had a showy and dramatic part, and Gwen Ffrangcon Davies gave a moving performance as the girl, assuming an extremely clever accent for the occasion.

Ralph Richardson played a small part in *Prejudice*, but we did not take much notice of one another. I should have been amazed to be told that we should one day be friends. Leslie Banks directed the play, and I liked working with him enormously. I had great hopes that some enterprising manager might transfer us to another theatre for a regular run, but it was not to be.

Red Sunday, by Hubert Griffith, was another disappointment. The play was much liked by the critics, and several managers made offers for it, but the Censor refused to pass it because the principal characters – the Tsar and Tsarina, Prince Youssoupoff, Rasputin, Lenin and Trotsky – were not then allowed to be shown on the English stage. In this production I again worked with Komis, and admired his methods as much as ever. The scenery was simple to a degree, but brilliantly suggestive and beautifully arranged and lit. There was a most vivid little vignette of the Tsar and Tsarina (Nicholas Hannen and Athene Seyler) in a room in their palace, seen from the audience as if through a balconied window. Komis conveyed exactly the atmosphere of grandeur and ceremony, in contrast to the mean room, lit by an oil-lamp, where I sat as Trotsky, dressed in shabby clothes (and looked even more like Val, in my black wig and spectacles, than I had as Trofimov) at a table littered with books and papers, while

1 Mother of Angela Lansbury.

Robert Farquharson, amazingly made up as Lenin, leered down at me over the rickety banisters. The scene of Rasputin's murder in the cellar of Youssoupoff's house was macabre and thrilling too, with the big supper table strewn with dishes where the officers sat, watching with strained panic-stricken faces while Rasputin ate the poisoned cakes. My part went right through the play from youth to middle age, and I enjoyed working out my make-ups, wearing a padded uniform in the later scenes to give the effect of a middle-aged 'spread'.

I hope I have not given the impression that Komis's greatest talent lay in lighting and *décor* and the arrangement of the stage, though he excelled in all these departments. I was more than ever impressed with his handling of the actors, and with his acute musical sensitiveness, which always enabled him to 'orchestrate' a scene to perfection, allowing the actors to feel instinctively that the pauses and business sprang naturally out of the dialogue and process of the action. The result was closely patterned rhythm flowing backwards and forwards between the characters, covering any weakness in individual performance, and shifting the focus of attention continually without breaking the illusion of continuous life and movement on the stage.

These Sunday performances were tremendously interesting but my professional career during the same period was disastrous. I played in three hapless plays in quick succession. First a farce, in which I was 'starred' for the first time in Shaftesbury Avenue, called *Holding out the Apple*, with Hermione Baddeley and Martita Hunt – 'You have a way of holding out the apple that positively gives me the pip!' – Then a thriller at the Shaftesbury called *The Skull*, in which I played an incredible detective who turned out to be the arch-villain. The scene throughout was a deserted church, with an organ played by ghostly hands. There was a comic spinster in difficulties, a somnambulistic *ingénue*, an old professor with a cloak, and a cockney sexton with a club foot. Finally I was in *Out of the Sea* at the Strand, a pretentious poetic melodrama by the American poet, Don Marquis, in which I played the Liebestod from *Tristan* by ear on the grand piano in the first act. In the last, the heroine, who was the reincarnation of Isolde, threw herself off a cliff while I sat glooming in a mackintosh on a neighbouring rock. This last excursion only lasted a week.

Mean while *The Lady with a Lamp*, Reginald Berkeley's play about Florence Nightingale, had been produced at the Arts Theatre, and I had attended a few of the rehearsals as I was originally cast for the part of Sydney Herbert. Then something happened to prevent my appearing, and I dropped out. The play was bought and moved to the Garrick, where it achieved a successful run, but Leslie Banks, who played Henry Tremayne (who, in the play, is in love with Florence Nightingale and is mortally wounded at Scutari), had to leave the cast, and suggested that I should take his place. The part was a short one and I was able to open with only a few rehearsals.

Gwen Ffrangcon Davies gave a most lovely performance in this play as Lady Herbert. It was only a sketch of a part, but she made it such a vivid thing that it seemed to stand out, in every scene in which she appeared, as a perfect foil to Edith Evans's performance as Florence. I had never acted with Edith before, but she and Gwen were old friends. I had seen them playing together brilliantly as Eve and the Serpent in the first part of *Back to Methuselah* at the Court, and had rushed home after the performance and written Gwen a five-page letter of wildly enthusiastic appreciation. Edith Evans fascinated me, but I did not get much opportunity of knowing her at the time of this first meeting. I was chiefly concerned in covering my arms and body with a large quantity of fuller's earth, so that I might appear convincingly filthy when I was borne in dying on my stretcher. Edith had sent strict orders that I must not present a romantically clean appearance, and so shatter the illusion of dramatic fitness which she had conceived in her playing of the scene.

One day, as I was lunching in the restaurant of the Arts Theatre, Harcourt Williams came across the room and asked me if I would consider going to the Vic, where he was about to begin working as director. I suppose I had met him before. Now it hardly seems possible that there was ever a time when I did not know 'Billee' Williams. At any rate I asked him to come and see me at the Garrick Theatre and we would talk the matter over.

In the meantime I asked the advice of most of my friends, as I always do on these occasions (though I can never decide whether I act on the opinions of others or merely use them to strengthen my own). I believe I was really attracted from the first by the idea of going to the Vic. I had had a drifting, unsatisfactory time since *The Constant Nymph*. It was no fun earning a big salary in a bad part, and although I had tried to do character work and act in as many different sorts of plays as possible, I found that managers thought of me chiefly as a 'type' for neurotic, rather hysterical young men. I was not gathering much strength in the West End theatre, and I believe I was secretly determined to reach a position where I might have some say in the handling of a production. I do not think I had ambitions yet to become a director, but I did not want to be nothing but a leading man, and I had begun to feel that acting eight times a week was hardly a full-time job. I was quite prepared to spend all day and all night in a theatre so long as I was making myself really useful and achieving results. Watching Banks and Faber and Komis and Granville-Barker, I realized that, in addition to their individual technical brilliance, a real passion for the theatre was the driving force behind all their work. If I could use my own enthusiasm, or find someone to teach me how to use it constructively, I might perhaps learn in time how to handle plays and actors too, and experiment in putting some of my own ideas to a practical test.

I went down the stairs after the matinée one day and knocked at Edith Evans's door. Edith always slept between the performances, and I am sure she must have been very much annoyed at my intrusion. But she was kind and helpful in discussing my problem, which was similar to the one she had solved so triumphantly for herself, not many years before, in her enormously successful Vic season. She had decided to go there, she told me, because, after playing Helena for Basil Dean in *A Midsummer Night's Dream* at Drury Lane, she felt that she did not know how to act Shakespeare and wished to gain further experience in his plays. Edith's early career had been an extraordinary one. She was working in a hat shop in London when her acting in an amateur performance brought her to the attention of William Poel, under whose direction she afterwards appeared in some special performances of *Troilus and Cressida*. Then she met George Moore. He also was greatly struck by her talents, and spoke about her everywhere. But even the recommendation of these two brilliant men did not bring her any immediate success. During the First World War she toured in the provinces with Ellen Terry, and afterwards worked in London, playing many kinds of character parts – elderly ladies in *Out to Win* and *Daniel* – and understudying with Dennis Eadie at the Royalty. Here another of Ellen Terry's pupils shared her dressing-room, a young actress named Lynn Fontanne. Edith made further successes as the governess, Charlotta, in *The Cherry Orchard* for the Stage Society, and as the old maid in Brieux's *Three Daughters of M. Dupont*. She played Nerissa at the Court with Moscovitch. Then Fagan and Shaw cast her for Lady Utterword in Shaw's *Heartbreak House*, and she had her first big commercial West End success in Sutro's *The Laughing Lady* at the Globe with Marie Löhr. Refusing to be typed in 'silly society' parts, she boldly refused the offer to play the character of the Duchesse de Surennes in Somerset Maugham's *Our Betters*, in which Constance Collier afterwards made such a great success. At last, at the Lyric, Hammersmith with Playfair, following her success at Birmingham, when she acted the Serpent and the She Ancient in Parts 1 and 5 of Shaw's *Back to Methuselah*, she achieved her greatest triumph as Millamant, and later as Mistress Page. But even at the end of all this varying experience, when her hard struggle had won her recognition and success, she had risked a year out of her West End career and salary to go and play for next to nothing in the Waterloo Road in Shakespeare.

Next day I went to meet Lilian Baylis and discuss my contract. I arrived at the stage door, and was shown into Lilian's office which has so often been described in the stories and descriptions of her. The Vic seemed cleaner than in the old days when I had walked on there, and all the dressing-rooms and most of the offices were new. Morley College was gone, and there was a big airy 'wardrobe' at the top of the new building, replacing the funny old warehouse round the corner, where I remembered rehearsing at nights in murky gloom amidst dusty piles of dress-baskets. Now the corridors behind the stage were painted and swept, and there was a faint smell of size from the painting dock, and of steak and tomatoes from the purlieus of the office, where Lilian's lunch was being cooked.

I was ushered in through the glass door, and found Lilian sitting behind her big roll-topped desk, surrounded by vases of flowers, photographs, two dogs and numerous cups of tea. I had on my best suit, and tried to look rather arrogant, as I always do when money has to be discussed. 'How nice to see you, dear,' said Lilian. 'Of course, we'd love to have you here, your dear aunt, you know – but of course we can't afford stars.' By the end of the interview I was begging her to let me join the company. We both evaded the question of salary as long as possible, and a little matter of fifty shillings, over which we both obstinately failed to agree, was settled by letters some days afterwards.

As soon as matters were arranged, I went to supper with Leslie Faber, whose advice I had asked. He had urged me to accept the engagement, and was delighted to hear that matters were agreed. I told him that the parts I was to play were not yet settled definitely. I was to open as Romeo, and I was promised Richard the Second, one of Leslie's favourite parts. But I was to play Antonio in *The Merchant of Venice*, which did not appeal to me very much, and the rest of the casting was to be decided later in the season. Lilian was not taking anything on trust. She always wanted to see how the Old Vic audience would respond to the new actors she engaged. 'I expect you'd like to play Hamlet, wouldn't you, dear, but of course Gyles Isham is coming to us too, and we shall have to see.'

Leslie Faber had moved into a new flat in Dorset Street. He had always loved music, and I had sometimes seen him at concerts or at the opera, sitting by himself. He had recently bought a gramophone and we shared our enthusiasms for new records and discussed hotly the respective merits of Bach and Wagner. Leslie gave me records of the enchanting songs from *Mariette* and *Mozart* made by Yvonne Printemps, and also some German recordings of Moissi's speeches, the 'To be or not to be' soliloquy from *Hamlet*, and a scene from Goethe's *Faust* with a background of bells. Even though I do not understand a word of German I realized that the vocal skill and power of these records was remarkably impressive. We would sit up very late at night over a cold supper talking of Gladys Cooper and Yvonne Arnaud, whom Leslie thought the two best actresses he had ever worked with, of the Danish actor Poulsen, of Wyndham and Hawtrey and Du Maurier.

Leslie Faber was making the film of *White Cargo*, playing the part he had also acted in the stage version. He took me to a studio in Wardour Street where we saw the picture in its silent form. It was an excellent film but, as talkies had just come in, it was decided to remake many of the scenes with spoken dialogue. The work was very tiring, and Leslie was still acting in *By Candle Light* eight times a week in addition to his long hours in the studio. He was very much fascinated by film work. He had just made a film for Rex Ingram, *The Three Passions*, in the South of France, and was very good in it. With some of the money he had been earning while doing this work he had bought a boat. He was passionately fond of sailing, and pictures of sailing-boats always hung over his dressing-table in the theatre. After a particularly tiring week's work, he went away for the week-end to enjoy a day's holiday in his new craft, and caught a serious chill.

I had been staying in the country, and read in the newspapers as I travelled back to town that he was ill and out of the cast at the Criterion. I called at his flat next morning, and inquired if he was better. The man answered, 'Mr Faber died this morning'. I turned mechanically and walked away down the street. It was not till five minutes later that I realized I should never see Leslie again. The doctors had performed the same operation which saved King George the Fifth, but it was too late to save Leslie's life.

I was surprised to read the obituary notices that appeared in the Press after his death. They described him as an actor who had always been eminently successful from his earliest days, and gave an imposing list of plays in which he had appeared as leading man. But I knew that Leslie's career was not in any way equal to his ambitions or his potential talents. He was almost too versatile, and had a curiously ascetic quality which prevented an audience from warming completely to his personality. He excelled as villains and seducers; in plays like *The Letter* and *The Sign on the Door* he was superb. As a character actor, his Dr Lomax in *The Ringer*, his mysterious Count in *In the Night* and his Henry Clegg were all equally different and equally brilliant performances. He failed, however, in heroic tragedy – as Jason, for instance, in *The Medea* – and, to my mind (though he himself thought it his finest performance), as Shakespeare's Richard the Second. On the other hand his Macduff, to James Hackett's Macbeth, was a beautiful piece of work.

He was not a happy man. Difficult, proud and shy, he antagonized many people, and I think he was conscious of this. He was vain, too, and hated the idea of getting old, but perhaps that was why he sought the friendship of younger people like myself, and gave them the privilege of his company so often. He had two unhappy marriages, and he must have been deeply affected by the blindness of his younger daughter, to whom he was devoted. And while he was in the trenches during the War, he received a telegram saying that his son had died suddenly of meningitis at the age of twelve.

By Candle Light had seemed to promise him a new era of success, and, if he had lived, he would, I am sure, have continued in management, surrounded himself with actors whom he admired and trusted, and perhaps he would have achieved at last, both as actor and director, some of the great ambitions he had always cherished. There is no friend that I have more often missed, no actor whose loss I have more often

regretted, than Leslie Faber. His death made me more
determined than ever to show at the Vic that I was really
worthy of the confidence he had placed in my ability, and to
try and emulate his artistic integrity.

Chapter 10

1929–30

I have always been fascinated by theatrical advertisements. When I was a child I used to stand staring in at the window of a ticket agency in the Gloucester Road, learning all the bills by heart. Later, when I went to Westminster School every day by tube, I used to stoop down as the train passed through Sloane Square Station, brushing all the nap off my topper and butting my fellow-passengers in the ribs, while I tried to catch a glimpse of the poster for Fagan's Court Theatre productions, printed in blue, with the picture of Shakespeare – or, was it Malvolio? – drawn in the right-hand corner of it.

When it came to the pleasure of seeing my own name on a theatre bill this obsession became more intense than ever. I was almost run over as I stood, speechless with delight, gazing at my name blazing in lights for the first time.

One evening, some weeks before rehearsals at the Old Vic were due to begin, I decided to walk across the river and look at the outside of the theatre. I pretended that my reason for going was that I had not been there for a long time, but all I really wanted was an excuse to see my name in print.

There are several ways of getting to the Vic. Another of my childish preoccupations, dating back, I fancy, to my dislike of those unswerving walks to kindergarten with Father, is my distaste for following the same route every day in travelling to and from my place of work. Going home from school I used to walk to different stations, Westminster, St. James's Park, or Victoria, on different days, and got out at either South Kensington, Gloucester Road or Earl's Court Station at the other end. Today I still go to the West End from Westminster, where I now live by different sets of streets on succeeding days, avoiding the same route with as much care as I avoid, if possible, wearing the same suit of clothes two days in succession.

From St. Martin's Lane to the Old Vic it is possible to go by several different roads – Northumberland Avenue – Whitehall and Westminster Bridge – the Strand and Waterloo Bridge – Villiers Street and Hungerford Bridge, the last my special favourite. There is something romantic about the steep wooden gangway below Charing Cross Station, leading up through murky Dickensian arches on to the narrow bridge, with its echoing wooden floor-boards and iron balustrade. Steps and bridges have always been a passion of mine. I used to think a design of Craig's called *Wapping Old Stairs* – a lovely and characteristic drawing – one of the most perfect ideas for a stage-setting that I had ever seen. Hungerford Bridge somehow reminded me of it. I used to love walking slowly home after rehearsal through the empty slummy streets behind Waterloo Station, climbing the bridge steps until I reached the top where the magnificent stretch of sunset river suddenly burst into view. There were never people about in the late afternoons, and I was able to slouch along mumbling the words of the part I was studying for the next play, without having to drag myself back to earth every few minutes to avoid attracting the attention of astonished passers-by.

It was by Hungerford Bridge that I reached the Waterloo Road that first September evening. I thought the whole place looked tidy and clean in comparison with the rather squalid, naphtha-lit thoroughfare I seemed to remember eight years before. There were still barrows and fish-shops round the corner in the New Cut, but the theatre itself looked bare and almost prim with the front entrance locked and no one going in or out of the stage-door. I scanned the bills on the walls excitedly. They announced a new season with opera in English and Shakespeare, but not a single name.

I walked home (across Waterloo Bridge) in a more mercenary and less romantic frame of mind. Was it for this that I had forsaken a good salary in the West End, a comfortable dressing-room to myself, new suits, late rising, and suppers at the Savoy?

Our first rehearsal took place in a big room at the top of the theatre, next to the wardrobe. It had iron girders in the roof which reminded me of the dormitory at Hillside, and there was a dreadful echo which Harcourt Williams silenced after some weeks by hanging canvas on the walls. A long high shelf ran down one side of the room, and on it perched the 'students', about twenty girls and two or three men. They carried Shake-speares of various shapes and sizes, and stared hungrily at us throughout the early rehearsals of every play. When they began to get bored with the production they all furtively, whispered, or fell asleep. It was rather like the classes at the Academy all over again.

Lilian Baylis arrived that first day and made her usual motherly opening-of-term speech, while we all stood sheepishly round summing each other up – Billee Williams with his eager, harassed face and the tin of Bemax under his arm, Martita Hunt and Adèle Dixon, both very smart and West End, little Brember Wills, Gyles Isham, Donald Wolfit, Leslie French. Billee discussed the opening play with us (*Romeo and Juliet*) and the Granville-Barker preface to it which he told us to read. He himself had just spent a week-end with Barker who had sent us his good wishes, and Gordon Craig had written wishing me luck. 'Stick absolutely loyal to H. W.,' he wrote, 'then great things are possible.'

Martita and I went out in the lunch hour and discussed everything excitedly. As we came back we looked into the auditorium together. The long empty rows of seats lay shrouded in dust-sheets, the boxes stood primly uninviting, with their ugly mouldings and hard gilt chairs, and the horse-shoe circle curved above our heads as we stood by the narrow lincrusta pillars underneath it.

I remembered Russell Thorndike as *Peer Gynt*, straddling like a scarecrow over Ase's deathbed, the painted beehives in Shallow's garden, Andrew Leigh singing his sad little snatches under the table in Goneril's hall, and, above all, Ernest Milton's tragic posturings as Richard the Second. I could see him crouching pitifully on the ground in the scene before Flint Castle, and standing alone, self-pitying but defiant, to give away his kingdom, dressed in a long black velvet robe with great ermine sleeves hanging to the floor.

As we climbed the stairs back to the rehearsal room, we passed the wardrobe door. I left Martita and slipped inside. Behind the nearest counter, like a magnificent grocer, stood Orlando Whitehead the wardrobe master, bald-headed, grinning, with a strong Yorkshire accent, wearing a white apron round his waist. Behind him and all around stretched the shelves and boxes and glass cases with their store of robes and crowns, helmets and swords and armour. Hanging among the other clothes, easily recognizable by its rich simplicity, was that same black velvet robe that had left its impression so vividly on my mind. The sleeves, at close quarters, were only made of rabbit, but their long sweeping folds were still sufficiently imposing and picturesque. In a few weeks, I thought, I shall be wearing that dress myself as Richard. The romantic tradition of stage finery, handed on from one actor to another in classic parts, moved me strangely, and I went back to the rehearsal bursting with a great desire to prove myself worthy of the noble inheritance I had come to the Old Vic to try and claim.

We were very busy. We were often very tired, but we never had time to be bored. We had our failures – in fact the first season opened in an atmosphere of gloom amid the execrations of most of the critics and many of the regular audience. Our great strength and rallying-point was Harcourt Williams. He ruled us by affection and by the trust he had in us, which was almost childlike in its naïvety. Any little instance of selfishness, of disloyalty to the theatre or to the play, would merely throw him into a mood of amazement or disbelief. I am sure we all still remember his little notes of good wishes and thanks to the company and staff on first nights (why were there never notes of abuse and disgust to balance them?), his vegetarian lunches which we could regard with such anxious interest, the occasional cigarette which he would light with an air of recklessness in a moment of extreme crisis, and his frenzied attempts to concentrate on the last rehearsal of a play, when the cast of the next one, to say nothing of the setting for the one after next, must have been causing him sleepless nights.

I know that Ellen Terry thought Harcourt Williams one of the most brilliant young actors of his generation. Her influence over his life showed itself in his straightforward manners, and in the fact that nothing which he accomplished in the theatre was tainted by cheapness or vulgarity. I am sure it must have been her sublime shrewdness and her artist's vision that guided his hand on the occasions during his four strenuous years at the Vic when his acute sensibility was often strained almost to breaking point.

Harcourt Williams quickly won our affection and loyalty, and we were all tremendously keen, for his sake as well as our own, that his plans should succeed. His ideas at that time seemed to be revolutionary,[1] though later it turned out that his Elizabethan productions, which preserved the continuity of the plays by means of natural and speedy delivery of the verse, and light and imaginative settings allowing quick changes of scene, were very suitable for modern needs. His work was to influence my own productions enormously in after years.

I have sometimes called *Romeo and Juliet* my 'milestone'. Four times in my career it has been an important play for me – but never a very satisfactory one from the acting point of view. For Romeo is a difficult, ungrateful part, needing wonderful natural qualities in the actor as well as skilled technique. In spite of the fact that the very name of Romeo would seem to arouse expectations of glamour in the breast of every schoolgirl, the opportunities which the part affords the actor are distinctly

1 Though Robert Atkins had already done fine pioneer work of this kind at the Vic in the twenties, producing every single play of Shakespeare, and doing away with cuts and traditional business

limited, and I don't believe anyone has been known to make stage history in it.

The production of the play at the Old Vic was very nearly a disaster. We gabbled in order to try and get pace and we were not yet used to working together – but our unfavourable reception seemed to draw us closer together, and we ranged ourselves behind Harcourt Williams with increasing devotion. Of course he felt that most of the blame fell on him, and he was much disheartened and hurt by the many angry letters he received, and by the rude remarks of a few furious fanatics who used to waylay him by the stage-door. His methods were to be carried to success, and he was to be hailed as an innovator before he left the Vic; in the meantime, we did our best to cheer him up and tried to conceal from him the worst of the notices.

It was in *Richard the Second* that I began to feel at last that I was finding my feet in Shakespeare. I seemed to be immediately in sympathy with that strange mixture of weakness and beauty in the character. I had seen both Faber and Milton play Richard, but, although their pictorial qualities had impressed me greatly in the part of the King, I had taken in nothing of the intellectual or poetic beauties of the play. But as soon as I began to study the part myself, the subtlety of the characterization began to fascinate and excite me.

The audience became a little more friendly towards us in *Richard the Second*. We thought that we had conquered some of their prejudices, and were rather dismayed to find that most of the critics were still in resolute opposition. I was astonished, in reading the notices again the other day, to find how unfavourable they were. Afterwards, when I had played *Richard of Bordeaux*, which was of course so much more popular, this earlier performance of the more difficult Shakespeare part was taken for granted. Actually, at the Vic few people saw me, as I only played Richard about thirty or forty times. In those days we only acted nine times a fortnight – an admirable arrangement for the actors in a repertory company, as we had occasional nights off, more time to study, and never two performances on the same day.

Our first real success came with *A Midsummer Night's Dream*. This time the public and critics alike applauded us enthusiastically. We were delighted for ourselves, for the theatre, but chiefly for Harcourt Williams, who had come through some dark hours before this splendid vindication of his methods. No one was more delighted than Lilian Baylis. She had left us alone and kept her own counsel, but I fancy she must have been slightly perturbed by the mixed reception and poor box-office returns with which our earlier efforts had been rewarded. All the same, she was not altogether in sympathy with farthingales in Athens and folksongs instead of Mendelssohn, though she never actually said so in public. But Billee was a little hurt when he overheard her say in a dressing-room, just before the dress-rehearsal, 'Well, I suppose I'm old-fashioned, but I do like my fairies to be gauzy'.

I was very happy in the part of Oberon. It is one of the few fine parts I have acted in Shakespeare that is not also a great physical strain, and I was learning to speak verse well at last. It gave me a wonderful sense of power to feel that I was beginning to control the lovely language which at rehearsals moved me so much that tears would spring to my eyes. I am always embarrassingly emotional at the early stages of a play, but Sybil Thorndike once told me at the RADA that the proper time to give way to emotion is at the early rehearsals. Afterwards one must put it behind one, study it objectively and draw on it with discretion.

The first season came to an end with two very important parts for me, Macbeth and Hamlet. I fancy that few people considered that Macbeth was within my range, and I was rather surprised myself when Billee allowed me to attempt it. But audiences are tolerant and helpful at the Old Vic once they have accepted you and are convinced that you can be trusted to do your best. I think I must have been successful up to a point for I have met several people since who liked me in this play.[1] I remember that it was a

1 Far more, on the whole, than in 1942 when I played the part again, directing the play myself, with Gwen Ffrangcon Davies as Lady Macbeth.

very exhausting part, but I don't believe I ever stopped to think how daring I was even to have attempted it at the age of twenty-five.

My physical picture of Macbeth was derived principally from the drawings by Bernard Partridge of Irving which I had seen in a souvenir of the Lyceum production. I made up for the last act with whitened hair and bloodshot eyes, trying to resemble as nearly as I could 'the gaunt famished wolf' of Ellen Terry's description of Irving, and in the opening scene of the play I carried my sheathed sword on one shoulder as Irving carries his in the picture. I knew this would look finely picturesque for my entrance but could not think how to get rid of it afterwards, until it suddenly occurred to me at rehearsal one day to drop it to the ground when Macbeth is hailed as King by the witches. This seemed to give Banquo a good reason for his line:

Good Sir, why do you start; and seem to fear
Things that do sound so fair?

It is always important to me, in a character part, to be able to satisfy myself with my visual appearance. I imagine at rehearsals how I hope to look, but if my make-up comes out well when I put it on for the first time, my confidence is increased a hundredfold. In the same way, the right clothes – especially in a part where they must be heavy and dignified – help me at once to find the right movements and gestures for the character. One's expression in a character part develops tremendously quickly after the first few times of making up. Photographs taken at a dress rehearsal only show a kind of mask, a sketch of the actor's intention, just like his performance at an early rehearsal. Photograph him again after he has been acting the part for a fortnight and the whole expression has deepened and developed into something much more complete, revealing the mental conception of the part in the eyes and mouth as well as in the lines and shadows that are painted over them. One afternoon, the famous critic, James Agate, bustled into my dressing-room half-way through the matinée performance. Although I knew him very slightly in private life, I was naturally never very much at ease in his august presence.

He began by saying that he had dragged himself to the theatre full of the direst presentiments; that I should fail as Macbeth had seemed a foregone conclusion to him. He then remarked: 'I have never seen the Murder Scene better done, and so I have come to congratulate you now. At the end of the performance I shall probably have changed my mind, for you can't possibly play the rest of it.' I murmured my thanks, and he went back to his seat. All through the second half of the play I was acutely self-conscious. I felt sure that I was over-acting every scene. I was amazed to read a favourable notice in his column the following Sunday.

In spite of the happy outcome of this particular visit, I never feel at ease if a critic comes to my dressing-room. Critics, like clergymen, always seem out of place behind the scenes.

Marion Terry was in a box one afternoon to see *Macbeth*. She had not appeared on the stage since she played the Princess in *Our Betters* in 1923. Six months later, illness had obliged her to leave the cast. Martita had been her understudy and had taken her place when she left. Soon afterwards, calling with flowers to inquire for Marion, Martita was shown into her bedroom. 'I hope, dear, you are playing the part exactly as I did,' said Marion and sank back on the pillows.

Both Marion and Fred suffered a great deal from ill-health during their last years, but they were both firm believers in the recuperative powers of 'Doctor Greasepaint'. Their work helped them to battle against weak hearts and exhausted nervous systems, which would have laid them low many years sooner if they had not both been people of quite extraordinarily determined character, with amazing powers of endurance and will-power. Fred would sometimes carry a stick during the first two acts of *The Scarlet Pimpernel* when his gout was troubling him, but by the middle of the play his indomitable spirit would have asserted itself and he would discard the stick and stride about the stage like a young man.

It was sad to see my wonderful Terry relatives sinking at last under the ravages of time. Marion could not manage the stairs to my dressing-room when she came to see *Macbeth*, and Martita and I went instead to her box, still in our make-up, at the end of the performance. She still looked immensely distinguished, though it was sad to see her with her back bowed and her hair quite white. It was the last time I ever saw her, and I do not think she was ever again inside a theatre.

The last time I saw Fred was in a theatre too. He came to see *Musical Chairs* two years after this time, in 1931, and sat in a box with his wife Julia. Frank Vosper and I dispatched a dresser to buy a big bouquet of carnations and sent them round with our love, and afterwards Fred and Julia came behind to see us. In the old days I am sure the frankness of Mackenzie's play would have shocked and disgusted Uncle Fred profoundly. I have never forgotten hearing him once hold forth on the vulgarity of the character of Linda, as played so grandly by Mary Clare in *The Constant Nymph*. But he had mellowed and softened in his last years and he was fond of Frank and me. He complimented us warmly and said he had enjoyed the play. I never saw him again, but I always think of him if I go down the long narrow corridor at the back of the Criterion Theatre. There he stood, framed in the iron pass-door leading from the stage, leaning on his stick, looking like a benevolent Henry the Eighth, with Julia by his side, still looking radiantly beautiful, with the flowers we had sent her held loosely in a dark mass against her light dress.

The last production of my first Old Vic season was *Hamlet*. It was exciting to have the chance of playing it after all, but I did not think it likely that I should give an interesting performance. I had no longer much confidence in playing 'romantic juveniles'. I had not made a success of Romeo, though I had played the part before, and I considered Richard and Macbeth, in which I had done better work, were both character parts. From my child-hood I had had some sort of picture in my mind of these two personages. I could imagine myself at once dressed in their clothes and tried, in rehearsing and acting them, to forget myself completely, to keep the imagined image fresh and vivid. To some extent I felt I had succeeded. Hamlet was different.

We began to rehearse. Some of the scenes came to me more easily than others; the first appearance of Hamlet particularly – one of my favourite scenes of all the plays I have ever read or acted – sincerity, real emotion, and marvellously simple words to express them in; the second scene, when Hamlet first sees the ghost, violent, sudden, technically hard to speak; the following ghost scene terribly difficult, intensely tiring to act, nothing to say then, after the ghost disappears, too many words. Impossible to convey, even with Shakespeare's help, the horror and madness of the situation, the changing tenderness and weary resignation.

The mad scenes. How mad should Hamlet be? So easy to score off Polonius to get laughs, so important not to clown, to keep the story true – then the intricate scene with Rosencrantz and Guildenstern, and my favourite prose speech in the play, 'What a piece of work is a man! . . .' – The arrival of the players easier again, natural true feelings, but the big soliloquy is coming in a minute, one must concentrate, take care not to anticipate, not begin worrying beforehand how one is going to say it, take time but don't lose time, don't break the verse up, don't succumb to the temptation of a big melodramatic effect for the sake of gaining applause at the curtain – Nunnery scene. Shall it be a love scene? How much emotion? When should Hamlet see the King? I feel so much that I convey nothing. This scene never ceases to baffle me.

Interval – The Advice to the Players. Dreadful little pill to open the second part, all the people coming back into their seats, slamming them down; somehow try to connect the speech with the rest of the play, not just a set piece; tender for the tiny scene with Horatio, a moment's relief – then into the Play scene. Relax if possible, enjoy the scene, watch the Gonzago play, watch the King, forget that this is the most famous of famous scenes, remember that Hamlet is not yet sure of Claudius, delay the climax, then carry it (and it needs all the control and breath in the world to keep the pitch at the right level) – No pause before the Recorders scene begins, and this cannot make the effect it should unless Rosencrantz and Guildenstern pull their weight and share the scene with Hamlet – Half a minute to collect oneself, and on again to the praying King. Such a difficult unsatisfactory scene, and how important to the play – but the closet scene is more grateful, and a woman's voice helps to make a contrast in tone and pitch. The scene starts at terrific emotional tension though, and only slows up for a minute in the middle for the beautiful passage with the ghost. The 'hiding of Polonius's body' scenes (this is The Entirety tonight – called The Eternity by actors) – and then grab a cloak and hat in the wings and rush on to speak the Fortinbras soliloquy as if it wasn't the last hundred yards of a relay race.

Now the one long interval for Hamlet, while Ophelia is doing her mad scene and Claudius and Laertes are laying their plot and the Queen is saying her willow speech. Last lap. Graveyard scene, with the lovely philosophizing and the lines about Yorick, and that hellish shouting fight and the 'Ossa' speech at the end, which takes the last ounce of remaining breath – Now for Osric, and a struggle to hold one's own with the scene-shifters banging about behind the front-cloth, and a careful ear for the first coughs and fidgets in the audience, which *must* somehow be silenced before the 'fall of a sparrow' (I remember one night a gentleman in the front row took out a large watch in this scene, and wound it up resignedly). And so to the apology to Laertes, with half one's mind occupied trying to remember the fight (which has been so carefully rehearsed but always goes wrong at least once a week) and on to the poisoning of the Queen and Claudius's death, and, if all has gone well, a still, attentive audience to the very end.

In rehearsing Hamlet I found it at first impossible to characterize. I could not 'imagine' the part and live in it, forgetting myself in the words and adventures of the character, as I had tried to do in my best work in other plays. This difficulty surprised and alarmed me. Although I knew the theatrical effect that should be produced by each scene, I could only act the part if

I felt that I really experienced every word of it as I spoke. The
need to 'make an effect' or 'force a climax' paralysed my
imagination and destroyed any reality which I had begun to
feel. I knew that I must act in a broad style, that I must be
grander, more dignified and noble, more tender and gracious,
more bitter and scathing, than was absolutely natural – that I
must not be as slow as I should be if I were really thinking aloud,
that I must drive the dialogue along at a regular moving pace,
and, above all, that every shade of thought must be arranged
behind the lines, so that nothing should be left to chance in
presenting them to the audience correctly and clearly in the
pattern which I had conceived. All through rehearsals I was
dismayed by my utter inability to forget myself while I was
acting. It was not until I stood before an audience that I seemed
to find the breadth and voice which enabled me suddenly to shake
off my self-consciousness and live the part in my imagination,
while I executed the technical difficulties with another part of my
consciousness at the same time.

Maurice Browne came to the Old Vic. He was an American
actor and director who had made money from the phenomenal
success of *Journey's End*, and had taken over two theatres, the
Globe and the Queen's, in Shaftesbury Avenue. He thought that
the West End ought to see our *Hamlet* and arranged to transfer
the production to the Queen's Theatre as soon as the Vic season
came to an end.

The first night in the West End gave the stage management
some alarming moments. The scene in the churchyard was
played on a platform. Below this was the real stage, which
served for the bottom of the grave. Here the skulls were
carefully placed. It seemed to me, when I walked on with
Horatio, that an air of thoughtfulness, one might have said of
strain, hung over the First Grave-Digger. I suddenly saw what
had happened a few lines before we came to the best part of the
scene. The skull was missing. And soon I must begin the 'Alas,
poor Yorick' speech, holding it in my hands. Should I orate over
an imaginary skull? I dared not hope that the audience's

imagination would follow me so far. I suddenly decided to cut out thirty lines. I jumped to 'But soft, but soft awhile – here comes the King', the words which introduce Ophelia's funeral procession which was fortunately forming in the wings at that very moment. There was a short pause while the surprised mourners hurried to their places, then the procession entered. I learned afterwards that owing to the rake of the stage the skulls had rolled out of the grave-digger's reach. There was nothing to be done, though the distracted stage manager had tried, without avail, to borrow another skull from the Globe Theatre next door, where Alexander Moissi was playing *Hamlet* in a German version.

Unfortunately, it turned out that Maurice Browne's faith in the drawing power of *Hamlet* in the West End was misplaced. Besides Moissi, Henry Ainley was also playing *Hamlet* at the Haymarket at the same time, so I had two rivals on this occasion. (Later, when I played Hamlet in New York in 1936, I was to have another rival in Leslie Howard.) It was only slightly gratifying to hear that the business at the other two theatres was no better than at ours. Our cheaper seats were always full, but the stalls and dress-circle public obstinately kept away. I was very much disappointed. What was the use of being praised, extravagantly perhaps, by the critics if one was to fail with the public? The cheers at the Old Vic had been so hopeful and encouraging that the atmosphere of failure at the Queen's Theatre seemed the more depressing by comparison. I was somewhat comforted by an elderly friend of mine, who said she had been too much impressed to move during my death scene, although a pipe had burst during the performance and water was creeping along the floor from one side of her stall and a mouse from the other!

The public was to flock to see me four years later as Hamlet at the New Theatre. But many people told me then, of course, that I had been much better in the earlier production which so few came to see. We tried to put the blame on the rival companies and on the heat-wave which added to our troubles but it was no use. I accepted another engagement, upon which the management immediately said (more in sorrow than in anger) that if I had not been so hasty they would have kept *Hamlet* on after all.

I was very sorry when the Old Vic company disbanded for the summer, but I was glad to know that I should be returning in the autumn. I had asked for a rise in salary as a condition of a second season, and when it was given me without a murmur – at the Vic, where money really was a most earnest consideration – I felt I must surely be something of a 'draw' at last. I had enjoyed our rehearsals, a new play every three weeks, the quick lunches at the Wellington Bar or the station buffet at Waterloo, during which we stopped arguing only when our mouths were too full of sandwiches and sausage-rolls to speak, and the rush back to the theatre to work until four o'clock. Afterwards I would go back to my flat and rest until the evening performance, play my gramophone, and perhaps have a drink with a few friends. On the evening when the Opera Company held the stage at the Old Vic we were free, and I was able to learn my lines or go to other theatres.

At our week-end dress-rehearsals at the Old Vic the company were permitted to invite friends and relations. My mother, I am sure, did not miss one of these functions. Besides friendly criticism she brought large supplies of food which she pressed on all the actors, and especially on Harcourt Williams, who used to say that her provisions saved his reason several times on these trying occasions.

Before our first nights it was a sort of ritual with some of us to have dinner at Gow's, a chop house in the Strand, but we were usually too nervous to eat very much. Old Vic first nights, although they occurred with such frequent regularity, never seemed to lose their novelty and excitement. There was a feeling of anticipation at the Vic which I have never encountered anywhere else, for the spirit of the place seemed so much stronger than any of the separate personalities who served it.

Before I went home after a first night I sometimes showed myself at the Savoy Grill for supper. This was pure snobbishness on my part, but I felt that it preserved my status as a West End actor, giving me the right to return one day to the bright lights of Shaftesbury Avenue, and I liked to be seen there with Martita Hunt. She and I were inseparable during this first Vic season, and besides her own brilliant performances in a variety of parts — especially as Helena in *A Midsummer Night's Dream*, Gertrude in *Hamlet* and as a vivid Lady Macbeth — she was unfailingly kind and wise in helping me in all my work.

I was not idle during the summer. Nigel Playfair proposed to revive Oscar Wilde's *The Importance of Being Earnest* in a stylized black-and-white production, and offered me the part of John Worthing. I accepted eagerly. Here was the sort of comedy-character I longed to play. I had once attempted the part when I was still an amateur, and it was amusing to change the black weeds of Hamlet for the top-hat and crepe band of Worthing's mourning for his brother. My recent association with the tragedy gave further point to Wilde's joke. I was very proud to have the opportunity of appearing for the first time in this production with my mother's sister, Mabel Terry-Lewis, who made a notable success as Lady Bracknell. Mabel was an instinctive actress, with a grace and skill which she inherited from her family. Her dignity and her beautiful voice reminded one of Marion, and she shared with Marie Tempest and Irene Vanbrugh that rare distinction of style, deportment and carriage which is so seldom seen on the stage today. Like Kate, her mother (and Ellen Terry too), a long retirement from the theatre after her own marriage did not seem to have impaired in the slightest the freshness and skill of her stage technique, and she took up her career at a higher point than she had left it. Her reappearance in H. M. Harwood's *The Grain of Mustard Seed* at the Ambassador's Theatre in 1920 after her husband's death was an immediate and distinguished personal success.

When I had worked with Playfair before, I had been very small fry indeed. I had been grateful for a smile or a nod from the other actors, and when Playfair had once asked my opinion on some detail or other at a rehearsal, I had been too shy to speak.

Now it was gratifying to play a leading part opposite such fine actresses as Mabel and Jean Cadell and to appear at the Lyric, where I had so often sat enraptured among the audience. Nigel Playfair was the first manager who ever made me feel that I was a star in his theatre. Of course, the Lyric, Hammersmith was too far west to be considered real West End, but this made the success of the revival all the more flattering.

The parts I played during the first Vic season were as follows: Romeo, Antonio, Cléante (in *The Imaginary Invalid* of Molière), Oberon, Richard the Second, Orlando, the Emperor in *Androcles and the Lion*, Macbeth and Hamlet.

It was a changed company that assembled at the Old Vic for the first rehearsal in the autumn. Martita Hunt had left. Her place as leading lady was taken by Dorothy Green. I had seen her play all the big parts in Shakespeare at Stratford-on-Avon in 1925, and had always hoped to act with her one day. Ralph Richardson now joined the company and I am delighted that I went back for another year if only for the reason that I was able to meet Ralph and win his friendship. He has told me since that my acting before this time used to keep him out of a theatre, and the knowledge that he would have to act with me almost prevented him from accepting the engagement. So are many good friendships brought about! Ralph and I formed ourselves into a kind of subordinate committee, and discussed and hinted and interfered generally over the productions. During the first season, Leslie French, Martita and I had always lunched with Billee and pestered him with our suggestions and advice, but he seemed to like talking over his plans beforehand, and we tried to make ourselves useful and not to let our enthusiasm run away with us too far. These 'conferences' about the Vic productions eventually gave birth to an intense longing in me to produce plays myself.

Ralph is a stimulating person in the theatre, and although we have not many tastes in common, with the exception of our love of Shakespeare – and of music, which he says he never cared for till I played my gramophone to him – we soon became fast friends. I found him in many ways curiously similar in temperament to Leslie Faber (who also shared my fondness for music). Ralph Richardson has great integrity both as an artist and as a man. He is, I think, one of our very best actors. He is inclined to despise the petty accessories of theatrical life which appeal so strongly to me – the gossip, the theatrical columns in the newspapers, the billing and the photographs in the front of the house – and it is probably only by chance that he has found a creative outlet on the stage. He might have succeeded equally well as a mechanic, a doctor, or an airman. Unlike me he is intensely interested in machinery and in all the intricate details of science and engineering. Once, when I was motoring in Cornwall, I met him unexpectedly. I had been enjoying myself quietly in my own way, admiring the scenery without inspecting any of it too closely, enjoying the air without wondering from which direction the wind was blowing, puzzling over various signs of industrial activity, such as slag-heaps, which I thought added to the picturesque effect though I had no idea what use they were.

Ralph soon transferred me from my own comfortable car to his long, low, wicked-looking racer, and proceeded to rush me through the air at ninety miles an hour. He could never pass a hill without insisting that we should get out and scale it on foot. Once, on the top of a cliff, he immediately decided that we should both struggle down it to the beach. We visited tin mines, salt mines, pottery works, and listened attentively for several minutes (at one of the slag-heaps I had noticed) while a workman explained the technical details of his occupation to us. Ralph never seemed to tire of long mechanical discussions, though I found these matters entirely beyond my grasp and felt painfully conscious of my one-track mind. Though I missed him as soon as he had left, I was secretly relieved when, later in the day, Ralph climbed back into his car alone, and almost immediately disappeared from view like a shell shot from a cannon.

Harcourt Williams introduced some plays of Bernard Shaw to Old Vic audiences for the first time while I was there. We had already given *Androcles and the Lion* and *The Dark Lady of the Sonnets* the season before. I had enjoyed myself immensely in the former playing the Emperor, with a red wig, a lecherous red mouth, and a large emerald through which I peered lasciviously. Now I was cast as Sergius, the mustachioed conceited major to whom Raina is engaged, in *Arms and the Man*. We were all very much flattered, and considerably awed, when we learned that Mr Shaw had consented to come and read his play to us. We waited for him in the theatre one winter morning. It was bitterly cold, and we sat muffled up in heavy overcoats and scarves. Punctually at 10.30 the great author arrived, wearing the lightest of mackintoshes. His reading of the play was far more amusing and complete than ours could possibly hope to be. He seemed to enjoy himself thoroughly as he illustrated bits of business and emphasized the correct inflexions for his lines. We were so amused that we forgot to be alarmed.

Later Mr Shaw came to a dress rehearsal. We could not distinguish him in the darkness of the stalls, but we saw the light of his pocket-lamp bobbing up and down as he made his notes. He assembled the company in the first interval, produced his written comments, and reduced everybody to a state of disquiet. Then he departed. Unfortunately I was not able to gather from him any hints about my own performance, as Sergius does not appear until the second act.

During my second and last season at the Old Vic, Lilian Baylis made the ambitious decision to re-open Sadler's Wells Theatre which had been restored after many years of disuse. The play chosen was *Twelfth Night*, in which I played Malvolio. There was a grand inauguration at our first performance. Sir Johnston Forbes-Robertson declared the theatre open and spoke of his master, Phelps, and Dame Madge Kendal was in the stalls. It was one of the last times either of them was to appear in public. The stalls bulged with celebrities, and the four front rows were like all the gossip columns come to life. The play was wedged between two grand celebrations, the first of which was almost an hour of speeches before the curtain went up, with rows of aldermen, mayors, and other officials sitting upon the stage, shirt-fronts and chains of office glistening above the footlights. But I was feeling that the play was the thing, and itched to speak my line, 'Have you no wit, manners, nor honesty, but to gabble like tinkers at this time of night?'

At the close of the performance the audience remained seated, and, after the curtain had been lowered for a few minutes, it went up again revealing the line of celebrities once more. Miss Baylis, imposing and academic in her robes of Master of Arts, with the Cross of a Companion of Honour on her breast, marched to the middle of the stage to make her speech.

The audience waited politely, and the line of celebrities sat, stiff and white-faced, rather like a cricket team about to be photographed. Lilian carried a huge basket of fruit in her right hand, and when she began her oration her gestures were somewhat hampered by her burden. However, she ploughed bravely on until, enthralled by the force of her own argument, she swept her right arm out impulsively. An enormous apple fell from the basket with a thud. There was a slight titter from the audience. Lilian looked at the basket, and then, edging towards the truant apple, tried to hide it with her robes. She went on with her speech, but soon sincerity overcame technique, and the basket shot out to the right to accentuate another point. This time a pear fell on to the stage. I gave one look at it and burst out laughing. The audience followed suit, and the solemnity of the occasion was irrevocably shattered.

How we all detested Sadler's Wells when it was opened first! The auditorium looked like a denuded wedding cake and the acoustics were dreadful. The only obvious advantages lay in the cleanness and comfort of the dressing-rooms. But we were never able to remember at which of the two theatres we were supposed to be acting or rehearsing, and no sooner did we begin to play to good business in one than we were transferred to the other, where the audiences promptly dwindled away. Patrons of the two theatres got muddled, and the famous green slips with details of the programmes which Lilian always insisted on enclosing in every letter that was sent from either theatre, became more complicated than Old Moore's Almanack. There were all sorts of debts incurred, and all sorts of economies invented to pay them off, but it always seemed that if Shakespeare was making money Opera was losing it, or vice versa. In later years the founding of the Ballet and a great deal of ambitious innovation on the Opera side made it possible for the Wells to be devoted entirely to the musical side of the enterprise.

It was a great triumph for Lilian to have carried through her cherished scheme of rebuilding and reopening Sadler's Wells, but it made my second season less successful and more exhausting than it might otherwise have been. We played eight times a week, instead of nine times a fortnight, and the weeks at the Wells were particularly strenuous, what with scanty houses and the strain of accustoming our voices to the pitch of the new theatre.

Still, *Henry IV, Part I, Antony and Cleopatra, The Tempest* and *King Lear* were all particularly successful, and Billee did some of his very best work in these productions.

Chapter 11

1930–31

The second season was drawing to a close. There had been a revival of *Richard II*. I had acted Hotspur, Benedick, Malvolio, Sergius, Lord Trinket in *The Jealous Wife* (great fun – I had almost forgotten him) and Antony in *Antony and Cleopatra*. This was one of Billee William's very best productions, founded on Granville-Barker's preface, and staged with Renaissance-Classical scenery and dresses in the style of Veronese. Needless to say, all this grandeur was achieved for a very few pounds by the ingenuity of Billee and Paul Smyth, the resident designer. Ralph was superb as Enobarbus. I wore a Drake beard and padded doublet and shouted myself hoarse but was very miscast all the same. I loved playing Prospero in *The Tempest* and thought I was good in that, helped by Billee, by Leslie French (who played Ariel beautifully), and indirectly by Komisarjevsky, who had suggested to me that I ought to look like Dante and not wear a beard. Ralph hated himself as Caliban but he was excellent in the part, with a wonderful Mongolian make-up that took him hours to put on every night.

My last part at the Old Vic was King Lear. It was distinctly ambitious of me to dare, at the age of twenty-six to try and assume 'the large effects that troop with majesty' as eighty-year-old King Lear. But I felt it would be a more exciting close to my two seasons than a revival of *Hamlet*, which was the alternative proposed. I was wholly inadequate in the storm scenes, having neither the voice nor the physique for them. Lear has to *be* the storm, but I could do no more than shout against the thunder-sheet. The only scene I thought I did at all well was the one with the Fool when Lear leaves Goneril to go to Regan: 'O, let me not be mad, not mad, sweet heaven—'. Ralph was fine as Kent and Leslie French moving and effective as the Fool.

It was not considered in keeping with the austere traditions of the Old Vic for audiences to applaud an actor's first entrance. But as Lear I came on in such splendour that, from the moment when Gloster announced 'The King is coming', the stage was mine. Trumpets blared in the orchestra and my way was cleared by spearmen; lords and attendants kept their distance behind my magnificent white robe. Sometimes the audience could not resist such majesty, especially in a farewell production, and at least three nights a week I came on to applause. This uncertainty started a little joke between Ralph Richardson and myself. He was on the stage before me, and as I prepared to enter, encumbered by my own magnificence, he would look slyly in my direction as I stood in the wings, hiding his smile behind his thick, mask-like make-up. (Ralph always designed elaborate make-ups, made careful drawings for them beforehand, and carried them out in great detail with shadows and highlights, scoffing at our comparatively slap-dash efforts at disguise. He achieved striking results, but his method stylized his appearance, and made him apt to look different from anyone else on the stage). In the meantime I was trying to amass my eighty years and my large effects of majesty in the wings. If I failed to get the round of applause as I mounted my throne the expression of amused triumph on Ralph's face would be almost too much for me. It was fortunate that I had to turn away from the audience for a moment before I faced them and began 'Attend the lords of France and Burgundy . . .'.

When *Lear* was over and my white robes were packed away, I crossed the river and came back to the West End once more. I had been asked to play in Edward Knoblock's stage version of J. B. Priestley's *The Good Companions*. How lucky I have been in the opportunity of doing so many different kinds of work! At that moment, I believe, I was almost the only man in England who had not read the book. I spent half the night skimming it through as quickly as I could, and next morning I called on Julian Wylie for the first time. His offices were in the Charing Cross Road. As I climbed the stairs, up which a hundred principal boys had borne their portly hips, I heard the sound of many pianos all being played at the same time. The sheet music of pantomime songs was ranged on racks on every landing, and I caught a glimpse of a boudoir as I passed, with Louis Seize decorations and a ceiling profusely painted with clouds and cherubs, the private sanctum of some lordly music-publisher who reigned in the offices below.

I was ushered in, ahead of the score of people waiting in the outer office. Julian Wylie sat behind a massive table smoking a big cigar, and the walls round him were covered with photographs of pantomime and music-hall favourites. Julian looked the typical impresario, but he was more than that. I liked him immensely – a sympathetic, cultivated man, who made the business of pantomime into a romance. He would digress upon its origins with an exact regard for tradition, pointing out that the Fairy Queen must always enter from the right, and the Demon King from the left – Why? Because it had always been so. But Wylie was not a reactionary, and, since pantomime had fallen upon less successful days, he skilfully led it towards revue and saved it. He was very broad-minded in his enthusiasms. I could not help smiling when I heard that he had been to the Wells to look at me with a view to my playing Jollifant, and had sat through my Lear with apparent enjoyment.

Wylie was very thorough in his methods. For two long weeks we read the play in the boardroom of the Dominion Theatre, after which we rehearsed for four weeks. The company then 'tried out' for three weeks in the Provinces with an understudy in my part but I played once at Birmingham and once at Leeds for single performances on the nights when we did not act at the Vic. Thus I appeared as Inigo Jollifant, King Lear, and Benedick (*Much Ado* was still in the bill for occasional matinées at this time) all in the same week – a record almost worthy of the old stock companies. But it was a mad rush, and I have no doubt that all three performances left a great deal to be desired.

The crowd scenes in *The Good Companions*, which were hailed as marvels of stage-craft, were rehearsed in exactly half an hour by Wylie and Knoblock, who divided the supers into groups and labelled them with numbers. Wylie was thus able to control them like a sergeant-major from his place in the stalls. There he sat, like some passionless Buddha, brushing the cigar-ash from his lapel with two fingers, a favourite and characteristic gesture of his.

I saw no signs of the temperamental storms and rages for which he was said to be famous among pantomime artists. Leslie Henson the great comedian, once told me of a rehearsal of *Dick Whittington*, in which he had appeared under Julian's direction. There was an unusually complicated change of set to be negotiated, from a 'Desert' scene to 'A Staircase in the Palace'. In the first there was a trap-door which had to be closed before the curtain went up on the second, in which a lady was discovered singing on the stairs. After a verse or two she was supposed to descend in stately fashion. But this she dared not do, fearing that the trap might still be open.

'For heaven's sake, come *forward*,' Wylie yelled each time.

But the lady demurred, and the change had to be rehearsed all over again. At last Wylie could bear it no longer. He bounded on to the stage with a roar, and immediately vanished into the still-open trap. There was a murmur of consternation. Then Julian's head suddenly popped up through the hole in the stage. 'I heard you laughing,' he announced, though actually everyone had been too much alarmed to see the joke.

I had to play the piano in *The Good Companions*. The music was by Richard Addinsell, whom I had known when he was an undergraduate at Oxford and used to play at parties. He kindly offered to teach me how to play his tunes, imagining, I suppose, that as I play tolerably by ear his task would be an easy one. Alas, my natural facility is a positive curse when it comes to learning correctly! I slaved away for days, just as I had done in *The*

Constant Nymph, when Elsie April had patiently guided my inexpert fingers. I cannot read a note of music from sight, and I can only play in certain keys — but the fact that I can easily transpose a melody and render it inaccurately with my own harmonies seems to make things all the more difficult for me when I have to learn correctly.

The scenes were very short and sketchy, and demanded a considerable readjustment of my style of acting. There was hardly any development of character. Jollifant in the play was a 'type' — a very ordinary juvenile who had to carry off a few slight love scenes and a couple of effective comedy situations with the aid of a pipe, undergraduate clothes, and the catchword 'absolutely'. Here there were no white robes and spearmen and lordly followers to bolster up my first appearance. The sets were enormous, the orchestra vast, and the stage as wide as a desert. I had learned from playing Shakespeare not to be afraid of acting broadly, and the size of the theatre did not dismay me as much as I had feared at first, but the manner and pace had to be very different from anything I had ever done before. I had to try and catch the audience's interest with the first word, and sweep my little scenes along to a climax in a few short minutes. However, though the robes and the large effects that troop with majesty had not come with me from the Old Vic, my followers had. On that exciting first night at His Majesty's, when my performance of Inigo might have been smothered under the reputation of Priestley's book, Knoblock's adaptation, and the immediate success of Edward Chapman and Frank Pettingell, at least a hundred of my staunch friends had crossed the river to greet me. My reception when I first appeared was out of all proportion, and I have no doubt that I deserved Mr Agate's flight of fancy in the *Sunday Times* the following week. He wrote:

The young man rattling away at the piano was Mr John Gielgud, and perhaps this time some of the applause might be taken as a tribute to all those kings over the water whose sceptres our young tragedian had just laid down.

I learnt some useful lessons during the long run of *The Good Companions*, for I was playing with actors of several different schools. Chapman and I had acted together years before, when we were both amateurs, in a performance of Noël Coward's *I'll Leave it to You*. Adèle Dixon had been my Juliet at the Vic, and some of the others I already knew. But there were one or two members of the company recruited from revue and pantomime.

In one scene a veteran actor ruined my lines by walking up-stage of me and standing against the backcloth. This is a well-known trick, even in straight plays, but not considered good art or good manners in any type of entertainment. I remonstrated politely, but without avail. One day I lunched with Fred Terry and told him of my nightly struggle in this particular scene. Uncle Fred pronounced his verdict grandly, as if it were the correct reading of some obscure phrase in the classics: 'Walk in front of him while he's speaking, my boy. He'll have to come down level with you then so that the audience can see him.' Next night I did as I was told, with immediate and gratifying results.

The Good Companions brought me my first real taste of commercial success. I was being well paid, and the play had a long run. Suppers at the Savoy were no longer a luxury, and sometimes I enjoyed hearing people say 'That's John Gielgud' as I passed. While I was basking in the comparative idleness of my leisure hours another piece of luck came my way. I was beginning to attract the attention of playwrights, and manuscripts arrived in increasing numbers. I was flattered to receive a few from established authors, bearing the exclusive stamps of the more expensive typewriting firms. Their pages were tidy and perhaps a trifle too self-assured. Others, from writers whose names were unknown to me, seemed more impressive because they were already printed, but I soon learned to become wary of these neat volumes. There was something cold and stillborn in their completeness. Most of the plays, however, came from begin-ners, some carefully typewritten, others tattered and covered with illegible handwriting. I perused them with an increasing sense of despondency as time went on. All actors must have shared my feelings. One can never dismiss a new play-script for fear that it may contain the seed of something good. Within a few weeks two packages arrived in my dressing-room at His Majesty's. One contained *Musical Chairs* and the other *Richard of Bordeaux*.

A letter arrived with the manuscript of *Musical Chairs*. The writer reminded me that he had been at 'prep' school with me at Hillside. At the end was the signature, R. A. Mackenzie. I remembered the initials at once, but at first I could not clearly envisage their owner. I picked up the play, however, and was intrigued to find that the action took place in Poland, the country of my father's family. I began to read. The first scene, with its masterly introduction of the characters and explanation of their relationships, interested me at once. When I reached the end of the first act I was enthusiastic, and I finished the play in a mood of great excitement. I wrote to the author immediately, inviting him to lunch.

I am afraid that our reunion was not a great success. I found Mackenzie waiting for me in a quiet room upstairs at the Gourmets restaurant in Lisle Street and at once recognized his blunt Scottish features and dark curly hair. He looked very much the same as the little boy who had been in my dormitory at Hillside. But he had had a hard time since our last meeting and he was bitter and cynical in his attitude towards the world. Also he was as shy as I was. I attempted to meet the somewhat aggressive air which he affected with a little charm. This he probably found thoroughly patronizing and obnoxious. I hoped the atmosphere might improve when we had ordered our lunch. Unfortunately, it turned out that Mackenzie was an uncompromising vegetarian. I felt greedy and superior as I tackled my steak. He glowered darkly at me over his carrots.

Towards the end of the meal he told me that he had been wandering all over the world, trying various professions with little or no success. He had never been able to make any money. He had worked on farms and in the logging camps of Canada. Then, on his return to England, chance had brought him in touch with the stage. He had been engaged as tutor to Owen Nares's two sons. He spoke to Mr Nares one day of his interest in the theatre, and obtained from him an introduction to Edgar Wallace, who gave him a job as assistant stage manager to a company playing *The Case of the Frightened Lady*. Later he occupied the same post at Wyndham's Theatre in another Wallace play called *Smoky Cell*. But he was very contemptuous of the commercial theatre and would sit in the prompt corner scribbling at his playwriting and reading Chekhov and Tolstoy. His own plays were written with tremendous care and the strictest economy. He rewrote every act two or three times and constructed every scene with the most expert skill.

I never got to know Mackenzie at all well. He was a difficult person, but he had tremendous talent and a fine instinct for the theatre. After some time, we discovered that we had musical tastes in common, and we used sometimes to meet in the same gramophone shop and discuss the records we were thinking of buying. The first thing Mackenzie did when his play was a success was to buy a large and beautiful new gramophone, which was still standing undelivered in the basement of the shop a few days after he was killed.

Although I was enthusiastic about *Musical Chairs*, I feared that it was not a commercial proposition. Actors need managers and backers as well as plays so I sent the manuscript off to Bronson Albery. I was very much surprised when he rang me up early next morning to say that he had read the play overnight and was anxious to put it on at the Arts Theatre, of which he was one of the directors, for a trial run of two special performances.

The moment I become excited over the manuscript of a new play I begin casting it furiously. This interfering side of my nature encouraged me later on, as soon as occasion offered, to try my hand as a director. As I had brought *Musical Chairs* to Mr Albery he allowed me to take part in the discussions of the way in which it should be cast and produced. Many actors take little interest in a play apart from their own individual share in it, but I enjoy every minute of the rehearsal period, whether I am directing the play or not, and my passionate interest in every detail compels me to watch and criticize and interfere in all directions. I am frequently a great nuisance, and entirely selfish in my desire to be consulted about everything that is going on.

I thought at once of Frank Vosper for the important part of old Schindler, my father in the play. Frank and I had been friends for four or five years. I had first met him at Lord Lathom's, and later, when I knew him quite well, I had taken over his flat, but we had never worked together before. He had made great successes with Barry Jackson, first as the sailor in *Yellow Sands* (in which he dressed with Ralph Richardson) and then as Claudius in the modern-dress *Hamlet*. He acted with Edith Evans, too, at the Old Vic during her season there – playing Romeo, Mark Antony and Orlando. (Of this last performance he said to me: 'I wore a red wig and looked like Fay Compton with goitre!')

Frank was always wonderfully good company. He loved ragging me about my highbrow activities, and pretended that, even in Shakespeare, he never knew which play he was in, or what the lines were all about. He used his shortsightedness to assist this impression of vagueness, peering at people through his glasses to avoid having to greet anyone he disliked. I was very fond of him. Some people thought him affected and rude, but I loved his sublime disregard for other people's disapproval and his really generous warm heart and sense of humour. When he first read *Musical Chairs* he said he thought it very depressing and difficult to understand, but gradually I discovered that he was quite intrigued with the play and anxious to create the part of Schindler. He behaved absurdly at rehearsals, singing snatches of grand opera to try out his voice, and imitating Fred Terry, for whom he had unbounded admiration. Mackenzie took a great fancy to Frank, and afterwards when he began to write his second play, *The Maitlands*, he built the part of the actor, Jack, round Frank's off-stage personality, with all the tricks and mannerisms he had used at the *Musical Chairs* rehearsals. I was very sorry, when the time came for the play to be done, that Frank was not available to play this part, in which he should have been inimitable.

I suggested that Komisarjevsky should direct *Musical Chairs*, and this turned out to be a most happy choice for everyone concerned. Although he could sometimes be capricious and difficult when he was dealing with the managerial side of the West End theatre, Komis had real sympathy with artists, and knew exactly the way to deal with awkward but talented young people in order to bring out the very best in them. He found himself in immediate sympathy with Ronald Mackenzie and his work, and at once agreed to direct the play.

There was originally an outdoor scene in the second act when the oil-well catches fire. This would have been difficult to stage in a small theatre. Besides, Komis thought that the change to an exterior setting would destroy the feeling of claustrophobia suggested by the small room in which the rest of the play took place, with the glimpse of mountains and flooded river outside the windows. An attempt to show all this more elaborately would have been most dangerous. So in the end the whole play was acted in the one interior scene. Komis devised this himself,[1] and added a little staircase which led to the door of the girl's room on one side of the stage. He used this with brilliant effect. Mackenzie had written a very conventional curtain to the second act which Komis developed into something subtle and original without adding a word, merely by the atmosphere which he created with pauses and effective lighting and grouping.

He was brilliantly clever in the way he helped me too. The plot of the play concerns a consumptive young pianist, whose fiancée (a German) has been killed in an air raid in which he was one of the bombers on the English side. At the first rehearsal Komis led me to the middle of the stage to explain the arrangement of the furniture. 'There is your piano, and there on it is the photograph of that girl who was killed. Build your performance round those two things,' he said.

He managed Mackenzie with consummate tact. The final curtain of the play was tried in several different ways, none of

1 At a cost, I believe, of only £12!

them entirely satisfactory. Komis had conceived a fine pictorial climax as the characters passed the windows dressed in black, and I begged him to bring the curtain down on this effective general exit. Mackenzie wanted an anticlimax, and had written a short scene to follow, between Anna, the maid, and the American commercial traveller. Frank, Komis, Mackenzie, Albery and I argued about this ending for half an hour after the dress-rehearsal, and finally two different versions were played at the Arts Theatre performances. I do not remember who thought of the father shutting the piano, which was the final 'curtain' as the play was eventually arranged. I should like to take the credit for it, but I think it is just as likely that it was suggested by Komis or by Frank. The title of the play was certainly mine. It was originally called *The Discontents*, a name which we all felt would not be thought attractive by the public. No one except me seemed to know what *Musical Chairs* meant, but it was an effective title and easy to remember. We always said at the Criterion that people booked for the play thinking it was a farce or a musical comedy. If so, they must have had a nasty shock when they arrived.

Mackenzie was at first inclined to be rebellious and obstinate about the alterations in his script. Then Komisarjevsky would say gently, 'But Mr Mackenzie, I assure you that we are doing this for the good of your play,' and then the young author's troubled frown would disappear, and his obstinate mouth would relax into a smile.

I was very pleased when, shortly after the successful Arts performances of *Musical Chairs*, Bronson Albery offered me a contract to appear in three plays, under the joint management of himself and Howard Wyndham. I knew very little about 'Bronnie's' activities (for he worked in an atmosphere of self-effacing anonymity) and I had hardly ever met him. Albery was the son of Lady Wyndham. She had spoken to him about me, it appears, after *The Constant Nymph*, and he had followed my career since that time at the Old Vic and elsewhere. I owe an enormous debt of gratitude to Mr Albery and his brothers, and I was very happy under their management. They allowed me a large share in the shaping of their policy while I was working at their theatres, and I learnt a great deal about the dangers and risks of management without having to contribute in any way myself towards the financial responsibilities of the productions with which I was so happily associated.

Musical Chairs had been a great success at the Arts Theatre, but we could not ignore the fact that it had attracted a specialized audience. By the time the dress-rehearsal before the regular run at the Criterion Theatre was upon us we were all plunged in gloom. The play was bitter and tragic, and the cast did not contain any dazzling and well-known names to attract people to the box office.

We say in the theatre that it is a good sign if dress-rehearsals do not proceed smoothly. The Criterion dress-rehearsal was chaotic. Throughout the early part of the play the audience had to be aware of thunder booming away in the distance. These noises had been timed most carefully during the previous rehearsals, but on this occasion they persisted in coming in at wrong moments, interrupting our best lines, and failing to materialize at all if we paused to allow them their full effect. The lighting went wrong. During one of my tensest love scenes with Carol Goodner I heard insistent hammering behind the scenes, and I lost my temper and shouted at the stage hands.

Only Komisarjevsky seemed to be satisfied and unperturbed. I watched him walk across the stage, just before the curtain went up on the first night and pin a fly-paper in a prominent position. He seemed delighted with this last-minute touch of realistic detail, quite absorbed and apparently oblivious of the feeling of tension all round him.

True to the traditions of the theatre the opening performance went like clockwork. The audience was delighted; Mackenzie was called for, and made an excellent and modest speech. His pleasure and gratitude were very touching.

One of the luckiest things that ever happened for me, and for the play and its author too, as it turned out, was the engagement of Carol Goodner for *Musical Chairs*. She played the American fiancée of the hero's brother, a distinctly unsympathetic character, who must, however, seem seductive and interesting to the audience.

I knew Carol Goodner by name, but I had never seen her act. Before she joined the cast, the part was offered to an English actress who thought it much too unpleasant. We had no other actress in mind, and we offered the part to Miss Goodner without any real knowledge of her capabilities, chiefly because we knew she was an American.

I had never before tackled such violent love scenes in a modern play, and the smallness of the Criterion Theatre, as well as one or two dangerous lines, had made me nervous at rehearsals. But when these moments held the house successfully on the first night I knew that all was well.

During the long run of *Musical Chairs* I became worried, as I have always done under similar circumstances, lest my performance should deteriorate more and more as time went on. I became very nervy, and looked so emaciated that people used to wonder if I was as consumptive as I appeared to be in the play. A charming lady said to Ralph Richardson: 'I went to see your friend Mr Gielgud act the other night. Tell me, is he really as thin as that?'

The Criterion is a small theatre, and my fatal habit of being too much aware of the audience became increasingly destructive to my concentration. *Musical Chairs* attracted the smart stall-public which likes to arrive late, and people would come pushing into the front rows, peering at us across the footlights. They were so near that we could have shaken hands with them, and we could hear their remarks as they rustled their programmes and asked each other stupid questions about the play.

My impromptu piano-playing in the part served well enough, but I became self-conscious about that too after a while, especially one night when I saw Artur Rubinstein sitting in the second row of the stalls.

Another evening I noticed Noël Coward in front. I recognized him immediately, became very nervous, and played the first act with one eye on him all the time. The curtain rose after the first interval, and I looked again in Noël's direction. He had not returned, and his seat was empty for the rest of the performance. For the next few weeks I was very hurt and complained to all my friends how rude he had been in walking out. At last I ran across him, and he said frankly, 'You were overacting so terribly that I couldn't have borne it another minute, and Frank Vosper's wig was so badly joined that it looked like a yachting-cap!' He also said (though not to me), that he would never have dreamed of leaving the theatre had he known that his exit would be noticed. 'This incident,' he remarked, 'has finally convinced me that I am really famous.' The same incident really broke me for good of my dreadful habit of looking at people in the audience.

I took a short holiday in the summer. While I was away, my part was played by another young man, John Cheatle, who had been at my preparatory school before the War, when he had played Portia to my Shylock. I went off to the South of France for a fortnight, but I did not get much rest. I stopped at hotels in noisy streets and stayed up all night gambling. On my way home I spent a night at Chartres, and happened to pick up an English paper in the lounge of the hotel just before I went to bed. There I read of Ronald Mackenzie's death in a motor accident. He also had gone on holiday (for the first time in eight years), and was motoring in France not a hundred miles from where I was. A tyre burst, the car overturned, and he was killed immediately.

Chapter 12

1931–32

During the run of *The Good Companions*, I had been given my first chance as a director. I was asked to go to Oxford and do *Romeo and Juliet* for the OUDS. This production was a first sketch for the one which was to be such a success in London in 1935. 'The Motleys', who designed the dresses, Peggy Ashcroft, who played Juliet, and Edith Evans, who was the Nurse, were all to be associated with me at the New Theatre four years later. Christopher Hassall, the son of the poster artist, was a splendid Romeo at Oxford. It is, in many ways, an ideal part for an undergraduate, whose natural attributes of youth amply compensate for his lack of professional experience as an actor. George Devine, who was president of the OUDS at this time, was a fine Mercutio, and William Devlin and Hugh Hunt played Tybalt and the Friar respectively, so I had a company bursting with potential talent.

'The Motleys', as we always call them in the theatre, have been associated with me in nearly all my productions, and any success I have had as a director I gladly share with them, for they are at all times the ideal collaborators. Their real names are Elizabeth Montgomery, Audrey and Peggy Harris. During my seasons at the Old Vic they had made some drawings of me as Richard, Macbeth and Lear, which they shyly brought to my notice. They were three silent and retiring young women in those days, and it was some time before I could get them to speak about themselves in their gentle, hesitating voices. I began to visit them in their tiny doll's house of a home near Church

Street, Kensington, and, although they were perfect hostesses I thought them strangely silent. They have since told me that my sudden and unexpected arrivals used to throw them all into paroxysms of shyness, as I hurled remarks at them over my shoulder and spoke so fast that they barely understood a word I uttered. At Oxford, when I produced *Romeo*, they did their first work for me in designing the costumes (but not the scenery). They were enormously helpful to me in the production, and tremendously popular with the company. The OUDS was split that term into rival factions by an intense political partisanship on the occasion of the election of a new president at the end of Devine's term of office. The visiting ladies of the company were taken out by the undergraduates between rehearsals. They listened sympathetically while the rival candidates were praised or abused. Edith would go marching along the Oxford Canal or drive out to Godstow for dinner with two or three members of the cast, while Peggy was soothing another party over an omelette at The George. I was only at rehearsal in the daytime, as I was acting all the week in London, and so missed most of this excitement. George Devine found the Motleys especially sympathetic, and when he went 'down' a few months later and decided to take up acting as a profession he also became business manager to the Motleys, who were then launching out as stage-designers on quite an ambitious scale. Later he married Sophie (Audrey), Harris, the eldest of the three.

Julian Wylie gave me the night off for the opening of *Romeo* at Oxford, and I sat in the pit and nearly died with anxiety and mortification when the curtain fouled, causing a two-minutes' wait towards the end of what should otherwise have been a non-stop production.

I was in an unusual state of nerves when I went on to the stage at the end of the performance. The graceful compliments I intended to distribute circled madly in my head, and I referred to Miss Evans and Miss Ashcroft as 'two leading ladies, the like of whom I hope I shall never meet again!'

In spite of this *gaffe*, my desire to continue as a director was unshaken. Working with amateurs had given me confidence, and *Romeo* was a play which I knew really well. Edith Evans had of course played the Nurse before at the Old Vic, and her superb performance freed me from the least anxiety in any scene in which she appeared. Not only was she friendly and encouraging to everyone, but she rightly insisted on a certain admirable discipline during rehearsals, which was exactly what the OUDS needed to ensure the best possible results. I knew Peggy's Juliet would be enchanting. I had first seen her as Desdemona, at the Savoy, in what I thought a very disappointing production of *Othello*, with Paul Robeson, Maurice Browne, Ralph Richardson and Sybil Thorndike. When Peggy came on in the Senate scene it was as if all the lights in the theatre had suddenly gone up. Later, in the handkerchief scene, I shall never forget her touching gaiety as she darted about the stage, utterly innocent and lighthearted, trying to coax and charm Othello from his angry questioning. Her Juliet, especially in the early scenes, had this same quality of enchantment, and she made an enormous success at Oxford.

I was happy to find that I got on well with the whole cast, and it was exciting to see some of my long-cherished ideas of production actually being carried out upon the stage. In private life I am never very good at giving orders and getting my own way. As a director I seemed for the first time to gain real authority. One of the most exciting moments came just before the first dress-rehearsal. The lights, the scenery, and the orchestra were all to be used together for the first time. I sat alone in the dress-circle with my note-book and torch. The house lights went down, the music began to play, there was a faint glow from the footlights. A wonderful play was about to be performed, and it was for me alone. I felt like Ludwig of Bavaria. On the other hand, my feeling of utter helplessness on the first night made me far more nervous than if I had been appearing in the play myself.

I began my career as a director of Shakespeare in the professional theatre with *The Merchant of Venice* at the Old

Vic. As usual I was doing two things at once, acting in *Musical Chairs* this time, and finishing a film of *The Good Companions*, which overran its schedule, so that instead of having three weeks for my production, I was only able to attend five rehearsals altogether. Once again I found myself indebted to Harcourt Williams, who took the rehearsals when I was kept away[1]. Many people told me that they enjoyed this production of mine, but I was accused of fantasticating the story too much, and of overloading it with dancing, music and elaborate decorations. I was impressed but not wholly convinced by my critics. What was wrong with the production was lack of rehearsal, and it was a marvel to me that the company were able in so short a time to give even a hint of the elaborate ideas which I had conceived.

In one respect at least we were most restrained. The Motleys' colourful décor, which some people thought affected and extravagant, cost only £90. These practical young artists were more than usually resourceful in discovering cheap and effective materials. Shylock's dress, for instance, was made of dish rags. I used a great deal of music in the play, chiefly from Peter Warlock's *Capriol Suite*, which fitted perfectly with the contrasting moods of the different scenes, bound the action together, and covered many of the deficiencies in my production.

Soon afterwards I directed my first modern play, *Strange Orchestra*. Rodney Ackland's plays have a distinctive rhythm. The moods and subtleties of his characters are delicately woven together. His vision is apt to be limited to his own particular type of atmosphere, but at least he deals with real people, struggling with the circumstances under which they live, unlike the creatures of so many playwrights' imaginations, who wander about the stage, well clothed and fed, with no visible means of practical support.

When I read *Strange Orchestra*, I thought I saw an opportunity of trying to put into practice for myself some of the methods which I had learnt from watching Komisarjevsky. My production was a direct imitation of his style as I remembered it.

---

1 Again I dropped one of my celebrated bricks in a first-night speech when I referred to 'Harcourt Williams, who has done all the donkey-work in this production!'

I discovered in Rodney Ackland another vegetarian play-wright. There, however, his likeness to Ronald Mackenzie ended. Ackland has a restless, excitable mind, and a lack of reserve which is sometimes frank and endearing, although it can be a little embarrassing on occasion. He too has led a struggling, difficult life, but the fact that he has spent many years in that most uncomfortable and nerve-racking region, the fringe of success, has not made him bitter. He tells stories against himself, and makes fun of his misfortunes, but I know that he is sensitive and feels very acutely in the production of his plays. *Strange Orchestra* takes place in a Bloomsbury flat, where the paying guests are young and poor. They are uncertain of their jobs, they quarrel, make love, indulge in scenes of hysteria, behave abominably to one another, perform deeds of unselfish heroism, and dance to the gramophone.

The principal character in the play was the owner of the flat, Mrs Vera Lyndon, a Bohemian, slatternly woman with a heart of gold. This was a gorgeous character, and I saw at once that much of the success of the play would depend on the actress who created it. I was very anxious for Mrs Patrick Campbell to play the part, and finally suggested it to her with some trepidation. She could be very stubborn, and her reasons for rejecting or accepting a part were peculiar to herself. She once came to me in a state of great excitement over a quite unsuitable play to which she had taken a fancy, and when I asked her why she was so anxious to do it, she replied: 'Because I should speak French and German, play the César Franck sonata in the second act, and Vosper could be my father.'

When to my delighted surprise, Mrs Campbell accepted the Ackland part provisionally, new doubts began to trouble me. I knew that she was liable to treat a producer as dust beneath her chariot wheels, and I had heard strange stories of her behaviour at rehearsals. Marion Terry had told me once that, in *Pygmalion*, when Mrs Campbell discovered that Mr Shaw intended coming to a rehearsal, she refused to act while he remained in the theatre. Mr Shaw sat still. Mrs Campbell strode to her dressing-room, locked herself in, and played the piano for hours, while the cast, who could not proceed with their work listened entranced.

When the first rehearsal of *Strange Orchestra* began, 'Mrs Pat' pretended that she did not understand the play. 'Who are all these extraordinary characters?' she demanded. 'Where do they live? Does Gladys Cooper know them?' she invariably arrived late every morning and we would hear her talking loudly all the way from the stage-door to the stage. She said to David Hutcheson, whom we got for a certain part after tremendous trouble: 'Oh, how-do-you-do. I hope you'll stay. We have had four already!' She kept on reminding us, 'I am leaving in a fortnight; you must get someone else to play this part.' Every afternoon she went off to sit with her beloved Pekinese, which had been locked up in quarantine on her return with it from America. Her distress about her pet was quite genuine, and a real obsession with her.[1] In the end she left us, as she had threatened to do, and I was in despair. She had rehearsed the part magnificently and I felt sure that if she would only open in it the play's success was certain. And how wise she was about all the other parts! Here, just as in *Ghosts*, she was extremely well-informed about every detail of the play though she pretended to be quite indifferent to everything that was going on. One day she was sitting at the side of the stage. I thought she was asleep. I was rehearsing another scene, and asked one of the actors concerned to cut a certain line. Suddenly the famous voice boomed out. 'You know his whole character is in that line; I shouldn't cut it if I were you.' Of course she was perfectly right.

After Mrs Campbell's departure, gloom reigned for several days. Our spirits revived somewhat when we succeeded in persuading Laura Cowie to take her place. I did not like asking another actress to take over a part which Mrs Campbell had given up, but she gave a fine performance, exchanging her own vivid beauty and distinguished manners for the slatternly blowzi-

1 She said 'I smuggled it once as a false bust, and once as hip-disease'. The third time she put it in her hat-box, and it barked and was discovered!

ness of Mrs Lyndon. When the curtain went up on the first night she was spreading jam on a piece of toast. Her hand shook with nervousness and some of the jam fell on to her stocking. Laura stooped down, lazily scraped it off, and put it back on the toast. This unrehearsed piece of business, so perfectly 'in character', opened the play with a roar of laughter.

I was proud to be associated with *Strange Orchestra*. The play was only a moderate commercial success, but it had great quality – 'as much superior to the ordinary stuff of the theatre as tattered silk is to unbleached calico' – as James Agate so aptly put it.

Sheppey was the last play of a famous and experienced author, Somerset Maugham. We had some difficulty in casting many of the parts. We finally selected Ralph Richardson for the title part, Angela Baddeley for Sheppey's pretentious, vulgar-minded daughter, Eric Portman for her caddish lover, and Laura Cowie for the street-walker who, in the last scene, appears as Death. Two very successful pieces of casting were Victor Stanley, as a sort of modern Artful Dodger, and Cicely Oates, who gave a lovely performance as Mrs Sheppey.

I have always been struck, in my career as a director, by the allround excellence of English character-actors. Their discipline is beyond reproach, and their knowledge of their work is an enormous help to a director. Cast them right and they will always be perfect; you need never worry about them. Cicely Oates had played Lady Montague (a part of two lines and a little wailing) at the Regent, the first time I acted Romeo. Though she was a fine actress, it was a very long time before managers seemed to be aware of her remarkable talents. She died not long after the run of *Sheppey*, just at the moment when success seemed to be coming at last to reward her for her many years of unrecognized hard work.

Maugham's play was difficult to direct, though. It was so well written and carefully constructed that any radical changes, except a few cuts, were out of the question. Sir Gerald du Maurier once said of another Maugham play, *The Letter*, which he was directing: 'I don't like this sort of play. There's nothing for me to do.' But *Sheppey* seemed to be conceived in an extra-ordinary mixture of styles, with a first act of Pineroesque comedy; a second of almost Shavian cynicism and drama, and a third of tragic fantasy. I had neither the courage nor the experience to make any drastic changes in the script, and Mr Maugham did not arrive till the rehearsals had been in progress for a fortnight. I was very nervous when I approached him first. He was charming, but seemed oddly devoid of enthusiasm. He made some practical and useful suggestions but did not comment at all on the work that I had done. He seemed quite untouched by the expectant atmosphere in the theatre.

I discussed deferentially with him the scene where Sheppey's daughter, furious because her father proposes to give away the fortune which he has won in a sweepstake, yet hopeful that, if the family can have him certified as insane, the money may still be theirs, wanders round the stage with her eyes closed repeating a prayer: 'O God, make them say he's potty'. I was doubtful of the effect of some comic lines at this painful moment in the play and said to Maugham: 'Do you want this scene played for comedy or pathos? As it stands, the audience will laugh in the wrong places, and make it very difficult for the actress.' Mr Maugham looked genuinely surprised as he answered, 'But I think the whole scene is very funny don't you?' The scene was played in the end with much power by Angela Baddeley, who gave a brilliant perfor-mance of a difficult part, but, though Maugham congratulated her, I never knew if he thought we had harmed the effect of the scene as he conceived it by the way we had handled it in production.

I have nearly always been acting in another theatre on the first night of other plays I have directed, and it is a trying business on these occasions to concentrate on the old work while the new is in progress at a theatre near by. On the first night of *Sheppey* someone rushed across the court separating the stage-door of Wyndham's from that of the New Theatre, where I was appearing in *Richard of Bordeaux*, to tell me that the lights had gone wrong in the last scene when Death appears to the sleeping

Sheppey. This mistake must have damaged the play considerably at this first performance.

Later, I asked Mr Maugham to come to a matinée of *Sheppey* with me, as I wanted his approval of a few slight cuts. We sat in a box together and he began to take notes. In the interval I thought, 'Now perhaps he will talk about his play to me'. But Maugham had an odd knack of drawing one out, while he remained practically silent himself. I found that, as usual, I was doing all the talking, and I had a sneaking suspicion that although his manner was studiously correct, my companion was extracting a certain amount of demure amusement from my eloquence.

When Maugham range me up a few days later and asked me to lunch with him at Claridge's, adding 'I have a little book that I want to give you', I went to keep the engagement with the liveliest expectations. But instead of the quiet *tête-à-tête* meal I had hoped for, I found that a large luncheon party had been assembled. Beverley Nichols and John Van Druten were present, as well as several other brilliant people, and I had to be satisfied with crumbs of polite conversation from my host, who sat right away from me on the other side of a large table. When the meal was over, Mr Maugham drew me into the men's room, where the murmured a few polite words as he pressed the promised gift into my hands. When I looked up to thank him, he was gone. The book was a first copy of *Sheppey*, and I found when I opened it that the author had dedicated the play to me. It was a charming gesture, but I should have been very grateful for an hour's talk with Maugham about the theatre. It is always difficult I find, to get on intimate terms with dramatic authors. I suppose my actor's egotism is to blame. I am not clever at drawing people out, and my friends tell me that I have no real interest in anyone but myself. I hope this is not the exact truth.

Chapter 13

1932–33

The manuscript of Gordon Daviot's *Richard of Bordeaux*, with its neat pages typed in blue, had lain in my dressing-room for several days before I found time to look at it. I picked it up in one of my waits during a matinée of *The Good Companions* and began to read it through. There was a long cast and a great number of scenes and I knew little of the history of Richard's time except what I had learned from Shakespeare. The opening scene of the new play was light and charming, and the description of Richard's appearance attracted me at once – I thought that perhaps the author had seen me in the part at the Vic[1] – but the council scene which followed seemed rather wordy and I could not at first distinguish the characters of the different councillors and uncles. It was not till I began reading the third scene, in Richard's palace after dinner, with Derby telling boring stories about the tournament on one side and Anne discussing fashions and religion with Lady Derby on the other, that my interest and enthusiasm were thoroughly aroused. I took the play home with me that night, and read it several times during the weeks that followed.

I realized at once that Richard was a gift from heaven, and I felt sure that Gwen Ffrangcon Davies would be exquisite as Anne, if she could be persuaded to play it. Originally the part was even smaller than in the final version, and it was essential that the actress who created it should completely fill the picture

1 It turned out later that she had!

in every scene in which she appeared as there was little other female interest in the play. I did not mean to direct it myself as I thought it would be too difficult a task for me in addition to playing such a long, exacting part. I hoped to get Komisarjevsky to undertake it, but he was abroad at the time. Bronson Albery liked the manuscript and offered to give performances at the Arts Theatre on two consecutive Sunday nights. I eagerly agreed, and asked Harcourt Williams to help me to direct the play.

These performances took place in the spring of 1932, when *Musical Chairs* was still running successfully at the Criterion. Joseph Schindler was a pretty exhausting part emotionally, but I was grateful for the chance of studying something new. I had shown the script of *Richard of Bordeaux* to the Motleys who were enthusiastic and full of ingenious schemes for saving time and money over the *décor*. Albery allowed us to spend £300 and lent us the New Theatre for the trial performances in order to give us more space to manœuvre the quick changes of scenery. However, what with casting, directing, and acting in two places at once, I was completely exhausted after the performances were over, and, although we had played to enthusiastic audiences, I felt that the middle part of the play was weak, and could not believe it had really much chance of commercial success. Mackenzie, I remember, disliked it intensely, and as I am always inclined to be more impressed by adverse criticism than by enthusiastic comments from my friends after an exhausting first night, I resumed the unbroken run of *Musical Chairs* without much regret and thought no more about the other play.

Soon after Mackenzie died, however, and when the nine months' run of *Musical Chairs* was coming to an end, Albery began pressing me to do *Richard of Bordeaux* again for a regular run at the New Theatre. For some weeks I was not at all enthusiastic about the idea as I still thought that certain parts of the play were weak, and I did not feel I had the energy to tackle it again so soon.

When we had started rehearsing the Arts Theatre production I had not met Gordon Daviot[1] at all. All the business negotiations were carried out by her agent, Curtis Brown, and it was only at the dress-rehearsal that a figure was pointed out to me sitting in the stalls, and I went down to meet my authoress for the first time.

We had already altered her play a good deal when she saw it first, yet she had nothing but praise for everything that we had done, and seemed ready to fall in with any suggestions for further alteration that might be thought necessary.

Gwen's share in the preparation and ultimate success of *Richard of Bordeaux* was incalculable. With her comedy, her pathos and her appearance in the rich simple dresses which the Motley's had designed for her, she might have stepped out of the pages of a missal. She was responsive to every mood and tone of mine as we rehearsed our scenes together. Every sweep of her dress and turn of her body was contrived with skill and grace. She helped me continually with my difficult part, just as she had done in *Romeo and Juliet* ten years before. In her own performance nothing was left to chance – she always wore a train for rehearsals, studied her costumes with extreme care so as to know beforehand exactly where they would help or hinder her while she was acting, and selected and economized her emotional effects from day to day, working with the other actors to share her scenes with them in the most helpful way possible.

After the two special performances were over, Gordon and I had talked together at some length about the play, discussing certain suggestions for improvements. There was a bad gap in the story at the end of the long first act, there was also a council scene later, after the Queen's death, which I did not think very effective. The last act needed strengthening, and two small intermediate scenes, we decided, ought to be cut altogether. One, describing John of Gaunt's death, seemed too close to

---

1 Gordon Daviot was the pseudonym of Elizabeth Mackintosh whose home was in Inverness. She wrote her plays under this name and, at the same time, wrote many successful thrillers under the pseudonym of Josephine Tey, including *The Daughter of Time*, a book about Richard III.

Shakespeare, and the other was not very successful in performance. I thought Derby himself should be given another scene instead. There was not enough of him in the play to give the audience a real interest in his final victory over Richard. Richard himself had so much to do that I felt certain it would help him if the characters of Anne, Robert, Mowbray, the uncles, and Derby could be more fully developed in contrast.

Gordon Daviot went back to Scotland after our conversation and I thought no more about it. Some weeks afterwards I said to Albery: 'I am not very keen to do *Richard* again. It will need a great deal of work and alteration, and then perhaps it will not come out right.' A day or two later I received a letter from Gordon enclosing a dozen pages of rewritten manuscript. Every single point we had discussed had been considered and remedied in the simplest and most effective way. There was a new opening to the second act. The council scene was gone. In its place was a scene at Sheen Palace in the winter, when Richard returns, for the first and last time, to the room where Anne had died a year before. Mowbray's character was elaborated in a few lines. There was a new scene in the last act for Derby and the Archbishop. I was delighted with the changes, and started to discuss the play again.

In the end I directed *Richard of Bordeaux* myself – a big responsibility, but by this time I felt I knew more about this particular play than anyone else except the author.

The cost of the whole production was extraordinarily little, though the scenery and dresses were of course elaborated from the 'one set with a few additions' which had served for the original performances. The final result was beautiful, even spectacular, and the Motleys established themselves, by their exquisitely graded colour scheme, and simple but brilliantly suggestive scenery, as designers of the very first rank.

In the manuscript, the scenes were labelled by the author, 'Conway Castle', 'The Palace at Eltham', 'The Palace of Sheen' and so on. We were therefore able to develop all the details for ourselves. Working with the Motleys, I planned out rough ideas for every scene – the council-chamber with a horse-shoe table, and banners hanging from the roof (I cribbed this effect of grouping, with the King on his throne seen through the backs of the councillors, from a photograph of a Reinhardt production of *Henry IV, Part I*, that had been done in Germany); the Eltham scene in a striped garden pavilion; the Palace of Sheen with white cloisters and a little tree. Then I was obsessed by the idea that I must walk down stairs at the end of the scene when Richard banishes Mowbray:

'So you never really trusted me, Richard?'
   'My dear Thomas, the only persons I trust are two thousand archers, paid regularly every Friday,'

– the line seemed to demand a slow descending exit, and so the scene was placed in a gallery overlooking a great hall. We suggested the festivities going on below by music under the stage, and by two or three richly dressed supers walking with us in procession across the front of the stage before the opening of the scene. The scenery throughout the play gave an admirable suggestion of the size and bareness of the mediaeval palaces of those days, with their high roofs and narrow corridors, steep steps, and embrasured windows. There was just the right amount of detail – a few simple pieces of furniture, rich hangings and table appointments, luxurious materials used for the lovely clothes, but nothing distracting or overdone.

There were some moments in the play which obstinately refused to come out right. During rehearsal one afternoon we were struggling with the Queen's death scene in a dark, depressing room in the back-streets of Soho. The stage direction suggested that Anne should be carried from the stage leaving Richard alone in despair as the curtain fell. Though this had seemed, in reading, one of those 'star curtains' which actors dream of, I began to be more and more certain that the audience could not be moved by the spectacle of my grief if the object of it was no longer there. With the centre of interest gone, I could not make anything of the 'curtain' by myself. At last someone suggested that the doctor should arrive and discover that Anne was dying of the plague. We improvised the scene in dumb show to get the right feeling and grouping for the situation, the authoress wrote two or three short lines of dialogue, and the trick was done.

Some of my other ideas were not so successful. I introduced two tableaux which were a complete failure, but had the sense to remove them (rather reluctantly and under pressure) at the dress-rehearsal. Gordon suddenly found her voice and called, 'Oh, don't cut them out, John has taken so much trouble with them'. I had thought it would be effective to show Richard setting fire to the faggots which were to burn down Sheen Palace, and had planned with the stage carpenter a magnificent stage effect, which he had invented some years before to burn Matheson Lang at the stake in *The Wandering Jew*. But this was not quite the same kind of play, and I realized, just in time, that tableaux were a little out of date, and quite inappropriate to this particular production.

The dress-rehearsal was a series of mishaps. I had spent the whole day in the theatre arranging the lighting. The dress-circle, where I sat, was in the process of being reseated by a battalion of workmen hammering and raising dust. I had to shout my directions to the stage-hands at the top of my voice and kept begging the workmen to extinguish their working lights every few minutes, in order to judge the effect I was trying to create on the stage below. By the evening I was too tired even to lose my temper. Instead I wore an expression of royal composure, suitable as I thought to the character I was trying to play. 'Surely there should be a blue spot there?' I said, pointing gently to a corner, as I lay on the floor at Gwen's feet attempting to act and watch together. 'It is lucky someone has a memory in this theatre.' Then came the incident of the tableaux, which I bore with comparative resignation, but in the final scene, as I opened my mouth to speak the last line of the play, the curtain suddenly descended. I was only able to murmur, 'If that happens tomorrow night we are all sunk!' and sweep, sad but forgiving, to my dressing-room. There is a superstition in the theatre that it is unlucky to speak the 'tag' line of a new play at the dress-rehearsal, and afterwards I wondered if there wasn't something in it after all.

The first night was not sensational, though the audience was attentive and enthusiastic. The strain of acting and producing the play had been very great, and I had practically lost my voice. To add to my troubles, I had quarrelled with one of the leading actors, who refused to see eye to eye with me in the way he should play his part. Fortunately, he was very well cast, and the faults in his performance, though irritating to me, were not detrimental to the general effect, as it turned out, or noticeable to the audience.

The notices were enthusiastic the following morning, and I spent the day thanking people who telephoned me their con-gratulations. However, when I opened the return for the second performance I found that there had been only £77 in the house. Such modest takings did not indicate the great success which some people had so confidently predicted. The tide turned at the first matinée. Business had been quiet all the morning, but at ten minutes past one the telephone bell in the box office began to ring. Queues formed outside the theatre, and so great and unexpected was the rush that it was a quarter-past three before all the members of the afternoon's audience were in their seats.

From that moment *Richard of Bordeaux* became what the Americans call a 'smash hit'. I travelled down to Brighton for the day on the following Sunday, and although I was physically dog-tired I felt so happy and exhilarated that I went for a long walk on the Downs in a heavy snowstorm.

I determined to make a gesture in honour of the play's success by giving a party. I borrowed the Motleys' studio, which had once been a night club, and sent out invitations to everybody I knew. The party was a great success both in numbers and distinction. 'Heavens, what a salary list!' somebody was heard to murmur. The Motley's model theatre was on view. A card had been placed in front of it with the words 'Do not touch' attached to the switch-board, but this awakened Leslie Henson's curiosity, with the result that the crowded room was plunged in darkness, and many of the best-known voices in London were raised in protest.

Richard of Bordeaux was the success of the season. From the window of my flat, I could look down St. Martin's Lane and see the queues coiled like serpents round the theatre. I was photographed, painted, caricatured, interviewed. I signed my autograph a dozen times a day, and received letters and presents by every post. White harts rained upon me in every shape and form, designed in flowers, embroidered on handkerchiefs, stamped on cigarette-boxes. When I left after the matinée the court outside the stage-door would be packed with people. It was rather embarrassing to find that some of my admirers had discovered that I lived near by, and I would often stagger up the street to my front door, with my hat over my eyes and my overcoat collar turned up, followed by a crowd of fifteen or twenty members of my enthusiastic audience. Of course I enjoyed it all at first. But after a time it became rather irksome when I could not go out of my flat without finding two or three 'fans' lurking across the street to intercept me, and several times a day I would open the front door to a complete stranger, or answer the telephone only to find that some importunate or impertinent schoolgirl was giggling at the other end, having 'had a bet with a friend that she would manage to speak to me'.

People came thirty and forty times to see the play. There were several changes in the cast during the run and the rehearsals kept us fairly fresh. In addition to this I was always watching the performance and making little additions and improvements which the 'regulars' were quick to appreciate. I was not so pleased when some of them wrote to me that I was becoming mannered and seemed emotionally exhausted. I fought hard against the boredom and fatigue of so many consecutive performances, and was dismayed to find that, in spite of all my efforts, I was becoming exaggerated and insincere. By the end of the run I had become acutely selfconscious in all the moments that people had originally liked best. But I nearly always enjoyed acting the last two scenes of the play, finding a way of playing these scenes in complete control of my own emotions although the audience became more and more affected to the point of tears. At last I felt I was learning to relax, which Komisarjevsky had told me was the secret of all good emotional acting, and to manage my audience instead of allowing the audience to manage me.

Just before Christmas of the *Richard of Bordeaux* year my voice began to give me a lot of trouble. I was given a fortnight's holiday, and went off on a motor tour through the West of England.

I stayed at a remote inn on Dartmoor, went for long walks, and ate enormous teas with jam and cream. I went to Plymouth and strode along the wind-swept Hoe. Next morning I crossed by the ferry and found myself in the strange foreign land of Cornwall. It was here that I met Ralph Richardson unexpectedly. We had dinner together, and drank champagne, and went cliff-climbing in the dark.

I was thoroughly enjoying myself, but I was conscious of a slight feeling of restlessness. Some time before it was really necessary I started back towards London again. At Bath the car broke down, and it was with a sensation which I recognized as relief that I proceeded to Brighton, where I decided to spend the last days of my holiday. But I found it impossible to keep away from the theatre, and rushed off in the evening to see a Charlot Revue which was being played at the Hippodrome. I must have been away from *Richard* for at least ten days, but although there were still several more left before I must return to the cast, I travelled back to London the next morning. Sneaking into the New Theatre in the evening, I sat behind a curtain in one of the boxes watching a performance of *Richard of Bordeaux* with Glen Byam Shaw, who understudied me, playing the King.

Richard was a wonderful part. It was perfectly suited to my personality and even my tricks and mannerisms did not seem to matter as much as usual. I was helped enormously by my costumes, which expressed exactly the development and gradual ageing of the character. Also the work I had been doing during the three previous years had been of great value to my acting taste.

Playing Shakespeare at the Vic had enriched my sensibility and developed my technique. Afterwards I had jumped into a completely different atmosphere and found a way of making the most of my shadowy part in *The Good Companions*. Finally, Komis's subtle production of *Musical Chairs* had demanded yet another method of approach, an inner understanding of character which I was able to carry a stage further than I had ever done before. I no longer fought shy of using my own personality, as I had at the time of the Vic *Hamlet*. On the contrary, I made full use of it for the first time as Joseph Schindler and gained confidence by doing so. Now, in *Richard*, I was able to gather the fruits of all this experience to give light and shade to a long and elaborate character study.

I have often wondered how *Richard of Bordeaux* stands in relation to the notable successes of the past, and what are its chances of survival. The majority of the plays in which Irving, Tree, Alexander and Wyndham appeared could now only be revived as curiosities.[1] I fancy we are unable to accept them today because their period is too close to ours, and also because they are associated in our minds with the great actors who created them. The theatrical successes of the Victorian age were essentially the products of single personalities. *The Bells* was Irving, and the public today would never accept another actor in the play. On the other hand, Gladys Cooper's revival of *The Second Mrs Tanqueray* in the twenties caused enormous interest, and though the play seemed rather old-fashioned it remained a finely constructed vehicle for acting.

In the future new players may interpret afresh some of the more recent works which now lie neglected on the shelf. Will

1 Since writing this we have had a notable spate of successful revivals. *Lady Windermere's Fan*, *Dear Brutus* and *Caste* among them.

those plays then become what we call 'classics'? I should not care
to guess the names of the plays of my generation for which this
honour waits – *The Circle*[1] perhaps, *The Vortex* possibly. Will
Musical Chairs or *Richard of Bordeaux* be among their number? And
shall I feel very jealous or only faintly patronizing if those plays
are revived during my lifetime with new players in the parts
which I created?

Richard came to an end at last. The final performances in
London were terribly tiring and emotional. The tour which
followed was a triumphant success, and at Golder's Green,
where we played the very last performance, the police had to be
called to keep back the crowd which surged round the stage-door
when Gwen and I tried to leave the theatre.

In the copy of the play that Gordon sent to me she wrote: 'I
like to think that, in time to come, whenever *Richard of Bordeaux*
is mentioned, it is your name that will spring to people's lips'.
How pleasant it was to be told that! But it was to the brilliant
inspiration and sympathy of Gordon Daviot that I owed the
biggest personal success of my career.

1 I revived this myself in 1944 with some success.

Chapter 14

1934

During the run of *Richard* I had made my first venture into management, greatly attracted by the charming atmosphere of a new play, *Spring 1600*, written by Emlyn Williams, who was at that time acting in Edgar Wallace's *The Case of the Frightened Lady* in New York. Emlyn had been an undergraduate at Oxford in the days when I was playing there with the Fagans, and I had sometimes seen him curled up in an armchair in a corner of the Clubroom at the OUDS. But I did not know him at all, though I had greatly admired his performance as Angelo, the Italian secretary to Tony Perelli, the gangster, in Wallace's *On the Spot*. I was aware that Fagan had given him his first chances, both as author and actor, by producing his first play *Full Moon* at the Oxford Playhouse. Since that time he had been acting and writing with equal success.

I was not able to interest Bronson Albery in *Spring 1600*, and after some thought I decided to present it myself, with Richard Clowes, a great friend of mine, as partner. I was also to direct the play. At first we found it extremely difficult to cast. Elisabeth Bergner had just arrived in England and had announced her intention of appearing on the London stage. I found out where she was living, and asked her to come and lunch with me. The childish figure who arrived, wearing a blue beret and a loose woolly coat, did not at all resemble the glamorous star of popular imagination, but she did look exactly like the young girl in Emlyn's play who runs away from the country and joins Richard Burbage's company disguised as a boy. She sat with me at

Boulestin's restaurant, with her red hair falling over one eye, talking eagerly in her precise attractive English and looking wisely at me as she picked at her very frugal meal. I was fascinated by Elisabeth Bergner, as I have been ever since.

She told me she had read three hundred plays since her arrival in London and had liked *Spring 1600* best, but she was greatly in the debt of Mr Cochran and could not dream of making her debut under any management but his. Why I did not immediately offer the manuscript to Cochran I cannot for the life of me imagine.

Spring 1600 was shelved for several months. I talked it over with Emlyn, and persuaded him to re-shape the last act completely and make other fairly drastic alterations. This method had been very successful in *Richard of Bordeaux*, but in this case my suggested additions overweighted the spectacular side of the play. The slender plot sank gradually deeper and deeper into a morass of atmosphere and detail. The Motleys designed elaborate sets, I engaged madrigal singers, a large orchestra, and a crowd of supers, Isabel Jeans, as Lady Coperario, had a magnificent-looking real negro attendant to usher her on to the stage, and a real black monkey (which promptly bit her) to carry on her shoulder. By the time the curtain rose on the first night we had spent £4000.

The most successful performance was given by Frank Pettingell, who was irresistibly funny as Ned Pope, a middle-aged actor in Burbage's company who had played Juliet's Nurse, and was delighted at the prospect of being offered the part of Gertrude, the Queen, in Shakespeare's new play. He was immensely sedate as he sat quarreling with the young boys who played the heroines' parts or sewing in a corner of Burbage's bedroom while a rehearsal was going on.

In spite of many hectic days in the theatre Emlyn Williams remained calm. He accepted most of my alterations and cuttings without demur, wrote in the extra scenes which I suggested and kept us all continually amused. One morning I approached him a little nervously and said that I thought the opening scene of the play was unduly encumbered with the names of flowers. Would he agree to my making a few cuts, as these repeated floral allusions rather held up the action? 'By all means', said Emlyn. 'We don't want James Agate to head his Sunday article, "Herrick, or Little by Little".'

We were only once in serious danger of quarrelling. 'The last act is thin. We must try to make the best of it,' I announced through my megaphone from the dress-circle, thinking that our author was miles away.

'I think we all know the act is thin, John,' said a voice at my elbow, 'but you need not announce the fact to the whole cast. You might wait for the critics to do that.' I felt very much ashamed of myself. But when I turned round to apologize I caught Emlyn's eye and we both burst out laughing.

The dress-rehearsal arrived. I was still playing in *Richard of Bordeaux* at night and was terribly tired with the double work. A few professionals came to the rehearsal, Frank Vosper among them. At the end he came to me and said, 'It's a lovely production, but you ought to cut twenty minutes out of the first act.' By some very careless oversight the play had never been timed, but I had chopped the text about so much that I did not dare to impose new cuts and alterations at the last minute, as there was no time left to rehearse them. I rushed off to the New for my own performance, leaving everything as it was and hoping for the best. Alas, I should at all costs have listened to Frank's admirable advice! On the first night, despite a most friendly and enthusiastic house, the first act hung fire badly, and the final curtain did not descend until 11.30.

I heard afterwards that the audience behaved with exemplary patience. They seemed to wish the play to succeed, and seized on the good things in it with pleasure and relief. When I read the notices the following morning, however, I knew the worst at once. The critics praised where they could, but it was obvious that most of them knew that something was amiss. Emlyn spoke to me on the telephone, asking my permission to make some cuts. I heard that afterwards he went straight to the theatre, borrowed the prompt copy of his play, and sat on a chair at the stage-door making the alterations he thought necessary. He had watched the first performance from the top of a ladder in the wings, from which point of vantage he was able to judge the audience's reaction to every single situation.

I had a matinée of *Richard of Bordeaux* that afternoon, and Emlyn came to see me after it was over. We found a subdued company waiting for us at the Shaftesbury Theatre. I think we all realized that our labours of the last four weeks had been for nothing, but the prospect of failure was never even hinted at as we gave out the cuts. How well actors behave on these occasions!

The very definite failures, which are taken off after a couple of nights, are easier to endure than plays which die a lingering death. A fortnight passed while *Spring 1600* perished slowly and miserably. The houses were poor, but not unenthusiastic, and several days of fog enabled us to blame the weather and continue to live in hope. But it was no use. Once or twice I looked in during a matinée, but the sight of so many empty seats drove me out into the murky streets again. But at least I had my own work to keep me occupied in the evenings, whilst poor Emlyn haunted the Shaftesbury Theatre every night. At last he could bear it no longer, packed his bags, and fled to Spain. A few days later the play came to an end.

I knew that Ronald Mackenzie had finished another play just before his death, though he had never shown it to me; and I had heard that he hoped to interest Leslie Banks in playing the leading part. But one matinée day, just before Ronald went on his fatal holiday, I had lunched at Rules with him and Komis. I was slightly disgruntled because I had not been asked to read the new manuscript, and as the conversation was chiefly centred on this topic I was not able to take much part in it. I left for my performance halfway through lunch, leaving Komis and Ronald glowering at each other across the table in a curiously glum but understanding manner.

A few months after Mackenzie died Komis sent me *The*

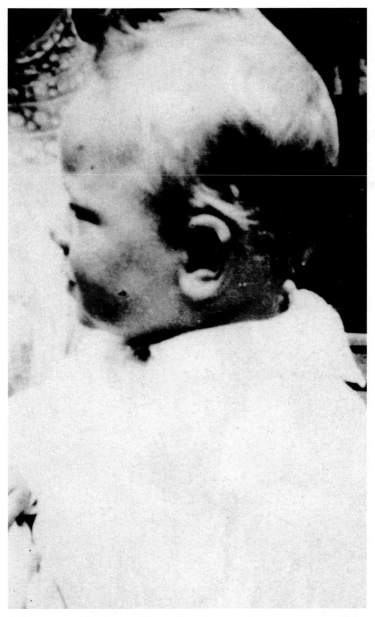

Arthur John Gielgud: one of the earliest photographs

The White Butterfly in *The Insect Play*, 1923.

Trofimov in *The Cherry Orchard*, 1925

The abdication scene, Richard II, 1929. Costume design by Elizabeth
Montgomery (Motley)

Richard of Bordeaux, 1933-34

Hamlet, 1934

Romeo, with Peggy Ashcroft as Juliet

irst major film role in *The Secret Agent*, with Peter Lorre, Madeleine Carroll and Robert
oung, 1935

Noah in the play of the same name by André Obey, 1935

Maitlands to read, and I thought it wonderfully good, though I understood immediately why the author had not thought me ideal for either of the two men's parts. I knew that Albery had bought an option on the play and proposed to present it at some future time. Now, more than a year later, it was decided to produce *The Maitlands* at Wyndham's as soon as I returned from my holiday.

Mackenzie had insisted that only Komis should handle the play, and I was not sure how much they had discussed together the details of the casting and production. I did not like to ask Komis too many questions on the subject, as he might have supposed me interfering. I knew he had been very fond of Mackenzie, and that he believed sincerely in the play.

The rehearsals began without me. I returned from my short rest, ten days later, to find the actors in position and all the preliminary work in hand, never a very satisfactory way to begin studying a new part. Komis orchestrated the action with his usual skill, but I did not think his cuts and rearrangements as successful as they had been in *Musical Chairs*. Again he ignored a change of scene demanded by the stage directions, and designed a composite set of great ingenuity, consisting of a sitting-room in the front of the stage with a dining-room in the background, and a hall, staircase and front door (all visible to the audience) on the right-hand side. There was a strange little door under the stairs, leading to the basement, round which a comic maid popped her head at various moments. The whole pictorial treatment conveyed a rather crazy, unreal atmosphere which I do not think the author intended, as the play was strictly realistic.

We opened on a terribly hot night. All day long the queues had waited patiently for the pit and gallery to open. My name was in large letters outside the theatre. After *Bordeaux*, everyone supposed that I must have chosen another big showy part for my next appearance.

When the curtain went up, I was discovered wearing rather shabby modern clothes, and a moustache (which I had specially grown for the occasion), with a trident in my hand and a paper crown on my head, being fitted for a Neptune carnival costume. There was tremendous applause at first. Then, either because my appearance disappointed those who thought I ought to look romantic, or because the regular first-nighters had been irritated and crowded out by a mass of *Bordeaux* enthusiasts, an uproar broke out in the gallery which lasted for several moments. Meanwhile I stood on the stage, paralysed with nervousness, waiting to speak the opening lines of the play. Calm was restored as soon as the dialogue began, and the performance continued without any other untimely interruptions. But at the end of the play, after many curtains, I stepped forward to speak about Mackenzie, when someone in the gallery shouted 'Rubbish!'

When I came out of the stage-door, half an hour later, the court was full of people looking curiously glum and disagreeable, though there was no demonstration of any kind. Next morning, however, the newspapers had headlines 'Dead author's play booed on first night', 'Wild scenes at Wyndham's' and so on. In spite of this unfavourable beginning, *The Maitlands* ran for ten weeks to average business, but it was never really a success. I hope it may be done again one day under happier auspices. It is a brilliant piece of work, full of observation and bitter wit, with an unerring quality of theatrical effectiveness, which was not, in my opinion, exploited to the full in the performance we gave.

I had an amusing encounter with Lilian Baylis about this time. The Vic was about to open again for a new season, and Lilian sent me one of her characteristic letters (neatly typed, with most of the typing crossed out and her own writing crowded in on top of it) asking me to come down to see her and discuss some of her plans. Delighted and flattered at being considered so important, I stepped into my car and drove to the Vic. I marched in to Lilian's office in my best West End style, with a new hat and yellow gloves held negligently in my hand. Lilian greeted me warmly and we talked enthusiastically together for half an hour. As I got up to go I said grandly, 'I should simply love to come down some time and act and direct again at the Vic for you if you'd let me, but of course I'm awfully busy for the next month or two'.

Lilian, looking steadily at my rapidly receding hair, said briskly, 'Oh no, dear, you play all the young parts you can while you're still able to!' I left the Vic in a distinctly chastened frame of mind, determined that I would never again attempt to impress so shrewd a judge of character as Lilian Baylis.

Ever since *Richard of Bordeaux* I had talked about *Hamlet* with the Motleys. We had sat in their studio over endless cups of tea, arguing about the ideal setting for the play, how it should be cast, what period of costume would suit it best, and so on. After the comparatively short runs of *The Maitlands* and *Queen of Scots*,[1] Albery suddenly decided to do *Hamlet* for me at the New. It was lucky that I knew the part and had been making plans on and off for nearly a year for this very play – otherwise I could never have hoped to tackle the tremendous job of acting in it and directing it as well with only four weeks' rehearsals.

Of course I was encouraged by the prospect of choosing a fine cast for myself, and I longed to see if my ideas for the production could be carried out as I had conceived them.

I have a particular aversion to the hackneyed Gothic style of decoration for *Hamlet*, in which the King and Queen look like playing-cards, and Hamlet like an overgrown Peter Pan. I described my ideas on the subject to the Motleys, and shortly afterwards they showed me some of the work of Lucas Cranach, a contemporary of Dürer. These drawings finally inspired the costumes which they designed for our production.

For the scenery a large rostrum was constructed, revolving on its own axis and moved by hand. It was quite easily pushed round by four or five stage hands. This rostrum (which looked by daylight rather like the body of a denuded battleship) provided slopes and levels, seen at different angles when the position of the rostrum changed, on which I could vary the groupings at different moments in the play. A cyclorama was used at the back for the exteriors – the platform, the graveyard, and the final scene, and painted canvas curtains, covered with a rich florid

---

1 Written for Gwen Ffrangcon Davies by Gordon Daviot. I directed it with a fine cast, including Laurence Olivier, but it only achieved a moderate success.

design in blue and silver, enclosed the stage or draped the rostrum for the other parts of the play. It was easy to raise or drop these curtains with only a few moments' pause between the scenes.

All the dresses were made of canvas, but trimmed with silk and velvet, and with rich autumnal colours patterned on to them with a paint spray. The cost of these clothes was amazingly little, and the result looked magnificent, thanks to the Motleys' labour and ingenuity. The finished costumes had the rich, worn look so difficult to obtain on the stage, where period dresses always appear to be either brand-new from the costumier or else shabby and secondhand. We wore great chains round our necks, which appeared imposing and massive from the front. Actually they were made of rubber, painted with silver and gold, and were as light as a feather.

The success of *Hamlet* at the New was a great pleasure and surprise to me. I have written at some length in Rosamond Gilder's book,[1] about my performance in this part, and discussed there most of my difficulties and conclusions in dealing with the inexhaustible problems of the play. I do not wish to enlarge on them again. As always happens when a production is hailed as a success, there was a good deal of conflicting opinion about the merits of the performance. Many people told me that they had preferred my own acting at the Vic when I had played the part for the first time. In the same way, Frank Vosper's Claudius was not so highly praised as it had been when he played it in modern dress at the Kingsway some years before. Jessica Tandy's Ophelia was dismissed as a complete failure by certain critics and highly praised by others. I liked it enormously myself. Almost everyone was agreed as to the excellence of George Howe's Polonius, Jack Hawkins was an admirable and sympathetic Horatio, and Laura Cowie magnificently sensuous in the part of Gertrude, playing with especially fine effect in her scenes with Vosper. They looked like a pair of cruel, monstrous cats, and their first appearance,

1 *John Gielgud's Hamlet*, by Rosamond Gilder. Methuen 1938.

seated on dull gold thrones above the bowing ranks of russet-tinted courtiers, with tall Landsknecht soldiers lining the steps behind them, was immensely fine and impressive.

One night, during one of the intervals in *Hamlet*, Frank was visited by an Army major who told him how much he was enjoying the performance. He was not the type of playgoer one would have expected to relish Shakespearean tragedy and we were all delighted to hear that he was enjoying himself. Then came the moment in the final scene when Claudius says, 'Cousin Hamlet, you know the wager'. None of us knew where to look when Frank, still thinking of his visitor and quite unaware of his mistake, demanded sonorously, 'Cousin Hamlet, you know the major!'

Hamlet was the last production in which I was associated with Frank Vosper. His tragic death in 1937 was a great shock to all his friends. He had inimitable gaiety and charm, was generous to a degree, a delightfully Bohemian and charming host and, as an artist, completely free from jealousy of any kind. Often he gave the impression that he behaved selfishly in doing exactly as he liked, but in reality he enjoyed nothing so much as giving pleasure to other people. As an actor he was often unequal, and sometimes his performances became exaggerated in the course of a long run, but his original creation of old Schindler in *Musical Chairs*, his Dulcimer in *The Green Bay Tree*, and his Henry VIII in *The Rose Without a Thorn*, could hardly have been bettered.

It is difficult to write in detail of these last four years of my career, for I was really too busy to observe their passing with much accuracy of detail. My time was taken up with casting, directing, acting. At the end of an exhausting run I was always in the throes of making plans for something fresh. My short holidays barely gave me time to recover from the hectic life I led in the theatre. I spent most of my spare time in sleeping a great deal, in taking care not to eat unwisely or too well (arranging one's menu is a great problem when one is playing exhausting classical parts eight times a week), husbanding my voice, and living in the country whenever I could.

Chapter 15

1935

While I was playing *Hamlet*, Rodney Ackland brought me a new play, an adaptation of Hugh Walpole's novel *The Old Ladies*. The book had always been a favourite of mine, and I had even been bold enough to call on Walpole himself a year or so before, and suggest with some temerity that I should collaborate with him on a stage version. We had a delightful talk but nothing came of the idea, as Walpole was busy with his Herries saga and I was full of other plans in the theatre at the time.

Again I found it impossible to discover a manager to share my enthusiasm. Albery and Horace Watson (of the Haymarket) both turned down the play, and I could not find anyone else willing to present it, so, for the second time, Richard Clowes and I decided to go into partnership. After a good deal of discussion, we managed to find a really perfect cast. There are only four characters in the whole play — one of them a charwoman who does not speak. We engaged Edith Evans for Mrs Payne, the old gipsy woman who covets the piece of amber owned by the poor faded gentlewoman Miss Beringer (Jean Cadell). The third old lady — Mrs Amorest, a motherly little widow whose hopes are centered in her adored son who is abroad and a tiny legacy which she is likely to receive from a dying cousin — was beautifully played by Mary Jerrold.

We started rehearsals without having been able to lease a theatre, and the cast worked away valiantly while we made every effort to obtain one. I felt sure that the play should be given in a small theatre, preferably the Criterion as, with only four characters, a small stage seemed essential. The faded gentility of the atmosphere, and the macabre scene of Miss Beringer's death in the last act, were considered to be dangerous ingredients for the box-office, and every day our search for a theatre became more and more despairing. We were terrified that our three fine actresses might be tempted by a more concrete offer to leave us in the midst of our rehearsals. The delay over the theatre finally resulted in our rehearsing the play for six weeks instead of the usual three and a half, and I believe this was one of the reasons why the production was such a complete piece of work when it was finished.

The Old Ladies was the first production in which I was able to carry out most fully my original intentions. Usually one begins with a number of exciting ideas which gradually get lost in the stress of 'putting on the play somehow' in a limited time.

The action took place in three rooms of an old house in a cathedral town. The script demanded that both the staircase and hall should be visible to the audience, and at first I pictured the stage with the rooms arranged symmetrically one above the other. One day we were rehearsing doggedly at the New, with our properties for *The Old Ladies* set up on the big uneven rostrum which was used for *Hamlet* in the evenings. Edith was sitting in a low rocking-chair on the highest part of the rostrum. A few feet below her, and a little forward on the stage, Mary Jerrold moved about, making cups of tea among her pathetic little sticks of furniture. The few feet of rostrum which divided them suggested immediately that they were in different rooms, though in reality a twelve-foot wall and a ceiling would have separated them from one another. I suddenly saw an extraordinary effect in this arrangement and rushed to the Motleys' studio, where I sketched them my idea on a half-sheet of paper. By next morning a new set had been designed showing the lower half of the house at the beginning of the play, Mrs Amorest's sitting-room, the hall, the foot of the stairs and the front door. After the first scene there was a short wait. While the curtain was down the top half of the back wall of the sitting-room was taken away to allow the floor of Mrs Payne's room to appear, on a slightly higher level, above and behind it, but several feet lower than it would have been if it had been built on top of the lower room. Miss Beringer's narrow attic was on the right of the stage on another level, sandwiched in between a little landing at the top of the stairs and the room next door where Agatha sat in her rocking-chair.

It would have been impossible for the actress playing Agatha to dominate the play, as Edith Evans did so successfully, if she had been 'skied' at the realistic level of the upper room for most of her important scenes. With the new arrangement of the stage the audience imagined the missing ceilings and found nothing strange, if indeed they noticed it at all, in the fact that the two principal rooms were built in an impossible architectural arrangement, one behind the other. When the curtain went up on the second scene of the play, showing the three old ladies dressing for Mrs Amorest's Christmas party in their three contrasting rooms, the effect was fascinating, like a Sickert picture, full of life and character and quite unlike anything I have ever seen in any other play.

The dresses were equally effective. Edith, on her first appearance, wore a sort of maroon-coloured dressing-gown, and in the last act she shuffled down the stairs wrapped in a dirty yellow velvet robe with a transparent shawl thrown over it on which sequins glittered menacingly. I was pleased with the moment when Agatha sat with her back to the audience, a huddled mass of shadow, waiting patiently outside Mrs Amorest's door till her victim should be alone. There was also a good effect when the two women's silent struggle for the piece of amber was disturbed by a sudden loud knocking at the front door which used to make the whole audience jump.

In the end, we were unable to obtain a small theatre for the play and, rather apprehensively, we opened at the New, which was far too big, though the setting looked very well on the wide stage. But, in spite of some fine reviews and encouragement from a few enthusiasts, the public did not care for the production and it only ran for a few weeks.

André Obey's *Noah* had been a great artistic success when it was played here at the Ambassadors Theatre, in French, by the Compagnie des Quinze, under the direction of Michel St. Denis. I went one afternoon to see it, and was deeply impressed by the dignity and naïveté of the play and by the superb teamwork of the actors. Some time after this I read in an American paper that Pierre Fresnay, a young actor of about the same age as myself, who had originally created the part of Noah in Paris (in London it was played first by Auguste Bovério, then by Michel St. Denis himself), had gone to New York in Noël Coward's *Conversation Piece*, and had afterwards played Noah in an English version there with great success. The account which I read of his performance roused my curiosity, and encouraged me to suggest to Mr Albery that we should try and get hold of the version that had been used in New York, and that he should present it at the New Theatre with me in the part of Noah. Albery, who had previously presented the Quinze in London, was enthusiastic about the idea, and so was St. Denis, who had lately arrived in England, with the intention of forming a school and a theatrical company here on the lines of the Quinze, which had been recently disbanded. This was a very daring scheme, particularly as at that time he knew very little English, though he immediately agreed to direct the London production.

The version of *Noah* arrived from New York, but it was far from satisfactory; strange Americanisms (among them the expression, 'Hey, you floozies!') had been used to translate the slang French phrases in the text, which, as St. Denis pointed out, was originally written in an alternately poetic and colloquial style. The charming speeches in which Noah talks to the Almighty were especially hard to express in simple English, and these passages were particularly important as they set the whole keynote of the play. We could not decide at first whether to get a completely new version done and to do the play quite differently as an English parallel to the Bible story, or to keep to the spirit and style of the French performance as nearly as possible. Not having very much time, we decided on the latter course, and I fear we were unwise in doing so. Noah, in the French version, was dressed in velveteen trousers, sabots and a fur cap; in fact he suggested in appearance a larger-than-life version of a French peasant. But when I appeared in these clothes people failed to see why the Patriarch, in the intense heat of the jungle, was apparently dressed as if he were ready for a trip to the North Pole! Fresnay, being a Frenchman, as well as a magnificent actor, probably wore this costume with more conviction in the New York performance. I believe now that the only chance for the play in London would have been to engage Charles Laughton or Cedric Hardwicke to play the part, with a costume, make-up, and speech suggesting the typical English country farmer, but this would have necessitated re-writing a great deal of the play.

We tinkered with the dialogue all through rehearsals, but the final English text had neither the charm and simplicity of the French nor yet the slangy vigour of the American. On the first night the play went marvellously, and it seemed that our fears had been groundless: from the moment that I appeared in my terrific whiskers, hammering at the ark and humming 'The Sailor's Hornpipe' (my sole personal contribution to the production), the house seemed to be entirely with us. But the audiences who came later never appeared to understand the swift transitions from comedy to pathos which were so attractive, and which had made their effect so easily at the first performance. The critics complained, with some justification, that the play had been elaborated scenically at the New, whereas at the Ambassadors it had been done in the simplest and most economical way. But at the same time they ignored a great many good points in our production. Though they had raved over the play itself when it was done in French, they never observed that, in our production, a large section had been revised and strengthened by Obey, notably the fourth act, which contained a completely new scene as well as some splendid new comedy at the opening of the second act, which increased the effect of the delightful episode later when the children play games and march round the deck to greet the sun after the forty days of rain.

I never satisfied myself as Noah, though I had many happy moments working at it. Physically, however, it was a perfect misery. The play was produced during a heat-wave in July, and I was covered with thick padding and enormously heavy garments which were completely soaked through at the end of each performance. Vocally and physically the part was a great strain, and in every scene I had to act with my body as well as my voice, swaying to and fro in the gale, balancing my unwieldy form precariously on a ladder, and in the last scene crouching doubled up on the ground.

Every detail of my performance was taught me by St. Denis, and it was several weeks before I found myself sufficiently at home in the part to add anything in the least creative of my own. Some of the critics who had seen the French performance saw at once how greatly I was indebted to my director, and I could not help feeling at times like a young painter trying to copy an Old Master. But it was a fine exercise in technique, and at least I succeeded in concealing my own personality completely, and creating an illusion of age and weight in a part for which I did not really carry sufficient guns.

How hard it is to know when to take notice of criticism, whether it comes from actors, laymen, or professional critics! It is nonsense to say that one is always the best judge of one's own acting. How many actors imagine they were giving their best performance on a night when they were afterwards told by the producer that they were playing particularly badly![1] When I worked at Noah I realized that mere histrionics would be of little use to me in the part, although a breadth and authority were needed which would be difficult for me to achieve without them. The opening speech of the play demanded a great comedian with

1 Ellen Terry says, speaking of this: ' "We all know when we do our best," said Henry once. "We are the only people who know." Yet he thought he did better in *Macbeth* than in *Hamlet*. Was he right after all?'

a very simple, natural method – a man like George Robey, who would have held the audience in the hollow of his hand, and forced them by sheer charm and good-humour to accept the very simple, almost child-like convention of the play. The other parts were not very happily cast in some instances, and St. Denis was hampered by the translation and by the fact that he had great difficulty in expressing himself in English at rehearsals. He was accustomed, with his own company, to a much longer period of preparation than he was allowed with us, and now, in so short a time, he had to try to teach us the special stylized technique, so perfected by the Quinze, which combined miming and rhythmic movements with natural comedy and dramatic emotion.

The performance that we gave on the first night was in some way inspired – largely, of course, by the sympathetic quality of the reception. St. Denis had warned us beforehand that *Noah* was a play of atmosphere, depending for its effect partly on the responsiveness of the audience. He said we could not possibly hope to act it really well eight times a week, and that the ideal way was to play it in a repertoire. We thought this rather a highbrow idea at the time, but when we had been playing for a few nights we realized that it was perfectly true. English people are easily embarrassed and put off by any humorous or fantastic approach to religion, though they will gladly swallow sensational plays on the subject (*Romance, The Passing of the Third Floor Back, The Sign of the Cross, The Wandering Jew*). They will also patronize plays of a more serious kind touching on religion (*St. Joan, Robert's Wife, Murder in the Cathedral*), but *Noah* did not fall into the same category as any of these plays, and only a superb company could have acted it, with the fullest effect, to the rather scanty and often suspicious audiences that came to see it at the New after the first night.

Stupid people thought it extraordinary that I should wish to disguise myself by such an unrecognizable make-up, and either stayed away or took a dislike to the play in consequence. Others were shocked by the comic scenes and failed to understand the miming.

At the final performance, Michel said to me, 'At last you are beginning to find the way to play the first act'. By that time I had such a respect for his idealistic attitude towards his work that I was encouraged rather than depressed by his remark.

Michel St. Denis was never entirely satisfied with his productions. In *Noah* he made me feel intensely lazy, ignorant, and self-satisfied, but I was terrified at first that he would also kill my self-confidence, and convince me that my talents were completely negligible. On the contrary, these doubts and fears made me work all the harder in my desire to overcome the technical obstacles which stood in my way. I never studied with Michel a part for which I was really well cast. In the two plays (*Noah* and *Three Sisters*) in which he directed me, my own physical and mental attributes were so much at variance with the characters I was trying to represent that I did not really succeed in giving anything but workmanlike character performances in either of them. On the other hand, I know that I learnt more from acting in these two plays than from others in which I have made a greater personal success.

During the rest of the summer following *Noah*, I worked on a version of Dickens's *Tale of Two Cities*, which I had long had in mind. Terence Rattigan, the young author of *French Without Tears*, wrote the dialogue, and I planned most of the scenario. We had various actors in mind for the principal parts, and tried to provide for them accordingly. The first two acts came out quite well, and I showed them to Bronson Albery, who was sufficiently enthusiastic to promise to put on the play for me in the autumn, provided that the last act came up to expectation. Rattigan and I rushed back to the country and completed the script in a little over a week. A number of actors were approached, and the Motleys completed several charming designs for scenery and costumes.

Suddenly I received a letter from Sir John Martin-Harvey asking me not to go on with the play. He said that he intended to revive *The Only Way* again shortly, and that another version of the story would ruin its chances of success. Rather reluctantly we abandoned our project, and our play was shelved.

At the board meeting at which this was decided I suddenly proposed an alternative idea. *Romeo and Juliet* had always brought me luck. Edith Evans and Peggy Ashcroft, whose lovely performances in the production at Oxford I longed to see again, were both disengaged, and I thought it would be interesting for me to alternate the parts of Romeo and Mercutio with another star. Robert Donat's name immediately occurred to me, but I found to my dismay that he was planning to present *Romeo and Juliet* himself. When we approached him he kindly agreed to abandon his own production but could not see his way to appearing in mine. My next suggestion was Laurence Olivier. I could hardly believe my ears when he told me that he too was planning to do the play. His scenery was designed, and he had worked out every detail for an elaborate scheme of production, but I refused to allow my plans to be altered a second time, and at last Olivier very generously agreed to give up his *Romeo* production and appear in mine, playing the two parts alternately with me, as I had hoped. We had only three weeks to prepare and rehearse the play, and I was due to begin filming with Hitchcock in *Secret Agent* directly *Romeo* was produced.

Romeo and Juliet is very difficult to stage from a scenic point of view. I was not altogether satisfied with the triple-arched set we had used at Oxford, yet it had obvious advantages in simplicity and speed. The Motleys worked furiously hard, and at the end of three days they had produced three different projects for a permanent setting. None of them, we all agreed, seemed exactly right. Sadly, we were looking over the neglected designs for the Dickens play lying in a corner of the studio when suddenly it occurred to us to make use of them in another way.

The scenery for the *Tale of Two Cities* was to be arranged on two sides of the stage, the action moving alternately from one to the other, with a few scenes played on an upper stage approached by a staircase in the middle. We adapted this upper stage for Juliet's balcony, always a terrible difficulty both for the producer and scene-designer. If the window is at the side of the stage the lovers can only be seen in profile throughout the scene. If the balcony is too low, it seems as if Romeo could easily climb up, and if it is too high people in the circles cannot see Juliet properly. The ball scene which comes just before requires a clear space for the dancers, and the noise of a heavy piece of built scenery being moved into position is a fatal interruption to the short 'front' scene in which Mercutio and Benvolio shout their bawdy jokes in the silence of the night. We decided to build our balcony in the middle and leave it there, concealing the upper part with shutters or curtains during the ball and street scenes, and adding to it for the second part of the play, when the whole of Juliet's bedroom was to be shown, as well as the balcony outside.

I was determined that the lovers should part, as I am sure Shakespeare intended them to do, on the balcony where they plight their troth in the earlier part of the play. With this arrangement Romeo is able to speak his final lines in view of the audience, whereas with an interior setting he disappears from view and the lines have to be spoken very tamely from behind and below the stage. In Shakespeare's day, of course, the lovers played the farewell scene on the upper stage and Romeo, presumably, climbed down, spoke his lines, and made his exit from the lower stage. Then, at the entrance of Lady Capulet and the Nurse, Juliet herself came down on to the lower stage, disappearing, one supposes, from above, and descending by a staircase behind the scenes. This convention would hardly be accepted by a modern audience, so I took a tip from the *Old Ladies*' set which, after all, had not been seen by many people, and devised that the whole of the interior of the bedroom should be seen above, on a platform, as well as the balcony outside the windows. Belowstairs there was a door leading to the street, and the acting thus moved effectively, helped by various changes of lighting, now from the bedroom to the balcony, now belowstairs where the preparations for Juliet's marriage were going on, and now to the Friar's Cell, which remained in place throughout on the other side of the stage, concealed by a curtain when it was not needed for the action.

Romeo and Juliet opened with great success, and I started on my film, playing Mercutio at night. I hoped, of course, that the filming would be over by the time I began playing Romeo, six weeks later but to my dismay I found the work stretching out day after day, and in the end it was thirteen weeks before *Secret Agent* was completely finished.

Altogether I made five films during the period this book covers. The first, *Who is the Man?* was a very imposing affair, adapted from *Daniel*, in which Sarah Bernhardt made her last appearance in London at the Prince's Theatre in 1921. The play (written by Sarah's godson, Louis Verneuil) centred round the character of Daniel, a morphinomaniac, who did not appear until the third and fourth acts, when he sat in a chair as the central figure in an emotional climax culminating in a dramatic death scene. This was the part offered to me in the picture, but of course I did not sit in a chair. Nothing of the kind. I was a sculptor in a beautiful smock, flinging clay at a half-finished nude lady. I had not sat to Epstein in those days and I had no idea of the way sculptors really work, but I made great play with a sweeping thumb and a wire-headed tool and hoped for the best. I had a wonderful stagey studio with a skylight and a sofa draped with shawls on which I flung myself at intervals and smoked a pipe of opium (in a close-up). It was very hot weather, and I exhausted myself acting in a highly melodramatic manner, inspired in my efforts by a piano and violin which played tear-compelling excerpts from popular melodies.[1] The director acted harder than I did, and exhorted me frenziedly through every 'take', waving his arms and shouting directions above the music. Some scenes at Le Touquet were needed to complete the film, and off we went one week-end to take the necessary 'shots' in the correct backgrounds. I acted in two short scenes, surrounded by gaping and delighted crowds, and suffered acute embarrassment marching about in a yellow make-up and attempting to drive a car (which is not one of my accomplishments) out of the gateway

1 This, of course, was a silent film.

of the Hermitage Hotel. In the finished film, this 'shot' lasted about five seconds (perhaps because of the obviously agonized expression on my face), and the background was indistinguishable, while the second 'shot' taken at Le Touquet showed a strip of sand and a bathing-tent and might have been photographed equally well at Margate. However, I had a very jolly week-end.

My second film was an Edgar Wallace thriller, *The Clue of the New Pin*. In this I played the villain, fantastically disguised in a long black cloak, black wig, spectacles and false teeth, and always photographed from the back, so that I could by no possible chance be recognized, even by the most adept villain-spotter in the audience, as the bright young juvenile whom I impersonated during the rest of the film. There was an endless 'sequence' in a vault in which I had to go mad and reveal myself as the maniac I really was. These were still the 'silent' days, and I thought I should really be sick by the time I had repeated a dozen times the peals of hysterical laughter, the moppings and mowings and extraordinary impromptu dialogue which the director, an actor (who had once appeared in Irving's company), demanded from me at this crucial moment.

My next film effort, *Insult*, was an adaptation of a play by Jan Fabricius that ran quite successfully for a time at the Apollo. This was my first 'talkie'. The director, an American named Harry Lachman, was also a painter. He had a great feeling for photography, and his arrangements of light and scenic composition were admirable — but as a director of acting he was rather eccentric. He had a wonderfully beautiful Chinese wife — who appeared occasionally in the studio — and a violent temper which he displayed four or five times every day. He used to go red in the face and scream at everybody, not so much from real anger, I think, as from a natural desire to ginger things up every now and again. The film was set in the East and Lachman suddenly had the idea of showing all the scenes in a certain 'sequence' through a veil of mist. Ten men would rush on to the set when all was ready for a 'take', brandishing foul-smelling torches filled with some nauseous substance which emitted clouds of smoke. We would all begin to cough and rub our eyes, and then, just as the fog was beginning to clear, there would be shouts of delight from Lachman, and the cameras would begin to turn.

Animals and a native crowd enhanced the charms of my long hours in *Insult*. There was a donkey, a monkey, and several horses, one of which I rode gingerly (in close-up) down a narrow studio village street, while a double stood close at hand to mount and dismount my fiery steed (in longshot).

I was fascinated and horrified by my acting in these three pictures – fascinated, because seeing one's own back and profile is an interesting experience usually limited to one's visits to the tailor, horrified at the vulturine grimaces on my face, and the violent and affected mannerisms of my walk and gestures. In the film of *The Good Companions* I had rather a better idea of what I was about, having played the part of Inigo for several months upon the stage. Also I liked working with Victor Saville, Jessie Matthews and Edmund Gwenn, and such scenes as I had were simple, light, charming and well-rehearsed. It was in this film that I played a short scene with the great music-hall comedian Max Miller. It was one of his first appearances in pictures, but he was quite undismayed by the new technique, rattling off impromptu gags each time the scene was rehearsed or photographed, while I tried to keep pace with rather lame replies whenever he paused for breath or seemed to need a 'feed' line.

There are many things about filming that I detest. The early rising, to begin with. Then the agonies of film make-up, by which a pleasant twenty-minute affair of conscience and vanity in the theatre every night is transformed into a surgical operation in the studio lasting forty minutes every morning. I loathe to be patted and slapped and curled and painted, while I lie supine and helpless in an equivalent of the dentist's chair. I hate the long endless days of spasmodic work – a week or more in the same set, littered with cables and lights and half-dismantled at every point except the small section on which the camera is directed. I detest the lack of continuity, which demands that I should idiotically walk twenty times down a corridor with a suitcase in my hand to enter the door of a room in which I played some important scene three weeks ago. 'Let me see, that was the suit you were wearing. Now do you remember your tie was hanging out, and your handkerchief was tucked into your pocket? Right. Shoot.' How I hate the meals in films, and the heat of the lights which makes them more disgusting! For a week, in *The Good Companions*, we sat round a huge table, with twenty or thirty arcs focused over our heads – two to each of twelve persons – while the food on our plates congealed every half-hour and was replaced by a fresh supply. In one scene I had to eat a piece of chocolate, and the moment I began to unwrap it it melted under the lights. A property man stood by with twenty spare bars and I chewed a bit off a different one in every separate 'take'. Then there is the discomfort of the 'dolly' shots – when a camera pursues you on a track while you are walking or dancing, or swoops down on you from a crane – and the close-ups, when the heroine is not called, and you play the big moment of your emotional scene with her in her absence, with the camera a yard away. 'Now please look just two inches to the right of this piece of paper. That represents Miss ——'s face. Just *think right*, and let the expression come into your eyes.'

Railway-train scenes are misery, because the actors are crowded together in a tiny space, carriages and corridors are just as cramped and uncomfortable as they are in real life, and the heat of the lights is worse than ever. There is also vapour to be blown across the window by a machine at the last moment, just before every 'take'. If I decide to have a cigarette in some scene (in order to make an excuse for smoking on the set, which is forbidden except 'when necessitated by the action') I regret it immediately, for, after several minutes' delay, the cigarette is burnt too far down to 'match' with the previous 'shot', and someone must stand by with relays of cigarettes cut to the right length which I must continue to smoke until my throat is sore. I decide to play a scene in an over-coat, and stifle, not for a few minutes, but for a week, while the 'sequence' drags to its interminable conclusion. If I think of a nice little bit of business to do in the close-up I must remember always to do it again in every 'take' and every 'long-shot' for fear it will not match.

In *Secret Agent* I lay for several days under iron girders and rubbish in a scene of a train wreck. Another day I sat for hours before a blank screen, while a short length of Lake Como was unrolled behind me in 'back-projection', a device which enables studio scenes to be played before backgrounds of places hundreds of miles away.

Victor Saville and Alfred Hitchcock were very good company, and, apart from the work, I enjoyed making films with them.

Hitchcock is famous for his practical jokes, and keeps everyone amused, but I find it quite impossible to rouse myself from the lethargy induced by hours of waiting, hammering and delays of every kind, and to work myself into a state of high tension and sincere emotion for about three minutes, only to follow it with another despairing wait of half an hour or more. The strain under which the director must labour, and the nervous power required by him to sustain the direction of such an enterprise over twelve or fifteen weeks, is more than I can understand. One must remember, too, that he has already worked on every detail of the picture for weeks before anything is photographed or a single actor is engaged.

Film people always think legitimate actors very odd in their enthusiasm for the theatre, much more so, I believe, than we theatre actors do observing their passion for the films. I was interviewed during the shooting of *Secret Agent* by Caroline Lejeune, a well-known film critic, for whose writing in a leading paper I had always had considerable admiration and respect. The Sunday before I met her she had made a thinly-veiled reference to my production of *Romeo* which she had been to see. I asked her immediately why she had not liked the performance. She seemed very embarrassed at my having found out which play she was referring to, and then said: 'Oh, but I always find it difficult to know what I am supposed to notice when the curtain goes up in a theatre. One is muddled by all the details. In films, anything important is shown in a close-up.' This point of view had never occurred to me before, but I suppose it must be shared by a great many people who go continually to the films, and seldom to the theatre.

Romeo and Juliet was an exciting play, with its street fights (resulting in casualties several times a week) and its murders and poisonings and lamentations, but it was extraordinarily restful after the chaos of the studio at Hammersmith where we were making *Secret Agent*. I used to rush away at 5.30, eat a hurried meal, sleep deeply for half an hour, and arrive at the theatre looking forward eagerly to playing before a real audience and to the pleasure of acting in an ordered play performed to schedule. Seldom have I more sincerely enjoyed speaking the words of Shakespeare, and I appreciated, more than ever before, the neatness and punctuality of the routine of a stage performance. I think it is the sprawling, untidy; wasteful atmosphere which gets on my nerves to such an extent in making films, and the mixture of extreme reality and outrageous fake which is combined in their paraphernalia.

Chapter 16

1936

Romeo and Juliet ran well into the spring. It was a happy time for me, only slightly marred by fatigue from overwork. *Secret Agent*, which had seemed to be finished just before the New Year, went wrong in the cutting-room, and eight weeks later I had to work for two more weeks filming a different sequence to replace one that had turned out unsatisfactorily.

My scheme of alternating the parts of Romeo and Mercutio with Olivier had proved very attractive to the public and showed that it was possible to play two great parts in completely different ways without upsetting the swing and rhythm of the whole production. The only trouble came in our scenes together, when we kept on trying to speak on each other's cues. Larry had the advantage over me in his vitality, looks, humour and directness. In addition, he was a fine fencer, and his breath-taking fight with Tybalt was a superb prelude to his death-scene as Mercutio. As Romeo, his love scenes were intensely real and tender, and his tragic grief profoundly touching.

I had an advantage over him in my familiarity with the verse, and in the fact that the production was of my own devising, so that all the scenes were arranged just as I had imagined I could play them best. I built my Mercutio round the Queen Mab speech, and enjoyed the lightness and gaiety of the part – surely one of the shortest and 'plummiest' in Shakespeare. But I was again disappointed with my performance as Romeo, and resolved after this to be done with it for ever, though I loved acting with Peggy. Her lightness and spontaneity were a continual joy and inspiration, and she won all hearts with her flower-like, passionate Juliet. She had already developed considerably in power and endurance since her first performance at Oxford. To me, acting with her, she seemed utterly natural and sincere.

But, after Hamlet, Romeo was not such a good part as it had seemed when I was young. It is badly placed in the play. The 'Banishment' scene, which would in any case be a difficult one for the actor, becomes doubly difficult following, as it does, right on the heels of Juliet's great lamentation scene with the Nurse, and the Apothecary scene (in which Irving is said to have acted so wonderfully) follows immediately on the long scene of wailing and grief over the supposed dead body of Juliet, which is apt to rob it of much of its effect.

The uncut versions of Shakespeare which we give nowadays show the plays to full advantage, but I suspect that the cuts and transpositions so much favoured by the Victorians were cunningly devised to allow the 'show' scenes of the stars their utmost value. I wonder how audiences today would enjoy a production of *Romeo and Juliet* in which only the principal and well-known *bravura* scenes were acted, tricked out with lavish scenery. In Irving's *Romeo* the 'cords' scene of Juliet and the Nurse was enormously cut, also the scenes with Capulet and the servants, while the final scene in the tomb after the death of the lovers disappeared altogether. Here a tableau was substituted, with the Prince speaking the four 'tag' lines of the play.

My second three-play contract with Howard Wyndham and Bronson Albery came to an end. Guthrie McClintic, the husband of the fine American actress, Katharine Cornell, and one of New York's best directors and impresarios, had spoken to me several times on his visits to London, of my playing Hamlet in America. Now he approached me again with a definite offer to do the play in the autumn, and with some hesitation I accepted. Guthrie was anxious to direct the play himself, and told me flatteringly that he could 'present' my performance to greater advantage than I had done in my own production. Lillian Gish was proposed for Ophelia, and Guthrie brought her to see me in my dressing-room. She was enchantingly dressed in a summer frock with short sleeves, her fair hair crowned with a big white straw hat with black velvet ribbons. I remembered the advertisement that I used to scan so eagerly on the Piccadilly Tube in the old days of the silent films – the backs of two little girls, both wearing straw hats with velvet ribbons, and a big question-mark, with an intriguing caption underneath, 'Two little strangers about whom all the world will soon be talking'.[1] When I spoke of this, Lilian said she had been afraid I should think her too old to play Ophelia, and had 'dressed the part' to make a good impression on me. I also met Judith Anderson, who had come over with Guthrie and was to play the Queen; and Jo Mielziner, who was to design the scenery and costumes, came to supper at my flat with his wife to discuss the *décor*, which was to be inspired by Van Dyck.

Meanwhile we planned to revive Chekhov's *The Seagull* at the New for a limited season. I arranged to leave the cast after eight weeks in order to have a good holiday before sailing to America. I had longed to see *The Seagull* done in the West End again with a fine company, and I had always wanted Komisarjevsky to direct it, as it was one of the few Chekhov plays he had never done in London. Edith Evans agreed to play Arcádina, and Peggy Ashcroft would obviously be well cast as Nina. I had always fancied the part of Trigórin for myself. After Romeo I was anxious not to play another heroic or romantic part before tackling Hamlet for the third time, and anyway I was really too old to act Konstantin again. Stephen Haggard was engaged to play this important part, and the rest of the cast was equally distinguished – Leon Quartermaine, Frederick Lloyd, Martita Hunt, Clare Harris, Ivor Barnard, George Devine. Komis brought us a new translation which he had made himself with a friend in Paris and designed his own beautiful and impressive scenery for the play.

The revival was a really big success, though most people

1 D. W. Griffith's film, *Orphans of the Storm*.

thought my own performance the least satisfactory in an almost perfect *ensemble* (the same success, and similar criticisms of my Vershinin, were to greet my revival of *Three Sisters* in 1938).

Now that I am considered to be a 'star', people cannot understand that I should sometimes play what may appear to be rather unsuitable parts in which I do not shine above the rest of the cast. But, as a matter of fact, I have been extremely gratified to find that it has sometimes been possible for me to make experiments in character work and to contribute in a supporting part without spoiling the balance of a fine team. I think it is fatal for a leading actor to appear in nothing but 'show' parts in which he can display his mannerisms and give an exhibition of virtuosity.

It was enormously interesting to work again in *The Seagull* and to see how differently the parts came out with a different cast. I remembered vividly all the performances when I had played Konstantin at the Little. Peggy was exquisitely eager and womanly in the first three acts, but could not efface for me entirely the vivid impression made by Valerie Taylor in the final scene of the earlier production when she returns to Sorin's house after Trigórin has deserted her. Nothing could have been more different from Miriam Lewes's striking performance than the brilliantly poised, temperamental Arcádina of Edith Evans. Miriam played the part as a tragic actress. She stalked on to the stage in the first act, angry and sullen, looking rather barbaric in appearance, dressed in a strange picture frock and pacing the stage like a tigress, violent in her rages and moody and self-accusing in her griefs. Edith, on the other hand, dressed the part like a Parisian, with a high, elegant coiffure, sweeping fashionable dresses, hats and scarves and parasols. On her entrance she was all smiles and graciousness, but one could see from the angle of her head, as she sat with her back to the audience watching Konstantin's play, that underneath all the sweetness she was a selfish woman in a bad temper. Her performance was full of the most subtle touches of comedy alternating with passage of romantic nostalgia, as when she listened to the music across the lake in the first act. In the scenes with Konstantin and Trigórin, in the third, she had sudden outbursts of tenderness followed by a show of violent possessiveness and self-justification. Her entrances and exits were superb, and I shall never forget the way she pointed the only moment when Arcádina and Nina are seen on the stage together in the second part of the play, just before Trigórin decides to run off with Nina. He is sitting at the lunch-table, and Nina runs off the stage when she hears Arcádina coming. The dialogue runs:

ARCÁDINA (to SORIN). Stay at home, old man. At your age you should not go gadding about. (*To* TRIGÓRIN.)
Who was that went out just now? Nina?
TRIGÓRIN. Yes.
ARCÁDINA. Pardon, we interrupted you. I believe I've packed everything. I'm worn out.

Her scornful look after the retreating figure, the weary harassed manner in which she sank into a chair, suggested all that had happened to Arcádina since the second act – her fear of losing her lover, her jealousy of the young girl, her weariness with the details of running a house and packing to leave it, her perfunctory affection for her old brother, her longing for attention and flattery, her dislike of being middle-aged.

Komis's garden for the first two acts made a lovely and romantic background, with its paths and pillars, banks of flowers and rustic bridge. I was surprised, however, to find him putting both acts into the same setting, as we had done at Barnes in the earlier production, with a neat little stage built for Konstantin's play, and a curtain drawn on strings to conceal it.

Chekhov's stage directions are – Act I: A part of the park on Sorin's estate. Act II: Croquet lawn of Sorin's house. In Stanislavsky's book there is a fine description of the setting for the first act at the Moscow Art Theatre. Remembering this, I always imagined the scene taking place in a damp and gloomy corner of the park, with wet leaves underfoot and slimy, overgrown foliage. Beyond the trees, a magnificent view of the lake, and, hiding it at first, a great flapping sheet hung between two trees. Here Arcádina must sit shivering in her thin shoes and evening dress while Konstantin declaims his prologue, and then the sheet falls, disclosing the placid lake and the figure of Nina, dressed strangely in some kind of modernistic costume, raised, perhaps, above the level of the onlookers on a clumsily contrived platform of planks and barrels. This is Konstantin's new theatre, so different from the conventional indoor theatre which he despises, the place where he can make love to Nina and lose himself in his romantic dreams.

In the second act there should surely be a great contrast – the croquet lawn with its neat beds of geraniums, hoops, mallets, deck-chairs and cushions, Arcádina's bourgeoise worldly atmosphere. Here she is mistress in her own domain, laughing at the slovenly Masha and making scenes with her servants. Here Konstantin is ill at ease and out of place with his old suit and his gun and his dead seagull, while Trigórin, strolling on the lawn with his stick and notebook, is in his element, master of the situation, easily able to impress Nina with his suave talk of the beautiful view over the lake and the anguish he suffers in the achievement of his successes as an author.

Apart from this purely personal feeling with regard to the scenery of the first two acts, I thought Komis's production magnificent. There was so much to admire – the double room, half library, half dining-room, seen from opposite viewpoints in the third and fourth acts, was so rich in atmosphere that one felt one knew the whole of the rest of the house. Then there was his masterly control of tone and pace, the groupings, especially in the first act of the play, and in the last, when the party sat round playing Loto, the handling of the whole contrapuntal scheme of the characters.

I conceived the part of Trigórin, with Komis's help, as a vain, attractive man, sincere in his insincerity, but not a first-rate writer by any means, really attracted by Nina in a weak kind of way, but not the professional seducer at all. In the last act Komis saw him as a tragic figure, aware of the disaster he has brought about, sorry for Konstantin (whose talent he recognizes as more important than his own), rather ashamed of his own return to Arcádina, and genuinely moved and horrified by the death of her son at the end of the play.

Sometimes I thought I conveyed this well, but many people disagreed with my performance, and complained that I was not enough the genius, that I was too smartly dressed, and that I was not passionate enough in the scenes with Nina. But Trigórin himself complains of his facile talent, says that he cannot write really first-class stuff. His innate weakness is shown in the two scenes with Nina at the beginning and end of the third act, and by his passive attitude in the scene with Arcádina which comes between. The difficulty, as always in a play, is to know how much of the real truth Trigórin reveals in his speeches about himself. Surely if Chekhov had meant the man to be a genius he would not have drawn the clear distinction and contrast between the two pairs of characters, Nina and Konstantin, both potentially brilliant but unsuccessful, and Trigórin and Arcádina, both successful but intrinsically second-rate. And what could be more second-rate than the existence of Trigórin, trailing like a tame cat at his mistress's heels – 'Again there will be railway carriages, mutton chops, conversations –!'

The atmosphere behind the scenes in a theatre varies curiously according to the mood of the play which is being performed there. In *Romeo* we were always visiting one another or joking in Edith's dressing-room. Edith herself would sit in the middle of her sofa, dressed up in her voluminous padded garments as the Nurse, wondering perhaps, what sort of madhouse this was in which she had suddenly found herself. In *The Seagull* the atmosphere was entirely changed. The wings were dark in two acts of the play, and in the gloom Edith would sail gaily by in her lovely Edwardian creations, whilst most of the rest of us sat about in groups whispering furtively. In the last act, with the wind and rain 'effects' whistling all around us, we were often subdued into complete silence, while Peggy, with a shawl over her head, slipped noiselessly to her place in the corner, where she would sit alone all through the act working herself up for her entrance in the big hysterical scene at the end of the play.

The weeks flew by, and before I could have believed it possible, it was time for me to leave the cast to go abroad for my holiday. I had had a very successful year, and for the first time I was able to rent a villa in the South of France, with a swimming-pool in the garden, and enough rooms for me to be able to invite five or six guests to stay. This holiday promised to be far more exciting than my previous visits to the Riviera, when I had lived in small hotels and counted my money every day for fear it would run out too soon.

Still, even with such a grand holiday in view, it was sad leaving the New after four years. It was the end of a big chapter in my career. There were friendly faces everywhere among the staff and in the front of the house; many of my best friends were in the company. It seemed almost flying in the face of providence to leave the play while it was still playing to capacity.

The following day I went to France by car. For three weeks I was utterly content, lying in the sun, bathing, and eating enormous and delicious meals cooked by a treasure of a cook, an elderly peasant woman, stout, with a fine face, wearing espadrilles on her bare feet. Every evening she set off to her house half a mile up the mountain at the back of the villa. Away she would trudge about ten o'clock of an evening, undismayed by the prospect of her steep climb in the dark, carrying a big lighted lantern, and looking for all the world like Juliet's Nurse on her way to visit Friar Laurence. After she had gone we would leave our dinner-table on the verandah and motor to the coast, where we would gamble and dance till the small hours. Coming back from the casino early one morning, I found myself, for the first time for many weeks, thinking of the theatre. I had secretly been dreading having to begin work again in the autumn, and the prospect of packing, sailing alone, and facing a new company and a strange audience in America had depressed me very much. Now I knew that this phase had passed, and that I was anxious to get back to work again. My holiday was over.

We motored slowly back through France. When I arrived in London, my new cabin trunks had already been delivered at my flat, and there were only two more hectic days left before I must sail. Peggy Ashcroft gave a farewell party for me at her house. My friends, the people with whom I had worked so happily in the theatre during the past few years, were there to say good-bye. I experienced my usual feeling of despair. I was certain that *Hamlet* would be a failure, and wished with all my heart that I had never agreed to go.

Next morning, at Waterloo, there were more farewells, Mr Tilden[1] (among the passengers), a belated photographer (who had *not* come to photograph me, as it turned out), and a film-star, who almost missed the train (and the photographer), making a terrific entrance on to the platform at the last minute with orchids, a coloured maid, and a large retinue of admiring 'fans'.

We arrived at Southampton in the dark, and chugged our way out on a huge tender to the *Normandie*, which was lying far out at sea, a mass of twinkling lights. My cabin was filled with flowers and telegrams, books and presents, and I felt very important but extremely lonely as the liveried page-boys dumped the last of my luggage and I felt the ship begin to move.

I was determined not to think of *Hamlet* till I arrived. The boat was immensely impressive. There was a theatre, a cinema, and a glass 'sun lounge' with an aviary of singing birds which were only removed, rather ominously, when it was going to be rough. The film star continued to make wonderful entrances, arriving every night for dinner, in a succession of terrific gowns just as everyone else was drinking coffee.

The voyage was soon over. I rushed to the upper deck to see the famous view which had impressed me so much eight years before. It was equally impressive now, but I got very tired of looking at it when the ship slowed down and took nearly six hours moving gradually up the Hudson River towards the dock.

1 Bill Tilden, the well-known champion tennis-player.

It was very hot. The pressmen had boarded our ship at Quarantine, and Phil Baker, the well-known American radio star, whom I had met during the voyage, came to find me. He took me off to be interviewed in a small cabin, where a number of ladies and gentlemen were gathered with drinks and note-books and cigarettes. I felt rather like a criminal at a 'line-up' before the police. I was sure that no one would be able to pronounce or spell my name properly or would know who I was or why I was coming to America. But I found everyone surprisingly amiable, I was asked no embarrassingly personal questions, and, when I read the interview in the newspapers next day, I was delighted to find them completely accurate.

Guthrie and his manager were on the dock to meet me and we drove to the McClintics' house in Beekman Place, where I had been invited to stay. The sounds and smells of New York came rushing back to me and I was surprised to find how familiar it all seemed – Third Avenue, with its clanking elevated railway and the iron pillars in the middle of the road, with the taxis swerving in and out between them, the long straight Avenues with their vistas of brilliant lights, the brick-fronted houses with steps and iron railings leading to the front doors, the little canopies outside the hotels and restaurants, and the restless shifting mass of foreign-looking faces in the crowded streets.

Guthrie's house was on the East River, and one of the oldest in New York. He lived there for many years. It had the atmosphere of a house in Chelsea, with panelled rooms, and bow windows looking out over a charming little garden. Beyond the garden wall I could see the lights of the boats going up and down, and a vague mass of buildings huddled on the other side of the river. It was wonderfully quiet and restful there having dinner out of doors, with candles on the table and deliciously strange iced food and drink. The stage manager was there to meet me, and after dinner Judith Anderson arrived, straight from the hairdresser, who had dyed and waved her hair in an elaborate new style for Gertrude. I stared at her and said, with my usual tact: 'Why not wear a wig? It looks better, and it's so much less trouble.' After we had dined we went out again in the car and drove through Broadway and Times Square. I dimly remembered some of the buildings and tried to recall the lay-out of the theatre streets. Guthrie pointed out the Empire, where we should play. We called on Jo Mielziner, who was working at the designs for the scenery in a studio twenty-three storeys up. Later we drove back to Beekman Place where I was shown into Katharine Cornell's bedroom. Miss Cornell, I hasten to add, was still on holiday. By this time I was very tired. I fell asleep at last, thinking it must surely bring me luck to spend my first night in America in Katharine Cornell's bed.

A week went by. I was measured for costumes, interviewed every day by pressmen and, oddly, I thought, by several of the leading dramatic critics. I searched for a hotel to stay at when I should leave Guthrie's hospitable roof. I went to the theatres in the evening. Maurice Evans telephoned me, and we dined together, and went to see *On Your Toes*. It was a perfect evening, and a wonderful production – the kind of thing at which the Americans excel, and which we do not do nearly so well in England. Jeanne de Casalis was with us too. (She had come over to produce her play *St. Helena*, in which Maurice was to play Napoleon.) She was as enthusiastic as we were, praising Mielziner's scenery, the choreography of Balanchine, and the brilliant performances of Luella Gear, Tamara Geva and Ray Bolger.

Another night I saw *Dead End*, with its wonderful realistic setting of a waterfront slum by Norman Bel-Geddes, and its fine cast of child actors, climbing and diving in and out of the river, which appeared to flow (with most realistic splashings and gurglings) between the front of the stage and the first row of the stalls. I saw Fannie Brice in a lavish but rather disappointing revue, and I discovered several restaurants which I remembered before as 'speakeasies'. On my first Sunday night I climbed the palatial stairs of Radio City Music Hall, gazed upon the mighty orchestra which rose like a phoenix from below the floor, gasped at the elaborate convolutions of the stage performance, with its acrobats and jugglers, at the 'Rockettes', a troupe of chorus girls who step-danced in such incredibly perfect unity that one quite longed for one of them to slip or make a mistake, and finally enjoyed the comparatively normal pleasure of watching Fred Astaire in *Swing Time*.

Next day I bought the records from this film and others from *On Your Toes*, and I can never hear any of these tunes now without being suddenly transported back to my sitting-room in the Hotel Gotham, with the skyscrapers outside the window, the cactus plants on the mantelpiece, and the portable gramophone grinding away in the overheated atmosphere. The music was a pleasant relaxation during the long evenings when Harry Andrews and I stayed in the hotel, trying to work at the scenes between Hamlet and Horatio. Harry and Malcolm Keen, who was to play the King, were the only other English actors in the company.

The first rehearsal drew nearer. The heat was terrific. Every day I shed more clothes. After a week I was walking, rather timidly, down Fifth Avenue in the sleeveless shirt and linen trousers I had worn in the South of France. Wearing these clothes in London I should have been stared at in the streets, but in New York everyone seemed too busy to take much interest in anyone else. Judith and I went to be photographed at three different photographers one boiling afternoon, she in scarlet velvet, I in black with my high white collar, cloak and sword. The car could not draw up at the door in the crowded street, and we braved the throng and rushed across Park Avenue in all our finery. No one even looked round.

The first reading took place in the bar downstairs at the Martin Beck Theatre. Judith and Lillian wore hats with enormous brims, and bent over their books, hardly murmuring their lines above a whisper. Flashlights clicked, interviewers came and went, Guthrie perched on chairs with his hat tilted on the back of his head, and everyone was frantically nervous and drank a great deal of water from the filter in the corner, varied with occasional draughts of iced tomato juice produced by Guthrie from a thermos.

For a fortnight we read and re-read the play, then we rose

shakily to our feet and began to rehearse. I enjoyed these first few days immensely. I was fresh from my holiday, found I knew every line of my part without the book, though I had not looked at it for two years, and acted my very best. If only it had not been quite so hot! Katharine Cornell returned from her holiday, and one day she emerged suddenly from the back of the dress-circle, where she had been hidden, watching the rehearsal without any of us knowing she was there. I had met her some years before in England, and again I was enchanted by her natural beauty and graciousness, and by the warmth of her affectionate, enthusiastic welcome. She took me to see the Lunts in *Idiot's Delight* and Helen Hayes in *Victoria Regina*, two evenings in the theatre that were unforgettable.

The days were passing quickly. A week before we were due to open in Toronto I was wounded in the arm rehearsing the fight. I fence abominably. In London I had nearly cut Benvolio's eye out at a rehearsal, and in *Romeo* I so badly wounded the actor who played Tybalt that he had to leave the cast for a week. In New York our instructor rashly allowed us to rehearse with real Elizabethan swords sharpened on both edges. This time I was the injured party. I was removed to a neighbouring surgery where I was given gas while several stitches were put in my arm. I was worried lest I should not be well in time for the opening performance.

A few nights later, when I had recovered, Alexander Woollcott came to a rehearsal. We acted the closet scene for him, and he appeared to be very much impressed, but made one or two good critical comments, and told me that I must pronounce 'satyr' 'sater' or nobody would understand me in America.

We arrived in Toronto at a skyscraper of a hotel amid very low-storied buildings. The town looked to me as if cowboys might appear in the main square at any moment (in the best silent-film manner), shoot off a bunch of revolvers in the air, and ride away again in a cloud of dust. The theatre was large and shabby, with looking-glasses all along the back of the pit in which I saw myself reflected six times over as I spoke my first soliloquy.

Guthrie sent out for felt and had them covered up. We had two dress-rehearsals in one day and opened the following night.

We played in Toronto for a week with apparent success. In between performances I read or slept in the hotel, emerging only to eat. Radio sets blared from every bedroom as I walked along the corridors. After a long journey we arrived at Rochester in time to open on the Monday night. The hotel was packed with a Masonic Congress. The theatre was huge, built as part of a big college institute. We dressed in a large communal room, with a few small dressing-rooms partitioned off. There was a yawning orchestra-pit between the stage and the front row of the stalls, with a Wurlitzer organ lying like a mastodon in the middle of it.

I caught a heavy cold. We acted only two performances, Monday night and Tuesday afternoon – an extraordinary feat of engineering and efficiency on the part of the stage staff and electricians, for we were due to dress-rehearse on Wednesday night in New York, and open on the Thursday.

We left on Tuesday night for the journey back. I lay in my berth exhausted but sleepless, trying to forget my cold and concentrate on *Gone With the Wind*. There were negro porters and a sleeping-car with flapping curtains and beds one above the other. As a good film-fan I should like to have taken stock of every detail, and at any other time I should have been fascinated by a night journey in America. But I had frightful claustrophobia, and found I could not open a window in the air-conditioned train.

We arrived in New York early in the morning. I got a taxi and drove to a small flat which I had rented where I went to bed for the day. My cold was better but I did not play at the dress rehearsal. The next day dawned. Somehow I got through the morning and the afternoon. I attempted to eat some food, walked about the streets, went to a cinema for an hour or so, and tried not to remember the ordeal that was to come. About six o'clock I could bear it no longer and went to the theatre. My room was packed with telegrams, a huge pile from England and another from generous Americans, many of them famous actors and actresses whom I had never even met. Guthrie came into my room and told me that the theatre was packed with celebrities – it was the first fashionable opening of the season. Lillian Gish brought in a Hawaiian 'lei' of white carnations, and hung it round my neck for a minute for luck. I made up slowly, and put on my costume. It was curtain time. The first scene came to an end, and I walked blindly to my place in the darkness. The lights rose on the second scene. There was a roar of applause from the audience, a warm, reassuring burst of welcome that brought a big lump into my throat. I gulped it down, took a deep breath, and steadied myself to begin to speak.

The cue came at last, 'But now, my cousin Hamlet, and my son –' and I heard my voice, far away in the distance, beginning the familiar words:

'A little more than kin, and less than kind.'
'How is it that the clouds still hang on you?'
'Not so, my lord; I am too much i' the sun . . .'

I have three besetting sins, both on and off the stage – impetuosity, self-consciousness, and a lack of interest in anything not immediately concerned with myself or with the theatre. All three of these qualities are abundantly evident to me in reading over this book.

No doubt it would have been better to have written in some detail of the technical difficulties and problems of the craft of acting. But it is not easy to describe how actors go about their business. Perhaps it is more seemly that these mysteries should remain a secret. No one can understand the technical side of the theatre until he himself comes to practise it; and in spite of imploring letters from inquisitive enthusiasts, we actors do not encourage members of the public to watch us at our rehearsals.

Of all the arts, I think acting must be the least concrete, the most solitary. One gains experience continually, both at rehearsals and in performance, from the presence of a large assembly of people, one's fellow-players and the audience in front. These are essential to the development of one's performance. They are the living canvas upon which one hopes to paint the finished portrait. These audiences, with their shifting variations of quality, are the only means by which an actor may gauge his acting. With their assistance he may hope to improve a performance, keep it flexible and fresh, and develop new subtleties as the days go by. He learns to listen, to watch (without appearing to do so), to respond, to guide them in certain passages and be guided by them in others — a never-ending test of watchfulness and flexibility.

But the struggles and agonies of the actor as he winds his way through this labyrinthine process every night upon the stage are of very little interest to anyone except himself. No one cares, or is even aware, that he works for many months to correct some physical trick, or fights against his vocal mannerisms, or experiments with pauses, emphases, timing, processes of thought. No one knows if he is suffering in his heart while he plays an emotional scene, or if he is merely adding up his household bills, considering what he will order for dinner, or regretting what he ate for lunch. Last night's audience, which he cursed for its unresponsiveness, may have enjoyed his performance every whit as much as tonight's, with which he seems to feel the most cordial and personal sympathy.

Actors talk unceasingly among themselves of all the varying feelings which assail them during the exercise of their craft; but the experience of each one is different, and nothing really matters except the actual momentary contact between actor and audience which draws the performance through its appointed action from beginning to end. At the close of each performance the play is set aside, for all the world like a Punch and Judy show or the toy theatre of one's childhood; and each time it is taken up again it seems, even in a long run, comparatively fresh, waiting to be fashioned anew before every different audience. This continual destruction and repetition make the actor's work fascinating, though it must always be ephemeral and often monotonous. The unending conflict in the player's mind as he tries to judge the standard of his work, wondering whether to trust in himself, in critics, in friends or in strangers, all this is bound to make it a disheartening and unsatisfactory business.

I have frequently envied painters, writers, critics. I have thought how happy they must be to do their work in private, at home, unkempt and unobserved, able to destroy or renew or improve their creations at will, to judge them objectively in their unfinished state, to watch their gradual development, and to admire their past achievements ranged in their bookshelves or hung upon their walls. I have often wondered how these artists would face the routine of the actor, which demands not only that he shall create a fine piece of work but that he shall repeat it with unfaltering love and care for perhaps three hundred performances on end. I have often wished I were able to rise in the middle of the night, switch on the light, and examine some previous performance of mine calmly and dispassionately as I looked at it standing on the mantelpiece.

In writing this book I have experienced for the first time some of the trials and anxieties of authorship, but now that I have finished it I feel little urge to penetrate deeper into the mysteries of the writer's craft. I am happier to return to the theatre, where nothing tangible remains to reproach me for bad work or carelessness, and where there is always tomorrow's audience and tomorrow's inspiration which may yet, I hope, surprise me into doing my very best.

Supplement to First and Second Editions: 1937–1952

My two seasons at the Old Vic in 1929–30 had given me confidence in myself and a new respect for integrity and team-work. The untiring example set by Lillian Baylis was never more modestly and faithfully followed in that theatre than by Harcourt Williams, whose simplicity and singleness of mind enabled him to guide us all in the way we should go, despite severe limitations of time and money. Trained by Benson and coached by Ellen Terry, he combined the new ideals of Poel, Craig and Granville-Barker with the best traditions of the theatre that preceded them – the theatre of Irving, Tree and Alexander – and so linked in his work the most valuable lessons of both generations. I had the inestimable opportunity of justifying his belief in me as an actor, and, after a little while, he began to encourage me to contribute ideas to the productions. We collaborated in the original Sunday-night performances of *Richard of Bordeaux*, and from that time onwards I began to work at directing with even greater enthusiasm than at acting.

The character parts which I played in my Old Vic seasons – Macbeth, Hotspur, Antony, Malvolio, Prospero and Lear – were very valuable exercises, for they enabled me to practise a considerable amount of impersonation and also developed my vocal range. I was thus, on the whole, better equipped for a variety of different kinds of work after I left the Vic, though the highly-strung, neurotic roles for which I was still being cast at this time brought me more noticeably before the public during the next ten years. I was fortunate in appearing in several plays in which there were very good parts of this kind. Hamlet and young Schindler in *Musical Chairs* were basically not so very dissimilar, and in the latter play I was able to use my experience in Chekhov to some advantage.

In playing these very tense emotional parts, however, I worked under an almost unbearable physical strain, trying to project myself with a nervous realism that exhausted me continually, especially in long runs. *Richard of Bordeaux* might seem, on first reading, to be simply another variation on the same theme, but actually it was not so. The lightness of the style, the economy of dialogue, the ageing and development of the character of Richard from scene to scene, and, above all, the humour of the part, made it infinitely easier, more attractive and more rewarding to the actor than Shakespeare's Richard, who carries such a load of exquisite (but utterly humourless) cadenzas in a stream of unrelieved self-pitying monotony. In *Richard of Bordeaux*, too, I began to gain confidence in my abilities for casting, directing other players, and generally ordering the stage. The arrangement of scene changes, grouping and lighting delighted me, and I was fortunate besides in finding an admirable cast of actors and actresses to work on such an original and charming play, which needed an acting style combining the best qualities of romantic melodrama and modern comedy. The productions of *Hamlet* and *Romeo and Juliet* which followed not only gave me further opportunities of testing my powers as actor-director, but also brought me into contact with many who were – or have since become – outstanding players: notably Edith Evans, Peggy Ashcroft, Gwen Ffrangcon Davies, Léon Quartermaine, Laurence Olivier, Ralph Richardson and Alec Guinness. I was also engaged to direct plays (in which I did not act myself) by Somerset Maugham, Rodney Ackland, Emlyn Williams and others, and I experimented for the first time in modern realistic work. *The Old Ladies*, with Mary Jerrold, Jean Cadell and Edith Evans, was, I think, my best production at the time in this new field.

Although I did not satisfy the critics greatly either as Mercutio, as Noah (in Obey's play), as the schoolmaster in *The Maitlands* of Ronald Mackenzie, or as Trigórin in *The Seagull*, yet these were all experiments somewhat away from my usual run of parts, and I learnt much from playing them. For I foresaw the time not far distant when it would be necessary to find a new line for myself, since I seemed to have already exploited to the full the pangs of hysterical youth. On my return to London in 1937 (after I had acted Hamlet for six months in New York) I had proof that these instincts of mine were not at fault, for I unwisely chose to reappear as a romantic half-mad princeling – the lost Dauphin of the Temple – in a play specially written for me by Emlyn Williams and directed jointly by us both. It proved a failure, though in manuscript it had seemed to provide us both with excellent parts and a number of effective scenes and situations. The withdrawal of this play after such a short time decided me to back my own judgement and go into management for a year with four classic revivals.

This season in management was a financial success, although the four productions had each of them to be paid for in advance before I knew whether the current play would show a profit. It is interesting to examine the budget of this season, only fifteen years ago. The most expensive production cost £2,200 (*Three Sisters*), the least expensive £1,700, and of the four plays presented only the Chekhov was a very great success. Each play only ran from eight to ten weeks and yet the final results were on the credit side. Such a programme today would be out of the question. It is impossible to stage a costume play in 1952 for less than £10,000, and, in addition to this sum, overheads would be four or five times greater than in 1937.

I was tired at the end of this energetic period, in which I had acted four big parts and directed two of the plays myself, as well as undertaking the extra burden of management – so, when I was offered a large salary to act in *Dear Octopus* (with Marie Tempest) I accepted the part, being also anxious for once to appear in modern clothes, though the character was not a very interesting one. The play opened on the night of the Munich pact, and, despite the anxieties of the time, was a huge success. I had arranged to leave the cast after nine months, and was rehearsing the part of Maxim de Winter in *Rebecca* (played eventually by the late Owen Nares) on the morning war was declared. The theatres in London closed and the play was shelved. Meanwhile I hastily got together a revival of *The Importance of Being Earnest* (which I had given for charity matinées a few months earlier), and this production toured successfully and afterwards played to full houses in London. I then returned for a short season to the Old Vic, playing King Lear and Prospero, rehearsing the former part for ten days with Granville-Barker who came over from Paris to help us. This was my only practical experience of the work of this great director, though we met and corresponded occasionally for some ten years before this time. His example was so powerful that I unhesitatingly consider him to have been the strongest influence I have known in the theatre, and his absence from it for the last twenty-five years of his life the most tragic loss our stage has suffered. As we laboured at the production of *Lear* during those fateful spring days of 1940, with Granville-Barker's masterly hand to guide us, the news-posters outside the Old Vic announced the fall of France. The fine company was disbanded soon after, and the Vic was closed. Shortly after the theatre was badly bombed and did not reopen till 1950.

The war years passed slowly, with endless difficulties of organization, makeshifts and emergency measures, but I was fortunate indeed in the quality of the artists who continued to appear with me and the standard of production maintained by H. M. Tennent, under whose management I worked from 1939 until 1950. Barrie's *Dear Brutus* and *Macbeth* were, I feel, more to my credit as productions than for the performances I gave in them, yet both plays ran for nearly a year in London and on tour. The choice of Congreve's *Love for Love* in 1943 was a fortunate one, and it was played continuously for more than a year. Rex Whistler, whose exquisite décor for this production was almost the last work he gave to the theatre he served so brilliantly, was killed in action in France during the run of the play – an irreparable loss.

Hoping to exploit the talents of the fine company working with me in *Love for Love*, I tried another experiment of four plays (in repertory, with a change of programme from night to night) in 1944 at the Haymarket Theatre. The choice of plays was perhaps not altogether happy, though *The Duchess of Malfi* was, I think, a bold experiment; although, ironically, I was rather against it at first, it was certainly the most interesting production. But somehow I lacked the necessary enthusiasm and inspiration to make the season a real success. I even found little pleasure in my favourite part of Hamlet – feeling confused and uncertain after so many previous productions with different directors. However, I left shortly after this on a tour of the Far East, when I acted *Hamlet* and Coward's *Blithe Spirit* to troops in India, Ceylon, Singapore and Egypt, and returned in 1946 to play Raskolnikov in Rodney Ackland's version of *Crime and Punishment* with Edith Evans. In this Anthony Quayle made a success as director, and, as he had acted in my companies before the war, we renewed a happy association which was to lead to my season at Stratford-on-Avon in 1950, where he had become director of the Memorial Theatre.

At the beginning of 1947 I took *The Importance of Being Earnest* and *Love for Love* to New York for a limited season. The first play was enormously successful, the second less so. I remained in New York for another six months to work with American companies for the first time, when I directed *Medea* for Judith Anderson, and played the ungrateful part of Jason for the first eight weeks of the run. Thanks to Miss Anderson's performance the play was a great hit, though my work in it was not much liked, and when I directed it again in England it failed.

Crime and Punishment, which I persuaded my American management to put on for me after I left *Medea*, with Komisarjevsky directing, was also a failure in New York. On my return to London I did not act for eight months – the first time in my career that I have ever had such a long period of inactivity. My luck seemed to be out for the time being, for I chose to reappear in a revival of St. John Hankin's *Return of the Prodigal*, with décor by Cecil Beaton and a fine cast headed by Sybil Thorndike. But this proved a disappointment – to the critics, the public, and, I need hardly add, to the cast and management as well.

The Lady's Not For Burning had already been commissioned and put on by Alec Clunes at the Arts Theatre while I was in America. I did not see the production, nor had I read the notices; but hearing from many sources of the quality of the play, I was lucky enough to obtain a chance to read it, and was immediately charmed and fascinated by it. It was bought for me by H. M. Tennent, but the production was delayed by the commitments of Pamela Brown (who was acting elsewhere), since the author and I both thought her engagement essential to the success of the play. This venture, which triumphed equally in London and New York, gave me enormous satisfaction. The work of Oliver Messel, who designed the décor, and the acting of a most happily chosen cast, gave me the opportunity of working, both as director and actor, in a new and exciting medium, and I shall always be proud of the result. I regained some lost prestige, and recovered confidence and enthusiasm. This was further enhanced by my work with Peter Brook in *Measure for Measure*, the play with which I opened at Stratford in 1950. Here too I played Cassius for the first time, as well as Lear (my third attempt, with intervals of ten years between each production), and revived my happy associations with Peggy Ashcroft, Gwen Ffrangcon Davies and Léon Quartermaine. While playing the Fry play the year before, I had also directed Anthony Quayle and Diana Wynyard in *Much Ado About Nothing* at the Stratford Theatre, and this production I repeated there in the 1950 season, with Peggy Ashcroft as Beatrice and myself as Benedick.

After a six-month season in America of *The Lady's Not For Burning*, I returned to play Leontes in *The Winter's Tale* with Diana Wynyard and Flora Robson at the Phoenix Theatre, and this production (by Peter Brook), followed by my own *Much Ado About Nothing*, broke records for both these plays in London.

Since 1933, when I first directed a play in which I was acting myself (*Richard of Bordeaux*), I have been repeatedly advised by many people to avoid the heavy responsibility of combining the task of actor and producer. Yet, whenever I have undertaken the double burden, provided there has been plenty of time to work at the production (both in rehearsal and on tour) before coming in to London, I have found the result to be reasonably successful. The actors in these productions of mine have shown great patience and restraint – for I work very broadly at first, suggesting and inventing business and movement of all kinds (from which I trust them to select to their advantage), and experimenting and changing continually from one day to another. My own performance is at first necessarily tentative and lacking in concentrated sureness of attack, for my mind in the first few weeks is busy with details of lighting, movement, and the performances of my fellow players. Yet from these muddled and clumsy sketches I have achieved a number of productions of considerable style and finish, and I have found that so long as the preliminary work on a play from the practical point of view – that is, the planning of the scenery, costumes, music and the technical details of presentation – has been thoroughly and efficiently carried out beforehand, it is permissible to shape the acting and movement (with many false starts, corrections and revisions) as the potential abilities of the cast and the holding power of the play itself develop in rehearsal and performance.

I have noticed, in books written by actors and actresses about themselves, that the later chapters are inclined to deteriorate into a bald list of plays and parts, and consequently lack interest for the reader. This is hardly to be wondered at. A professional critic can write more or less objectively about the contemporary theatre. Indeed, it is his business to do so. The professional player cannot. He can look back on the early years of his career with some measure of detachment, but he cannot write with any sort of discrimination about the people with whom he is working every day. Some of them are more, some less successful than himself. To praise or criticize one's contemporaries is an impertinence, and one can neither see one's own work nor judge it with any kind of impartiality.

The theatre in London, as everywhere else, has changed enormously in the fifty-odd years during which I have worked in it. But changes, though far-reaching, are subtle and gradual, the trend of things difficult to summarize in a few sentences. Owing to various circumstances, some of chance and some of choice, I believe I have had some influence in reviving the popularity of the classics. This has been of value, I think, at a time when a dearth of contemporary playwrights would have otherwise given the best players of our time a very limited field in which to display their talents, and deprived the public of seeing them in the great parts which have always been the test of the leading actors and actresses of past generations. Working in my early days in many classic revivals, in repertory and at the Old Vic, I acquired a taste for Shakespeare, Congreve, Wilde and Chekhov (though not for Ibsen or Shaw), and dreamed of ways to stage them, and I determined then that if I ever reached the position in which I had the power to decide what plays I would direct and act in, then certain plays of those authors would be my first consideration.

Between 1930 and 1944 I achieved my ambition: besides creating three or four fine parts in plays by modern authors, I took part as actor and director in revivals – most of them successful – of nine or ten of my favourite classical plays. But by the close of the Second World War I had reached the end of this list, compiled so many years before, and I found myself tired, empty of ideas, less adventurous, more apprehensive of choosing badly.

Abroad, when actors have achieved a successful classical performance, they seldom play it for a long run, but alternate it with several other parts, gradually creating a repertoire of half a dozen contrasting plays, which they are able to repeat over a number of years, and which continue to stand them in good stead for foreign tours and revivals until they are too old to play them any longer. At the end of the last century Irving had created such a repertoire and continued playing it (until his stores were burnt), and even in my own time, as I have said elsewhere, Fred Terry and Martin Harvey still toured the provinces with their successes of thirty years before.

To my mind, the economic conditions of today make such a programme, though superficially an easy and attractive one for a leading actor, most difficult, if not impossible. I am not prepared to revive old successes without an equally good company and very full and careful rehearsals. Often one needs to take more pains than before. The excitement of the first conception, evolving slowly, and gradually coming to completion, with everyone concerned contributing their enthusiasm, is hard to recapture with a set prompt book. Preconceived results are death to spontaneity and inspiration. It is very hard to cast a number of plays adequately from the same company of actors without several parts being miscast. Deliberate compromise is far more damaging in the theatre than the compromise of emergency, which may justify itself at a critical moment in a new production but seems wilfully perverse when the impulse is no longer the original one. One must move on, find a new line, tackle different problems, act in the plays of new authors, beware of repeating one's effects, resist the temptation to imitate one's youthful performances without the youthful instinct which gave them vividness and life.

Ours is a paradoxical profession. On the one hand I enjoy the punctual routine of a successful run, the security of a steady salary, the nightly exercise and experiment of my craft. On the other I love the unexpected, the manuscript that appears suddenly out of the blue and sets my imagination racing off in a new direction, the making of plans far ahead, casting, discussing possible schemes of production with designers and musicians, the uncertainty of the future.

In some ways it might be pleasant to become an actor-manager, to be host in one's own theatre, with a permanent company and a settled policy – some ideal five-year plan of classic repertory alternating with modern work – and of course I have often hoped for this. But the financial organization of such a scheme is an added burden. I have no talent for it, and in actual practice I dread the responsibility of committing myself for more than a few months ahead, lest my own enthusiasm may wane before I have completed my task, and so bring the whole project to disaster. I do not believe in commissioning authors to write plays to measure for me, even if there were authors available and willing to do so. If a new play I have read appeals to me as a play, I like to direct it, or act a part in it if I think there is one that will suit me. There are many players with whom I enjoy directing and acting, but I think we work better together if we are not together for too long. I have no 'theory' of production or acting, but I believe a certain kind of play needs a certain kind of playing which rarely suits the capacities of a group of actors, however talented, who have just been playing a different kind of play. Besides, one cannot expect young players who make conspicuous successes in smaller parts not to become restive and move on to more ambitious work. The cinema, radio and television continually rob the theatre of writers as well as actors. The overheads and production expenses mount with terrifying and increasing regularity, while the money taken at the box-office cannot exceed the existing capacity of the theatres. One's duty to a new author and to the management obliges one to contract oneself to appear in a successful play for six or eight months at least, in order to repay its initial cost and make a profit. One may therefore be bound by success to a long period of comparatively monotonous security, or alternatively find oneself completely at a loss for a new play. After acting in the great classics it is more than ever difficult to find the suitable modern part in which one may display some range. One may disappoint the public and do the author no good service by appearing in an unsuitable modern play. It is tempting to fall back on old successes, but I do not believe this is the way to develop one's powers.

I hope in the years to come to make some more interesting experiments as a director, to work with designers and actors that I admire, to discover new talent, and to act myself when I can find a part. The line of my career has developed luckily for me hitherto, but I do not think I have ever been able to see clearly the way that I was going. Perhaps I should have had a duller time if I had planned more practically, though perhaps, on the other hand, I might have worked to a more constructive pattern, building a company or making a more definite contribution in a single direction. But the child in me (as I believe in many actors) still longs for great days, unlooked-for surprises, sudden and unexpected developments. Without the stimulus of such uncertainties I believe I should find the theatre a dull and drab professional business, instead of the magical absorbing hobby that, to my own continual amazement, it still remains for me today.

Backward Glances

To Gwen and Peggy,
my two dear and lovely Juliets

Acknowledgments

I would like to thank Messrs Mander and Mitchenson for their invaluable help in supplying the illustrations.

I would also like to acknowledge Sotheby's for permission to reproduce the photograph of Edith Sitwell by Cecil Beaton, and the Radio Times Hulton Picture Library for the photograph of Elizabeth Bergner.

Foreword

In 1971, when I was acting at Chichester, I celebrated my fiftieth year as a professional player. During my leisure hours that summer I amused myself by concocting a small book of reminiscences, recalling a number of actors and actresses whom I had known and admired in my earlier years, but all of whom are now sadly dead.

Since that time I have written various tributes and short pieces for various newspapers and magazines, and now these seem to have accumulated over the years into quite a considerable number. Hodder & Stoughton have thought fit to wish to re-publish these in the form of one book, as well as to reprint my first autobiography *Early Stages* (1939) and a further book, *Stage Directions*, which I wrote in 1963. Both are now in paperback. With the help of Edward Thompson, an old friend (and my editor at Heinemann Educational Books who first published the other books), I have chosen and rearranged these later writing efforts of mine into a collected shape.

The second part of this book is a direct reprint of my third book *Distinguished Company* (1972). The first part contains the various pieces, all connected with the theatre (but some only distantly so), and I am giving the whole book the title of *Backward Glances*, which I hope may convey an appropriate summary of its contents.

I have also to thank the original publishers who have allowed me to rescue many of the new excerpts from their archives.

JOHN GIELGUD, Wotton Underwood, August 1988

Chapter 1

Edith Evans: A Great Actress

How shall we best remember her? As heavenly Rosalind, or the lumbering peasant that was Juliet's Nurse? As one of her 'lovelies' as she used to call them: Millamant, Mrs Sullen, Daphne Laureola, Orinthia in *The Apple Cart*? Or as one of the working women she drew so well – the maid Gwenny in *The Late Christopher Bean*, and her two great performances on film, as the saviour of the village in *The Last Days of Dolwyn* and the crazy old lady in *The Whisperers*?

I first saw her act when I was a schoolboy towards the end of the 1914 war. Then she was playing supporting parts in various long-forgotten plays – spinsters, companions and even mothers in white wigs. The dragonfly had not yet emerged from the cocoon.

The eccentric William Poel had discovered her, and cast her as Cressida (after rehearsing her first in several male parts in the same production). It was he who encouraged her to leave the Belgravia hat shop in which she had been working and become a professional actress.

At that time she was considered plain, and leading ladies were expected to be beautiful, as they usually were. (Whether they could act as well was of course another matter.) Edith Evans was no beauty in the conventional sense. Her eyes, with their heavy lids, one set slightly lower than the other, gave her face an enigmatic originality. It was a fascinating canvas on which she soon learned to paint any character she chose.

In 1923 she was offered the showy part of a pork-packing

Duchess with a gigolo in the original West End production of Somerset Maugham's *Our Betters*. But she turned it down, saying she refused to be typed in vapid society roles, and decided instead to go to Birmingham, where she triumphed as the Serpent (doubling with the She-Ancient) in Shaw's *Back to Methuselah* pentateuch. In her next big part, as Millamant in Congreve's *Way of the World* under Nigel Playfair at the Lyric, Hammersmith, she took the town by storm. It was a unique and exquisite performance. She purred and challenged, mocked and melted, showing her changing moods by the subtle shifting angles of her head, neck and shoulders. Poised and cool, she stood like a porcelain figure in a vitrine, as she handled her fan (though she never deigned to open it) in the great love scene, using it for attack or defence, now coquettishly pointing it upwards beneath her chin, now resting it languidly against her cheek, while the words flowed on, phrasing and diction balanced in perfect cadences, as she smiled and pouted to deliver her delicious sallies.

She showed her superb taste by brilliant timing and control, never stooping to indulge an over-enthusiastic audience, and disdaining any temptation to overstress an emotional moment or allow too many laughs to interrupt the pace of a comic scene.

Only tragedy eluded her, and this was perhaps because her nature was essentially sunny and resilient, besides which her voice, however athletic and articulate, lacked deep notes that she could sustain in her lower register. She always refused to attempt Lady Macbeth, whose explicit admission of evil she could not bring herself to accept. She grew to hate her success as Lady Bracknell, though it was perhaps the most popular and famous of all her great impersonations. She was staying at my cottage in Essex one weekend just before the war when I suggested a possible revival of the Wilde play. I took a copy from the bookshelf and we read the bag scene together to the guests. After the hysterical laughter had died down, Edith handed me back the book and remarked gravely, 'I know those women. They ring the bell and tell you to put a lump of coal on.' But in the end she had to play the part too often – in a film, for the gramophone and on radio, as well as for several long runs in the theatre, and she firmly refused my entreaties to repeat it in New York. She disliked the imitations of her trumpet tone in the famous 'A HANDBAG?' which many people seemed to think was the alpha and omega of her performance as Lady Bracknell. For me there was so much else to admire, exquisite details of observation and execution. The sly look of suspicion, for instance, as she glanced at the armchair she had chosen for the first interview with Worthing in the first act. In those few seconds she managed to convey both appraisal and approval, to reassure herself of the suitability of that particular piece of furniture before it should enthrone her corseted dignity as she lowered herself into the seat.

She disliked the trappings of a great star, the gossip, the private anecdotes made public, the intrigue, scandal and petty-mindedness. One always felt one must approach her with respect and restraint. She hated gush, was wary of strangers and conventional compliments, striving to create her performances from an inner conviction, trying to find the 'bridges', as she called them, to achieve progression and climax in the characters she was determined to bring to life. 'I never make effects,' she used to say. Of course she did, but with what subtlety, skill and artistry she set about it.

In 1929 I first acted with her, for only a few weeks, in a play about Florence Nightingale called *The Lady with the Lamp*, and she advised me then to go to the Old Vic, a decision which was to further my career to unexpected advantage.

Three years later I was asked to direct (for the first time) by the young undergraduates of the OUDS., a production of *Romeo and Juliet* at Oxford, a play I already knew and loved, and found myself enriched by the privilege of working with Peggy Ashcroft as Juliet and Edith Evans as the Nurse. Of course I was greatly in awe of her at first. I timidly suggested that she might perhaps be doing needlework in her opening scene with Juliet and Lady Capulet. I pictured her, I suppose, with a tapestry in a frame and a large needle threading in and out, typical romantic costume play 'business'. I was quite wrong. She kept a tiny piece of material between her hands which she handled very sparingly (almost hiding it in her long sleeves), using a gentle rhythmic movement to give a slight counterpoint to her first long speech without in the least detracting from it. It was my first glimpse of her remarkable instinct for selectivity.

She seemed to prefer to move very little. I do not remember any swift entrances or exits in her performances, but she taught me to give up my own impatient inclination to drive actors about the stage in order to give a scene excitement long before the dialogue demanded it. You could not hurry her or muddle her with too many suggestions before she was ready for them. The character and its truth, the pattern of the syllables, the give and take of the vocal exchanges – these were slowly taking shape during the early rehearsals, and from these basic foundations she began to develop her performance. She governed her audiences and refused to woo them, though her wooing scenes as Millamant, Rosalind, Orinthia, were miracles of coquetry and provocation. She was baleful in *The Old Ladies* and *The Witch of Edmonton*, overwhelmingly touching in simple characters – as the Welsh housemaid in *The Late Christopher Bean* for instance. She could be aristocratic (and absurdly autocratic) as Lady Bracknell, and equally well bred (and even sometimes ridiculous) in *The Chalk Garden* when her brilliant technical skill never failed to fascinate me. As she heard of her butler's death in the last act, I never tired of watching her as she switched from comedy to pathos and back again in the course of a scene of only a few lines.

She had real humility. I could feel this even in the honest reluctance with which she took her curtain calls – a polite but restrained acknowledgment of the applause, with none of the affectation or smugness which sometimes mar the behaviour of lesser artists on these occasions. She had enormous authority but also intrinsic shyness. Not until the part she was rehearsing really possessed her would she completely sweep in to her performance. She could not, as actors sometimes do, patch together material tried out successfully in other plays, in order to achieve a superficial shortcut to a new creation.

I think she found it difficult to expose her feelings in private life, and she was reluctant to give opinions unless she felt them with great certainty. She had no wish to be misquoted by making unconsidered or hasty remarks. About the acting of her colleagues she was always extremely reticent, though praise from her was as precious as it was rare. I was never sure just how much she was aware of what was going on around her on the stage. Admittedly she was supremely self-centred, but she was neither selfish nor jealous, though occasionally prim and narrow. Strong but uncertain of herself, formidable yet easily melting, proud yet meek, she was an extraordinary mixture. She sometimes longed to lead an ordinary life, to dance and skate and lark, to be a housewife, to look after a husband, to cook and farm and live in the country, but her talent for acting was too strong to enable her to succeed anywhere but in the theatre. She was inclined to defy tradition (though of course she created it herself). No chestnuts for her about Mrs Siddons and Mrs Bracegirdle, no reading up of old stage 'business'. I remember her being quite sarcastic at the grandeur of Bernhardt's dressing-room and large bathroom when she occupied it in Paris where we once played together. She always liked to boast of her early apprenticeship in the West End ('I never had to tour and get into all those bad habits!') with Dennis Eadie, Charles Hawtrey and Gerald du Maurier, whose fine manners and professional courtesy she always quoted with admiration.

She hated slovenliness, unpunctuality, rudeness and careless talk. She disliked extravagance, had a reputation for stinginess, but did many generous actions in strictest secrecy. She tried as far as possible to divide her own life and her life in the theatre into completely separate compartments. I do not think she had more than a dozen intimate friends. Her letters were few, but one felt proud to receive one, knowing that it cost her an effort to put pen to paper. She was often witty and pungent, and could be great fun if she was in the mood. But she was intensely fastidious and abhorred cheapness either in talk or action.

She once paid me a sublime compliment which I shall always

cherish. 'Your Benedick, Johnnie,' she said once, after a rather stormy argument we had had about the playing of comedy, 'that performance you know, was seven-eighths perfection!'

Observer, 17th October 1976

Chapter 2

Sybil Thorndike: A Great Woman

In 1922 she came to the RADA and rehearsed our class in scenes from the *Medea*. She had sandy hair in those days, arranged in coils round her ears, like radio receivers, and wore long straight dresses in bright colours with strings of beads round her neck. She told me that Jason was a self-righteous prig and I must play him so. She exuded vitality, enthusiasm, generosity, and we were all spell-bound as we listened to her.

I do not remember seeing her on the stage until *Saint Joan* in 1924, when I was lucky enough to be at the opening night, sitting with my parents in the dress circle of the New Theatre. It was an inspiring occasion – play, production, décor, acting, it all seemed perfect to me – and, at the end of the evening, when Sybil Thorndike led on the weary actors to take a dozen calls, all of them suddenly looking utterly exhausted by the strain of the long performance, I realised, perhaps for the first time, something of the agonies and triumphs of theatrical achievement.

She was surely the best-loved English actress since Ellen Terry, and these two great players shared many of the same fine qualities – generosity, diligence, modesty, simplicity. Both were demons for hard work – Ellen Terry called it her blesséd work, but that could be taken with two different meanings, for like Edith she often longed (or said she longed) to live in the country and forget the theatre. But her own private life was not destined to bring her great happiness, and she was to become, alas, a somewhat tragic figure in her old age.

It was quite otherwise with Sybil Thorndike. The theatre was the breath of life to her – the theatre, music, and her deep religious faith. Blessed with immense talent, boundless energy, unremitting application and splendid health – until the last few years when she learned to triumph over continual pain and increasing disabilities – she fought her way, helped by the devotion of a brilliant husband and loving family, to worldwide recognition. Her good works were manifold, her influence for good shone from her like a beacon, but she hated to be praised and to be thought sweet and saintly. 'I hate pathos,' she said once. 'It's soft and weak. But tragedy has fight.' And in Lewis Casson she had a superb partner and a tremendous fighter, though his temperament was often inclined to be moody and pessimistic in contrast to Sybil's radiant determination to see the best in everyone and everything around her. He argued with her endlessly, criticised her ruthlessly, and tried to control some of the more eccentric enthusiasms and outbursts of exaggeration which sometimes tended to mar her acting. Outrageous she could certainly be at times, playing to the hilt some second-rate vehicle which gave her an opportunity to let off steam in some particularly repulsive or wildly melodramatic character. But Sybil would be the first to admit, with a hoot of laughter, that it was all such fun, and apologise ruefully for overacting at a matinée with the excuse that a cherished grandchild had been in front.

In her long life there was no moment wasted, never a thought of boredom, laziness or surfeit. She and Lewis cared little for money, clothes, rich food or social grandeur, though they were perfectly willing to enjoy such things occasionally when they came their way. Sybil, someone said once, had no airs, only graces. She could be perfectly at ease with Royalty, poets, politicians or men of letters, and equally natural sitting on the doorstep of a miner's cottage in Wales, chatting to the wives and telling them the story of Medea. But you would hardly expect to find her at Wimbledon or Ascot – more probably at home, doing piano scales and voice exercises, learning a new part, studying a new language, reading aloud to her grandchildren, or arguing furiously with Lewis.

Intensely feminine in her maternal and womanly qualities, she could not on the stage be coquettish or swooningly romantic. During the Great War she played several male parts in Shakespeare at the Old Vic and found the experience a thrilling one, but she never attempted Juliet or Cleopatra. 'I can't be sheer femininity,' she said. 'Feminine wiles I can't manage and I don't want to!'

Both she and Lewis had a passion for words. Fanatical about speech, rhythms, phrasing, diction and modulation, they were inspired disciples of Poel, Granville-Barker, Shaw, Gilbert Murray and their voice-coach, Elsie Fogerty.

She was very fine, though to my mind unequal, in her playing of tragedy, but she was one of the few actresses of her generation who dared even to attempt it. She took the stage, whether in Lady Macbeth, Queen Katharine or Hecuba, with a splendid stride, faultless phrasing and diction, and riveted her audiences with superb authority and vocal power. In comedy she was sometimes tempted to hit too hard, but, as the years passed her skill and control, under Lewis' iron hand, restrained and refined the execution of her art to a marked degree.

Saint Joan of course was written for her, and it was her acting masterpiece, though she must have got sick and tired of hearing people say so. Her performance was unrivalled. Here she did not need to play for sheer femininity, nor for masculinity either. Her tearing up of the recantation in the trial scene was a moment of really great acting that I shall never forget, but she was equally convincing in the slangy colloquial passages as in the great poetic speeches, blending the different sides of the character with unerring judgement, and never for a moment allowing sentimentality or sanctimoniousness to intrude on the simple directness of her attitude.

In her private life she managed somehow to retain a certain reserve and dignity, despite an ebullient façade. She had beautiful manners. Genuinely interested in everyone she met, strangers as well as friends, she could bounce and flounce without ever losing her modesty and basic humility. And the moment you were lucky enough to work with her in the theatre, you knew she was a leader, a giver, not self-centred – professional to her fingertips, disciplined, punctual, kind. She confessed to having a terrible temper but I never saw a sign of it myself.

To me the most perfect examples of her acting were in some of the comparatively restrained characters in which she displayed her essential womanliness. Jane Clegg, Miss Moffat in *The Corn is Green*, Mother parts in *The Distaff Side* and *The Linden Tree*, and her lovely performances in the two Hunter plays, *Waters of the Moon* and *A Day by the Sea*. 'When Lewis died,' she said, 'I became a bit tired of myself.' But we could never tire of her as we watched her rallying her forces in those last splendid years, still eager to understand new styles, appreciate new talents, to lend shrewd advice and criticism, fearlessly honest about everything she saw and read.

Her beauty grew, as it had every right to do, in her old age, and her noble head, veiled in the white silk scarf she came to wear always, picked her out in any gathering, whether at theatres or parties or in church, as she listened and watched and walked, more slowly now, with an unerring sense of any occasion she was honouring with her presence. During these last years, it was sad to see her the victim of continual pain. But how magnificently she rose above it. 'My piffling arthritis,' she would say. With what unforgettable dignity she led her family up the long nave of the Abbey at the memorial service for her husband. How eagerly she followed every moment of the service, and how like her to wait afterwards to greet a great crowd of friends. One day not long afterwards I called on her at her flat in Chelsea to find her sitting in an armchair, reading Sir Thomas More. On another I found her lying on her bed, evidently in great pain. 'A bit tired today,' she said, 'for it was Lewis' anniversary yesterday, so I got them to drive me up to Golders Green and sat there for half an hour.' But she announced defiantly that she intended to come to see me in Pinter's *No Man's Land* the following week. I begged her not to make the effort and thought no more about it, but when the evening came, sure enough, during the interval, I heard over the loud-speaker, above the chatter of the audience, her voice, unmistakably clear: 'Do you know my daughter-in-law Patricia?' Ralph Richardson bounded into my dressing-room. 'She's here after all', and of course we both had letters afterwards. George Devine told me that she came to see every one of the new plays he was then presenting at the Court, and would always write him vivid and constructive criticism as soon as she got home.

How fitting that her very last public appearance should have been at the Old Vic on its farewell night when, at the end of the performance, she was wheeled down the aisle in her chair to smile and wave for the last time to the people sitting in the theatre she had always loved so well.

Lively and personal, passionate and argumentative, always practising her piano, cooking her dinner, making her bed, travelling, acting, learning a new language or a new poem, simple clothes, simple tastes, a magnificent wife and mother – surely one of the rarest women of our time.

'O Lewis,' she cried once, 'if only we could be the first actors to play on the moon.'

Sunday Times, 13th June 1976

Chapter 3

Ralph Richardson:
A Great Gentleman, A Rare Spirit

He was my friend, faithful and just to me,
But Brutus says he was ambitious . . .

But Ralph was not, I think, a predominantly ambitious man, except in his lifelong determination to perfect his art. He was never satisfied with a single one of his performances, but would go on working to improve what would seem to me a perfect interpretation, however often repeated, until the very last time he came to play it.

Besides cherishing our long years of work together in the theatre, where he was such an inspiring and generous partner, I grew to love him in private life as a great gentleman, a rare spirit, fair and balanced, devotedly loyal and tolerant and, as a companion, bursting with vitality, curiosity and humour.

A consummate craftsman, endlessly painstaking in every detail where his work was concerned, he was something of a perfectionist in many fields outside the theatre. He read voraciously. Two or three different books – a novel, a classic, a biography, a thriller – these would, during a long run, be propped up on shelves and tables for him to peruse during his waits in the dressing-room. His beautiful houses were filled with furniture, ornaments and pictures which reflected his unerring individual taste.

He loved to discuss his motorbikes and cars, his clocks and pets, to argue about films and plays he had been to see. He never cared for gossip, and would avoid, if possible, giving adverse criticism of other players, though he could tell a good actor at a glance and shrewdly sum up an indifferent one equally quickly. He was a wonderful influence in a company, punctual, concentrated and completely professional, patient and courteous in delays and crises, critical (and intensely self-critical) and never malicious, taking his own time to consider questions and answering them patiently with grace and wisdom.

On the very few occasions when I saw him in a rage, he suddenly showed a formidable strength, but the mood would quickly pass, and he never harboured grudges.

When we first acted together at the Old Vic in 1930, I little thought that we might be friends. At first we were inclined to circle round each other like suspicious dogs. In our opening production I played Hotspur to his Prince Hal, and was relieved, though somewhat surprised, to discover that he was as reluctant as I to engage in the swordplay demanded in the later underrehearsed scenes at Shrewsbury. On the first night I was amazed at his whispered instructions — surely, I thought, the audience must hear them too — 'Now you hit me, cocky. Now I hit you.'

A few weeks later, as we moved into rehearsals for *The Tempest*, I rather hesitatingly ventured to suggest to him a private session for examining one of our scences together, and he immediately agreed with the greatest modesty and good humour. This was, as he has often said himself, the beginning of a friendship that was to last for fifty years.

There are many things about me that he must have found deeply unsympathetic, but his sensitive generosity has never faltered. When we ventured into the avant-garde together in *Home* and *No Man's Land* we both felt we were paddling dangerously in uncharted seas, but our shared success in both plays was a lively encouragement as well as a refreshing challenge after the more conventional ups and downs of our past careers.

I think he was fundamentally a shy man, and in his later years he cultivated a certain delightfully eccentric vagueness, especially when he was cornered by strangers or failed to greet someone he had not noticed. Once, when an understudy, whom he had never seen before, went on for one of the two supporting parts in *No Man's Land*, Ralph absentmindedly congratulated a stagehand who happened to be standing near him after the curtain fell.

But actually he was intensely observant and extremely farseeing. He warmed immediately to a sympathetic author, or to a new director whom he decided to trust – Lindsay Anderson, for instance, Peter Hall and, I am proud to say, myself. He was never jealous or spiteful, never bitter or attempting to blame anyone but himself after his occasional failures, always eager to set to work on the next venture, fighting his gradual difficulties in learning a complicated new text by writing it out in huge letters with coloured chalks and pinning it on boards all round his study walls.

He could give delightfully comical advice. 'How many clubs do you belong to, Ralph?' I once asked him. 'Three,' he replied. 'But, you know, you should never go to the same club more than once a week.' 'Aren't your subscription bills rather heavy?' 'Oh, I just write out a banker's order.'

How sadly I shall miss his cheerful voice on the telephone, telling me of a new book he had just finished reading (a copy would arrive by the next post) and his patience with my chattering tongue. When we appeared together on talk shows in America, his pauses and slowness would make me nervous and, fearing to bore the listeners, I would break into a torrent of anecdote which I kept trying to control lest he should think I was trying to steal the show. But he would cap my gabble brilliantly with a look and a short comment, well-considered, which threw the ball back into his own court with unerring skill and deftness. When I was directing him in a play he learnt most cleverly how to make use of the few good suggestions I made at a rehearsal and discard the many bad ones.

One of the few arguments I ever had with him was over his first entrance in *The School for Scandal*, as Sir Peter Teazle. Ralph argued every day, and we could not begin to rehearse the scene. 'Should I have a newspaper in my hand? A walking-stick? Or be taking snuff perhaps?' At last one morning he leaned across the footlights and said, 'You know, Johnnie, I prayed to God last night to tell me how to come on in this opening scene. And this morning God answered, "Do what it says in the text, just come on." '

The loss of a most dear friend is only equalled by the loss of him as a great man of the English theatre. His Falstaff, Peer Gynt, the drunken actor in *Eden End*, Borkman, *Early Days*, all these superb performances, as well as those in plays and films when we have appeared together, are unforgettable memories for me and will always remain so. I hope the happiness of his married life and the great successes and popularity which he achieved, especially in his later years, consoled and gratified him after the long struggle he won so patiently in the early days of his career.

The Observer, 16th October 1983

Chapter 4

Elizabeth Bergner

Elfin-like, volatile, mischievous, fascinating. Elizabeth Bergner had all these qualities. But the huge public that had raved over her performance in Margaret Kennedy's *Escape Me Never* in 1934, both in London and New York, took little notice of her death in 1987. Only one or two actors besides myself were present at her funeral, though the German Government had sent a huge wreath, as well as rewarding her with the Duse Memorial shield, during her last years, evidence that she was still gratefully remembered in the country which she had been one of the first actresses to leave when Hitler came to power. But though she often talked in her last days of going back to live in Berlin or Vienna, she remained and died in London.

I had a long and unforgettable friendship with her, though I could never be certain of her moods. She had been a great star, with all the spoilt trappings of a gifted celebrity, from the time of her earliest successes on the continent – some under Max Rheinhardt – and I was not altogether surprised to read, in Count Kessler's memoirs, that during a performance of *Romeo and Juliet* (with Franz Lederer and Elizabeth) the manager had come before the curtain to announce that Miss Bergner was so exhausted by the big scene she had just played that there would have to be a short interval to enable her to recover her energies – a somewhat unusual emergency it seemed to me.

In 1934 I met her, just before she first appeared in London, at Boulestin's Restaurant, when Emlyn Williams and I had asked her to lunch with us to suggest she might star in *Spring 1600*, a play of Emlyn's which I was about to direct. It was, of course, an idiotic idea, as the leading character was an English country girl, and her accent would have been an impossible barrier, but we were fascinated by her all the same.

She cleverly chose C. B. Cochran to sponsor her début in England, as he was to do years later in *The Boy David*. Komisarjevsky, who directed her in both plays, told me that on the first night in Manchester (of *Escape Me Never*) he had to push her on to the stage from the wings, since she was paralysed with nervousness. But when I saw the play one afternoon in London, she acted enchantingly, but spoilt her most dramatic scene in the last act by giggling, though this did not seem to deter the audience from wild applause and endless curtain calls at the end of the performance. As I walked down Shaftesbury Avenue afterwards, I heard a tremendous roar behind me, and, looking round, I saw an open taxi slowly driving along, and Elizabeth sitting on the hood with flowers in her lap, waving to a mass of shouting fans who were following her, crowding the pavements on both sides of the street.

Her husband, Paul Czinner, directed all the films in which she starred with great réclame: *Escape Me Never, Catherine the Great*, and a better forgotten *As You Like It*. Her German-speaking film *Der Träumende Mund*, had already been seen by cinema buffs in London, who praised it greatly and all the English film and stage critics (except James Agate, who always pugnaciously refused her his approval and dismissed her as being 'mousey-pousey') were unanimous in extolling her talents to the skies.

She forfeited her popularity, however, when, at the outbreak of the war, she was to be one of the stars in a film of Michael Powell's, *49th Parallel*. The scenes she was in demanded some days on location in Canada, but after a few days she suddenly threw up her part and fled to Hollywood, with the result that the whole sequence had to be scrapped and reshot with Glynis Johns. (Gracie Fields, who left for the States at about the same time with her new husband, Monty Banks, became equally unpopular in consequence – the mill girls in Lancashire were even said to have broken all her gramophone records – but she reinstated herself a few years later at a huge concert at the Albert Hall – in which I made a short appearance – under the auspices of Basil Dean, who was then to direct her in several successful films.)

Meanwhile, in California, Elizabeth made an English film version of *Der Träumende Mund* (Dreaming Lips), and *A Stolen Life* with Michael Redgrave, and remained in America for several years. She acted in a sex melodrama *The Two Mrs Carrolls* on the Subway Circuit, and appeared in New York, for a short run, in an ill-conceived version of *The Duchess of Malfi*, adapted by W. H. Auden, and directed by George Rylands of Cambridge, who came over (with Arthur Marshall as assistant). The cast included a black actor, Canada Lee, as Bosola, playing in white face!

Czinner had bought the scenery and costumes we had used in our production of the play in London the year before, but Elizabeth commissioned new costumes for herself and gave Peggy Ashcroft's dresses to the ladies-in-waiting.

She lived for some time in Princeton, renewing friendships with Brecht, Einstein, Mann and other distinguished European refugees, but I could never persuade her to talk about them, or even to tell me stories of her early triumphs before she came to England.

She flattered me greatly when, in 1937, she asked me to direct *The Boy David*, which Barrie, who had fallen in love with her, had written especially for her, but I could not care for the play when I was sent it to read. When Elizabeth came to my flat to dine with me and discuss the matter, I hedged at criticising the text of the great man, but said I would only consider the task she offered me if I could count on her support in suggesting changes. But at this point, Elizabeth broke a string of beads which she was wearing round her neck and dived under the sofa to retrieve them, and I at once made up my mind to doubt the likelihood of her using any influence on my behalf, and demurred at the responsibility of working with such eminent seniors as Cochran, Barrie, and Augustus John, who was to design the décor. Barrie died just before the London opening and the production was postponed, after a try-out in Edinburgh, when Elizabeth fired the director, H. K. Ayliff, and temporarily retired into a nursing home. When she emerged, Komisarjevsky was engaged to re-direct, and Ernest Stern and the Motleys were brought in for the scenery and costumes. But the play was damned by the London critics and lasted at His Majesty's for only a few weeks, despite a fine cast, including Godfrey Tearle, Ion Swinley, Sir John Martin-Harvey and Jean Cadell. Elizabeth made her entrance on a donkey and was said to have amused herself by crouching at Tearle's feet and pulling hairs out of his leg to make him laugh.

Barrie had left a legacy to Elizabeth in his will, and there was some rather spiteful speculation in the press at his neglect of the leading ladies who had played Peter Pan in so many years of successful revivals. Elizabeth told me this episode had upset and embarrassed her very much. But she would also boast of her behaviour at a matinée of *Saint Joan* at Malvern when she got bored and proceeded to cut the famous Bells speech, unaware that Shaw was in the audience. 'He came round,' she said, 'and threw the book at me.' 'What on earth did you do, Elizabeth?' I enquired. 'I threw it back,' she replied with her inimitable giggle.

When she finally reappeared in London after many years, she rashly chose for her vehicle a translation of Molière's *Malade Imaginaire*, which failed completely, though she had some fun in trying to upstage the redoubtable old warhorse A. E. Matthews, who was far too experienced a performer to let her get away with it. She could be very unpredictable as a colleague, though enchantingly courteous towards players she admired. Irene Vanbrugh and Léon Quartermaine were both devoted to her, and the young Irene Worth, who acted with her when she was quite a beginner, and was later to become an intimate friend, told me how much she had learned from working with her.

After Paul Czinner's death she continued to live in her elegant flat in Eaton Square, where she had nursed him devotedly through a long illness. She had recently become a Christian Scientist, and at her cremation service the ceremony was half Scientist and half Jewish.

I only acted with her once myself in a television version of Shaw's *In Good King Charles's Golden Days* when I had suggested her for the part of Catherine of Braganza, who has a charming scene with the King in the epilogue (the part had been created in the theatre by Irene Vanbrugh, who must have been almost as unsuitably cast as Ernest Thesiger, who played the King). Elizabeth gave an exquisite performance, though she was difficult and evasive during the rehearsals, begging me to rehearse alone with her without the director, suggesting cuts and transpositions, and avoiding meeting the other members of the cast, and she never referred to the episode again. But she was an intensely generous friend, always giving me valuable presents, but very difficult to please when I tried to think of suitable tokens in return – flowers seemed to annoy her, though her drawing-room always seemed packed with flowers, books, and cards, though she did seem to like a present of chocolates. But she was apt to keep her friends in separate boxes – Irene Worth, Michael Redgrave, and myself, for instance, whom she would never invite together. Increasing deafness, I think, made her reluctant to entertain more than one person at a time. Usually wearing horn-rimmed spectacles, with grey hair not touched up, and dressed in exceedingly becoming trouser-suits, beautifully simple and well cut, she was still the most delightful and attractive hostess.

Quite often she would go back to Germany, to act there in *The Deep Blue Sea* by Terence Rattigan, and the Shaw-Campbell duologue *Dear Liar*, as well as a number of films, few of which were shown in this country. But she seemed to find little pleasure in these visits, and seemed to long to appear again on the London stage, though I tried in vain to interest her in plays that I thought might suit her (one especially: *La Monstre Sacrée* of Cocteau). But she had no use for any of them.

Meanwhile she booked seats – always in the front row so that she could hear better – for concerts and plays of all kinds, and she read voraciously and took enormous interest in the experimental theatre, as well as in films, museums and picture exhibitions. She talked of playing in a new piece at the Royal Court but turned it down in the end. Then she appeared in a translation of a Hungarian play called *Cat's Play* at the Greenwich Theatre, in which she was helped through by the director, Robin Phillips, and in which she was brilliant as ever, but very unpleasant to the distinguished actress with whom she had important scenes to play. This last appearance in London made very little stir. Finally, she decided – also at Greenwich (where evidently her remarkable gifts had not gone unappreciated), to play the drug-taking wife in Eugene O'Neill's sequel to *Long Day's Journey Into Night*, called *Fading Mansions*. But in the rehearsals of this play she proved so undisciplined that it was decided to drop her from the cast, and another actress was secretly engaged. I was dismayed to be the person to break this news to her, but to my amazement she shrugged the insult off, and went into roars of laughter at the news. I could not help admiring her remarkable courage in facing old age and losing her great reputation, and I continued to visit her quite often and sometimes I took her to the theatre. Then I was told, when I telephoned, that she had become very ill, and I never saw her again.

Chapter 5

Vivien Leigh

What seems to me most remarkable, as far as her career was concerned, was her steady determination to be a fine stage actress, to make her career in the living theatre, when, with her natural beauty, skill, and grace of movement, gifts which were of course invaluable in helping to create the magic of her personality, she could so easily have stayed aloof and supreme in her unique position as a screen actress. Of course she will always be remembered as Scarlett O'Hara, as Lady Hamilton, and later for her wonderful acting in the *Streetcar* film. But these screen successes by no means satisfied her ambitions, and she had a lifelong devotion to the theatre, and determined to work there diligently through the years in order to reach the heights which she afterwards achieved. Though in her first big success, *The Mask of Virtue*, she had taken the critics and public by storm, she knew that her youth and beauty were the chief factors of her immediate success, and she was modest and shrewd enough to face the challenge of developing herself so as to find the widest possible range of which she was capable.

Her marriage to Laurence Olivier was an inspiration to her qualities – not only as a devoted pupil but also as a brilliant partner. Her performance in their seasons together, not only at the St James's Theatre (whose untimely destruction she tried so gallantly to prevent), but also at the Old Vic and Stratford, and in tours all over the world – in Russia, Australia, Europe and America – added fresh laurels to her crown. Besides the classic parts, she delighted everyone too in the modern plays she chose, each of which made different demands upon her versatility — *The Skin of Our Teeth, The Sleeping Prince, Antigone*, and later *Duel of Angels*.

She had a charmingly distinctive voice. On the telephone one recognised it immediately — that touch of imperiousness, combined with a childlike eager warmth full of friendliness and gaiety. But she was determined to increase the range of it for the theatre, and in Shakespeare's Cleopatra, in which I thought she gave her finest classical performance, she succeeded in lowering her whole register from the natural pitch she was using as the little girl Cleopatra in Shaw's play — a remarkable feat which few actresses could have sustained as successfully as she did. Her Lady Macbeth, too, showed an astonishing vocal power and poignancy of feeling — and it is a thousand pities that the project of filming her performance of this was abandoned, for I believe it would have created worldwide admiration.

Her manners both in the theatre and in private life were always impeccable. She was punctual, modest, and endlessly thoughtful and considerate. She was frank without being unkind, elegant but never ostentatious. Her houses were as lovely as her beautiful and simple clothes. Whenever she was not entirely absorbed in the theatre she was endlessly busy, decorating her rooms, planning surprises for her friends, giving advice on her garden, entertaining lavishly but always with the utmost grace and selectivity.

I had never thought to become an intimate friend of hers. My first meeting with her was at Oxford in 1937, when she played the little queen in *Richard the Second* with the students. I was acting in London at the time, and so only met her when I was directing the rehearsals. The part is not a very interesting one, though she managed to endow it with every possible grace of speech and movement, and wore her medieval costumes with consummate charm — but I never got to know her in these days.

A few years later, during the war, I acted with her in *The Doctor's Dilemma*, when another actor was taken ill, and from that time we began an acquaintanceship which slowly ripened into a deep friendship and affection, and it is a wonderful happiness to me that during her last years I had the joy of seeing her so often and came to love her so well.

Of course she was restless and drove herself too hard. Although she seemed so astonishingly resilient, she often suffered ill health and fits of great depression, but she made light of the fact and rarely admitted to it or talked about it to other people. Her courage in the face of personal unhappiness was touching and remarkable. She always spoke affectionately of those who had first recognised her talents and helped her to develop her natural gifts. She studied and experimented continually, and always brought to rehearsal a willingness and technical flexibility which was the result of unceasing self-criticism and devotion to her work.

As she grew older she acquired a new kind of beauty, without any need of artifice, and she seemed to harbour no resentment against the competition of younger beautiful women. She was always enormously interested in everything, people, places, changes of fashion – and she had friends of every different sort and kind in London, in her country homes and in America and Australia. How delightfully she would talk of her Japanese admirers, who wrote her such charmingly phrased letters, and of those in Russia, where her film *Waterloo Bridge* is still considered a classic. She had the most punctilious and gracious way of answering letters and of dealing with strangers, admirers, newspaper men and women, and she was loved in the theatres she worked in for her sweetness to staff and company alike.

Her magic quality was unique. A great beauty, a natural star, a consummate screen actress and a versatile and powerful person-ality in the theatre – she had a range that could stretch from the comedy Sabina in *Skin of Our Teeth* to the naturalistic agonies of Blanche DuBois in *Streetcar*, and the major demands of Lady Macbeth and Cleopatra. Even in *Titus Andronicus*, when she had only a few short scenes, she contrived the most beautiful pictorial effects. Who can forget the macabre grace with which she guided the staff with her elbows to write in the sand with it, a ravished victim gliding across the stage in her long grey robe.

We who loved her must be always thankful for knowing her and working with her, and salute her for all she gave the world, so generously and so gaily.

Now boast thee, Death, in thy possession lies
A lass unparallel'd.

Chapter 6

Gwen Ffrangcon-Davies

In the early Nineteen Twenties, when I first came to know her, she was already something of a cult personality in the London theatre, to which she had graduated, after an improbable apprenticeship touring in musical comedy successes, to establish herself as leading lady of Sir Barry Jackson's repertory company at Birmingham. Daughter of a fine and well-known singer father, her success at the Glastonbury Festival in Rutland Boughton's opera, *The Immortal Hour*, led Sir Barry to present her in London in the same part – the fairy princess Etain – at the Regent Theatre, opposite King's Cross Station (long pulled down) for a short season, to be followed by a production of *Romeo and Juliet*, in which, after several nerve-wracking auditions, I was finally engaged, as a nineteen year old novice, to play Romeo – Gwen had already played the part with success in Birmingham.

I do not believe Gwen herself was present at my auditions, and I had to deliver my speeches, in a large empty auditorium, to Sir Barry and his director, H. K. Ayliff (a tall, grim figure with a toupée, dressed in green tweeds and brown boots) while a stage-manager fed me from the wings with Juliet's lines. Gwen afterwards told me that she had seen me as the Poet Butterfly in Capek's *The Insect Play* – my first professional engagement in London two years before – and thought me disastrously bad. Consequently she was dismayed to hear I was to partner her. (She evidently had not been consulted in the matter herself.)

However, after a few days' rehearsal she decided to put up with me, and helped and encouraged me in every possible way, though my performance was very inadequate, and the production, a rather chilly affair except for Gwen's enchanting Botticelli Juliet, greatly praised by a few discerning critics and her growing band of devoted admirers, only lasted for a few weeks, two of which I was to miss owing to illness. I fainted one day during the balcony scene but managed to finish the performance (and hoped that the audience might have thought me to have swooned with lyrical ecstasy). My understudy was incompetent, and Ion Swinley and Ernest Milton were hastily summoned to replace me, for a week each, which must have created a series of emergencies for all concerned.

Throughout her long career, Gwen's skillful voice-control and graceful movements, as well as her unusually talented gift for wearing period costume, made her greatly in demand, especially for Shakespeare. She appeared as Titania, Cordelia and some years later as Ophelia, and the beautiful photographs of her in those busy days show how great was her appealing personality, though she never made claim to being a raving beauty. Laura Knight painted her as Juliet as she stood in her petticoat in the dressing-room, and when she played Isabella the She-Wolf for the Phoenix Society's special performances of Marlowe's *Edward the Second*, she was immortalised by Walter Sickert in a magnificent portrait which now hangs nobly in the Tate Gallery.

But she was equally successful in many contemporary plays, including some of Shaw's best women's parts – Mrs Dubedat, Eliza Doolittle, and the young Cleopatra when her Caesar was Cedric Hardwicke, a partnership that was to continue some years later, with great advantage to them both, in *The Barretts of Wimpole Street*.

But one of my favourite memories of her is also in a Shaw play, when she was Eve in the Garden of Eden scene in his pentateuch *Back to Methuselah*, with Edith Evans as the hissing Serpent. In the second part of this play she was the old Eve, trying to cope with a rebellious Cain, and in this scene she was movingly effective. Then, in the last Methuselah play, she acted the Newly-Born, emerging from a huge property egg and tottering about with bare feet in a long white nightie, while Edith Evans appeared as the She-Ancient wearing a bald wig and hideous rags. She and Gwen were to be cast in plays together many times, and were devoted friends in private life, though I always felt that, in the theatre, Edith was inclined to under-rate Gwen's brilliant talents and was sometimes inclined to patronise her.

In 1928, Gwen and I acted together in a modern piece called *Prejudice* of which I remember little, save that I had to be Jewish, and Gwen a New England country girl, for which she assumed a most authentic-sounding accent. I had thought I was going to be very good, and was duly brought down from my high horse when, lying in bed after the first performance and eagerly sitting up to open the newspapers, I sank back on my pillow murmuring, 'Christ! Gwen's got the notices!'

But we remained as good friends as ever, and when, in 1932, after her triumph in *The Barretts*, I offered her the comparatively small part of the Queen, Anne of Bohemia, in *Richard of Bordeaux*, she accepted it eagerly, and her enchanting performance proved to be an invaluable contribution to the success of the play.

Her vivacity and enterprise led her to undertake a remarkable range of entirely different plays and characters. She played Tess in an adaptation of the Hardy novel, and she and Ion Swinley went down to the country and acted a scene from the play on the hearth rug in the great man's drawing-room. She was a Marseilles prostitute in *Maya* at the Gate Theatre Club (public performance banned by the Lord Chamberlain), a servant drudge, Elsie, in an adaptation of Arnold Bennett's *Riceyman Steps*, and Magda in a play by Sudermann which had been famous in the repertories of Duse, Bernhardt, and Mrs Patrick Campbell. And she was memorably effective in *The Lady with the Lamp*, a play by Reginald Berkeley about Florence Nightingale, played by Edith Evans, with Gwen as Lady Herbert. In the last two scenes of the play, in which both actresses were required to span many years, Gwen was (as she had in Eve) given a fine opportunity to show her consummate skill in developing her

characterisation, and her elderly lady was even better than
Edith's.

In 1937 I began to plan a season of four classic plays, to be
given, with a permanent company, for runs of six to eight weeks
each. Gwen and I were on tour together in a play by Emlyn
Williams, which turned out to be a complete failure in London,
when it ran for only twelve performances, but though I had
discussed my projected season with Gwen many times in my
usually thoughtless way, I proceeded to engage Peggy Ashcroft as
my leading lady, and the choice was eagerly seized on in the
press. Half way through the season, Michel Saint-Denis agreed to
direct the third play *The Three Sisters* of Chekhov, and we both
agreed that Gwen would be ideal as the elder sister Olga. When I
received from Gwen the only disagreeable letter I ever had from
her. I realised how tactlessly I had behaved, and was duly
mortified.

Everything, fortunately, was to turn out well. Michel went to
see Gwen, who found him fascinating, and his tact and enthusiasm quickly persuaded her to change her mind. She was
typically affectionate and forgiving when we started to rehearse,
and made immediate and lasting friends with Peggy, while the
production turned out to be the biggest success of the whole
season.

She continued her immensely varied career in a long series of
successful performances, among which I much admired her as the
tortured wife in Patrick Hamilton's *Gas Light* and as a stylishly
subtle Gwendolen in *The Importance of Being Earnest*. In Graham
Greene's *The Potting Shed* she was my mother, and in the
Stratford *Lear* she was my daughter Regan, venomous and
deadly. In 1942 she played Lady Macbeth with me, a fine
performance underrated, I thought by the critics, who would
never accept a small feminine actress in the part until they came
to relent at the surprising success of Judi Dench a year or two
ago. I had the joy of directing Gwen (Judi was the Anya) in a
production of *The Cherry Orchard* at the Lyric, Hammersmith, and
thought her Madame Ranevsky finer even than the often brilliant

performances of Edith Evans, Peggy Ashcroft and Athene Seyler in different versions of the same play.

I was very sorry to be out of England when she played the drug-taking wife in O'Neill's *Long Day's Journey Into Night*, for many people told me it was the finest performance of her whole career. Today in her nineties, she has remained indefatigably energetic. Though living alone in her Essex cottage, she has lately appeared on television and radio; has given talks at the National and at Stratford; entertains guests at weekends and has made new friends while steeling herself gallantly to the loss of many old ones. Practical, shrewd, philosophical and so greatly talented, she is surely a unique example of a great actress, a generous warm professional colleague, and a most dear and cherished friend.

Chapter 7

Golden Days: the Guitrys

It was in the early 1920s that the Guitrys – father and his son
Sacha – first appeared in London with their enchanting leading
lady, Yvonne Printemps, giving a short season of repertoire
under the banner of C. B. Cochran. They were acclaimed by the
press and became immediate favourites with the public. Lucien
made a tremendous impression with *Pasteur*, a play in which he
delivered a long monologue, addressing the theatre audience as if
they were students attending a lecture. My parents described this
performance to me in some detail, but I was not lucky enough to
see it myself.

However I have a most vivid recollection of Lucien's acting in
a drama called *Jacqueline*, in which he played an elderly roué who
was destined to strangle his mistress in the final scene. It was the
preparation for this dénouement in the second act that impressed
me most. The scene was a hotel bedroom at Le Touquet where
he had taken the girl for a weekend. As Guitry stood over her as
she lay on the bed, she suddenly shrank from his embrace crying,
'Oh–! You terrify me.' For a few moments – seconds perhaps –
he seemed to grow inches taller and became a towering and
sinister creature. Then, suddenly breaking the tension completely, he resumed his normally charming manner for the rest of
the scene. I watched him most intently, and am convinced that in
fact he did absolutely nothing, moving neither his hands, his face
or his body. His absolute stillness and the projection of his
concentrated imagination, controlled and executed with consummate technique, produced on the girl and on the audience an

extraordinary and unforgettable effect. I knew I had seen a great actor.

Lucien was evidently a tremendous figure both on and off the stage. It was said he could eat twelve dozen snails for supper after a performance. (Fortunate for his stage colleagues that it was not beforehand.) And I once saw a film of contemporary celebrities, including Renoir, Monet and Bernhardt, called *Paris 1900*, compiled by Sacha, which included a fine close-up of Lucien, wearing a big sombrero, with a monocle hanging from the brim on a narrow cord. Both he and his son were great dandies, affecting frilled shirts, fur coats, opera cloaks and elegant walking sticks, obviously proud to be immediately recognisable (even off the stage) as the distinguished personalities they were.

Sacha was enormously talented and prolific, turning out dozens of plays, films and operettas over the years, as well as directing and acting in most of them himself. Yvonne Printemps was said to have been Lucien's *chère amie* at first. Whether this was true or not, she married Sacha not long after his father's death and returned with him many times to London to delight the public with various pieces artfully concocted to display both of them to the best possible advantage.

Yvonne Printemps was a *soubrette*, with a trim, elegant figure, appealing spaniel eyes, and a broad turned-up nose not unlike that of our own Gertrude Lawrence, and her acting had the same inimitable brand of impish sentimental comedy. But unlike Gertie Lawrence, whose singing voice, fascinating as it was, could be distinctly unreliable and wobbly, Printemps' tones were exquisitely delicate and true. She was sometimes tempted, perhaps, to prolong her top notes unduly in order to show off her brilliant breath control, and to yield rather too easily to demands for encores. But in *Mozart* (for which her songs had been composed most skilfully by Reynaldo Hahn) she seemed ravishingly youthful and touching in her powdered wig, black knee breeches and buckled shoes, while Sacha hovered about her with avuncular authority, not attempting to try and sing himself, but contributing a kind of flowing, rhythmic accompaniment with his own speeches, delivered in a deep caressing voice.

In another play with music, *Mariette*, Sacha, as the Emperor Napoleon the Third, sat in a stage box, half hidden by the curtains, his great hands emerging at intervals in their white kid gloves to applaud the heroine as she stood on the stage within a stage; while, in the dressing-room scene that followed, she parried his advances in captivating roulades as he murmured in baffled tones of royal entreaty, 'Venez souper avec moi.'

The gramophone records of Printemps, especially some excerpts from *Les Trois Valses*, which unhappily she never played in London, can still give us a nostalgic memory of her inimitable quality as a singer. But in Noël Coward's *Conversation Piece*, which he wrote specially for her, and which she played with success both in London and New York, she had to learn her part in English, parrot fashion, and was considerably hampered by her difficulty with the language, though her best scene at the climax of the operetta was sung in French.

I was only near her once, when she and Guitry were guests of honour on one of their annual visits, at a dinner dance, given (rather improbably) by the ex-students of the RADA. I timidly ventured towards the high table where she was sitting, beautifully gowned and bejewelled, but Sacha, seated beside her, guessed at my impertinent intention, and growled imperiously, 'Madame ne danse pas', at which I hastily bowed myself away with my tail between my legs.

Sacha was obviously compulsively jealous as a husband, though a notorious ladies' man, and married again several times after Yvonne Printemps finally left him to elope with the actor Pierre Fresnay. But he had evidently taught her to be somewhat possessive herself, since she insisted that Fresnay should never kiss another woman on the stage after she had married him, and he obediently resigned himself to playing saints, priests and confirmed bachelors for the rest of his distinguished career.

I only met Sacha on one occasion. In March 1939 Peggy Ashcroft and I were invited to appear at a gala, to celebrate the state visit of the French President. We were asked to play the balcony scene from *Romeo and Juliet* as part of an entertainment to be given at the Foreign Office in London, the courtyard of which had been covered over and transformed into a theatre for the occasion. It was a tremendous affair, the last of its kind before the war, and I could not help referring to it afterwards as the Duchesss of Richmond's Ball. There was a magnificent profusion of flowers edging the balconies, and a positive thicket of madonna lilies dividing the stage from the auditorium.

Before the performance, the guests – glittering with tiaras, long gloves and fans for the women, and uniforms, medals and sashes for the men – distributed themselves on small gilt chairs. Everyone rose as the royal family entered by different doors, Queen Mary from one, the Duke and Duchess of Kent from another, and lastly the King and Queen, who conducted the President and his suite (which included the nefarious Laval) to their armchairs in the front row. We actors dragged ourselves reluctantly away from the peepholes in the curtain and the entertainment began.

It was a long and somewhat patchy programme, as is usual on such occasions. The audience, exhausted by a long day of official functions – a visit to Windsor, the National Gallery, and a state banquet to follow – became increasingly restive in their tight clothes. Several elderly gentlemen seemed to be in some danger of falling asleep and slipping off their chairs, and Peggy Ashcroft and I did not feel that our Shakespeare excerpt was very successful. No doubt we were somewhat inaudible as well, but we were politely received. Edith Evans appeared with a group of distinguished actresses representing the wines of France. But the most strikingly effective moment was the entrance of a band of Scottish pipers, magnificently kilted and bonneted, who swung on to the small stage with a great swirl of bagpipes, marched round it, and swung grandly off again, as everybody woke up and applauded vigorously for the first time.

Sacha Guitry had been invited to appear with Seymour Hicks in a sketch written by them both. Hicks was a great admirer of

Sacha and had acted in English versions of several of his plays. The humour of their joint endeavour was supposed to lie in attempts by Sacha to speak English and Hicks to reply in French, but both actors were exceedingly nervous and obviously under-rehearsed. I watched them from the wings as they kept drying up and killing each other's laughs, which were not very plentiful in any case. Appearing with them was Sacha's latest wife, Geneviève Sereville, an extremely young and pretty girl. At the morning rehearsal Peggy and I had been asked to come on to the stage to be introduced to the distinguished visitors. Mademoiselle Sereville was dressed in a very short skirt, and her stockings were rolled below the knees like a footballer's, showing a considerable expanse of bewitching thigh. We stammered a few polite words in our halting French, to which M. Guitry, magnificent with his fur collar and gold-topped cane, made suitably gracious acknowledgment. As we moved away to find our dressing-rooms I ventured to remark to Hicks, 'I say, sir, that's a remarkably attractive girl with M. Guitry don't you think?' and was rewarded by the trenchant comment, 'Try acting with her, old boy. It's the cabman's goodbye.'

Chapter 8

Eminent Victorians: Sir Squire Bancroft, Sir Johnston Forbes-Robertson, Dame Madge Kendal

As a young man I often caught a glimpse of two of the great theatrical figures of my parents' time, Sir Squire Bancroft and Sir Johnston Forbes-Robertson. I would pass them as they strolled along Piccadilly in their curly-brimmed top hats and frock coats, the one with wavy white hair and a monocle dangling on a moiré ribbon, the other cadaverous, with sculptured Burne-Jones features. Both men, in their seventies, remained slim, upright, and immensely distinguished.

Of course I never saw either of them on the stage. But I heard glowing praise of 'Forbie' from Léon Quartermaine, who had been an enthusiastic member of his company, and from his daughter Jean, so like him in appearance and so gifted as an actress throughout her brilliant but eventually tragic career. Forbes-Robertson writes in his autobiography that he was only happy in his youth, when he was a painter, and that he left the theatre with intense relief. I was lucky enough on one occasion to hear him give one of the great Hamlet soliloquies in a lecture, and was enormously impressed by his grace and eloquence. A silent film which still exists, though photographed when he was sixty, gives proof of his picturesquely gothic gestures and princely bearing.

Bancroft had retired with a fortune many years before I was born. The number of his productions is surprisingly small, but he revived them many times and they never failed to continue to attract the public. *Diplomacy* (a melodrama adapted from Sardou's *Dora*) was his most notable success. When Bancroft and his wife decided they were too old for the youthful roles they had created, they re-cast them with players of promising young talent and appeared themselves in the older character parts — a very sensible decision. Gerald du Maurier, Owen Nares, and Gladys Cooper appeared in various revivals of the play, which still held the stage as late as the Nineteen Thirties.

When Lady Bancroft, a skilful comedienne in the Marie Tempest manner, died, Sir Squire went to live in Albany. From there he would walk each morning to his bank, when he would demand a slip with the amount of his current balance, which he diligently perused before proceeding to lunch at the Garrick Club. Somewhat morbidly fascinated with mortality, he always visited the bedside of friends who were ill bearing a large bunch of black muscat grapes. He was also a faithful attendant at funerals and memorial services (as well as fashionable theatrical first nights) and was heard to remark, on his return from a cremation service — still something of a novelty in the Twenties — 'A most impressive occasion. And afterwards the relations were kind enough to ask me to go behind.'

But to me the most august figure of the last *monstres sacrés* of the Victorian era was Dame Madge Kendal. I once saw her driving down Shaftesbury Avenue, redfaced and imposing in full evening dress. For some unknown reason her car was lighted up inside, and there she sat, bolt upright, her hair parted in the middle and screwed back into a bun, her neck and shoulders in handsome décolleté. With a sparkling necklace at the throat, and her bodice tightly corseted, with the cleft between her breasts exposed like a portrait by Ingres, she was an awe-inspiring sight.

As a girl she had made her first successes acting at Bristol in a company that included Ellen Terry. Her brother Tom Robertson was the author of *Caste* and other 'cup-and-saucer' plays, as they were called, which inaugurated a completely new series of realistic ensemble productions. Later she married William Kendal, and together they went into management, achieving a hugely successful partnership which rivalled that of the

Bancrofts, and the couple were able to retire in early middle age, just as the Bancrofts did, with comfortable bank accounts and legendary reputations.

Many people, including my father and James Agate, considered Mrs Kendal the finest actress in England, a mistress of comedy and domestic drama even surpassing Ellen Terry. She seldom ventured into the classic field, however, and the photographs of her as Rosalind/Ganymede – with Kendal as Orlando sporting a resplendent Victorian moustache – suggest a rather over-corseted, buskinned Amazon. But she triumphed in Tree's famous *The Merry Wives of Windsor* for the Coronation of Edward the Seventh in 1902, when she and Ellen Terry shared the honours with him, though Mrs Kendal had always disapproved of Ellen's divorces, love affairs and illegitimate children. Tree hid in a box to watch their reunion at the first rehearsal, chuckling with glee at expected tantrums, but the ladies seem to have behaved to one another with admirable restraint. The subsequent publicity and box-office returns did much, no doubt, to sweeten their differences, though I noticed that in the revival of the same production the following year, Mrs Kendal did not appear.

On her eightieth birthday Dame Madge (as she was by now) being asked to record a speech for broadcasting, chose to read the epilogue from *As You Like It*. Arriving at the BBC she was received with respectful ceremony. The director showed her where to stand and pointing to the microphone explained politely 'and that, Dame Madge, is your Orlando'. To which the old lady replied with a gracious smile, 'Ah, my husband was better looking than that.'

Her autobiography is sadly disappointing reading, showing her to have been a tremendous snob, and full of self-pity about her children's treatment of her. She even refers to herself as Mater Dolorosa, though actually she herself had treated them very cruelly. But evidently she was a brilliant and professional artist, a fine director and trainer of young talents (Marie Löhr and Mary Jerrold both spoke of her with affection and respect) and in her last years she was an amusing and impressive personality,

speaking at public dinners (I once heard her imitate Phelps
playing Macbeth) and making appeals at charity matinées. Having
been shown the box where she was later to be received by
royalty, prior to one of these occasions, she announced, 'I must
go down to the stage for a moment. I haven't felt my roof.' And
descending to the footlights she gazed towards the gallery, where
the cleaners were working busily, and called out in silvery tones,
'Ladies, can you hear me?'

She wrote several amusing letters to the newspapers deploring
the behaviour of the Bright Young Things, and castigating the
new fashions – cigarette smoking, short skirts, lipsticks, and
making-up in public. To the end of her life – as one can see in
Orpen's splendid portrait of her in the National Portrait Gallery
– she always wore Victorian bonnets decked with flowers and
tied under her chin.

When I was playing Benedick at Sadler's Wells in 1930,
Dorothy Green and I were summoned to her box during an
interval, where she greeted (and shortly afterwards dismissed us)
as if she were royalty, with a few patronisingly gracious remarks.
But Seymour Hicks tells a tragic story of his last meeting with
her. Mortally ill, she sent him an urgent message, and he arrived
at her house in Portland Place and was shown in to an empty
room with all the blinds drawn. Dame Madge rushed in a few
moments later, haggard and dishevelled in a dressing gown, and
fell to her knees, exclaiming, 'I have wronged my children. I am
a wicked woman.' Mater Dolorosa indeed.

Quite recently she was depicted as a character in a new play,
and afterwards a film, *The Elephant Man*, about a poor deformed
creature whose horrific appearance created great publicity at the
turn of the century. It seems that Mrs Kendal visited and
befriended him, as did also Queen Alexandra. Two of the film
critics referred to the character playing the visiting lady – one as
'Mrs Kendall', the other as 'Mrs Kemble' (could they have
mixed her up with Sarah Siddons perhaps?). Such is the ephemeral nature of theatrical memories. Dame Madge would not have
been amused.

In the film she was played with considerable glamour by the American film star Anne Bancroft, but I thought a great effect had been missed by not depicting the severe, buttoned-up dignity of the original actress, for whom the episode must have been a most painful and rather courageous experience, but also showed there must have been a compassionate streak in her apparently rigid nature.

28th January 1978

Chapter 9

Aunt Mabel Terry-Lewis

My Aunt Mable was the youngest of my mother's three sisters.
She was also the prettiest and the most elegant. Somewhat sharp-
tongued and opinionated, she darted in and out of my parents'
house when we were children, and at my grandmother's house
there was a full-length portrait of her by John Collier that I much
admired in which she was sitting in an imposing chair, dressed in
a long black velvet teagown.

As a boy I was particularly fascinated by her because I knew
she had formerly been an actress. But when I first knew her as a
boy she had been married for several years and given up the stage
to live in the country with her husband, a captain of Territorials
and, presumably, well-to-do. They had no children. My father
told me that Mabel had once been engaged to his own brother,
but he had evidently found her somewhat too demanding. On
one occasion, when he was to escort her to a ball, she had sent
him back half-way across London to retrieve the gloves which
she had left at home.

She had made her stage début in the Nineties, when her
mother (my grandmother Kate Terry) had emerged, after many
years' retirement, to help launch her daughter in a long-
forgotten piece called *The Master* with Sir John Hare. The play
only lasted a few weeks, but Mabel's talent was immediately
recognised, and she appeared subsequently in a number of good
ingénue parts, among them the young girl in Pinero's *Gay Lord
Quex*. But I was surprised to find that her attitude towards the
theatre was curiously patronising. She told me once that she had

been in love with Guy du Maurier, the author of a well-known war play, called *An Englishman's Home*. 'But what about his brother, Gerald?' I enquired, 'weren't you in love with him too?' 'In love?' replied Mabel sharply, 'with an *actor*?'

She and her husband lived in Dorsetshire, and when I was in my early teens they invited me down to stay with them. There were white doves on the lawn, a dairy where I licked cream off my greedy fingers from the open bowls, and delicious meals. But I was absurdly homesick and dismayed by the quiet of the country where I had seldom been except on family holidays. I can remember sitting in the downstairs lavatory gazing ruefully at a decorative plaque over the washstand which announced in raised capital letters EAST OR WEST, HOME IS BEST.

But I liked helping to pick mushrooms in the wet fields and bringing them back to eat for breakfast, almost as much as I disliked accompanying Mabel's husband, when he went out shooting, attended by several spaniels – one of them with a raw wound on its back which glittered repulsively in the sunshine.

In the evening, however, Mabel would descend in a becoming teagown and lie on the sofa with her feet up. Reassured by her charm, I became more than ever convinced that the theatre must somehow be the career I was determined to pursue. To my great delight my aunt decided to stage a series of performances of a one-act play by Gertrude Jennings called *The Bathroom Door*, considered at that time, I suppose, the least bit daring, since all the characters appeared in dressing-gowns, night-gowns and pyjamas. In this I was to play the juvenile and Mabel herself the Prima Donna (the leading lady naturally), and we acted in village halls for the benefit of the local Women's Institute where it was all a great success.

Mabel was something of a snob. She loved titled folk and Royalty. Lord Ilchester was one of her neighbours and she was very much the Lady of the Manor, patronising bazaars and point-to-point meetings and giving bridge and tennis parties. But when, after the first war, her husband died, she suddenly decided to employ her boundless energies by returning to the stage. It may be that she needed money too.

She reappeared in a political comedy by H. M. Harwood, called *A Grain of Mustard Seed* in the early Twenties and made an immediate personal success. Her style and technique were quite unimpaired by her long absence from the theatre. Her carriage and diction were always faultless, and she continued to act for twenty years, both in London and New York, in a succession of aristocratic roles which fitted her to perfection. She was quite without humour and amazingly self-contained. She demanded (and obtained) permission to be absent from the cast at a matinée in a du Maurier revival of *Dear Brutus* because she had arranged to go to the Derby. She also insisted on driving a very shabby car with several spaniels on her lap and an array of rubber sponges lashed to the wheel to counter her rheumatism.

I doubt if she ever read a book. When she played Lady Bracknell in *The Importance of Being Earnest* with me at the Lyric, Hammersmith in 1929, she had no idea that her lines were funny. 'What on earth are they laughing at?' she used to say. And since, with a rather shaky memory, she would frequently have to be prompted by one or other of us in the cast, we were further dismayed to discover that, during the second act, in which Lady Bracknell does not appear, Mabel had lain down amongst the spaniels on the floor in her dressing-room and enjoyed an hour's nap, returning for the final scene more vague and absentminded than ever. Nevertheless, she made a great success of the part, which she played with her usual grace and distinction, and only the definitive creation achieved by Edith Evans in the 1939 production eclipsed her performance completely, which must have been somewhat galling to her vanity, though she was far too dignified ever to mention it to me.

Unhappily, her last engagement led to a very embarrassing situation. Hugh Beaumont engaged her to play the Duchess of Berwick in a 1946 revival of *Lady Windermere's Fan*, which was to open in Manchester for a short provincial tour before coming to the Haymarket Theatre, and I was asked to direct the play. At rehearsal, Mabel was quite unsure of her lines and made endless pauses and mistakes, even calling characters by the wrong names, which was somewhat confusing to the plot. She crossed swords with Cecil Beaton over her costumes, which she thought over-showy and unbecoming, and thwarted all my attempts to persuade her to rehearse and memorise correctly, spending her days on tour motoring about to look at houses and visit friends. This resulted in her giving a more confused performance than ever, though her elegant period manner and grace of movement won her a round of applause on her exit almost every night.

Finally we decided we had no choice but to replace her, and Beaumont agreed to go to Leeds and break the news, a mission which I was too cowardly to undertake myself but which I am sure he carried out with great reluctance and considerable tact. It was an extremely sad ending to a distinguished career, and I was ashamed to be involved in it, only telling myself that the theatre had never meant anything deeply serious to my aunt. All her life she had scattered her talents and interests in too many directions. She painted miniatures and was an expert needlewoman. Her houses and gardens were somewhat ramshackle but always cosy, attractive and charmingly arranged. She inspired great devotion in the servants and companions who ministered to her with such affectionate attention, and was always kind and amusing in a superficial way. But I found it sad that her professional efficiency and inherited instinct for the stage never seemed to fire her ambitions and allow her to take her work more seriously.

Chapter 10

Annie Esmond: The Old Character Actress

In the last year of the war I was acting every night and rehearsing during the day, so I was very reluctant to comply when the secretary of the management for whom I was working suddenly telephoned me, saying, 'You ought to go and see Annie Esmond. She wants to see you, and I think she is dying.' With my usual dread of hospitals and nursing-homes, I finally braced myself to the ordeal, and have been thankful ever since that I did so, although the poor old lady was the colour of mahogany, gasping for breath, and obviously drugged and desperate, only able to mumble a few almost incoherent words. I sat at her bedside for twenty minutes, while she held my hand tightly and gazed at me beseechingly. Later that day I was told that she had died.

I had never known her except when I worked with her in the theatre, though before I became a professional actor, when I used to see every play I could, I had admired her acting in a number of plays in the West End, supporting famous stars such as Charles Hawtrey and Lilian Braithwaite. She was unusually tall for a woman, with a somewhat formidably grim appearance but a charming smile. I met her first, for a couple of special performances for the Stage Society, in an early O'Neill play called *The Great God Brown* in which she played my mother, and we all carried masks which we assumed at intervals throughout the play – a rather pretentious and unsatisfactory affair, it seemed to me.

She confided to me at that time that she had a tremendous admiration and affection for two leading players of the period, Leslie Faber and Yvonne Arnaud, both of whom I also greatly admired, and of course I was much impressed to share her enthusiasm for them both. We did not meet again until 1938, when we were both engaged to appear with Dame Marie Tempest in Dodie Smith's *Dear Octopus*. Annie played the children's Nanny in the large cast of this family play, which, though it opened on the night of Munich, had an enormous success with the public and ran for more than a year – but I hardly remember talking to her, as we had no scenes together and so many other people were involved. I left the play when the war broke out, and did not see her again until 1942, when I was planning a production of *Macbeth*, which I was to direct and appear in for a long provincial tour before bringing it to London.

I suggested Annie Esmond for the Second Witch, and she immediately agreed to accept the part, even though the designer, Michael Ayrton, had created for the character a grotesque headdress of stag's antlers surmounting bare legs and ugly rags. The rehearsals, held in the draughty wastes of the Scala Theatre in Charlotte Street (long pulled down) were infinitely depressing in winter weather. We tried to make the best of it, and christened Annie 'Sitting Bull' as she squatted beside the witches' cauldron, and we laboured for hours trying to synchronise the rhyming lines of her few scenes to the recorded background of William Walton's music.

The usual disasters of tradition occurred during the tour, when two of the cast died, and there were replacements, accidents, and other complications. Someone told me that Annie had trudged round Glasgow trying to find cheaper digs. I gave her lunch occasionally and became as fond of her as ever, and I was very glad to be able to insist, when the production eventually opened in London, that she should have rather more important billing and a less inconvenient dressing-room, as she well deserved. In the following year, after I had played in and directed a revival of Barrie's *Dear Brutus* in London, I took the production to several military camps to play it to the troops. Mary Jerrold, an enchanting Barrie actress, had to leave the cast owing to her husband's sudden death, and Annie readily agreed to replace her.

One afternoon, when we were acting at Cheltenham, she suddenly surprised me by asking to see me in private. She produced the official form which had to be filled in before setting off on the ENSA tour and burst into tears. 'What can I put down?' she sobbed. 'I have never known who my father was.' I tried to calm her, assuring her that her stage name would surely be accepted without question, but realising of course that she had been evidently ashamed of her illegitimacy all her life and had probably never confessed it to anyone before.

In 1944 I gave a season of four plays in repertory at the Haymarket Theatre, but, when Annie came to see me begging for a part, however small, I was very sorry to have to admit that there was nothing I could offer her. The air-raids and buzzbombs were still a continual menace, and Annie, who lived alone, wore a whistle round her neck for fear she might be buried alive. Finally I suggested apologetically that she might care to walk-on in *Hamlet*, play a part (of one scene) in *Love for Love* as the Nurse, and understudy her adored Yvonne Arnaud in Maugham's *The Circle*, and she agreed immediately, glad to be relieved of the loneliness which coming to the theatre and mixing with the company would remove.

She must have been already ill that year, for at the dress rehearsal of *The Circle* in Edinburgh she suddenly rushed on to the stage, snatched the hat from Yvonne Arnaud's head, and cried out, 'I have no costumes provided for me in case I ever have to go on.' The matter was quickly seen to, and we opened the play in London, but after a few nights I was told that Annie had been suddenly taken ill, and she never appeared in the theatre again.

Some months after her death, I received a solicitor's letter telling me she had left me £5,000 in her will, the exact amount I needed to pay for the premium on a house I had just taken in Westminster, where I was to live for the next thirty years. There was an equal sum left to Edna May (the star of the famous Edwardian musical comedy about the Salvation Army), and a number of smaller bequests to various friends which were able to be increased, since her estate amounted to £15,000. Yet she had

lived alone for years in a single room. I never opened my front
door in Cowley Street without thinking of her touching generosity and her professional dedication to her work.

Plays and Players, 1984

Chapter 11

The Wigmaker

Willie Clarkson was a somewhat preposterous Dickensian figure, part Fagin, part Quilp, with a dash of Mr Mantalini. As he entered a theatre on a fashionable first night he would be greeted by a slight flutter of applause from the occupants of the pit and gallery, though their warmest outbursts were reserved for the theatrical celebrities of the day – the leading ladies and actor-managers – who timed their entrances so discreetly and turned towards the cheaper parts of the house to bow their acknowledgements as they took their seats.

Willie was short and plump. Beneath his black satin stock his chest protruded like a pouter pigeon's, decked in an elaborately frilled shirt with diamond studs over a brocaded waistcoat. His waist was tightly corseted and his stumpy bow legs ended in tiny feet encased in glossy high-heeled boots. He wore white kid gloves with black stitchings on the back of them and carried ivory opera glasses on a long gold handle. His red hair, curly moustaches, and full Edwardian beard, were dyed and crimped, his face patently rouged and powdered, and as he bustled in, waving his opera hat in all directions, he nodded and lisped greetings to the people sitting round him in the stalls.

I saw him again one night at the Chelsea Arts Ball, an annual jamboree held at the Albert Hall every New Year's Eve, where everyone wore fancy dress, and the night's revels usually ended in something of an orgy. Clarkson appeared leading the procession which paraded round the Hall just before midnight. He was dressed as a Sultan, with wide silk trousers tied with a huge sash, and curly-toed slippers. On his head was an enormous turban, in the front of which a tall aigrette was fastened by a gigantic property jewel. He was attended by a cortège of extremely unattractive ladies (probably assistants at his emporium in the daytime), clad in gauzy veils and yashmaks, and clattering with beads and bracelets. Willie marched round the Hall in front of the group, brandishing a long ebony stick with a cluster of false diamonds attached to the top of it, grinning and gesticulating like the Demon King.

I have no idea how old he must have been when I was first aware of him, but he was *the* theatrical wigmaker right up to the 1920s, when Madame Gustave, who soon after this time opened a rival wig shop in Covent Garden, began to surpass him with more modern merchandise and greater efficiency of workmanship, losing him a number of his former customers.

Clarkson was already famous right back in the Nineties, when Queen Victoria, after so many years of complete retirement, began in her old age to encourage private theatricals and tableaux vivants performed by her children and courtiers when she was at Windsor. She even commanded professional companies (Irving and Ellen Terry, the Kendals, the Bancrofts, and others), to mount miniature copies of their London successes and appear before her in the Waterloo Chamber at the Castle, thereby greatly increasing their professional reputations.

Russell Thorndike told me a fantastic (and I fear quite apocryphal) story of an afternoon when, as an apprentice choirboy to the Chapel at Windsor, he was told to go down to the station to meet Clarkson, who was due to arrive with his wigs, costumes, and make-up boxes to supervise one of the fashionable private performances. According to Russell, Willie was suddenly taken short as he puffed up the steep incline to the Castle. Fortunately Russell was able to direct him hastily to a small lavatory nearby and Clarkson dashed inside. At this very moment, a bathchair, with the Queen herself sitting in it, attended by the Munshi, her Indian servant, was seen descending the slope in the direction of the convenience. Russell hissed through the keyhole, 'The Queen is coming. It's the Queen.' On which a voice came lisping through the locked door. 'It'th all right, your Majesty. Only old Willie Clarkson thitting on his own inithials!'

There is another similar story told of him at Windsor. (Lavatory jokes were evidently popular at the turn of the century.) 'I was just going along a passage in the Castle,' Willie said, 'when who should I thpy but Her Majesty herself coming out of a thertain apartment!' 'What on earth did you do, Willie?' 'Oh, I jutht murmured, "Honi thoit qui mal y penthe, Your Majesty" and thwept on!'

Under Royal Patronage, of course, Willie's fame and fortune grew and prospered. He created wigs for Sarah Bernhardt, and even flew over to Paris in one of the early aeroplanes to attend one of her dress rehearsals. She opened his shop in Wardour Street (long since demolished and rebuilt) where the plaque she unveiled to celebrate the event could still be seen till quite recently on one of the pillars of the portico. As a student at Drama School, and for several years after I became a professional actor, I would go to the shop to hire wigs or buy grease-paints (sticks of Leichner were what we used in those days). Clarkson also sold the big oblong tinned japanned make-up boxes with flexible shelves and compartments which many actors then used in their dressing-rooms. When I went on tour for the first time, my parents gave me one as a present and of course I was immensely proud of it.

Clarkson's shop was rather spooky; poorly lit, with stained-glass windows on the steep stairs to the first floor, dusty and cluttered with suits of armour, weapons, play bills, masks – a positive Aladdin's Cave of theatrical paraphernalia, and the walls covered with signed photographs of Willie's most famous clients, presented to him with flattering dedications. Clarkson lurked in the recesses of the shop, but nearly always darted out when he heard the bell which rang as the front door was opened. He would sometimes proffer free theatre tickets, as well as a stream of snobbish reminiscence and encouragement, to young male customers, and we always took care to avoid getting too close to him, in case his hands should become unduly familiar or a visit to his private sanctum be proposed, though I never heard of him actually making a pass at anyone. The best one could hope for would be that youthful looks might be a passport to a rather better wig, since the stock ones usually provided for the hoi polloi were inclined to be shabby, much worn, and unattractive both in quality and in appearance.

Stage wigs in those days nearly always had forehead pieces of pink linen which had to be joined cunningly with grease paint to the make-up on the rest of one's face, a difficult and often unconvincing process, especially for young beginners. The foundation of the wig was thick and one sweated profusely in hot weather. In the last fifty years, of course, the whole art of wigmaking (like that of theatre and film make-up as well) has been completely modernised, and today wigs are very light and easy to wear as well as being completely convincing for the audience. But even as late as 1931, Noël Coward came to see *Musical Chairs*, a play in which Frank Vosper was playing my father. When the curtain rose on the second act I was dismayed to observe that he had disappeared. Meeting him a few weeks later, he apologised, remarking, as he wagged a reproving finger, 'Couldn't bear to stay. You were overacting so disgracefully, and Vosper's wig looked like a yachting-cap!'

Clarkson was reputed to be extremely disreputable and extremely rich. His star clients were attended by his head assistant, Mr Sussex, a gloomy-looking, elderly man with a huge Kitchener moustache and a long white apron, but we small fry were not considered of sufficient importance to be candidates for his ministrations.

Willie's end was sudden and dramatic. He became somewhat involved in a blackmail case. Then a fire broke out on his premises which no one seemed to be able to account for, and soon afterwards he was found dead in bed in his flat above the shop. I have no idea whether he left a fortune or whom he could have bequeathed it to if he did.

I have always thought what an effective central character he would make in some lurid thriller, for he was certainly an amusing old rip – a mysterious, highly coloured eccentric of the deepest dye.

Chapter 12

The Tea Ceremony and The Sitwells

I have always been astonished at the English passion for drinking tea, a beverage that I have never found essential to my own well-being. Yet almost everyone I know seems to demand it at regular intervals throughout the day, beginning with a cup brought to them by some willing hand, if possible, before they even rise from bed. There are compulsory tea-breaks in factories, rehearsal studios, building-sites and offices, yet I cannot but resent the ever-present recommendations of a 'cuppa' which greet me on hoardings and try to woo me in television commercials. I was once dismayed to find so fastidious a writer as the late Somerset Maugham, remarking (in his determination to be an adept observer of up-to-date colloquial slang) in one of his later novels that a character is 'not his cup of tea'.

However, I have to admit that in my own boyhood and adolescence, when tea was an established meal as well as merely something to drink, I looked forward to indulging in its more solid adjuncts with unmitigated greed. Nursery tea – strong and Indian, with rock cakes (buns and crumpets in wintertime), china and dainty sandwiches for the grown-ups. Teashop outings with my mother, at the Devonshire Dairies, opposite Selfridge's in Oxford Street, with clotted cream, scones, and raspberry jam. High teas on holidays in the country – shrimps, hard-boiled eggs, salad and cold meat. Rich teas at Gunter's – ices slightly flavoured with salt. Elaborate teas at Rumpelmayers, where one walked up the length of the room to a platform where an array of cakes were spread out on tables, and one stood choosing greedily, plate in one hand, fork in the other, and returned with a heap of richness piled up, nervously glancing to right and left and hoping the other customers were not taking too much notice. Even Maison Lyons in those days could proffer varied, though somewhat less patrician, confections – ice cream sodas, knickerbocker glories and banana splits. An actor friend of mine, lured there after a matinée by an adoring fan, was momentarily taken aback when she politely enquired: 'Do you prefer cake or gâteau?'

I don't think my parents ever drank tea at all themselves, though of course they provided it for guests, but my eldest brother, who was somewhat fastidious in his tastes, taught me to like very weak China tea with a slice of lemon, though I always felt somewhat shy at asking for it away from home. Badly wounded in the First War, he used to beg the orderlies in the hospital not to give him the strong Indian brew which everybody else appeared to relish, and they would stare at him in bewilderment and say, 'Don't you even like to taste the tea, sir?'

The Victorians and Edwardians, of course, considered afternoon tea an established fixture in their daily curriculum of gargantuan repasts, and their tables groaned with an elaborate paraphernalia of kettles, silver, cakestands, spirit-lamps, tea caddies, doilies, lace table-cloths and rich displays of food.

Two tea parties have always been among my cherished memories. I was playing Hamlet in 1944 at the beautiful Haymarket Theatre, where my dressing-room – where I sometimes fire-watched also – was on the top floor up a long flight of shallow stairs. (In winter there was even a coal fire in the grate, a privilege long since abandoned.) One evening an elderly lady climbed those stairs at the end of the performance. Her name was Mrs Carnegie, and she was certainly in her eighties. I immediately recognised her as the wife of Canon Carnegie, whom I had once seen, when I was still a boarder at Westminster School during the Great War, sitting with her family in the Norman undercroft in the Abbey cloisters. Her husband, magnificently tall and distinguished, was also part of the group, and they shared the shelter with other clerics and their families as well as some twenty of us schoolboys, all of whom were ordered to leave our dormitories in Dean's Yard and to take refuge there whenever the zeppelin raids occurred. We would occasionally dash into the cloisters to watch the searchlights and the flash of gunfire over the Abbey roofs, though, of course, such rashness was discouraged by the master in charge of us.

Now, so many years later, I ventured to remind my visitor of this episode as she congratulated me on my acting, and she promptly invited me to call on her for tea the following day. Her house in Egerton Crescent was elegant and beautifully kept. An elderly butler ushered me into a drawing-room full of presentation scrolls and caskets (I realised by this time that Mrs Carnegie had formerly been the wife of Joseph Chamberlain, the eminent Birmingham politician and father of Austen and Neville), and above the fireplace was a striking portrait of my hostess which appeared to be (and probably was) by Sargent. The only concessions to wartime conditions were evident in the white linen loose covers which shrouded the chairs and sofas.

A large tray was brought in, and Mrs Carnegie, talking busily all the while of her American grandchildren, whom she hopefully expected to spend the coming Christmas with her, proceeded to warm the cups with hot water, from the silver kettle, before mixing different blends of tea from silver caddies. There were hot scones under a covered dish, sandwiches and cakes. I sat entranced.

It so happened that I was rehearsing at the time a revival of Wilde's *Lady Windermere's Fan*, which I had been engaged to direct, and the scene in the first act, when the heroine has to play a flirtatious exchange at the tea-table with her would-be seducer, was proving very difficult to bring to life. I told the young actress playing Lady W. of my visit to Mrs Carnegie's, and begged her to introduce the detail I had observed with such fascination. But, alas, she refused to be fired by my enthusiasm. 'Oh no,' she cried. 'I could never manage it – all those bits and pieces to handle and manipulate as well as timing that complicated dialogue!' But I still hope to see the tea ceremony correctly reproduced on the stage in some Victorian or Edwardian revival.

My second tea party was to take place, many years later, when I was acting in New York. I had been given an introduction to Mrs Murray Crane, a wealthy elderly lady with a spacious and beautiful apartment on Fifth Avenue, and she too invited me to tea, when she entertained me with similar elaborate trappings — menservants, silver, covered dishes and exquisite china. Most of the male guests were officials from museums and galleries, and the occasion was crowned by the presence of two legendary ladies, Dame Edith Sitwell and Baroness Karen Blixen-Finecke.

I had first met Dame Edith at luncheon in London (at the house of Sibyl Colefax, the famous lion-hunter) and had been amused and surprised to find her so congenial, as she talked freely — and somewhat slyly — about her own taste in clothes and jewellery.

The Sitwells

It was during the early Twenties, when I was acting at Oxford, an earnest beginner and a member of J. B. Fagan's Repertory Company at the Playhouse (which included Flora Robson and Tyrone Guthrie among its members), that I had first become aware of Edith Sitwell.

I had recently made the acquaintance of a number of undergraduates of my own age who were then making their mark in the aesthetic circles of the University. Among them were Evelyn Waugh, Robert Byron, the notoriously decadent Brian Howard, and Harold Acton, who is exactly the same age as I am. The latter always delighted me by his meticulous pronunciation and elegant deportment. He would usually carry a walking-stick, and would bow courteously as we passed each other in the street. It was he who described to me a recent visit of the poetess Edith Sitwell to lunch with him in his rooms, where an intimate circle of his friends had gathered to receive her, and who rose politely as she appeared in the doorway, looking, he said, like Edward the

Second in the last act of Marlowe's play, with her long green gown splashed and muddied from the puddles in the Quad, while Harold, advancing with outstretched hands murmured, 'Ah, dear Edith, welcome to our unhappy Gothic midst.'

In those far-off days I was sublimely ignorant of the many-sided talents of the Sitwell family. Not long afterwards, sitting in the pit of the Duke of York's Theatre, I laughed uproariously at one of the most successful items in Noël Coward's first revue *London Calling*. Coward had written all the songs and scenes himself, and he acted, sang and danced as well. (He had been coached by the great Fred Astaire, and was partnered by the brilliant Gertrude Lawrence.) I was greatly impressed by his all round versatility, little thinking that a year or two later I should have the luck to understudy him in his first big dramatic success *The Vortex*.

In the skit which was a feature of the revue, two brothers, Gob and Knob, performed on weirdly sounding musical instruments, dressed in velvet jackets and check trousers, accompanying their sister Hernia Whittlebot (in the person of the splendid matronly comedienne Maisie Gay) as she spouted a series of preposterous verses, swathed in purple draperies, with a wreath of grapes and vine leaves tipped roguishly over one eye.

I was not aware until long afterwards how deeply the Sitwells had resented this unmannerly caricature of their recent controversial recital of *Façade*. Indeed, it was not until Coward wrote a letter to Edith Sitwell not long before her death that a reconciliation was achieved, followed by a tea party at her flat during which they gracefully agreed to bury the hatchet.

In my extreme youth I had the pleasure of meeting Osbert and Sacheverell at a supper party in a studio near Bond Street, and was dazzled by the brilliant conversational power and generosity which they extended to me, a complete stranger. I remember thinking, when I returned home that night, that the talk of Wilde and Alfred Douglas, Robert Ross, and Reggie Turner, must have had that kind of sparkle and repartee, and I regret that I never wrote any of it down to remind me of the subjects that were discussed during that evening, which I have always remembered with delight. How rare it is to sit at a table with really witty and generous guests, who can shine so spontaneously and rivet one's interest without making one feel totally inadequate oneself.

All three Sitwells, if they happened to like you (but of course they could be very cantankerous if they didn't!) always struck me as superb conversationalists. The Russian painter, Pavel Tchelitchew (a great friend of Edith Sitwell's, with whom he enjoyed a long and stormy friendship and who I met in New York long afterwards in 1936) had also an amazing descriptive talent as a talker, and I remember an afternoon in his studio when he not only described in detail his mother's wedding dress, but also a performance which he had attended in his youth, at the Opera in St Petersburg, when the prima ballerina, smothered in real jewellery, danced on point on the sloping deck of a sinking ship.

But it was not until, just before the Second World War, that I sat next to Edith Sitwell at one of Lady Colefax's fascinating lunch parties in Lord North Street, and was amazed to find her so human and agreeable. She even made fun of the immense rings and necklaces she was wearing that day, and immediately charmed me with her beautiful manners. Some years later she dedicated a poem to me, sending me the original in her own handwriting – a highly surrealist piece which I could not pretend to understand, much as I appreciated the implied compliment.

As I began to meet her more often, she would sometimes write me amusingly characteristic letters about plays in which she had seen me act, and in 1955, when I was playing King Lear in a very abstract and avant-garde production, she came round to my dressing-room after the performance and discussed the play with me at some length. Once or twice she invited me to luncheons at the Sesame Club in Brook Street, where I sat amongst poets and literary lions whom she delighted to entertain there from time to time.

The lady members at the other tables would sink into hushed silence as we trooped in behind our hostess, splendidly gowned and turbanned, with huge aquamarines displayed on her beautiful hands. At the end of one of these occasions we were ushered upstairs to listen to Mrs Gordon Woodhouse playing Bach and Couperin on her clavichord, though only those close enough to the instrument could hear the tinkling music properly against the competition of the traffic roaring past outside.

One year when I was acting in New York, I called on Dame Edith at the St Regis Hotel. She and her brother Osbert were engaged on one of their poetry-reading tours, and were being duly lionised by New York literary society. Edith seemed to me touchingly out of place in the conventional grandeur of her hotel suite, and I found her struggling with a very dull lady visitor (perhaps a distant relation or merely an ardent fan) and admired her patience as she sat bolt upright, tolerating her guest, who kept up a flow of flattering platitudes punctuated by embarrassed pauses. She seemed very pleased to be interrupted by my arrival, and invited me to a preview of a reading of *Macbeth*, which had been arranged to be given in her honour at the Museum of Modern Art at eleven thirty a few mornings later.

This was a very strange, and not very happy, occasion, though it had its amusing side, though less so perhaps to its participants.

The cinema hall in the basement of the museum had been arranged for the recital, with two imposing desks on the raised platform. Edith made a most impressive entrance through the auditorium and received a great ovation from the fashionable audience. She wore a turban and a huge enveloping robe of figured brocade, looking like a spinster Pope as she took up her position in sole possession of one of the desks. Several feet away she was flanked by Glenway Westcott, who was to read the part of Macbeth, and wore a dinner jacket, with a discreet gold neck chain peeping beneath the collar of his frilled shirt – and the third member of the company (who shared his desk), was a fluffy-looking lady in evening dress with flowing skirts, who was to read the part of Lady Macbeth's Gentlewoman and any other odd lines required to give necessary cues to the two principal performers. The reading started very shakily. Edith muddled her pages and fumbled with her spectacles before announcing in ringing tones: 'Act three, scene two – *No*, Act *two*, scene *one*.' Her reading of the verse was sensitive and meticulous, but curiously lacking in dramatic power, and the whole performance seemed to me sadly incongruous and ill-advised.

At the celebration of her seventy-fifth birthday there was a great gathering at the Festival Hall. Edith was brought on to the stage, now sadly enthroned in a wheel chair, wearing a golden gown and a round golden hat, worn like a halo high above her noble forehead. She raised her arms in a wild kind of Papal blessing in acknowledgement of the applause that greeted her appearance, but the microphone attached to the front of her dress slipped out of place almost as soon as she began to speak, and little of her reading was audible in the big auditorium. After the performance, in which *Façade* was read by Sebastian Shaw and Irene Worth, and pieces by William Walton played by the orchestra, she proceeded to give a huge dinner party in the restaurant upstairs.

I had hoped to be able to slip away, but finding I had been allotted a place at Edith's own table, did not like to seem discourteous, and found myself sitting next to Edith's nurse, who delighted me by telling me what a splendid and courageous patient she had the privilege of tending.

After her death, when Osbert began to suffer from his long and protracted struggle against Parkinson's Disease, he remained gallant and determined as ever. I used to have my hair cut at Trumpers in Curzon Street in those days, and Osbert would always greet me and his barber and chat to us both with the greatest liveliness and good humour, though he could hardly walk and trembled violently all the time he was being shaved. He even invited me to supper one evening at Carlyle Square, and insisted on getting up from the table several times to pour wine and serve the food with infinite tact and care.

My final memory of him was at Brighton, just before he was to leave England for the last time. We were both staying at the Metropole Hotel, and every morning he would sit in his wheel chair in the hall, beautifully shaved and tidy. Twice he asked me to have lunch with him, but these were agonising occasions, as he could not help spilling his food, and his voice would suddenly fail him soon after he had begun an anecdote, making it very difficult to know how to answer.

I was acting at the Theatre Royal, Brighton in Chekhov's *Ivanov* and Osbert's male nurse told me one day that he would like to come to a performance. Of course I arranged aisle seats at the end of the row, to enable him to manipulate his chair, and at the end of the play I received a message asking me to go to speak to them in the stalls. As I came into the empty auditorium, there they were, he and his male nurse, sitting waiting for me, both dressed in dinner jackets, a superb touch of courtesy which moved me very much – 'The Grand Manner' as my father used to say.

Chapter 13

Lady Bountiful

I could hardly fail to notice her as she sat, several times a week, in the middle of the front row of the stalls at the New Theatre where I was acting in *Richard of Bordeaux*. Sometimes she came alone, sometimes with parties of friends, always elegantly dressed in black lace or white satin. Soon I began to receive charming notes of appreciation which I would answer in suitably polite acknowledgment, and finally I invited her to visit me in my dressing-room.

She was then I suppose in her late sixties, imposing, dignified and motherly, with a charming pussycat smile and a golden plait binding her white hair like a tiara, and her head was apt to shake a little as she talked with great enthusiasm and vitality.

Lavish presents began to arrive at my flat several times a week – fruit, flowers and books in expensive bindings. Soon she invited me to lunch at her beautiful house in Charles Street, where the banisters were curved outwards to allow easy passage to hooped skirts and crinolines, and there were menservants and elaborate meals beautifully served. She told me she had once lived in Berkeley Square, and had given a cotillion party for the then Prince of Wales, for which she had arranged that two flower shops should remain open all night to provide fresh bouquets and buttonholes for the guests. She was incorrigibly generous. Once she took me to Partridge's in Bond Street and walked me through all the departments, asking me to choose anything I liked. Of course I blushingly refused, but she insisted on sending me a huge parcel of glass and china to help furnish a cottage which I had just taken in the country, and she would encourage me to bring my friends so that she might entertain them as well as myself when I came to her house. Taking a great fancy to one of them who was knowledgeable about the Turf (she had been a great huntress in her youth), she proceeded to present him with a horse.

Our friendship prospered for several years. She had a fine Lutyens house near Hastings, to which she would invite me for weekends, with glasshouses, rhododendrons and a water garden. Her Rolls, driven by an elderly and trusted chauffeur, would be waiting at the stage-door, and she would greet me, in jewels and evening dress, on the doorstep at one o'clock in the morning, with a hot supper waiting to be served as soon as I arrived.

She told me she had been married to the 'richest commoner in England' but I gathered she had not been greatly fond of him, and she hinted at a passionate love-affair with one of her grooms, whose subsequent death had shattered her. She also had several daughters to whom she referred with considerable disapproval, but I never met any of her family.

She was extremely good company, suddenly surprising one with frank and unexpected remarks delivered without a hint of malice. 'He powders his face. I fear he will have to go,' she murmured to me one day as the butler was busy at the other end of the table. On another occasion, when a young priest was one of the guests she announced to the assembled party, 'Father B. is a saint. He has started a Home for Unwanted Boys. Imagine anyone not wanting a boy.' And once I heard her remark, as one of my actress friends was out of hearing, 'Ah, I fear it is evident that C. aime les femmes.'

She took me several times to Glyndebourne, then in the great inaugural days of John Christie, Busch and Ebert, and during the interval we walked across the garden to a field close by, where a sumptuous supper was laid out, specially sent over from her house in a horse-box, with flowers, silver and a lace tablecloth, upright chairs, and a footman to wait on us.

About this time, however, her interest began to seem some-

John Gielgud as a boy

Ellen Terry as Queen Katharine and Edith Craig as her lady-in-waiting in *Henry VIII* at the Lyceum Theatre, 1892

Below left: Fred Terry

Below right: Marion Terry with A.E. Matthews in *Peter's Mother* at Wyndham's Theatre, 1906

John Gielgud and Mabel Terry-Lewis in *The Importance of Being Earnest* at The Lyric, Hammersmith, 1929

Edward Gordon Craig, 1956

This page

Left: Lilian Braithwaite and Gerald du Maurier in *Nobody's Daughter*

Below: Madge Titheradge A Doll's House, November 1925

Opposite page

Top left: Lady Tree, 1935

Top right: Mrs Patrick Campbell, 1913

Bottom: Viola Tree, C.B. Cochran, Sacha Guitry and Yvonne Printemps

Above: Cedric Hardwicke and Gwen Ffangcon-Davies in *The Barretts of Wimpole Street* at the Queen's Theatre, 1930. *Above right:* Charles Hawtrey in *Ambrose Applejohn's Adventure* at the Criterion Theatre, 1921.

Below left: Nöel Coward and Gertrude Lawrence in *Private Lives* at the Phoenix Theatre, 1930. *Below right:* Vivien Leigh

n Barrymore as Hamlet, Theatre Royal, Haymarket, 1925

ow left: Esmé Percy *and below right:* Edith Sitwell, 1928

Above: Ada King in *The Queen Was in The Parlour* at St. Martin's Theatre, 1926

Above right: Haidée Wright and Robert Loraine in *The Father* at the Everyman, Hampstead, 1927

Below: Hugh Sinclair and Elizabeth Bergner in *Escape Me Never*

what less concentrated where I was concerned, for she had been greatly attracted to a young Indian just down from Oxford, and I was somewhat dismayed when, during one of the opera performances at Glyndebourne, she slipped a flask of perfume into my hand, whispering that I should pass it to him to sprinkle on his hands. He had aspired to become a ballet dancer, but it soon appeared that he was not strong enough to lift his partners and was forced to abandon his ambitions in that direction. He was certainly strikingly good-looking, and changed his suits and jewellery several times a day, but I was not greatly sorry when his reign appeared to be over and I was restored to the best bedroom, from which I had been temporarily superseded, when I went to stay.

In 1936, when I went to New York to play Hamlet, my benefactress soon followed me in order to be present at my first night. She stayed at the Plaza Hotel, accompanied by a maid who sat with the chauffeur as she drove about the city, shopping and visiting museums and galleries and investigating religious groups. When the great night arrived, she appeared in the foyer, splendidly arrayed, some minutes before the rise of the curtain, and was immediately interviewed and photographed by reporters who were convinced she was my mother. On my return from America she insisted on giving a big dinner party in my honour, to which she invited my parents and a dozen of my best friends.

When war broke out in 1939, she was still going strong. Of course I never knew her real age, but she had joined the WRNS as an officer, and very fine and dignified she looked as she greeted me at the door in her uniform and tricorne hat worn with a martial air. I do not remember seeing her again after that day, for she died while I was abroad, and the short obituary that was afterwards forwarded to me gave little information about her early life. Her houses were both sold soon afterwards, the Sussex house dismantled and the gardens and grounds hacked up for a building development, which would have made her very sad. I still possess a number of charming presents that she gave me at various times. Several of my most elegant books are dedicated in

her characteristic manner, and the sight of her strong handwriting always reminds me vividly of her energy and charm, her
endless generosity, the way she accepted so many of my friends,
never dreaming of interfering, influencing or intruding in any
way. She was known in her heyday as 'the fascinating Mrs – and
that is how I shall always think of her.

Chapter 14

Queen Mary

The Royal Family, with the notable exceptions of Queen Elizabeth the Queen Mother, and the late Queen Mary, have not been very enthusiastic playgoers during the last fifty years, though Queen Victoria loved the theatre in her youth, and as an elderly lady commanded quite a number of plays to be performed for her at Windsor, when the Waterloo Chamber was temporarily transformed, and the Court sat deferentially anxious, waiting to see whether her Majesty was amused or moved. The actor-managers, Irving, Hare and others, had simplified scenery specially made for these occasions and closed their London theatres for the night in order to comply with the Royal Command.

Edward VII was mostly fond of comedies, and basked in the lighter aspect of the Paris theatres, where he was often to be found both in the auditorium and behind the scenes (he is even said to have once appeared as the dying husband in the first act of Bernhardt's *Fedora*, where the character lies in a bed at the back of the stage), but Queen Alexandra was very deaf and preferred opera to the straight theatre. She herself had been an enthusiastic amateur pianist, and I once met an old lady in Washington who told me she used sometimes to be invited to stay at Sandringham in order to play duets with her while King Edward was out shooting.

But Shakespeare and the Classics have always, I fancy, been somewhat of a strain upon Royal endurance. (The Duke of Windsor once asked me about the plays of T. S. Eliot. 'Were they not in verse?' he wanted to know. I replied somewhat nervously that I believed Eliot himself referred to them as 'staggered verse'. 'Ah, yes,' he said, 'of course a lot of Shakespeare's in verse, too.') Queen Mary had been an ardent playgoer in her young days, and sometimes attended Henry Irving's Beefsteak supper parties after visits to his Lyceum productions with her mother, the Duchess of Teck. Later, when she became Queen, she was obliged to be seen at a few serious plays, as well as greatly enjoying light comedies and even thrillers. In her last years she went a great deal to the theatre, and her approval of a piece called *Pick-up Girl*, which she visited on more than one occasion, brought headlines in the press and a corresponding reaction at the box-office.

King George V, like his mother, was deaf, and was said to enjoy his playgoing chatting about racing with Sir Edward Elgar at the back of the box. Arriving for a charity matinée of *Hamlet* at the Haymarket Theatre one afternoon, Queen Mary asked the head of the Reception Committee what time the performance would be over. 'You see,' she said, 'the King always has to have his tea punctually, and he is so anxious not to miss seeing the girl with the straws in her hair.'

King George did not accompany the Queen when she went to the Old Vic one evening, and Lilian Baylis, standing beside her in the box as the sad little orchestra squeaked through the National Anthem, was heard to remark comfortingly, 'You see, madam, we always play your husband's little tune.'

Queen Mary had a wonderful presence, and the audience (as well as the players, if they dared) delighted to watch her, as she sat with her opera-glasses raised steadily in a white gloved hand, during the whole performance. I was lucky enough to be presented to her several times when she came to see plays that I was acting in, and I have a vivid picture of her in the retiring-room at the Globe Theatre, when several of us had been sent for after the first act of *The Importance of Being Earnest*, just before the war. The Queen, half a head shorter than Edith Evans, looked almost like her on a small scale, and when Edith curtseyed one felt she should really have curtseyed back.

When she came one evening to Chekhov's *The Three Sisters* at the Queen's Theatre, a year or two earlier, we all wondered what she would make of the Russian gloom. I was to be presented after the second act, and sent word asking if I might bring my four leading ladies with me. Of course the answer came back 'yes', but I went up to the retiring-room alone while the ladies changed. Queen Mary came out from the box and I gasped in admiration at her appearance. She wore a glittering dress of black paillettes, and a magnificent set of aquamarines with matching earrings, necklace, and bracelets. Perhaps a tiara, too, but I am not sure of this. I know I longed to touch her to see if she was real. She was exceedingly shy and I fancy she spoke with a faint German accent. At any rate her voice was gruff and rather brusque. The ladies arrived and we made desultory conversation, mostly about their stage costumes, for five minutes or so. The Queen then said she felt sure we must get back for the next act, and there was some confusion as we all tried to back out of the retiring-room together through a very small door. One of the ladies, Carol Goodner, an American, who was particularly nervous and excited, backed through the wrong door to the Royal lavatory and had to be extricated before she could beat a hasty retreat. Then, as I was leaving with a bow, the Queen remarked with an enchanting smile, 'Well, I suppose it all ends very badly.' Not a bad summing-up of Chekhov after only two acts.

During the war years when she stayed at Badminton, Queen Mary was fond of giving lifts in her car to soldiers she met on the road, which, naturally, endeared her to the whole neighbourhood, and she often asked actors who came to play at the camps to give performances for her and her entourage at Badminton House. She even came to some of the troop shows and sat amongst the men in a big armchair.

My favourite story of her may or may not be apocryphal. Walking one day in the garden at Buckingham Palace, King George enquired why his usual equerry was not in attendance. He was told that the man was ill and the King asked what was the matter. 'Oh, the universal complaint, sir,' was the evasive reply. Next day Queen Mary remarked to someone, 'I hear the King's equerry is ill. What is the matter with him?' 'A severe attack of haemorrhoids, I'm afraid, ma'am.' 'Oh!' said the Queen, 'why did the King tell me it was the clap?'

My last memory of her was in 1951, when she came to a matinée of *The Winter's Tale* at the Phoenix Theatre. Diana Wynyard, Flora Robson, Lewis Casson and I were presented during the first interval when just after Leontes accuses Hermione of adultery she swoons and appears to be dead. The Queen seemed very interested in the play. She shook Lewis Casson warmly by the hand. 'Of course, I've often seen you before.' Then turning to Diana Wynyard, 'You wrote me a very nice letter when the King died. I hope you got my answer.' And finally to me. 'Well, it's extremely well done, your part, but extremely unpleasant, of course.'

Chapter 15

New York

I have always loved cities – first London, where I was born and lived for seventy years, then Oxford, New York, and Venice, in that order. I had always longed to work in America, and it has never disappointed me, from the first time I went there, so long ago, in 1928, to act in a play which only ran a week.

Luckily, however, before I went back home (since I could not, at that time, afford to stay) I saw something of the Broadway theatre, flourishing and lively as it was in those days – Helen Hayes in *Coquette*, Judith Anderson in *Behold the Bridegroom*, and, standing at the back of the orchestra in the new Ziegfeld Theatre among a packed matinée audience, I watched with rapture the original production of *Show Boat*, with Norma Terris, Howard Marsh, Charles Winninger, Jules Bledsoe, Edna May Oliver, and, best of all, Helen Morgan as Julie singing 'Bill' on the top of a piano with a long chiffon handkerchief dangling from her wrist. Mabel Mercer was at Tony's in 52nd Street and there were speakeasies, the Cotton Club, evenings in Harlem, the dining room at the Hotel Algonquin packed with celebrities, and unexpected meetings with English players I knew who were acting in New York. No wonder I have always vividly remembered that first short visit with wonder and delight. Today, after living there very often over many years, I am still stimulated by the unpredictable, electric liveliness of the city, despite the extremes of heat and cold, cramped taxis and sweltering buses, the squalor of the subways, the steam-heating and air conditioning, the friendliness and politeness (as well as the occasional rudeness), the foreignness mixed with familiarity. I love the brilliant quality of the New York lights, from twinkling towers as they begin to glitter on Central Park South round six o'clock on a winter evening – and the strip of sky which one can always see in four directions even from the deep canyons of the avenues. The vista of Fifth Avenue from St Patrick's Cathedral to the Plaza Hotel is, to me, one of the finest sights in the world, with an elegance that our own Bond Street used once to have but has now lost forever, smothered as it is today by so many cheap new shops and unimaginative modern buildings.

American theatres dismayed me at first with their extreme width of auditorium and shallow stages – no bars or proper lounges (save for those cavernous overheated cellars, with queues lining up for the telephone in the intermissions) and the disagreeable men who tear up one's tickets as one passes through the doors in the narrow entrance halls. Yet the sense of expectation in an American audience – especially at matinées when the women predominate, screaming and waving greetings to one another across the aisles, and wildly applauding every entrance and exit, song or dance – is wonderfully infectious and finally rewarding, both for actors and spectators alike, and infinitely preferable to the scene in London, where trays of tea are shuffled in and out over people's heads, and the elderly ladies sit munching with dogged indifference, often slumbering and even snoring as the afternoon wears on.

I have, alas, no memories of seeing the great actors and actresses of America as I have of so many in England, though Guthrie McClintic used to entertain me with wonderful stories of Mrs Fiske and Emily Stevens, Nazimova and Laurette Taylor, all alas before my time.

Pauline Lord, John Barrymore, Jane Cowl, Leslie Howard

I happened to be present on the first night of a new play *Salvation* by Sidney Howard at the Empire Theatre in New York. I remember little of the play save a splendid performance by

Osgood Perkins father of the film star Anthony Perkins as a newspaperman, and the strange broken syllables and emotional power of Pauline Lord, who played the leading part.

I had seen her once before at the Strand Theatre in London (also, oddly enough, on the opening night) when she played O'Neill's *Anna Christie* and took the town by storm. But when Greta Garbo made her huge success in the film version of the play, Pauline Lord's wonderful acting was soon forgotten, though not by me. Years later, I was leaving the Plaza Hotel in New York by a side door one afternoon, when I recognised Miss Lord, sitting in an armchair in the passageway, looking extremely sad and lonely. I ventured to introduce myself, and her face lit up with pleasure when I reminded her of her triumph in London. But she told me she had lost heart for the theatre, and had just returned from playing Amanda (the mother) in a tour of Tennessee Williams's *The Glass Menagerie*, which I imagine she must have acted brilliantly, though eclipsed, I suppose, as far as New York was concerned at any rate, by comparison with the great Laurette Taylor who created the part on Broadway, an actress whom, alas, I never saw. Pauline Lord's pathos was extraordinary, individual and evocative, and I often think of her strange beauty on the stage.

I greatly admired John Barrymore as Hamlet when I saw him in London in 1926, and once heard him speak at a Sunday Dinner Club, but I never met him, though he sent me a page-long telegram when I was honoured ten years later at a dinner in New York by the Players Club. His famous sister Ethel I met several times at George Cukor's house in Beverly Hills in her last years, but I never saw her act except on the screen.

Jane Cowl I met in London, and saw her when she played Noël Coward's *Easy Virtue* there in 1926. Miss Cowl was most effective in the Coward play, and adapted her acting style to great advantage in modern plays after successes in New York both as Juliet and Cleopatra. She was also very dramatic in private life. She fainted one night when she was in the audience watching John Barrymore in Galsworthy's *Justice*. A few weeks later someone told Barrymore 'Jane Cowl is in front again.' 'Is she?' Barrymore remarked airily. 'I do hope she'll give a good performance.'

While she was in England, Miss Cowl wrote a play under the pen name C. R. Avery entitled *Hervey House*. It was presented at His Majesty's Theatre in May 1935, with an all-star cast headed by Fay Compton and Gertrude Lawrence. (I was nearly in the play myself in the role eventually played by Nicholas Hannen.) Margaret Rutherford made one of her first successes in a supporting part, as did Alan Webb, but *Hervey House* did not achieve a long run although it was brilliantly directed by Tyrone Guthrie. During the weeks they were awaiting rehearsals, Fay Compton and Gertrude Lawrence made a tour of Devonshire riding bicycles, while a Rolls-Royce followed them distantly in case they became tired.

The year 1936 when I played Hamlet at the Empire Theatre in New York for Guthrie McClintic (with Lillian Gish, Judith Anderson, and Arthur Byron) was, of course, one of the most exciting of my life, though I was placed in a somewhat embarrassing position when Leslie Howard appeared during the same season in his own production and with a number of English players in his cast. (Malcolm Keen and Harry Andrews who played the King and Horatio respectively were the only English actors in mine.)

Howard had announced that he had decided not to put on the play before I had agreed to come over in the spring of that year, but later changed his mind, and I was upset at having to compete with a fellow countryman whom I did not know but greatly admired, and who was also an internationally popular film star. The reviews for my performance were encouraging but not wholly enthusiastic, and I was expecting a run of not more than a few weeks. When Howard opened, however, a few weeks later, and was poorly received, our performances began to sell out almost immediately. The press tried to persuade us to meet and give interviews about one another, but we stuck to our own guns and behaved with as much dignity as possible. Still, the Battle of the Hamlets was quite a popular topic in the city for several months. Beatrice Lillie played in a sketch about us in a revue, and even the taxi drivers used to ask which of the Hamlets I was when I directed them to the stage door of the Empire. The abdication of the Duke of Windsor, which happened at the same time, helped to fascinate the New York public with England and Royalty, everyone arguing and taking sides.

I have been lucky enough, through my work in the theatre, to meet four American Presidents. Lillian Gish took me to see President and Mrs Roosevelt at the White House, and I met Truman, Johnson, and Kennedy on different occasions when they came to see plays that I was appearing in. During the *Hamlet* run I did not keep a diary, and find it hard to remember the many fascinating and illustrious visitors who were kind enough to come round to see me.

But two amusing incidents have always remained with me. One night, when I was very tired at the end of two performances, Maria Ouspenskaya, an elderly Russian actress, was announced. I had greatly admired her in films, particularly *Dodsworth* and *The Rains Came*, and she had recently been acting in the theatre in New York in a Greek tragedy, though I had not been fortunate enough to see it. She came into the dressing-room, a formidable and striking personality with a long cigarette holder in her hand, looking very distinguished and escorted by an elegant young man who leaned gracefully against the wall behind her. 'Oh, Madame Ouspenskaya,' I burst out, gathering my dressing gown about me and wondering if I ought to kiss her hand, 'I am so sorry to think you were in front tonight. I was dreadfully tired and I know I played so badly!' On which Madame nodded her head twice in profound approval, turned around, and left the room without a word.

On another evening, Judith Anderson brought in a friend of hers to see me, a Swedish Countess beautifully bejewelled and dressed. She seemed greatly moved by the performance and, as she was leaving, murmured, 'I would like to give you something in remembrance of this great experience,' and, putting out her hand, began to take off a most beautiful square cut emerald ring that she was wearing. I nervously began to put out my own hand, but, just as I did so, she hastily drew her ring back on to her finger and made a graceful exit. I thought I must have imagined the whole episode, but Judith Anderson assured me afterwards that it was perfectly true.

The generosity of the leading players in America has always charmed me. When I opened in *Hamlet* I received telegrams of good wishes from a number of stars whom I had never even met, and on the last night, Helen Hayes, who was playing *Victoria Regina* so brilliantly at the Broadhurst Theatre just opposite, sent over a tray, with a bottle of champagne and glasses, saying how sorry she was that I was leaving this neighbourhood. I have the happiest memories of the Players Club, the courtesy of its late presidents, Walter Hampden, Howard Lindsay, and Dennis King, and the dinners given there for me, and on other occasions for Alfred Lunt and Lynn Fontanne, and for Howard Lindsay just before his death. I was given a degree a few years ago at Brandeis University in Massachusetts and made a freeman of the City of Philadelphia, and I need hardly say that I have always found America, and Hollywood too – on the few occasions I have worked there – to be immensely kind and encouraging. I shall always look on that country as my second home, where I have made so many delightful friends among my fellow players and the audiences for whom I have played.

Chapter 16

Promenade

In July 1919 I was still a schoolboy of fifteen, a dayboy at Westminster, living at home with my parents, but proud possessor of my first latchkey. Already irredeemably stagestruck, I was bent on designing scenery and costumes for the stage, torn between admiration for the drawings of my cousin, Gordon Craig, and the romantic and more conventional staging of *Chu Chin Chow*, the oriental musical pantomime which reflected the illustrations of Edmund Dulac and Kay Nielsen that I had so loved as a boy, and which I had even tried to copy in my own amateurish way. I had bought several volumes of Aubrey Beardsley drawings too (which I found wildly exciting as well as somewhat decadent and improper) and had become an eager admirer of Compton MacKenzie's *Sinister Street*, with its nostalgic picture of pre-war Oxford and later excursions into Bohemian London, especially as I had caught one of the masters at my prep-school reading the novel surreptitiously, hidden discreetly beneath a brown paper cover. In short, I was longing to experience every kind of adolescent discovery, especially with regard to the theatre, though I had yet no desire or thought of becoming an actor myself.

I was a great walker in those days, finding my way all over London – Lincoln's Inn, Chelsea, Chiswick, Kew Gardens and Hampton Court among many favourite excursions – but my Mecca was the West End and the triangle of streets radiating from Piccadilly Circus, where so many theatres stood. Were those old women in straw hats and shawls still sitting round the

base of Eros selling flowers, in those last years of the Great War?
I well remember seeing them there, but perhaps it was at an
earlier period in my boyhood.

How I used to love jumping on to the top of a number 14 bus
near our house in South Kensington and jumping off again at the
top of Piccadilly. On the way we passed Devonshire House, then
an imposing edifice behind its elaborate gates, and Solomon's the
grand fruit shop next to the Berkeley Hotel, its windows
crammed with peaches, pineapples and muscat grapes. Once
arrived at the Circus I would begin my favourite round. I would
glance up the curve of Regent Street for a glimpse of the portico
of the Café Royal, where I had once been taken by my brother
when he was on leave during the war. Here I had gaped at
Augustus John, in a black sombrero and gold earrings, sitting
with his cronies among the marble-topped tables and gilded
caryatids, and there was a kiosk with all the foreign newspapers
on the ramp which led from the street up to the brasserie,
where, hanging on the walls, the letter 'N' (for Nicole) was
surrounded by gilt laurel leaves. 'What does "N" stand for?' I
asked my brother. 'Nature,' he replied, and led me to the Men's
room.

I would walk up Shaftesbury Avenue, skirting on my left the
narrow streets of Soho (where I had occasionally ventured, to
show off my growing independence by ordering a delicious lunch
for seven and sixpence in an atmosphere mysteriously foreign)
but ignoring, to the right-hand side, the temptations of Gerrard
Street and Lisle Street, where the tarts lingered provocatively all
day long, as well as at night, attempting to inveigle every man
who passed. At Cambridge Circus I would turn to the right down
Charing Cross Road, with its seedy but fascinating secondhand
bookshops, and stroll down St Martin's Lane as far as Trafalgar
Square. Back again up the Haymarket, and then through Panton
Street to Leicester Square. These walks round theatreland (still
rather prim and dignified in those days) allowed me to examine
minutely all the photographs and bills outside the playhouses,
while I tried to decide which seemed the most likely to

encourage me to invest my pocket-money and to savour the never-ending delight of standing in a queue for several hours waiting for the pit and gallery doors to open.

There were four theatres in those days in Leicester Square. Daly's (replaced today by the Warner Brothers' Cinema) stood close by the Hippodrome. A few doors off was the Empire, then a famous Music Hall, whose notorious promenade was closed to ladies during the 1914 war, expelling the throng of pretty ladies, who plied their trade there into outer darkness and the rainy streets.

In the middle of the square stood the statue of Shakespeare, improbably surveying his somewhat raffish surroundings. The statue still remains today, flanked by a few trees, some ill-kept grass, and two prominent public lavatories. But where the Odeon Cinema now rears its majestic front, on one side of the Square, was the old Alhambra Theatre, a pseudo-Moorish edifice crowned by twin domes with gilded crescent moons decorating their tops.

The theatre had mostly housed revues during the First War, its most successful productions being *The Bing Boys are Here* and *The Bing Boys on Broadway*, both of which starred a famous team of comedians, George Robey, Alfred Lester and Violet Loraine. The great song hit, *If You Were the Only Girl in the World*, sung by Robey and Miss Loraine in the first revue, was soon to be sung and whistled all over the world. Inside, the building was crammed with arches, mosaics, and tiled walls, and there was a big circular promenade at the back of the stalls, similar to the one at the Empire, from which women had been excluded after considerable publicity and fuss. Here the admission price was five shillings. You could lean on the cushioned edge which ran all round the back of the seats and there were banquettes against the wall behind you and big glass doors through which people slipped into the great bar.

I had been once to *The Bing Boys on Broadway* at a matinée, sitting grandly with my family in a box near the stage, but the Promenade was quite a new point of vantage, and it was to the

Promenade that my father decided to take me, on that memorable summer evening in 1919, to see the Diaghilev Russian Ballet Company for the first time.

I always regretted bitterly that I was too young to have seen the legendary genius, Nijinsky, who had left Diaghilev just before the war, but I had seen Anna Pavlova on one or two occasions, and had been ravished by her brilliant personality, though unimpressed by her material, which seemed, even to my young eyes, somewhat conventional and unimaginative, and by her supporting company, which I felt to be somewhat second-rate. What I was to see tonight was something very different. The programme consisted of three halfhour ballets – *Carnaval, La Boutique Fantasque* and *Prince Igor*, wonderfully contrasted in style and content, each one more thrilling than the other. Karsavina had returned to the Company, but was now only playing second parts. Leonide Massine was the new principal male dancer and choreographer, and Tchernicheva and Lopokova, two of the leading ballerinas, were to vie for my affections for many years to come.

I had no knowledge of the technique of ballet dancing, and to this day I am no judge of the fine points which are so dear to critics and true balletomanes alike. But the entrancing mixture of music, mime and spectacle enraptured me immediately, though at first I was somewhat puzzled by the décor – by Bakst for *Carnaval*, Derain for the *Boutique*, Roerich for *Igor*. The last was more immediately appealing – a line of low tents under a lowering smoky sky. But *Carnaval* was set in high flats of bluish-green wallpaper with a pattern of huge flowers, almost like cabbages, sprawling over it, and towards the back of the set two small blue sofas, in the Biedemeyer style, stood side by side on an otherwise empty stage. For *Boutique* the scenery was extremely avant-garde. A strange drop curtain, with exaggerated figures drawn on it, rose to reveal the interior of the toyshop, with enormously high windows at the back through which one could see a painted steamer. Shelves and plates, chairs and curtained windows were drawn on the side-wings. It was all quite unrealistic and at first I found it difficult to accept. But it did not take me long to change my mind, for the combination of elements was immediately entrancing. The ballets still used a lot of pantomime (especially of course in story ballets like *Cléopâtre, Thamar, Schéhérazade, Petrushka* and *The Good-Humoured Ladies,* all of which I was to see and love on later visits), but, even on this first experience, I was able to appreciate the acting as well as the dancing, which seemed to merge together with incredibly skillful ease and grace. Pierrot, in *Carnaval,* trying to catch a butterfly in his cap, and the parents of the children in *Boutique,* in which Cecchetti, the great choreographer for Diaghilev and his elderly wife, gave inimitable performances as non-dancing characters. The detail was as fascinating as the verve and brilliance of the ensemble. The elegance of *Carnaval,* the high spirits of *Boutique,* with Lopokova as the chief Doll, in a white flounced dress, with a white and pink wreath on her head, rioting through the cancan to a sensational finish ending in the splits, and Massine — chalk-white face, long sideburns and a black velvet suit — a superbly accomplished partner, flinging himself about in his white socks and flying coat-tails. Finally the savage dances in *Prince Igor,* with the women spread out across the stage, waving their arms seductively, as the men, with their fierce moustaches and bows and arrows, leapt wildly up and down, now advancing on the girls, now jumping over them towards the front of the stage till one felt they would hurl themselves across the footlights into the auditorium, as the music crashed out with increasing shrillness and the curtain fell to tumultuous applause.

I left the theatre in a dream. Soon I was to become an aficionado for all the Diaghilev seasons that were to follow during the next three years, but nothing could ever quite equal the first sight of their originality and glamour. Standing in the Promenade beside my father and walking about with him in the intervals among the cigar smoke and clinking glasses all round me, I felt I had really grown up at-last.

I seldom go to ballet any more. My memories of that first impact are too vivid and nostalgic, but they gave me an experience that has stayed with me unforgettably ever since.

Chapter 17

Curtain Calls

But what if there is no curtain, as is so often the case nowadays? The re-entrance of the cast for instance, as well as their subsequent difficulty in retiring at the end of the calls without turning their backs upon the audience, is quite a complicated manoeuvre on the wide expanses of the National Theatre's Olivier stage. And it is even more difficult for the stage management to judge the length of time to be allowed, according to the response of the spectators – whereas it is possible to gauge things more exactly with a curtain to rise and fall, and the actors can remain or redistribute themselves tidily on stage between times.

In America much attention is paid to the convention. Some years ago, when I was asked to direct a musical there (and was eventually sacked with some justification before it opened in New York) I quarrelled furiously with the impresario, who wasted valuable rehearsal time in devising elaborate curtain calls, though I ventured to protest that the old-fashioned 'walk down', so familiar to us in England in revues and pantomimes, would surely be a perfectly simple solution to the problem.

In the West End of London, during the early years of my career, the pit and gallery were always the accepted arbiters of applause, as well as making their voices heard if they considered the play unworthy of their approval. On first nights they would make their presence felt by greeting the celebrities among the audience as they made their way into the stalls. At the rise of the curtain there would be more clapping as a handsome setting was revealed, especially in spectacular costume plays and melodramas, while the entrance of the star would evoke a big round of applause, which the star would often acknowledge with a slight but gracious bow before he or she began to speak.

Right up to the early Thirties curtain calls were expected after every act, though the custom was gradually abandoned and began to be reserved for the end of the play. I remember being somewhat disconcerted when, in Sybil Thorndike's production of *Henry VIII* at the old Empire Theatre in the Thirties, Buckingham, Wolsey and Katharine each took individual calls immediately following their death scenes. And once, at a performance of *Tosca* in Verona, I was amazed to see the prima donna, after a passionate aria which ended in a fall to the ground, rise from the floor to bow in acknowledgment of the rapturous applause, and then resume a languid pose upon her sofa, from which she proceeded to repeat the aria, using exactly the same gestures and movements as before, and ending as before with a similar fall which left her prone upon the stage!

Three supreme exponents of the art of taking curtain calls were none of them straight actresses. Best of all, perhaps, was the great dancer, Anna Pavlova. After endless bows and the gracious acceptance of a mass of flowers, she would suddenly leap into the wings with a graceful bound, returning a few moments later from some other entrance at a different part of the stage. The applause would grow more and more frantic as she floated on and off, running, tiptoeing, or leaping, surprising the enraptured audience with every reappearance. Something of the same hysteria would greet the similar means used by Marlene Dietrich at the end of her solo performance, many years later, to encourage the applause. She too would leave the stage for several minutes, while the audience became gradually more insistent, and reappear unexpectedly from different entrances. She would allow a full twenty minutes for her calls, and managed the whole ceremony with a perfection of timing and execution. Maria Callas, on the other hand, would accept her ovations with an extraordinary command of personality;

combining queenly dignity with an effect of grateful, and even humble, appreciation.

In my early days in the theatre, the curtain calls at the end of a play would sometimes degenerate into something of a shambles, as the director of the play – and the author too in a contemporary piece – were led on to the stage by the leading lady. Ill at ease in the glare of the footlights, and looking oddly inappropriate among the actors in their make-up and costumes, they were apt to be unrecognised by the audience. Their speeches too were often inept, and sometimes inaudible, and the leading players would follow them by obliging with a few tactful words. On a famous occasion, the opening night of Noël Coward's *Sirocco* – one of his few sensational failures – Frances Doble stepped forward and began. 'This is the happiest moment of my life' – to be speedily interrupted by yells of derision from the gallery.

But many of the star performers of that period were experts in delivering the curtain speeches so often demanded of them. Fred Terry, Martin Harvey and Matheson Lang charmed their audiences with appropriate compliments, and Donald Wolfit, who had studied their methods when he had been apprenticed to two of them, would stand, shaking the curtain to encourage the applause, before emerging in front of it to speak, dishevelled but triumphant and gasping with exhaustion. Marie Tempest would always grace her final curtain with an elegant curtsey, whereas Edith Evans seemed rather to disdain the whole convention and would acknowledge the audience with an air of somewhat tolerant resignation.

My own dislike of over-elaborate curtain calls springs perhaps from a production of *The School for Scandal*, at the end of which Tyrone Guthrie had spent much time in posing the actors in amusing groups. I remember that as Joseph Surface I had to wait until the cast was all assembled and then pop my head up over a screen – and *The Times* critic remarked, not unfairly, that after a rather untidy performance of the play itself, the company had evidently decided to join the Russian Ballet.

We know, of course, that in the eighteenth century the

audience loved to applaud any points or innovations of business created by the great actors – Garrick, Macready and Edmund Kean – and they took calls after every scene.

It is curious that in America the custom of greeting favourites with applause is still continued, whereas in England it has markedly diminished. The hysteria of audiences seems to be reserved in this country for pop concerts, where the interruptions continue unceasingly before, during, and after the performance. Now that films and television have dispensed with audible reactions, applause may perhaps become less and less to be expected. And the lack of a curtain may necessitate a return to the directions of Shakespeare, for bodies must be ceremoniously borne off at the end of the classical tragedies. Otherwise the director must have recourse to a blacked-out stage, while the poor corpses must scurry into the wings in ignominious half-obscurity, before returning, safe and sound, to receive the plaudits of the audience.

But there is little doubt that most of us players can hardly fail to enjoy the age-long custom of curtain calls, and would feel cheated if they were obliged to forego them altogether. Audiences, too, perhaps. As Fred Terry used to say proudly in one of his curtain speeches:

> 'If there is anything an actor values more than your applause, it is your silent attention to detail that enables us to give you of our best.'

Plays and Players, 1985

Chapter 18

Pause and Effect

Today, when we are so overwhelmed by sound of every kind – aeroplanes, traffic, television, radio, transistors and loud-speakers all day long – the effect of silence, both on stage and screen, seems sadly to have become infinitely more significant than ever before. Many people find it menacing, lonely and depressing, but its power is undeniable. Strikingly used, it can be tragic, terrifying, nostalgic or evocative.

It can be comic, too. The great comedians – Chaplin, in whose performances silence is everything, George Robey, who paused as he surveyed the audience and had them roaring with laughter before he uttered a word – these geniuses and their successors can use the pause and illuminate a silence with an individual magic beyond words, while the new playwrights have learned to entrust their interpreters with equally pragmatic opportunities.

Modern playwrights make a tremendous effect with pauses, as I realised very quickly in the two plays *Home*, by David Storey, and *No Man's Land*, by Harold Pinter, in which I was lucky enough to appear. Pinter even prints his pauses explicitly in his texts, and the 'Pinter Pause' is now a kind of copyright in the theatre world as it was once the traditional property of the actor Macready in the nineteenth century.

'Pause' was the favourite interruption of the Russian director Theodore Komisarjevsky, when I first rehearsed for him in some early London productions of Chekhov in the Twenties. He was determined to orchestrate his productions as significantly in the silences as in the dialogue.

Bernard Shaw, on the other hand, though equally musical, demanded continual attack and speed, though his ear was impeccably accurate and his text demanded extremely accurate execution. But in the acting of his wordy plays there is no time to waste, nor can one find an excuse for slow delivery and lengthy pauses in acting Congreve, Sheridan, Wilde, Maugham or even Noël Coward.

With Shakespeare it is another matter. The old actors seem to have made immense pauses to gain their best effects – Macready, Kean and especially Irving, whose diction and vocal weakness were evidently a continual hazard in his reading of the verse. Shaw was always attacking him for putting his Shakespearean performances in between the actual lines, and even Ellen Terry confessed to being obliged to change her timing to disadvantage when she played Portia and Beatrice in his productions.

Both Irving and Tree cut the Shakespearean texts ruthlessly in order to interpolate elaborate stage effects, and it was not till Granville-Barker's 1912–14 Savoy productions that audiences were allowed to hear full texts spoken at great speed, though, because of this innovation, the actors found it difficult to sustain the pace demanded of them, and the critics and public, used to the old-fashioned deliberate declamatory style, found the experiment new-fangled and complained of inaudibility.

Actors set great store by the art of timing. By this they mean the way they judge how to gain the most telling result from the speaking of a text at different speeds, in emphasising a particular word or phrase, and learning how to gauge their delivery with flexibility and skill, according to the reactions of their fellow players and the audience at every different performance.

The live rapport between a player and his public is a continual challenge and refreshment, and he is intensely receptive to the varying temper of the public as well as to the difference in the sizes of the theatres he may appear in, which may demand broader or more intimate methods.

In filming and television, of course, the art of timing is largely a matter for the director. The actors still rely on one another in their interplay, but the effects they achieve can easily be changed, without their knowledge, in subsequent cutting and editing. The timing of laugh-lines, in particular, is different and more uncertain without the reactions of a live audience, which is why, presumably, studio laughter and applause is so often dubbed in afterwards to create a more lively atmosphere in television comedies.

Chapter 19

W. Graham Robertson

In the Tate Gallery there hangs a portrait of the young Graham
Robertson, one of Sargent's most striking successes – an
aesthetic-looking young man in a very long black overcoat
carrying a jade-handled ebony walking stick with a grey poodle
stretched out at his feet. (Robertson told me that Sargent insisted
on his taking off his clothes under the over-coat in order to look
more slender in the portrait.)

It was in the early 1930s that I met him first, by then a rather
portly figure (though still addicted to wearing a Spanish sombrero and a caped cloak), very benevolent and distinguished and
living in a high narrow house on Campden Hill.

I knew he had been one of Ellen Terry's greatest admirers,
and his reminiscences of the Lyceum (in his charming book *Time
Was*) during the great Irving days recall her with vivid accuracy
and grace. In the early years of this century she had become one
of his greatest friends, and had appeared at His Majesty's as Aunt
Imogen in his children's play, *Pinkie and the Fairies* which was
produced there by Sir Herbert Beerbohm Tree one Christmas
with considerable success. After her death in 1927, Graham
began to take a great interest in the young players who were then
beginning to be successful in London, and he numbered Jean
Forbes-Robertson, Eric Portman, Ernest Milton and Marie Ney
among those whom he watched in the theatre and encouraged
and entertained at his home. He also wrote to me (I was then
acting at the Old Vic) and I went to tea with him in Kensington
several times. I was fascinated by his nostalgic anecdotes and was

lost in admiration of a water-colour by William Blake which hung over his mantelpiece, 'The River of Life', which depicted a young woman swimming with two children, and bearded elders in two temples on the bank looking on.

When Robertson left London for good he gave his splendid Blake collection to the Tate Gallery. He was a very rich man, but always seemed to me unostentatious and warmhearted, though Gordon Craig writes bitterly in one of his books about Robertson's refusal to back one of Craig's few London productions at the beginning of the century. I imagine that, like most of Ellen Terry's friends and advisers, he had little confidence in giving money to her son, who was generally supposed to be suspect, unpractical, and extravagant, and had already squandered much of his mother's hard-earned savings in the unhappy season at the Imperial Theatre in 1901, when he produced Ibsen's *The Vikings* and *Much Ado* for her. Actually these failures were to be remembered long afterwards as important innovations as regards scenery and lighting and undoubtedly brought new originality, selectivity and a use of space to counteract the Edwardian fashion of elaborate display and attempted pictorial realism in the theatre.

Graham Robertson retired to live at Witley in a small house, with a charming garden and studio attached. Here he had always painted, and enjoyed producing several pageants featuring local talent. Ellen Terry would often stay with him there in her old age, when she had few men friends left. He was one of the oldest and most dependable who could still be relied on to give her rest and sympathy.

In 1942 I was suddenly invited to come down to Witley one Sunday with Alan Dent (then secretary to James Agate and theatre critic of the *News Chronicle*) and we set off together, standing in a crowded train, to be met by Robertson with a taxi at the station. We had been told beforehand that the war was a subject not to be mentioned, and he behaved as if the great crisis of the world had completely passed him by. He talked happily of his devotion to Alfred Lunt and Lynn Fontanne, who had recently become his friends when they had come over to act in London, and Ellen Terry's photograph stood in a place of honour on a little table with the inscription 'How happy I am to be at Sandhills!'

An elderly manservant opened the front door and later served a delicious lunch. But first we were taken into the kitchen to meet the cook, Mrs Cave, an august figure in black bombazine with a gold chain round her neck, and, I suspected, a handsome red wig. 'She nursed Carlyle when he was dying,' Graham whispered, and then, as we were ushered to a bedroom where a jug of hot water stood on a washstand with a towel folded over it (there was no hot water laid on in the house) he called out from below, 'The Blakes get less good as you go upstairs.' He walked us round his domain when lunch was over, and we had a most enchanting day. When I wrote afterwards to thank him, he wrote back: 'Perhaps you realised that you left London in 1942 and arrived some time in the 1890s.

My mother, usually so appreciative of everyone, surprised me considerably, when I spoke to her with such enthusiasm of my new friendship, by saying 'Oh, yes, I remember him as being a very mother-ridden young man whom I sometimes used to meet sitting about in actresses' dressing-rooms.' But how well he was to write about these actresses afterwards!

Robertson was certainly no great painter, to judge by the pictures of his that I have seen, and he was, I suppose, something of a dilettante. But his taste was as evident as was the simple elegance which emanated from his distinguished personality, and I was very proud that he should take an interest in my own budding career. His writing has enormous charm and I am delighted that it should now engage the attention of a new generation, evoking, I hope, the same enthusiasm and enjoyment which I felt on reading it when it was published first.

October 1980

Chapter 20

The Glass of Fashion

Buried today in the drawers and cupboards of theatrical costumiers lie the paraphernalia of accessories, once so much a part of everyday use, in private life as well as on the stage, at the turn of the century and in the years before the First World War.

The muffs and fans (alas, Lady Windermere), the elbow-length gloves and cardcases, the button boots, braces, and spats, monocles, pince-nez and lorgnettes, the powder-puffs and cigarette-holders, inkwells, blotting pads and sealing wax, sugar-tongs, sock suspenders, collar studs, all these are forgotten now. Whatever became of the smart shops which specialised in these objects, once so greatly in demand? With what delight, as a young playgoer, did I watch the elegant deportment of the older actors and actresses, as they sat on chairs and sofas, straight-backed with pointed feet, while the younger members of the cast lounged about, challenging their prim behaviour, the girls crossing their legs in their short skirts, while the young men, in their blue blazers and flapping white flannel trousers, charged through the inevitable french windows, brandishing their tennis rackets, balancing jauntily on the furniture, tapping their cigarette-cases to point their lines and blowing smoke through their noses as they offered a 'fag' to their partners.

No longer can one see a witty actress dabbing her nose with a tiny handkerchief trimmed with lace, so useful to tease and provoke their partners in scenes of flirtation, quarrelling, or social chit-chat, while the men would also produce large white handkerchiefs from sleeve or starched cuff wherewith to mop their brows or proffer to a damsel in distress. Kleenex, however useful and hygienic, is hardly a very attractive substitute.

At what date, I wonder, did ladies, and especially actresses, begin to admit that they suffered from poor eyesight? In 1934, when I was beginning to venture into the task of directing plays, the beautiful Isobel Jeans, whom I had so often admired as a young playgoer, agreed to appear in a play of Emlyn Williams which I was to stage. After the first rehearsal she drew from her bag a pair of large green horn-rimmed spectacles. When she was not peering through them to correct her lines, she would take them off from time to time and gesticulate with them to great effect.

Women on the stage never wore glasses unless they were playing frumps, and even in real life they would carry a lorgnette for use in the street or shopping, and opera glasses when they went to the theatre. Only very old ladies were occasionally to be seen wearing gold-rimmed spectacles (elderly men often wore monocles) and schoolgirls were often made to wear them by their parents, though they appeared to have discarded them for ever before they 'came out'. (The strange fad of 'granny-glasses' affected by young women only a few years ago did not, I am glad to say, appear to catch on.) Fashions have changed too in the discussion and portrayal of many other afflictions, and our permissive age has completely removed any hesitation to write about them, in plays as well as books, and we can refer to them unashamedly even in mixed company.

Blindness was always a sure engager of sympathy, especially in melodrama, though cripples could be pitied or equally arouse terror, from Richard the Third to The Hunchback of Notre Dame. False teeth were never mentioned of course, in polite society and Somerset Maugham, in his comedy *The Circle* produced at the end of the First War, created a sensation (only equalled by Shaw's 'Not bloody likely' in *Pygmalion* as far back as 1915) when he made one of the characters rush out of the room with 'My damned teeth are coming out!' The music-hall comedians had of course found them a good excuse for laughter many years before (as well as mothers-in-law and kippers). In 1954, the authoress of *The Chalk Garden*, Enid Bagnold, demanded that her leading lady should announce her first entrance from off-stage, calling to her factotum, 'Are my teeth on the table? My bottom teeth . . .' and the management were doubtful of persuading any leading actress to accept the part. Fortunately Edith Evans in London, and Gladys Cooper in New York, managed to surmount embarrassment with remarkable expertise and handled the episode with remarkable grace and tact.

Deafness was always a good card to play. Feydeau employed it a great deal, and the Victorians sometimes used ear-trumpets, though I rarely remember seeing one in my youth. I imagine that Evelyn Waugh, who carried one and used it ostentatiously in his latter life, must have ordered it specially.

During the last few years there have been a succession of books, plays and newspaper articles, dealing with every kind of physical experience, deafness and dumbness, childbirth, operations to be read about and seen in the theatre and the television, to say nothing of morgues, funerals and masturbation.

Chapter 21

My Favourite Room

For an actor, his dressing-room, in my case at any rate, is the centre of his existence during the hours he is committed to spend in it. So I can honestly call it my favourite room, though its features, in the many hundred different ones I have occupied over more than sixty years, must necessarily vary enormously from one theatre to another.

Of course in my early days I was always obliged to share a dressing-room with other actors, and was immensely gratified to have reached the privilege, in the late 1920s, of being given a room to myself, with my name proudly displayed upon the door.

My favourite room is in my favourite London theatre, the Haymarket. Although ideally it is preferable to dress as close to the stage as possible, this particular room is situated at the very top of the theatre, with a long flight of stairs leading up to it. It is almost like a small flat, with an anteroom and bathroom leading out of the main room, which has windows looking on to Suffolk Street far below. There are plenty of shelves and cupboards, chairs, a sofa and writing desk – even, until recent times, a coal fire in winter – and it is therefore possible to install oneself there comfortably, even occasionally in the daytime when there is no performance.

Here I dressed for a number of years in various productions, and in 1944, when the buzzbombs were such a disagreeable interruption, I would firewatch several nights a week, sleeping in my dressing-room at intervals. Garlands Hotel, only a few yards away, was hit and finally completely destroyed in two successive air raids, and I dreaded lest the theatre – so happily constructed, but mostly in wood and plaster – should also become a victim. I always wondered, too, if I should meet the famous Haymarket Ghost, during the watches of the night (said to be a famous old actor), but I never succeeded in seeing him, though Margaret Rutherford once claimed that she did.

The privacy of a star dressing-room gives its occupant a very pleasant promise of relaxation, although the routine of making-up, now a much simpler process than was once thought necessary, demands the necessary tedium of looking at one's face in the glass for half-an-hour or so. But this is perhaps a less depressing prospect than the similar routine while shaving every morning.

The other London theatres in Shaftesbury Avenue and Charing Cross Road, mostly built at the turn of the century, are fortunately pretty well equipped with spacious and convenient dressing-rooms, whereas at Stratford-on-Avon, and more recently, at the mammoth new houses at the National and the Barbican, they are amazingly ill-designed, cramped and uncomfortable. One cannot imagine that the plans for them would have been passed by experienced eyes.

The Broadway theatres in New York are also, for the most part, equally gloomy and claustrophobic, while in Philadelphia I once played in a theatre where the dressing-rooms had been forgotten altogether, and the actors had to content themselves with rooms on the other side of the street and toil along a passage underground in order to reach the stage.

But I have always looked forward to arriving at the stagedoor, well before curtain time, to find my dresser laying out my dressing-table and costumes in correct order, to put on a dressing-gown, open my mail, and sit before the mirror knowing exactly how long I need to prepare for my performance. Even in times of great stress, nervousness, despondency, failure or success, my dressing-room is a refuge from outside interference and I even resent it when the telephone rings.

In the old days I always anticipated the callboy's knock with a mixture of pleasure and dismay, although that long-established character has now ceased to exist, and the insistent barking of the tannoy system which has replaced it is for me a most unattractive and impersonal substitute in this progressive world.

With regard to dressing-room visitors I have rather mixed feelings, knowing that they can often mislead one into supposing that a performance has been very successful when it has been nothing of the kind. They feel they must attempt to be tactfully complimentary at all costs, and one is apt to be suspicious if they are unduly enthusiastic. Interviewers with tape-recorders, long-forgotten acquaintances, insincere flatterers, importunate authors with their manuscripts, and the occasionally impertinent unknown fan – these are occupational hazards, and one needs a devotedly tactful dresser to deal with them and ration their intrusions to as short a time as possible. And yet one is vain enough to be somewhat disappointed if no one comes to the dressing-room at the end of the performances, so long as they have the sense not to outstay their welcome.

The traditional ghosts at the Haymarket and Drury Lane are curious reminders of the great players who appeared in those theatres so long ago. At Her Majesty's and Wyndhams I dressed in rooms once occupied by Herbert Tree and Gerald du Maurier, and I felt proud to use those rooms so many years afterwards. And, in the last play in which I appeared in London, I found myself working for the first time in the Duke of York's Theatre, where I had seen my very first play *Peter Pan* when I was still a boy. So that those rooms backstage will always have a particular nostalgia for me, especially in the West End of London, where I so longed to appear and finally achieved that ambition over so many years. Will my own ghost linger in some of those dressing-rooms one day, I wonder?

Chapter 22

On Acting Shakespeare

A discussion with George Rylands

GEORGE RYLANDS: What were your first important Shakespeare roles, who directed them, and where were they played?

SIR JOHN GIELGUD: I played Romeo when I was nineteen at the Regent Theatre, long pulled down, under Barry Jackson's management, with Gwen Ffrangcon-Davies as Juliet. H. K. Ayliff, who was Jackson's great stand-by as a director, directed it. He was very hard with us, and I remember we played the dress rehearsal with the safety curtain down because Jackson had invited an audience and Ayliff thought the play was not ready for the audience. It wasn't very helpful for the poor actors to play to a safety curtain, and it was a pretty good disaster; it only ran about six weeks. I found it frightfully exhausting. I was very fond of myself at the time and fancied I was going to look very romantic, and found I didn't when I was made-up. It was fun in a way, but I got very bad notices, and it was after that, when I went to Fagan's repertory company in Oxford that I began to learn to act a bit. It was really much too soon to play such an important part, and so it was a big set-back for me, which I think did my conceit a lot of good.

RYLANDS: But Romeo is a poet and this might have been the moment when your famous speaking voice first made its impact on the world?

GIELGUD: I don't know. Ivor Brown said I was like Bunthorne, I remember; and I played Romeo after that two or three times and never felt I had a success in it. And when Laurence Olivier and I played Mercutio and Romeo alternately in 1935 in a very successful production, I was enraged by the fact that he, who I knew didn't speak verse as well as I did, was so much better as Romeo, because, as I think Richardson said to me at the time, he only had to stand against the balcony to convey the whole passionate emotion of this animal lover. I was very cold and very voice-conscious and very self-conscious, so I never really had a success with the part of Romeo. But we were a very good team and it was one of the first big productions when I directed myself as well as acted.

RYLANDS: Did you find that to direct yourself in Shakespeare is dangerous?

GIELGUD: It is dangerous because I pay far too much attention to the lights and the other people. On the other hand when it comes off, as it did I think in *Much Ado* many years later, you have the feeling you are the controlling force all over the stage. You also have the fun of playing every night and checking what goes on around you. Every few nights I make a few notes – a very few – and if you go on doing that carefully for a month, you find the improvement all round is enormous; whereas if suddenly the director comes from outside and says the whole show's gone to pot, you have a rather lazy and sullen rehearsal and often you can't get the show back into its proper state. On the other hand, of course, one is inclined, through doing that, to pay too much attention to the others and not to concentrate on one's own part, which is a dangerous thing to do, particularly in a big Shakespeare part.

RYLANDS: What other great productions have there been in your whole career?

GIELGUD: The first time I worked with Peter Brook we did *Measure for Measure*, in a season when I played Angelo, Cassius, Benedick, and Lear at Stratford in 1950, and they were all, if I may say so, more or less successful. Brook was awfully clever at knowing when I was false. One wants to be told when one is bad and false, but one doesn't want to be put down so that one loses confidence. And he has a way of doing that, as Barker had and as you had; which is very important – otherwise it's very easy to feel that you can't do it at all, and then you lose all confidence and can't do it.

RYLANDS: What about some disasters?

GIELGUD: There was the Japanese *Lear*, which was considered to be a great disaster; we toured it on the Continent and played at the Palace Theatre in London to packed houses, and the young people and the avant-garde saw there was something to it. I was accused of terrible gimmickry and the only thing that pleased me about it was that, when Brook did his *Lear* with Paul Scofield years later, he said to me very generously that it was our *Lear* which had given him the basic idea for his production, which was acknowledged to be enormously successful, and it was true. The great mistake I made in the Japanese *Lear* was a purely technical one. Noguchi, who was a sculptor, designed the sets and sent them to us and we thought they were thrilling and I still think they were, but I did not know at the time that he had never designed costumes. He arrived with no costumes, he designed them very hastily, he left before he had seen the fittings, he was not at the dress rehearsal or the first night. We all looked so strange and peculiar and I remember saying to George Devine who was directing the play: 'Don't you think we could discard all the costumes and get some rubber sheets and make them into drapes and all wear sort of nondescript cloaks? I believe with this scenery that might work.' And I still believe it might have done; but we hadn't the courage at the last moment to make such a drastic alteration, so I went through with it because I felt Noguchi was too individual and brilliant a designer to throw overboard completely, or half throw overboard which would be even more dishonest.

RYLANDS: Yes, you couldn't do that. Now, one more disaster if you can bear me to mention it, and that is the Zeffirelli *Othello*.

GIELGUD: This was a bitter blow to me because I've wanted all my life to play Othello, although I'm quite sure the public would never think me a satisfactory Othello in every way because I haven't got what Agate used to call the thew and sinew. Zeffirelli made the fatal mistake of dressing me as a Venetian, so that I looked, as many of the notices said, like an Indian Civil Servant. I didn't stand out from the others. Desdemona was over-dressed, I was under-dressed, there was much too much scenery, there were I think very damaging cuts, and certain other members of the cast were to my mind fatal. And it was terribly badly lit, which was very strange for Zeffirelli. He had dark scenery, so that with my dark face and dark clothes people couldn't see me – and when one feels one is not well lit, one is immediately at a disadvantage. He also did some terribly dangerous things like putting me far too much upstage; he had a wonderful-looking scene with a huge table and imprisoned me behind it so I couldn't get any contact with the audience or with the other actors. I felt that I only succeeded in the last scene of the play, when the poetry could carry me along. He had never seen me act, he had only seen me do the Shakespeare recital, so I don't think he knew at all what my dangers are when I act in a play, and he wasn't able to give me – or even Peggy Ashcroft – the right sort of confidence. We both suffered bitterly although we were both devoted to him and he had boundless universal charm. He consulted me to some extent over the cuts, but he put the intervals in fatal places. He insisted on having an interval after the first act, which he put at the end of the Senate scene where the play has hardly begun, and then we had a twenty-five-minute interval before Cyprus, which was disastrous. And he had very elaborate sets in the last act which made pauses between every scene – of course in opera houses, which he is used to, scenery can be moved more quickly and there can be much longer intervals. In Italy they have no idea of time, everything begins half an hour late and the intervals don't seem to matter because they're always great social occasions.

RYLANDS: You did a *Lear* production in which Granville-Barker had a hand, didn't you?

GIELGUD: He refused to take the full responsibility for it. This was just at the time of the fall of France in 1941. Tyrone Guthrie and Lewis Casson agreed to try to get Barker to come and work on the *Lear*, so the three of them really did the *Lear* together, but Guthrie and Casson were absolutely thrown out of the window by the force of Barker's personality, though they did an awful lot of the hard work for him, and it was a great pity that he wasn't completely concentrated on doing it himself, because the actors found him absolutely magical and illuminating.

RYLANDS: Can you just describe what the magic was?

GIELGUD: It was the Toscanini authority mixed with a curious humanity and an enormous knowledge of the scaffolding of the work, not only as a student, as a professor, but also as a stage manager and a stage director; but as well as that there was a feeling that he was ready to improvise and that he summed up your possibilities almost the first-day. I remember him coming to a production of mine of *Hamlet* before the war and giving me notes. He said, 'Well, Laertes is no good; we won't discuss him. Now the King is a cat, you see, and he ought to be a dog' – things like that. It was so quick, and he had only just made a few notes, and it immediately gave me a clue about what to say to the actors afterwards. I found all his notes for *Lear* and I have republished them[1]; I hope people will be interested to read them, because the two or three words he said about many lines in the play were so pithy and clear and such wonderful direction for any actor, that I think it will be thrilling for people just to read them in print and see what a really brilliant mind like that can do. I remember very well in the last scene of *Lear* I said, 'Do you think I could find the rope that had hanged her in the soldier's hand at the back of the stage when I'm wandering around; could this be perhaps effective?' He said, 'Oh no, it's very Tree. You can't do that. It's like the old-fashioned thing.' Then, after two days, he suddenly said, 'I rather think that was a good idea you had about the rope.' This gave me enormous pleasure because he had somehow woven it into his conception of the scene. Nothing is more flattering to an actor than when he invents something and

1 In *Stage Directions*

can be allowed to use it with such authority. When Barker told me anything was good I never wanted to change it again, whatever the people said from the front or the critics or anybody who came round. You had this feeling of absolute confidence in his criticism.

RYLANDS: I suppose you have read all Barker's prefaces?

GIELGUD: Yes indeed. I always enthuse about them whenever I'm doing a production; everybody reads them.

RYLANDS: How much Shakespeare criticism do you normally read, or have you read in your life?

GIELGUD: The man to whom I always go back and whom I really love, perhaps because I only met him once or twice, is John Masefield, who wrote short essays.

RYLANDS: They are brilliant.

GIELGUD: I once went to see him; it was during the war when we were doing *Macbeth*: I wanted advice about it and asked him if he would see me and I went down and had lunch with him. I shall never forget the way he spoke of *Macbeth*, almost as if he had written it himself. He spoke of each line with such love and tenderness and understanding that you really felt he had lived with this play all his life and it was as dear to him as a child; it was extraordinary, it was so wise.

RYLANDS: That Home University Library book of his is about fifty years old.

GIELGUD: He told me he wrote it in three months on a commission from some publishers when he was twenty-six.

RYLANDS: And every single thing in it tells and is so original.

GIELGUD: Oh, so brilliant; and it is easy for actors to read it because it isn't complicated and long-winded, and even the little précis of the plays at the beginning of each one are awfully good.

RYLANDS: What do you think about Shakespeare between the wars, and Shakespeare since 1945 or 1950? Has the old tradition broken, is there a new tradition and is it a good one?

GIELGUD: It's very hard to tell. It seems to me there has been much too much done, since the Vic and Stratford have become established. I suppose I feel a bit jealous of the panoply of the modern Shakespeare set-up in England, because when I was at the Vic at the end of the Twenties it was so exciting to do these plays, not to have the critics come on the first night and sometimes not to have them come at all, to play a thing about thirteen times and to have a production costing £15. It made it such an adventure and such an experiment: you felt you could sort of try your wings and if you fell down a bit they would still forgive you, and if you did succeed it was frightfully exciting. Whereas now the whole standard is much higher. On the other hand, you cannot expect to get more than one good production in three years, because there is too much done and people either fall back on hack work or on gimmicks.

RYLANDS: On the other hand the last twenty years have brought forward plays which have been totally neglected since Shakespeare's time.

GIELGUD: Yes, his less-known plays have certainly come into their own for the first time, and the young directors like Peter Hall are frightfully interested in doing plays that are not completely smothered in stage tradition because they find that gets in the way both of their actors and of their own ideas about direction.

RYLANDS: And this has altered everybody's feeling about Shakespeare?

GIELGUD: I would say so; and I think the radio has done a tremendous amount to popularise it, people are more familiar with the plays. I mean it was people like Churchill – the old-school Establishment people – who knew their Shakespeare by heart; they say Churchill could go and prompt at Olivier all through *Antony and Cleopatra* which I well believe, because he knew every line.

RYLANDS: He said he learnt all he knew about English history from reading Shakespeare.

GIELGUD: I don't think that people used to know Shakespeare as well as they do now; but now they do hear it on the radio continually and usually see three or four productions a year. And schoolchildren see much more finished productions. I saw the

Youth Theatre production of *Julius Caesar*, and I thought that really was a step in a completely fresh direction: it was better than anything I have seen at either university, and it had the most amazing pace and skill. It was not well acted, but it had a marvellous understanding of the text. I understood everything everybody said.

RYLANDS: Pace and clarity are what Barker was very keen on, and what I think has been sacrificed at the present time.

GIELGUD: Of course.

RYLANDS: Do you think that there is now a slight antipathy to poetry as such, a sort of feeling that Shakespeare is poetical and 'may God forgive you for speaking blank verse' – that there is a certain hostility to that as being Victorian?

GIELGUD: Yes, the young actors all want to try to make it more colloquial, but the great danger is that they are inclined to kill the pace by putting in realistic pauses to make it as if they had really thought it at that moment. Instead of which I've always said that if you lie on it, like lying on the water when you are trying to swim, it sustains you, and if you kick about and make holes in the water you go down and drown.

RYLANDS: I don't know whether you remember, some years ago you gave me a book by Stark Young, that American dramatic critic who died not long ago, which is called *The Flower in Drama; and Glamour* which you said was very good and which absolutely bowled me over. He has in it a chapter entirely about the voice in the theatre, in which he says that in our theatre sound is almost forgotten, that every dramatist has his own voice, every language has its own voice, and an actor's voice is his most important medium, the tone an actor uses can move us more than any other thing about him: our theatres cultivate the eye and not the ear. I think this is absolutely true, and this brings me to your recitals where the eye goes into the background and it is the ear which counts.

GIELGUD: On the other hand I think it is also the Ancient Mariner's beady eye on the audience which holds them there, so that one cannot entirely discard the personal contact of the actor with the audience, which to me is greater in that recital than in any performance I have ever given of Shakespeare; because I play the whole recital to the audience or to myself, but not to other characters. They never lose my face for a single moment and that is one of the reasons why I'm sure it holds so well; and they are so surprised to hear every word. Nearly always in Shakespeare they miss a lot through the movement and through the colour of the costumes and people turning upstage with their backs to them, and so on. And that's why people want the apron stage, and the semi-circular and the rostrum. In a soliloquy you can come near to the audience: I once gave a performance in a sort of senate house in Madras during a monsoon, and the stage was so far back that obviously nobody would hear; so we quickly redirected *Hamlet* in about two hours by having a little stage built over the orchestra pit; and that was to me one of the most thrilling performances I ever played in. The audience was not really on three sides, it was in a semi-circle as in the Sheldonian Theatre, and one was able to get very close to them and look round during a soliloquy and really take their eyes right round the stage and rush off at the side. It was interesting to see how the closeness of the audience seemed to give one much more contact. In the repertory theatre at Birmingham, for instance, which is built on that sort of plan, you get a very good contact and the Mermaid is the same – two of the best modern theatres, merely for the fact that the auditorium is steeply raked, and when you are far downstage you really have strong control of the house, more I would say than in a semi-circular theatre like Chichester, where members of the audience see one another across the stage, and where the actors are continually having to turn in order to be seen: that seems to me very difficult.

RYLANDS: Your Cassius in the *Julius Caesar* film was very powerful and effective. Did you learn anything about Shakespeare from doing a film?

GIELGUD: Yes, I did to some extent. I'm sure I wouldn't have played it so well if I hadn't known the part complete. Brando, who was so brilliant in moments, didn't know the line of the

Forum scene. The director fondly hoped that by making him do it in tiny bits, he could give the whole effect of the scene, but as Marlon Brando didn't know the whole play – didn't know where the climaxes really came in these speeches – he went in and out and round about and was in complete confusion; the scene lost its impetus altogether, because he didn't know where he was going in the part. If you've played one of those great parts right through, you know where the beginning and the middle and the end come, and the same thing with all the speeches. I find that in the recital I have to be terribly certain where I begin, where I'm going to and where I'm going to finish, and this thing must have a line. I think it was Barker who told me, 'You must have a line of a speech, and inside that line you can have any number of variations and cadenzas. Don't bother about the peak moment, don't bother about how you're going to say "to be or not to be", but worry about everything round it so that when "to be or not to be" comes you empty your mind and do it the best way for that particular performance; some days it will be very good, other days it will fail, but it will always be of a certain quality, because you've placed it in the right place.' You must of course have a regular performance so you won't disappoint the customers but in a great poetic part you can only hope to reach the heights once or twice, perhaps, in the whole run, or certainly not more than once or twice a week, however carefully you plan it and however successful you are generally in playing it. You've got to hope that the gods will descend on you.

The *Listener*, 23rd April 1964

Chapter 23

Overture – Beginners

My first play – *Peter Pan – The Boy Who Wouldn't Grow Up*. I must
have been seven years old at least when I saw him first. (Actually
he was born the same year that I was, in 1904.) Pauline Chase
played Peter, Hilda Trevelyan was Wendy, and Holman Clark
was Hook. There was a drop curtain painted to look like a huge
sampler, and a mysterious character called Liza who ran across at
the beginning and was supposed to have written the play. I was
thrilled by the first entrance of the Pirates, drawn on a kind of
trolley with Hook enthroned at the centre of the group, and the
sinister song that heralded them as they approached from behind
the scenes. I loved Nana taking the socks in her mouth from the
nursery fender. Was she a real St Bernard, I wondered, or a man
dressed up and walking on all fours? But I resented the wires on
the children's backs which I could see glittering in the blue
limelight, and guessed that their nightgowns had bunched-up
material on the shoulders to hide the harness they wore underneath. And I wished the wallpaper at the top of the scenery didn't
have to split open, as well as the tall windows, when the time
came for them to fly away. Trap doors immediately fascinated
me – the one in *Peter Pan*, through which the little house rose
slowly at the end of the play, with Peter and Wendy waving to
the audience from its windows, and the one in *Where the Rainbow
Ends* which suddenly whisked the wicked Aunt and Uncle to the
nether regions. And of course I loved the fights in both plays:
Peter and Hook, St George and The Dragon King, and the
double scene above and below ground in *Peter*, and the hollow

tree with stairs inside it, with Hook in a green limelight leaning over the low door at the bottom, leering at the children as they lay asleep.

I never much cared for pantomimes. The story was always so disjointed, and the Principal Boy who was a girl, the Dame who was a man, and the knockabout comedians and topical songs, made the whole thing very confusing and difficult for me to follow.

These are early memories, of course – childhood treats when my grandmother or my parents always accompanied me. But later in my school days, with a latchkey in my pocket and a few half-crowns carefully saved up from my allowance, I would spend long impatient hours waiting in a queue for the pit or gallery of a theatre, with my brother Val or a schoolfellow for company. After our long hours of waiting we would hear the doors being unbarred at last and would shuffle slowly along in line to pay our money.

In those days the strange method of admission was not by paper ticket but by a metal disc, which was shovelled out from the booking-window after we had paid our shilling or half-crown. Then, clutching our disc, we had to drop it back into the slit of a wooden box a few yards further on before we were finally admitted. We rushed along a dark passage to a flight of steep steps leading down to the pit, or climbed several long flights of stone stairs to reach the gallery. The seats, when we clambered into them at last, were hard wooden benches, sometimes with iron back-rests, sometimes without, so that the knees of the people sitting in the row behind us would press sharply against our shoulders. As we looked down from the gallery the floor of the stage looked absurdly raked, and the actors at the back of a scene were often only visible from the waist downwards, while from the pit our view of the stage was often blocked by tall people sitting in the stalls and by late-comers pushing past them to reach their seats.

In some theatres the underside of the dress circle hung very low, and from the pit the top of the proscenium was cut off completely, and there were often pillars which one had to dodge in order to see the stage at all. If the play was a great success extra rows of stalls would be added and the pit reduced to a few rows at the very back of the theatre, while the second balcony (the 'upper' circle as it was called in those days) was often enlarged during a successful run, and the gallery pushed back till it consisted of only a few seats close up against the roof.

Advertisements, bills, and programmes were designed individually, and I always connected certain colours and typesetting with various managements and their respective theatres. His Majesty's used buff colour, with red and black print in very bold readable lettering, and the Haymarket, Wyndham's, and the St James's all had their own particular types of bills. Then there were boards outside the theatre which displayed only one name, known, when I learned theatrical jargon, as 'double-crowns'. On these bills the name of each star in the play would be printed singly (as well as in lights, along with the title of the piece, over the main entrance), but a few of the principal supporting players would also be featured on individual boards, and when an actor began to be cast in more important parts he would look forward to the moment when the management might think him sufficiently important to merit one all to himself.

Shaftesbury Avenue, Charing Cross Road, and St Martin's Lane looked much as they do today, though one no longer sees tramps and down-and-outs sleeping on newspapers in the alleys at the back of the theatres. But Soho (with its three-course meals in the little restaurants for a shilling or two) was still like a discreet foreign village, and the clutter of cheapjack advertisements, reeking food counters and shoddy porn shops, were not to disfigure the neighbourhood for many years to come. Charing Cross Road was filled with respectable second-hand book shops, and the less discreet 'rubber shops' did not begin till you had passed the Palace Theatre on your way to the Tottenham Court Road.

The Café Royal was still one of the sights of the West End, frequented by a crowd of painters and Bohemians. The main brasserie was approached by a long ramp leading from the front doors in Regent Street past a big kiosk selling foreign papers and magazines, and my eldest brother took me there one day in 1915, when he was on leave, and pointed out Augustus John holding court, with his earrings, red beard, and wide black felt hat. On the following afternoon we went together in a box to the Alhambra to see *The Bing Boys on Broadway* (arriving, to my dismay, nearly half an hour late for the performance after a festive lunch party at the Gobelins Restaurant in Rupert Street where I had sat fidgeting and agonisingly looking at my watch). George Robey leaned over the footlights and picked up one of my chocolates, grinning and raising his huge black eyebrows, and Violet Loraine sang one of her songs, as I thought, looking especially in my direction. How did I react, I wonder, to this early experience of audience participation? Fascinated, perhaps, but a bit alarmed as well.

First nights in London used to be such great occasions – at least I thought so. The queues would begin to form outside the theatre several hours earlier than usual, though they behaved in a more orderly fashion than in Victorian days (as my father used to describe them to me) when the men had to move their ladies into the centre of the crush, and protect them by shoving with their elbows in the stampede that always took place as soon as the doors were opened. My father first admired my mother, before he ever met her, when he saw her from the Lyceum pit as she sat with her mother and sisters in a box at one of Irving's first nights.

I came to recognise many of the habitual first-nighters – the critics, including A. B. Walkley of *The Times* and Malcolm Watson of the *Morning Post*, Edward Marsh, with his pointed jutting eyebrows and a monocle, Willie Clarkson, the wig maker, Courtenay Thorpe the actor, with a frilled shirt and false white-gloved hand, quizzing the house through a gold lorgnette, and Mrs Aria, who had been Irving's last devoted friend and was a famous wit. ('In all matters pertaining to Sir Henry,' she once observed to a young lady who repeated some indiscreet gossip at a party, 'I believe I am considered to be the past-mistress.') Various leading actors and actresses – one of the Vanbrugh sisters perhaps, Marie Tempest, or even Ellen Terry, were quickly recognised as they entered the stalls or boxes (they timed their appearances with care so as not to divide the interest of the pit and gallery) and would be greeted with excited cries and enthusiastic applause which they would acknowledge gracefully, bowing to the audience as they took their seats. The curtain would rise at least ten minutes late, and there would be more excitement as the scenery (also applauded if it was at all spectacular) was disclosed, and more clapping as each of the principal actors made their entrance. In the intervals I looked forward to the buzz of argument and comment in the foyer and, at the end of the performance, the shouts of approval (or perhaps booing) from the gallery, and speeches from the star, the director (dragged on and usually ineptly inaudible) and sometimes from the author (whom the audience often failed to recognise). Then, after it was all over, the long journey back to South Kensington by tube or bus, dead tired but still arguing excitably all the way.

Chu Chin Chow

1916, and His Majesty's Theatre packed with uniforms. I am twelve years old, sitting with my parents in my favourite seat, the middle of the front row of the Dress Circle. The lights go slowly down and music plays. Clouds of delicious incense are wafted from the stage as the gold fringed red velvet curtain rises on a dazzling palace scene, a dark blue banqueting hall with marble steps and a frieze of peacocks that looks like beaten gold. Negro slaves, led by a major domo in a huge turban carrying a wand, parade with covered dishes. 'Here be oysters stewed in honey', they sing, 'all for our great Lord Kassim.' Oscar Asche makes his entrance, huge and impressive, with long moustaches and gilded fingernails, rattling his Chinese fan, and Lily Brayton, his wife, in a great wig of frizzed black hair, swathed in veils and jewels and transparent gauzes.

Courtice Pounds as Ali Baba singing (with Aileen D'Orme) the hit song of the evening 'Any Time's Kissing Time'. Sydney Fairbrother[1] as Ali Baba's comic wife Mahbubah. Frank Cochrane, as Kassim Baba, murdered in a cave full of jewels at the end of the second act, reappears in the part of a blind cobbler in the third. 'And as I cobble with needle and thread, I judge the world by the way they tread.' There are two real donkeys, several goats, some sheep, and at least one camel. The next time I come to see the play again – I shall see it nearly a dozen times – I shall have the added pleasure of watching the animals arriving at the stage-door as I stand waiting in the long queue, listening to the buskers and exchanging theatre gossip with my neighbours.

Chu Chin Chow ran for years, but it always seemed fresh and fascinating to me, even when a dreaded slip in the programme would announce that one of my favourite players was ill or taking a holiday. But the lighting and scenery appeared as beautiful as ever, and a bill announcing 'New scenes, New songs, New costumes', issued after two years' run, sent me scurrying off to His Majesty's once more. The piece was nothing in itself, simply the old fairy tale of *Ali Baba and the Forty Thieves*, but Asche had made it into a brilliant fantasy, part pantomime, part romance, part musical comedy, and had also written the book with the composer Frederic Norton, whose music was so charming and so hugely popular. Black velvet Moorish shutters (a kind of false proscenium) slid together at the end of each full scene, and opened to reveal insets on little rostrums where duets were sung while another full scene was prepared behind, an infinitely more attractive solution than the flapping front cloths which had always been accepted before this time in plays demanding elaborate scenery.

Besides an excellent cast of players and a most convincing group of extras drilled to perfection, Asche had taken care to engage a number of beautiful girls, whom he deployed in the

1 A brilliant eccentric actress – she was apt at rehearsal to produce live mice from her sleeves or bosom – adored dogs – and wore very strange clothes. 'Don't care for jewellery, dear,' she said to me once – 'Beads can't resist them!'

slave-market scene wearing spectacular and scanty costumes, a kind of London version of the Folies Bergères. This episode was naturally one of the production's most popular features, especially to the men on leave who crowded the theatre. Sir Herbert Tree, who had built His Majesty's, returned from America, where he had gone to recoup some past failures, to find his 'Beautiful Theatre' packed to the doors with *Chu Chin Chow* and sat among the audience murmuring sadly, 'More navel than millinery.'

It was in the same year that I saw the revue, *Vanity Fair*, produced by Alfred Butt at the Palace Theatre. The opening scene was set in Piccadilly Circus, and Arthur Playfair and Nelson Keys, two brilliant comedians, acted in a hilarious skit called 'Two-chinned-chow' – Playfair imitating Oscar Asche, while Nelson Keys, in an enormous fuzzy wig, with bare legs, his arms covered with bracelets and hands spread out with palms downwards in Cleopatra style, ran coyly round the Eros fountain, his body swathed in black wrappings with two large yellow hands embroidered on them, appearing to clasp him round the waist. He gave a brilliant caricature of Lily Brayton's way of talking in the play, with a lot of pseudo-Oriental jabber, and the scene ended with the Forty Thieves entering from the back of the stage, carrying on their shoulders the sandwich-boards which were commonly used to advertise plays in the streets in those days. The boards were printed in large letters in the colour and type of the posters for His Majesty's, and read, 'Stalls Full', 'Dress Circle Full', 'Gallery Full', 'Awfull'.

Shakespeare Tercentenary Performance 2 May 1916
Drury Lane Theatre, A Gala Matinée

My brother Val and I sit with our parents, in the Upper Circle this time, as seats for such a grand occasion are very expensive. King George and Queen Mary arrive in the Royal Box and the whole audience rises to greet them. Sir George Alexander has arranged the performance, as Tree (considered to be the leader of the Profession) is still in America. The programme is a formidably long one, nearly half an hour of orchestral pieces and some solos by various eminent singers, followed by the whole of Shakespeare's *Julius Caesar*, and a pageant to finish up with, as well as speeches from Sir Squire Bancroft and Mrs Kendal. But of course we sit spellbound from beginning to end. The Forum scene is magnificently played, with a great crowd of distinguished citizens led by Gerald du Maurier and Edmund Gwenn. We quickly decide that Henry Ainley, stripped to a leopard skin for the games in the opening scene, is an ideal Mark Antony, and Arthur Bourchier a rather dull and heavy Brutus. Also that Cassius, superbly played by H. B. Irving, is the best part in the play, an opinion from which I have never wavered since. The Alma-Tadema scenery, designed for Tree's production at His Majesty's years before, is used again, with solid-looking palaces, balconies and awnings, pillars, perspectives, and blue skies.

During one of the intervals we hear a great outburst of cheering from behind the curtain, and someone comes out to tell us that Frank Benson, who is playing Caesar, has just been sent for to the Royal Box, still in his corpse-like make-up as the Ghost, to be knighted by the King with a sword hastily borrowed from Simmonds, the theatrical costumier's round the corner in King Street. The audience cheer wildly at the announcement, taking up the applause from the huge crowd of delighted players behind the scenes.

The great pantomime was still being presented every year at Drury Lane by Arthur Collins, an experienced master of such productions, and the previous Christmas he had used a massive pillared set for the finale – wide steps stretching from under the stage close to the footlights from the open trap, rising to the very top of the huge stage, with two broad landings to divide the ascending flights of stairs. The same set is used again for the Shakespearean pageant this May afternoon. Groups of characters from nine or ten of the plays emerge in procession, coming up from below with their backs towards the audience. On reaching the landing they turn and reveal themselves – Ellen and Marion Terry as Portia and Nerissa, Fred Terry and Julia Neilson as Benedick and Beatrice, and dozens more. Every star of the legitimate and musical stage in London at the time is recognised and greeted by the enraptured house. The clapping never seems to stop. When all the players in the various tableaux have been applauded and have stepped aside, curtains on the top landing are drawn back, revealing a bust of Shakespeare on a plinth. Flanking the bust are the figures of Comedy and Tragedy – Ellen Terry in white and Geneviève Ward in black – and the huge cast of players begin to move slowly up the last flight of stairs to lay wreaths at the foot of the plinth. Finally with the singing of the National Anthem, the curtain falls and the performance is over.

Percy Macquoid, the great furniture and costume expert, who was also an experienced man of the theatre and had helped Tree and Alexander in many of their finest productions, was a great friend of my parents. He told us afterwards some funny stories of the great occasion. How Evelyn Millard, who played Calpurnia, begged, 'Oh, Mr Macquoid, couldn't I have a different to go?' and that Bourchier, when Macquoid remonstrated with him for wearing white socks with his sandals, looked very cross and demanded, 'Ain't they right, old boy?' Geneviève Ward (who had played Queen Eleanor in *Becket* at the Lyceum with Henry Irving) was evidently something of a terror, and had made a fuss at being asked to share a dressing-room with a number of other distinguished actresses, not having bothered to read the imposing list of names pinned to the door. Ellen Terry, who was already in the room, making up quietly in a corner, was heard to murmur softly, 'You always were a cat, Ginny!'

Miss Ward was however a fine tragedienne, a famous Volumnia in *Coriolanus*, a part she often played with Benson's company, and the first actress to be made a Dame. But Ellen Terry was not similarly honoured till several years later, presumably because of her marital irregularities, and the title only came to her when she was too old to take much pleasure from it. The whole theatrical profession was deeply indignant that she had not been the first actress to be singled out. As the two actresses stood opposite to one another at Drury Lane that afternoon, I remember watching Ellen Terry, as she held the mask of Comedy for many minutes in her outstretched hand, restlessly dropping it to her side from time to time, while Geneviève Ward stood like the Rock of Gibraltar, holding her Tragic mask with a grip of steel.

Chapter 24

Family Portrait

Fred, Marion, and Dame Ellen Terry

'Ladies and gentlemen. If there is anything an actor values more than your applause, it is your silent attention to detail which enables us to give you of our best. On behalf of my dear comrade Julia Neilson and all the comrades of my company, I thank you from my heart.' This was one of Fred Terry's characteristic curtain speeches.

He was an imposing figure, my great-uncle, when I first became aware of him at my parents' Christmas parties, built on generous lines, with fine hands and red curly hair. Extremely shortsighted, and wearing gold pince-nez like his master, Henry Irving, he behaved, as he acted, in the grand manner, jingling the sovereigns in the pockets of his striped grey trousers – worn with a black stock, tailcoat, and button boots – the typical Edwardian actor-manager.

He loved his work with a dedicated devotion, and was touchingly sincere and simple in his attitude towards it. For him heroes and heroines were always white and villains always black. A faithful disciple of Irving, Tree, and Alexander, in whose companies he had so often appeared in his first years as a young actor, he followed their example by embellishing his own productions with fine scenery and lavish costumes, and drilled his crowds and ensemble scenes with loving care, perfecting elaborately worked-up entrances and effective 'curtains' and using music to give background to dramatic or sentimental scenes.

Max Beerbohm, writing of his performance in a drama entitled
Dorothy o' The Hall (in which Dorothy Vernon danced with
Queen Elizabeth), remarked, 'Mr Terry . . . hiding behind a
bower of roses, thrust his face through the flowers, in sight of the
audience, without seeming ridiculous. Mr Terry thrusts his face
thus and stays thus, for several seconds: and yet manages to
remain, as he would say, "mahnly". It is a remarkable achievement.'

Jolly, warm and generous, he was also a man of violent
prejudices, and subject to sudden and violent fits of apoplectic
rage which quickly passed like clouds before the sun. His
language could be sulphurous, though he managed to restrain
it in front of ladies, to whom he was always extremely
courteous. He was fond of gambling, and would spend long
hours playing bridge at one of his London clubs (he was a great
clubman) or swearing furiously if he played badly on the golf
course or backed a loser on the race-course. On one occasion,
feeling it was necessary to call a young actor to order for using
bad language in the Green Room Club, he sent for the young
man in question and spoke to him severely. 'Well,' said the
culprit, 'I seem to remember, Sir, that I have sometimes heard
you use fairly strong language in the Club yourself.' 'God all
bloody mighty,' retorted Fred Terry, 'I'm the f . . . President.'

He believed completely in the romantic nonsense in which he
acted so successfully, but in modern clothes he knew he could
not achieve the splendid panache which so delighted his audiences
when he was in period costume. He knew just how to swing a
cape, flourish a feathered hat, sweep a magnificent bow, dance a
minuet, spit his opponent with a flash of his rapier, or light up a
commonplace scene with his lively presence and ringing laugh.
But he thought Ibsen decadent and Shaw discursive. Clean, full-
blooded romantic melodrama was his acknowledged field, and he
revelled in it all through his theatre life, and occasionally in his
private life as well.

Marion, his favourite sister, who acted so delightfully in plays
by Wilde and Barrie, had also been beautifully trained in

Shakespeare and costume plays. She too was somewhat narrow in her outlook and lacked humour in private life, where she demanded a good deal of flattery and attention. But she was a brilliant actress, shrewd enough to adapt her technique to a more realistic manner as time went by, even succeeding (as Lilian Braithwaite, who had often worked with her, when she herself was an *ingénue*, was also to do in *The Vortex* some twenty years later) as 'the woman with the past', when she created the part of the adventuress, Mrs Erlynne, in Wilde's *Lady Windermere's Fan*. Her last appearance in London was in Somerset Maugham's *Our Betters*, as the Princess, one of the only two respectable characters in the comedy, which was considered at that time (1923) to be extremely daring, and I always wondered what Marion herself must have thought of the play when she agreed to act in it. Fred would most certainly have disapproved of it profoundly.

It is sad that Ellen Terry, the greatest and most famous of the Terry family, could not succeed in finding vehicles for her talent after leaving the Lyceum, whereas her sister and brother – Fred was the youngest of the family – continued to appear in London and the provinces right up to the Twenties. Ellen was to triumph only once more for a season at His Majesty's as Mistress Page with Tree (though Irving was still alive), in his Coronation production of *The Merry Wives of Windsor* in 1902. In this she appeared with Mrs Kendal, her life-long rival and, according to my father, the best actress in England, though never to be compared in popularity with Ellen Terry. In 1905 Tree also presented *The Winter's Tale* for Ellen at his theatre though he did not himself appear in it (Charles Warner was Leontes), but she seems not to have made any great impression as Hermione. Her memory, as with all the Terrys, was treacherously uncertain, and her concentration easily disturbed, though she continued to the end of her life to enchant the public whenever they were lucky enough to see her on or off the stage.

Ellen Terry drew her characters, with instinctive genius, in broad strokes and generous flowing lines, but she seemed too restless to be confined within the walls of drawing-room comedy or even in contemporary heroic drama. Her failure as Hiordis in Ibsen's *The Vikings* (which she daringly produced in 1903 under her own management chiefly to display the scenic talents of her son Gordon Craig) must have made her wary of venturing into more experimental work. She had listened too late to Shaw's entreaties, and stayed too long at the Lyceum, with its fading fortunes, out of a strong sense of professional discipline and unwillingness to dissolve her long and triumphant partnership with Irving.

She could not help loving to be loved, and, as the public always preferred her to make them laugh or cry (they would have none of her as a tragedienne, either as Lady Macbeth or Volumnia), she went on playing Goldsmith's Olivia and Nance Oldfield,[1] with Portia and Katharine of Aragon to bring her back to her beloved Shakespeare from time to time so long as the passing years allowed. In her seventies, when I heard her give her Shakespeare lecture readings, she could still give radiant glimpses of her former glory, and one could understand the older generation of playgoers who said, 'She speaks Shakespeare as if she had just been talking to him in the next room.' But the only two contemporary plays in which she appeared at the turn of the century, Barrie's *Alice Sit By The Fire* (1905) and Shaw's *Captain Brassbound's Conversion* (1906), proved something of a disappointment, and her divine gifts of tears and sunshine never seemed to inspire a new playwright to provide her with adequate material.

I think both Fred and Marion were always somewhat afraid of their elder sister, perhaps because she was apt to be slyly amused at their immense seriousness and respectability, and was basically far simpler and more unashamedly Bohemian than they were. When she was engaged by Doris Keane in 1919 to play the Nurse in *Romeo and Juliet* – her last professional appearance in a London run – she wrote with glee, 'I am keeping all the rude bits in!' – a remark which would certainly have shocked her brother and sister. But perhaps the shade of Irving would have chuckled.

1 *Olivia* by Wills adapted from *The Vicar of Wakefield*. *Nance Oldfield*, a one-act play by Charles Reade.

Himself a somewhat bitter and ironic humorist, he had never been able to resist her enormous sense of fun, even when she arrived late for rehearsals and broke up the other actors by fooling during a performance, behaviour which he would never have countenanced from anyone else within the sacred portals of his theatre.

All the Terrys had healthy appetites, enormous courage, and staying-power – especially in honouring their acting commitments – poor eyesight, bad memories, and intermittently indifferent health. They all possessed expressive hands – Fred's were beautiful (but Ellen's were not, though she used them wonderfully), and they all contrived to move with unfailing grace. Marion took the stage with immense distinction, even when bowed with age (there was a sensational moment one Christmas, when my mother warned us that Aunt Marion's hair was white and we must not appear to notice; she had always dyed it red which of course we had not realised), while Ellen appeared to dart across the scene, giving an impression of dragonfly swiftness and outdoor freedom. 'But look where Beatrice, like a lapwing, runs close by the ground to hear our conference.' Even when I saw her at the Coliseum and another time at a theatre on the West Pier at Brighton, during the First World War, acting the Trial Scene of *The Merchant of Venice* and some scenes as Mistress Page (with a young Edith Evans as Nerissa and Mistress Ford), she seemed to bring a breath of fresh air with her the moment she stepped on to the stage.

Ellen, Marion, and Fred – all three spoke with unerring diction, phrasing, and flow of thought, in the melting beauty of their inimitable Terry voices. As one can see from Ellen's rehearsal-scripts, she would rewrite and rephrase her lines as she tried to memorise them, in order to make them sound spontaneous and more natural, managing to breathe life into the stilted speeches allotted to her, even in fustian plays like *The Dead Heart* and *Ravenswood*, the later Irving productions at the Lyceum. Irving himself had always used the same method with his most famous parts (in his melodramas, *The Bells*, and *Louis XI* for instance), and Fred used to follow the same example, cutting and adding continually over many performances to build up the effects he needed, though of course this was an impossible method to use in Shakespeare or in a really well-written modern play.

Fred could add grace to the most commonplace lines. As he leaned over the back of the garden seat in the scene at Richmond in *The Scarlet Pimpernel* and said to Lady Blakeney 'Madam, will you not dry those tears? I could never bear to see a pretty woman cry,' he would suddenly lower his voice a whole octave and a hush would spread over the entire audience.

He loved to help young people if he possibly could, with money, encouragement, and good advice. He once sent for a young actor whom I knew and advised him to leave his company to take an engagement in the West End (this was towards the end of his own career, when he was touring with cheaper actors than before). He told the boy that he was ready to better himself and could learn no more from him. He helped to train the young Donald Wolfit, who always acknowledged all he had learned from him. When he was not acting himself he would go to see the current successes in the London theaters, standing at the back of the pit so that he could slip in and out unnoticed. He once engaged his nephew Gordon Craig to design a scene for him, though I doubt if he really understood his work. But he could never bring himself to appear in plays that he could not pretend to like and, in spite of recurring ill-health which he resisted with the greatest courage, he remained in management with his wife, acting in the vehicles they had always loved and in which they felt they both showed to the best advantage. They continued to give regular seasons in London with varying success, and managed to recover the losses of their occasional failures by touring the big provincial cities, where their arrivals and departures were always something of a royal progress.

Of course Fred should have played Falstaff in his later years, and he would have been a magnificent Sir Peter Teazle. But he preferred to act Benedick, for which he was then too old, and

Bothwell and Henry the Eighth in two indifferent melodramas, probably because they gave equal opportunities to his wife. He had appeared as Charles Surface in his young days, and told me that once, acting in the Screen Scene with the famous old actor William Farren as Sir Peter, Mrs Patrick Campbell, hidden behind the screen as Lady Teazle, became exasperated by their slowness, and boomed out, 'Oh, do get on, you old pongers!' Someone congratulated him on the way he flicked his lace handkerchief over his uncle's portrait in the auction scene, but Fred only said modestly, 'Ah, that's Coghlan's business.' It was always touching to hear the respect and admiration he expressed for Irving and his famous predecessors of the past.

When he first produced *The Scarlet Pimpernel* in the provinces, it was not much liked, and Fred realised instinctively that as nearly all the action took place offstage, a more lively scene to open the play might get it off to a better start. So a prologue was introduced, set at one of the Gates of Paris, with the Pimpernel, disguised as an old woman, driving a ramshackle cart in which, of course, the aristocrats he was saving from The Terror were concealed. The new opening proved an enormous success and the play was to stand him in good stead for twenty years and more. As soon as it became talked about, everyone got to know that the hag in the Paris scene was Blakeney, despite his disguise of a false nose and shabby bonnet, and the entrance of the cart (drawn by a real horse – ever a hazardous but popular addition to any drama in those days) always drew a round of applause to greet the star. But Fred soon decided that he need not trouble to add to his labours by the task of making a quick change of clothes and make-up so early in the evening, and after a few weeks preferred to entrust the part of the old hag to his obedient understudy. Of course the audience were unaware of the deception and applauded just the same. But Fred instructed his dresser to stand in the wings at every performance and solemnly hand the Terry pince-nez to the understudy as he dismounted from the cart. It is not recorded whether the company were deceived by this charming little trick.

Fred's historical romances were always strictly wholesome, even at the expense of authenticity. Lady Castlemaine and the Duchess of Portsmouth were only malicious ladies at the court of the Merry Monarch, Nell Gwynne herself merely the King's great-hearted friend, who foiled the wicked Judge Jeffreys by dressing up in his wig and gown, making great comic play as she wielded a scratching quill pen and sneezed loudly after taking huge pinches of snuff. At the end of this scene she was triumphantly carried from the stage in a sedan-chair, waving her huge cartwheel feathered hat out of the window. She danced with two of her former actor cronies, accompanied herself on a spinet, and in the last act rushed breathlessly up a staircase from below in a magnificent dress which billowed round her, crying, 'The Queen is too ill to see me. What's to be done?' The part of King Charles, with his real spaniels, was something of a holiday for Fred, but he wore a splendid make-up and played it to perfection, even when one of the dogs bit off the end of his false nose and jumped off his knee to vanish with it through the stage fireplace, to the audience's great delight.

He once mounted a production of *Romeo and Juliet* for his daughter Phyllis. He had intended to act Mercutio, but became ill during rehearsals and finally directed the play without appearing in it himself. A shy young actor, engaged to play the part of Paris, was given an elaborate Carpaccio costume to wear — parti-coloured tights and an Italianate wig falling to his shoulders. Some of the older members of the company, with whom he shared a dressing-room, mischievously drew attention to the inadequacy of his make-up, and finally persuaded him to add mascara to his eyelashes, rouge to his lips, and a dangling pearl to his right ear. Deeply self-conscious in all this finery, the young man slunk timidly on to the stage at the dress, parade and bashfully announced himself. Fred, who was asleep in the darkness of the stalls, woke suddenly, rammed his glasses on to his nose, and, roaring with laughter, shouted out, 'My God, it's a tart I once slept with in Bury St Edmunds!'

At the old Borough Theatre, Stratford (long since torn down), on a foggy afternoon after a matinée, he came to the stage door, still dressed in his Pimpernel costume, to press a gold sovereign into my schoolboy hand. On another day he gave me a rich lunch at his Club, and afterwards climbed many flights of stairs in my parents' house to look at my model theatre and the clumsy scenery which I had painted to embellish it. Later, when his daughter had generously given me my first professional engagement, and afterwards, when I had arrived at some success, he never failed to encourage me and write me delightful letters. In one of them he praised my Hamlet, to my great delight, comparing it to that of Irving and Forbes-Robertson and the other great ones who had played the part. And though he professed to be deeply shocked by *The Constant Nymph* (with its Gordon Craig-like character of the Bohemian Sanger, with his mistress and brood of illegitimate children) when he saw it in 1926, he seemed strangely tolerant of an equally ambiguous atmosphere when he came to see me act in Ronald MacKenzie's *Musical Chairs* in 1931. But by that year he had aged considerably, mellowing as his time grew short.

Narrow but generous, simple, direct, and deeply honest – a 'prince of good fellows' (as he once called the Prince of Wales at a Public Dinner, only to find his Royal Highness furtively picking his nose as he sat beside him in the place of honour) he was a noble figure of the theatre, a consummate romantic actor, and a great gentleman besides.

To Act A New Part

The life of Ellen Terry has already been recorded in a number of vivid and informative memoirs – notably her Autobiography, first published in 1908, and reissued in 1933, with notes and a record of her later years (she died in 1928) by her daughter Edith Craig, in collaboration with Christopher St John, who had worked as 'literary henchman' on the original memoir and was a close friend of both mother and daughter. Naturally Mr Manvell, in his new life of the great actress,[1] has drawn

1 *Ellen Terry* by Roger Manvell. Heinemann 1968.

extensively on these two books, as well as quoting freely from the Shaw-Terry correspondence, the letters and diaries of Graham Robertson, the two Irving and Terry books of Gordon Craig, the fine biography of Henry Irving by his grandson Laurence, Marguerite Steen's *A Pride of Terrys* and my own mother's autobiography. He has been extremely adroit in compressing and sorting this mass of relevant detail into a highly readable and straightforward account, and has added interest to it by shedding fresh light on many of the episodes which were suppressed or glossed over in the earlier books in order to avoid giving offence to surviving personalities or their families in the tactful conventions of the time.

The new book is greatly enriched by admirable sketches of Frederick Watts, Charles Kelly and James Carew (the three husbands of Ellen Terry); of her lover, the father of her two children and great love of her life, Edward Godwin (the architect and decorator); and of the great Henry Irving, her partner for so many years of splendour and success at the Lyceum Theatre. Mr Manvell sides with Laurence Irving (and against Marguerite Steen) on conjecturing that Irving and Ellen were never lovers. This is a fascinating riddle, still unsolved. Even members of Ellen's family – my own mother and Gordon Craig especially – defiantly rejected it all their lives, though there are two letters from Irving in Mr Manvell's book which I should have thought clinched the certainty of a love affair, during a few years or months at least, of their early partnership in the theatre.

The strictures of Henry James on both Irving's and Ellen Terry's acting talents create an admirable critical balance for readers of today, and show that, amongst the almost unanimous public adulation accorded them both for so many years, they were not without their detractors among a number of discerning playgoers. I find a certain coldness in the book which may largely be accounted for by the fact that, because of my own relationship to Ellen Terry, my lifelong pride in her achievements and my own personal remembrances of her magical charm and humour (even though I only knew her in old age when I was still a schoolboy), have given me a sense of affinity with her that has made me feel that no one could understand her character and talents quite as well as I do.

Gordon Craig, her son (whom I began to know only when I was middle-aged and he was an old man) had a marvellous sense of humour – a rather wicked and yet childishly attractive kind of fun and defiance – which reminded me strongly of his mother as I remember her, though in his case this was allied to a certain malice which I do not at all connect with her, and which seems to me more likely to have come from Godwin, the father whom he knew so little, and idolised yet resented, I fancy, all his life. (Shaw once said cleverly that Craig never quite forgave his mother that Irving was not his father.) Ellen's best known sister and brother, Marion and Fred Terry, were both fine players and enchanting personalities (the one stingy, the other extravagantly generous), both Philistines, somewhat snobbish, typical late Victorians in their outlook, tastes and prejudices. But Ellen was magnificently impulsive, wise (except for her own emotional recklessness), a simple, honest woman – Bohemian and great lady at the same time, she could move in any direction that once engaged her intelligence and common sense. One felt immediately that she had a modern point of view, a desire to understand new people and new trends.

It was only sad that her faculties began to fail her in her last years, making her dependent on people who guarded her of necessity, but also troubled her by that possessiveness and jealousy which so often surrounds a uniquely magnetic personality. She had always been fond of the company of men. They stimulated and delighted her, and in old age she was always hemmed in by women. I cannot resist quoting from a superb essay, written for the *New Statesman* in 1941 by Virginia Woolf, which I have always kept in my own copy of Ellen's biography (which she gave me herself in 1917), for it seems so extraordinarily perceptive:

Which then, of all these women is the real Ellen Terry? . . . Is she mother, wife, cook, critic, actress, or should she have been after all, a painter? Each part seems the right part until she throws it aside and paints another . . . Shakespeare could not fit her; nor the nursery. But there is, after all, a greater dramatist than Shakespeare, Ibsen, or Shaw. There is Nature. Hers is so vast a stage, and so innumerable a company of actors, that for the most part she fobs them off with a tag or two. They come on and they go off without breaking the ranks. But now and then Nature creates a new part, an original part. The actors who act that part always defy our attempts to name them. They will not act the stock parts – they forget the words, they improvise others of their own. But when they come on, the stage falls like a pack of cards and the limelights are extinguished. That was Ellen Terry's fate – to act a new part – and while other actors are remembered because they were Hamlet, Phèdre, or Cleopatra, Ellen Terry is remembered because she was Ellen Terry.

New Statesman, 12th April 1968

Chapter 25

Brother and Sister

Edward and Edith Gordon Craig

Edward and Edith Gordon Craig, the children of Ellen Terry by Edward Godwin, the architect and designer to whom she was never married, were a fascinating pair. The boy was something of a genius – a promising actor who became dissatisfied with acting, and became a brilliant designer, scene-inventor, etcher, wood-cutter, and an accomplished and original writer; the girl, equally frustrated, was also an actress *manquée*, handsome, though less physically attractive, and gifted, like her brother, with consider-able talents for which she failed, on the whole, to gain the recognition she deserved.

They were both devoted to their mother, but resented the absence of the father whom they had hardly known. Ellen's second husband, Charles Kelly, and afterwards Henry Irving, became substitute father-figures to them both, but they were difficult children to manage and were to cause their mother continual anxiety as they grew older, even though her growing success and popularity, and the large salary which she earned at the Lyceum, enabled her to lavish much care and money on their education. She was inclined to spoil them, though she tried to be very strict. Ted escaped from home and married young, after a turbulent career at various schools and a long restless apprenticeship at the Lyceum, but Edy remained in her mother's house, failing to achieve an early ambition to become a professional pianist through a rheumatic condition which developed when she was studying in Germany.

Ellen Terry, remembering no doubt the failure of her own marriages (the first, to the painter Watts, had been contracted and dissolved when she was little more than a girl), is said to have interfered on two occasions when Edy fell in love. A clique of women friends who flattered and adored her gradually began to influence her strongly, and were apt to involve her mother (whom they also adored) in jealous intrigues and possessiveness. Ted never lived in England after his early years, and, though Ellen loved him devotedly and treasured his occasional visits, she had mostly to be content with paying his debts, sympathising with the various women with whom he was associated at different times, and housing his children when he appeared to be too busy to look after them himself.

The brother and sister were basically very fond of one another, but when they had worked together, under their mother's management, at the Imperial Theatre in 1903, Ted designing and directing and Edy in charge of the costume department, they had failed to get on for various reasons, and Ted soon escaped abroad after the season had proved a disastrous financial failure. Though many had admired and praised the ideas which he conceived in the few productions he had actually carried out in London, he was obviously much before his time, and it was said that no management had sufficient faith to engage him, as he was reputed to spend money extravagantly and demand to be given complete authority in any theatre in which he worked.

Ted and Edy had both appeared in minor parts with Irving and their mother at the Lyceum. Both became devoted to him, though the experience did not seem to give them great confidence in their own abilities as actors. Surprisingly for that strict time, they were accepted everywhere in society for Ellen Terry's sake, but there is no doubt that the slur of their illegitimacy, as well as a favouritism which they resented, helped to disturb their youthful development.

Edy was not aggressively masculine in personality, though she was sometimes brusque and rude, and very autocratic in dealing with those who worked with her. She was a very clever costume designer, and later an original stage director, but in her best years she was evidently too managing to be tactful or popular. Living in the shadow of Ellen Terry's overwhelming charm, she probably developed a complex about being considerably less attractive than her mother. She had a slight lisp which was hard for her to overcome, and she earned the reputation, as she grew older, of being a kind of dragon, apt to exploit her mother, bullying her, sometimes in front of other people, and forcing her to go on appearing in the theatre when her memory and eyesight were too weak to allow her to shine with her former lustre. Chris Marshall (who changed her name to Christopher St John when she was converted to Catholicism) was Edy's greatest friend, and as devoted to the mother as she was to the daughter. She was the 'literary henchman' who collaborated with Ellen in the writing of her splendid autobiography in 1906, the time of Ellen Terry's Jubilee. After Ellen died in 1928, she and Clare Atwood, the painter, helped Edy with devoted pains to perpetuate her memory, arranging Ellen's Smallhythe Farm as a beautiful museum, and adapting the old Barn which stands in her garden as a small theatre where they organised a matinée every year on the anniversary of her death. Christopher St John also revised Ellen's first book of memoirs and annotated it admirably, while Edy, despite bitter recriminations from her brother (who retorted with a book *Ellen Terry and Her Secret Self* giving his own account of his relationship with his mother), persuaded Bernard Shaw to let her publish the fascinating correspondence between himself and Ellen Terry, which had originated when Shaw was a musical critic and Ellen was still leading lady at the Lyceum.

Edy was as industrious as her brother, and continued working almost till her death, producing plays in churches and pageants in parks and gardens. To me she was always most sympathetic and kindly, a picturesque figure whether in her country smock or rather striking bohemian clothes, delivering her views with brisk authority. In old age she grew to look very like her mother.

Many theatre people admired and respected her, though they were somewhat wary of allowing her too much rein for fear of upsetting her collaborators. She was unlucky to have lived at a time when women were not greatly trusted with leading positions in the world of the theatre (except as actresses) and in consequence she always had a good deal of suspicious resentment to contend with. Her mother became fretful and forgetful, and it was necessary for Edy to take every care of her. Her family resented this as an intrusion and criticised her accordingly, but there is not doubt that Ellen and Edy loved each other to the end, in spite of many difficulties and heart-burnings on both sides, fanned by the interference of well-meaning relations, as well as by enemies and devotees.

I appeared under Edy's direction for the first time at a matinée to help some Children's Charity at Daly's Theatre in the early Twenties. There were tableaux of famous Saints (Gladys Cooper as St George, Sybil Thorndike as St Joan) with groups of small children, dressed as cherubs and angels, in the main feature of the programme, a Nativity Play. The Virgin was to be played by Fay Compton, and I was asked to be one of the three shepherds. We had, I think, only one rehearsal, the usual half-baked muddle in some bleak room or other, with half the cast failing to put in an appearance. My own few lines were, I was told, to be spoken as the shepherds walked from the footlights across the stalls on a gangplank stretching to the back of the theatre. We had to sit down near the footlights, munch some food we had with us, and then see the Star in the East and move through the auditorium towards where it was supposed to be.

On the afternoon of the performance the house was not very full. In fact there seemed to be more people on the stage and behind the scenes than in the audience. The mothers of the children who were appearing kept rushing from their seats in the stalls, pushing through the pass door into the wings to attend to their offsprings' manifold emergencies. Stage-hands were trying to find their way among the crowd of actors and actresses who were greeting one another to loud stage whispers. Two huge wolfhounds were held on leashes by Esmé Percy, who was Herod, and George Hayes, his decadent son. Edith Craig herself, with her devoted friends, Christopher St John and Clare At-wood, dressed in voluminous monks' robes, were issuing orders in all directions. As the afternoon wore on and a number of mistakes began to occur, they drew their hoods over their heads and pressed their way on to the stage among the performers. I entered with my two companions, and we proceeded towards the footlights, where we sat to begin our speeches, to find, to our dismay, that slices of delicious soft bread, hunks of cheese, and apples had been realistically provided in our haversacks. These, rashly crammed into our mouths, made our enunciation almost unintelligible. However, we hastily finished our lines (and our food) and progressed gingerly towards the doors at the back of the stalls, only to find them locked impenetrably against our exit. So we had to walk back along the ramp the way we had come, and sneak as unobtrusively as we could round the characters on the stage who were already engaged in playing another scene.

After the episode in which Joseph and Mary arrived at the inn and were given shelter in the stable, there was supposed to be a blackout, during which the Child was born, to be discovered later in the manager with the Virgin and the animals. But the light cues were fatally mismanaged, and the gauze, supposed to conceal the stable during an interlude played in front of it, suddenly became transparent. Fay Compton could be plainly seen picking up the doll representing the infant Jesus by its heels out of the crib and swathing it with a napkin before setting it on her lap. Ellen Terry, who had been brought by her daughter to make an appeal at the beginning of the performance, and was now sitting in the prompt corner, eagerly listening to all that was going on, peered through her thick spectacles at Fay Compton and called out in her famous Terry whisper, 'Do tell that child to take all that red off her lips.'

Ted Craig was a great disappointment to me when I met him first. C. B. Cochran had invited him to England to design an opening production for the Phoenix Theatre, which had just been completed in 1930. Sidney Bernstein had built it and had engaged Komisarjevsky to decorate it. Sidney lent Craig his London house to stay in and he was given *carte blánche* by Cochran to decide on the play he would choose to design and perhaps also to direct. I was acting at the Old Vic at the time, my second season there, and *The Tempest*, in which I was playing Prospero, had just been added to the repertoire. Of course I was greatly excited at the prospect of meeting my famous second cousin. As a schoolboy I had devoured his books, the more enthusiastically since Ellen Terry herself had given me one of them, *On the Art of the Theatre*, as a Christmas present with a dedication written on the title page. Craig invited me to lunch at the Café Royal. With him was Martin Shaw, a clever musician and one of Craig's oldest and dearest friends. They had produced *Dido and Aeneas* and *Acis and Galatea* together in Hampstead at the beginning of the century. Martin Shaw was disfigured by a large birthmark on one side of his face, and, according to one account, Edy had once been in love with him, but Ellen had considered him too ill-looking for her daughter.

Craig treated me somewhat patronisingly at this first meeting. He said, 'I felt we ought to get to know each other, as you seem to be quite popular here in London.' He went on to say that he had rushed from the Old Vic in horror after seeing only the opening scene of *The Tempest*, though Harcourt Williams, who had directed the production, was one of his old friends and fellow actors. Ted had written to him several times during our rehearsals, wishing him luck and predicting success for him, and Harcourt Williams had continually held him up to us all as a great man and an acknowledged genius of the theatre, so I was naturally very hurt by his airy dismissal of Lilian Baylis, the Vic, and all it stood for. Naturally, too, my vanity was piqued that he had seen so little of my own performance. I asked him shyly what play he was proposing to do for Cochran. 'Oh,' he answered vaguely, 'I am not sure yet. Perhaps *Macbeth*. I have many schemes and designs for that play. But, you know, what I do look forward to is inviting any artists or friends who may be in London at the time to sit with me in the Royal Box and watch rehearsals. ' I took this remark with a grain of salt, but throughout our meal I felt that he was probably posing a good deal and pulling my leg. Still, I went away with a great sense of disappointment. Not long afterwards the whole project with Cochran ended in smoke and Craig went back to Italy, and it was many years – twenty-two to be exact – before I was to see him again.

In 1953 I had rented a villa in the South of France for a summer holiday, and decided to look him up in Vence, where he was living on little money at a small pension. My sister and I drove up a steep lane to find it, and there, standing at the top of a flight of stone steps, was Craig – unmistakably impressive in a broadbrimmed straw hat, with a walking stick (probably Irving's) in his hand, large tortoiseshell spectacles on his nose, a scarf thrown round his neck, and a frieze Italian cloak flung back over a white coat like a surgeon's, with a high collar, and some kind of medallion on a black cord round his neck. He looked very like the famous Toulouse-Lautrec poster of Aristide Bruant. He seemed enormously pleased to welcome us, sang snatches of music-hall songs, cracked jokes, and told us the best restaurant to eat at. Of course we took him there immediately and helped him to enjoy a delicious meal. Then he took us back to the pension and showed us his small room, touchingly simple and beautifully arranged. Small photographs were pinned on a screen and above his narrow little bed with its folded rug. Pipes, drawing instruments, knives and chisels, all impeccably tidy, were laid out in order on his desk. He had created a little world of his own in those modest surroundings. On a shelf were copies of mid-Victorian farces which he had collected on the quais in Paris and bound and annotated himself. Books were piled everywhere but he seemed to know exactly where to find any reference he wanted. He seemed contented and delightfully affable, and when he came to see us at our villa a few days later he charmed us as greatly as before. I noticed that he never spoke French – even in the restaurant, where the proprietress and waiters knew him well – and he seemed amazingly well informed about the theatre in London and indeed everywhere in Europe. He had met Laurence Olivier in Paris, where he had seen him play Richard the Third, and thought his performance fine and Irvingesque. I told him I had heard he had gone to see it several times. 'Yes,' he replied, 'I am getting deaf you know, and they used to let me pop into the prompter's box so that I could see and hear really well.' 'Surely not *every* night,' I said. 'Well, occasionally I used to slip out and sit for a bit of a smoke in the box-office,' he admitted, chuckling. 'And do you know, about nine o'clock every evening a man would come in and take a big bag of money away with him. Of course that impressed me every much!'

We had broken the ice at last on these two visits, and I was deeply touched when, at a time of great trouble for me in London a few months later he suddenly wrote me a letter enclosing a card in Ellen Terry's handwriting, which she had sent to comfort him on some occasion, years before, when he had been involved in a disturbing crisis of his own.

After that time we wrote to each other fairly often, and I went to see him again whenever I was in the South of France. After long negotiations he had managed to sell his fine library to a French collector, and with the money had bought a small bungalow on the outskirts of Vence, where he was looked after by his daughter Nellie, a charming middle-aged woman, about my sister's age, with a great look of her grandmother and a gentle voice. He was ninety now, deaf, toothless, and very frail, but still full of energy and fun. He was lying on his bed when we arrived to take him out to lunch, reading a little book of Elizabethan poems. I asked Nellie to come with us (at which she seemed rather surprised, as she had expected to be left at home) and we got into the car with Ted in front. He chose a restaurant some fifteen miles away and seemed delighted at the prospect of quite a long drive. 'Don't talk at the back there,' he shouted to us, 'I can't hear a word you're saying.' Then he handed the book of poems to me across the back of his seat. 'Read this one,' he said, 'it's supposed to be by Walter Raleigh, but it's far too good for that. I bet it's Shakespeare. You ought to read it in your Recital, John, I hear you're having a great success with your readings.' 'All right,' I said, 'if you'll copy it out in your beautiful handwriting and send it to me.' But, alas he never did.

We chattered and laughed together over an enormous lunch, and it was after four o'clock when we got back to his little villa. When I said goodbye he put his hands on my shoulders and kissed me sweetly on both cheeks, and I felt sure I would not see him again.

Was Craig a genius? Thinking of him the other day I suddenly wondered why on earth I did not ask him to design *Macbeth* for me when I directed and played in it in 1942 – but then of course the war was raging, and he could not easily have come to England. (He was actually interned in Paris by the Nazis, but released after a few months with the help of Sylvia Beach, the publisher, and some Germans who had always admired his work.) But I fancy he would always have proved very difficult to handle if he had ever got down to the concrete task of producing a play. He was didactic and uncompromising, but also frivolous and unpredictable, as one can easily see from his son Edward's superb biography. Apart from the management who engaged him would he have known how to deal with actors and actresses? Would he have been patient and tactful enough to direct them, as he always seemed to expect to be allowed to do, as well as collaborating successfully with the technicians in creating the décor and lighting? He suffered from persecution mania, relying on other people yet trusting hardly anyone. He could not bring himself to confide in those who tried or offered to carry out his ideas for fear they would steal or misinterpret them. Autocratic to a degree, wildly egotistical, fickle and utterly unprincipled where money and women were concerned, he still created for himself a mystique of enduring proportions. A master without a school, an Englishman hardly acknowledged in his own country, he influenced the whole development of the theatre both in Europe and America. He abolished footlights and experimented with the spatial limits of the stage both in his designs and in one or two of the few productions which he actually achieved, framing his scenes in higher and wider proscenium openings and creating effects of simplicity and grandeur. He used a cyclorama for the first time, and the movable screens which he designed for the Moscow Arts production of *Hamlet* by Stanislavsky (though they failed to be completely successful on that occasion through lack of technical equipment to manipulate them), were a really magnificent invention. His passion for research was indefatigable. He was a voracious reader and an untiring worker. Very beautiful as a young man, his features still had a certain weakness which remained even when he was very old. Temperamental, crackety, with a charming voice and aristocratic manner, he was an artist to his finger tips. His thumbs however were rather sinister — unnaturally broad and thick. Quarrelsome and tender, violent one minute and gentle the next, he must always have been what nurses used to call 'a handful'!

Chapter 26

Three Witty Ladies

Mrs Patrick Campbell, Lady Tree,
and Dame Lilian Braithwaite

Mrs Patrick Campbell

'Stella – Stella for Star,' cried the heroine of Tennessee Williams's *Streetcar Named Desire*. And I thought at once of another star – Stella Beatrice, the great actress Mrs Patrick Campbell. Brilliant, impossible, cruel, fascinatingly self-destructive, witty (especially when she had a foreman worthy of her steel – Herbert Tree, Bernard Shaw, or Noël Coward), devastatingly unpredictable, she could be grandly snobbish one minute and generously simple the next. She despised people who were afraid of her, would patronise an audience if she felt them to be unsympathetic, and make fun of her fellow actors if they failed to provide her with inspiration. I once saw her walk through the whole of the first act of *John Gabriel Borkman*, ignoring the other players and taking every other line from the prompter, only to electrify the house in the next scene when she was partnered by an actor she admired. Her stage movements were expressive and unlike those of any other actress. I can see her now in *The Second Mrs Tanqueray* (late in her career, on tour at a theatre in Croydon), peeling muscat grapes with her fingers and cramming them into her mouth, 'I adore fruit, especially when it's expensive'. Stabbing the hat on her lap with a furious hatpin as Mrs Cortelyon felt the stage in the second act, and gazing at her face in a hand-mirror at the end of the play just before her final exit. I see her opening champagne in *Ghosts*, laying a table, cooing to a baby, and digging into a hamper of old clothes in *The Matriarch*, knitting in the last act of *Pygmalion* with a look of unutterable boredom on her face, airing her newly taught society accent in hollow, supercilious tones.

She was beginning to be fat when I met her first, and would make constant references to her fast-vanishing figure. 'I look like a burst paper bag,' and, 'I must borrow a chair with a high back so that I can hide my chins behind it.' She nearly always wore sweeping black dresses and hats with shady brims (she once told me proudly that the hat she was wearing that day looked so much better since she had trimmed the edges of it with a pair of nail-scissors), and her flowing velvets were usually sprinkled with the white hairs of Moonbeam, her beloved Pekinese. But she still appeared majestic as she swept down in the hotel lift to enthrone herself in a New York taxi, where she would proceed to chat with the driver on a variety of topics – the stupidity of Holly-wood, the Abdication of the Duke of Windsor ('Such a gesture has not been made since Antony gave up a Kingdom for Cleopatra') or the necessity of a halt to walk her dog. 'Who's responsible for this?' the man demanded as he discovered a puddle on the floor of his cab. 'I am,' replied Mrs Campbell, as she alighted calmly.

Everyone referred to her as Mrs Pat, but I always hated the familiarity, and took care always to address her by her full name until the day when she rewarded me by asking me to call her Stella. I had been introduced to her, in the early Twenties, at a luncheon party in Brighton in a private suite at the Metropole Hotel given by a Lord who loved the stage. She was playing Hedda Gabler at a theatre on one of the piers (why didn't I go to see her in it?) and someone told her that the performance was a *tour de force*. 'I suppose that is why I am always forced to tour,' she replied mournfully. Her company dreaded her, except for the few worshippers who dared to stand up to her when she was in a bad mood. She loved rich and titled people and would allow them to give her presents and entertain her, but she was very proud with younger folk and generous both in advice and criticism. She could be wonderful company, though I think she was often cruel to men who fell in love with her – even Forbes-Robertson and Shaw – and sometimes even more unkind to her women friends, letting them fetch and carry for her for a time and then making fun of them or casting them aside. But somehow I was never afraid of her, though the only time I acted with her, as Oswald in *Ghosts* in 1929, she played some alarming tricks and made a fool of me at one performance. The dress-rehearsal had gone off without mishap, and Mrs Campbell was word perfect and sailing through her scenes. At the first performance, however, she seemed less at ease, though still charming to me at the fall of the curtain, when she graciously thanked me for having helped her through. I beamed with delight and thought I had passed my test. At the second performance I was sitting at a table smoking. No ash tray had been provided, and I looked helplessly round when the cue came for me to put out my cigar. Not daring to leave my chair, for fear of complicating the moves that had been arranged by the director, I stubbed it out on the chenille tablecloth and dropped the butt under the table and then, a few moments later, stupidly put my hands on the table before lifting them to cover my face. Mrs Campbell, turning upstage, shook with laughter for the rest of the scene, and pouted, 'Oh, you're such an amateur!' as the curtain fell. During the second interval my aunt, Mabel Terry-Lewis, never famous for her tact, burst into my dressing-room. 'Tell her we can't hear a word she says,' she announced, 'the Charing Cross Road is being drilled outside!' This counsel I naturally preferred to ignore, though it hardly tended to improve my already shaken confidence. But worse was yet to come. At the end of the play Mrs Alving stands aghast, staring at her son as he mutters, 'Mother, give me the sun. The sun! The sun!' In her hand she still holds the box of pills which she does not dare to give him. Mrs Campbell had evidently decided suddenly that she must make the most of this important final moment. With a wild cry, she flung the pillbox into the footlights and threw herself across my knees with her entire weight. 'Oswald. Oswald!' she moaned. The armchair (borrowed by Mrs Campbell herself from a friend, because, as she said, 'the back is high enough to hide my chins') cracked ominously as she lay prone across my lap, and as I clutched the arms in desperation for fear they might disintegrate, she whispered fiercely, 'Keep down for the call. This play is worse than having a confinement.' Yet she had been of the greatest help during rehearsals and I always thought she could, if she had chosen, have been a fine director herself.

It was very difficult to judge the extent of her real talents in those later days. Of course I never saw her at the time of her early triumphs, when she was slim and elegant and Aubrey Beardsley drew her, willow-slender, for an exquisite study in black-and-white. I think she never took much exercise – the leading ladies of her day didn't deign to walk – and she was very fond of food. During the rehearsals of *Ghosts* we would lunch together, and she would sit in the Escargot Restaurant, devouring snails by the dozen. One day, while we were there, a striking-looking lady, with black hair parted in the middle and drawn back in a great knot at the nape of her neck, appeared in the doorway, attracting considerable attention from everyone in the room. 'Surely that is Madame Marguerite D'Alvarez, the famous singer,' I ventured to remark. Mrs Campbell lifted her eyes from her plate and murmured in tragic tones, 'Ah yes, Me in a spoon.'

I thought she did not much care for the Terry family, for my great-aunt Marion had been a famous rival of hers. She had played Mrs Erlynne on one occasion in Dublin to Mrs Campbell's Lady Windermere, and taken over her part at the last moment when Mrs Campbell quarrelled with Forbes-Robertson during the rehearsals of Henry Arthur Jones' *Michael and his Lost Angel*, though Marion proved to be ill-suited and the play was a complete failure. They were to play together once more in the 1920 revival of *Pygmalion*, and I fancy that she and Mrs Campbell must have worked on this occasion with velvet gloves.

But she always spoke to me of Ellen Terry with great admiration though she could not resist one crushing remark about my mother's family. I had been distressed to find her in New York (this was in 1936), living without a maid in a second-rate hotel room, clothes and papers strewn everywhere, laid up with influenza. She wrote afterwards to Shaw that my eyes had filled with tears when I arrived. 'All the Terrys cry so easily,' was her typical comment. But when I tried to send her a cheque as a Christmas present she refused to accept it and sent it back.

One afternoon, while I was playing *Hamlet* in New York, Mrs Campbell offered to take me to visit Edward Sheldon, the playwright. This remarkable man had been a youthful friend of John Barrymore, and had encouraged him to further his stage career by the brilliant series of classical revivals and romantic plays (*Richard III, Hamlet*, Tolstoy's *Living Corpse, The Jest*) in which Barrymore triumphed in the early Twenties. Sheldon was also the author of two sensationally successful melodramas, *Salvation Nell* for Mrs Fiske and *Romance* for Doris Keane, with whom he had been very much in love. He was now completely paralysed and blind as a result of some petrifying bone disease, but, despite his infirmity, he retained all his intellectual faculties, and continued his friendship with all the most brilliant players of the New York theatre, who went continually to see him and greatly valued his advice.

I realised, of course, that it was a great compliment to be given the opportunity of this meeting, and arrived punctually at the address in the East Sixties where he lived. Mrs Campbell was not yet there, and I was somewhat dismayed to be shown up to the penthouse, where I was ushered into a big lofty room with many windows looking out on to a terrace. Flowers, photographs, and books were everywhere, and there was no feeling of a sickroom except for the great bed, covered with a dark brocade coverlet, on which Sheldon lay stretched out, and his head tilted back at what seemed a dreadfully low and uncomfortable angle. His smooth face was beautifully shaved and he wore a neat bow tie and a soft shirt, but his eyes were covered with a black mask, and his hands were invisible beneath the coverlet.

Of course I was very shy at first, but as soon as he began to talk (though with a grating tired voice) he managed immediately to put me at my ease, and by the time Mrs Campbell arrived we were chattering away as if we had known each other all our lives.

Books and newspapers were read to him every day, and he was amazingly well-informed, especially about the theatre, and seemed to know everything that was going on. He asked me if I would come again one day and act some scenes from *Hamlet* for him, and of course I promised to do so. Again, he contrived to put me at my ease, and I never played to a more sensitive and appreciative audience.

In the years that followed he never forgot me, sending cables and messages even during the war years (he was destined to live longer than Mrs Campbell, who died in 1940) and when I was acting in Congreve's *Love for Love* in 1944 I received a telegram 'How I wish I could see you in Valentine's mad scene.'[1]

On that first afternoon, Mrs Campbell appeared ten minutes after I did. I fancy Sheldon had asked her to be late, so that he could break the ice with me alone. She was in one of her complaining moods, pouting and holding up her Pekinese against Sheldon's face, sighing that nobody wanted her any more in the theatre now that she was old and fat. Sheldon suddenly grew very quiet, and I noted how quickly she changed her manner and began to behave and talk in the fascinating, brilliant way that showed her at her very best. When we went away I tried to tell her how much I appreciated her charming gesture in taking me to see Sheldon and how delightfully she had helped to entertain us both. 'Ah,' she said, with real sincerity, 'one has to be at one's best with Ned. After all, we are all he has left. Think of it. There he lies in that room up there which he will never leave, and here we are walking in the street in the sunshine.' I never loved her more than on that day.

1 The remarkable memories of the older well-educated generation are very striking. Mr Justice Frankfurter, a famous American High Court Judge, quoted verbatim the whole opening scene of *Love for Love* when I met him in Washington at supper after the performance.

In a lecture recital which she concocted in the early Thirties, I realised that she was a complete Pre-Raphaelite. Neither Shakespeare nor the Bible served to exhibit her to real advantage. She boomed too much, sometimes even verging upon absurdity. I once saw her attempt Lady Macbeth, appearing with the American actor James Hackett, and she evidently did not care for acting with him. She had one fine moment at the end of the banquet scene, when she wearily dragged the crown from her head and her black hair fell to her shoulders as she sat huddled on the throne. But on her first appearance, looking like the Queen of Hearts about to have the gardeners executed, she swept her eyes over the stalls, graciously bowed to acknowledge her reception – leading ladies always entered to applause in those days – and, solemnly unrolling a large scroll (which, as one critic remarked, it would have taken a whole monastery a month to illuminate!), she read out Macbeth's letter with stately emphasis but ill-concealed contempt. In her recital, however, the excerpts from Pinero, Shaw, and Ibsen were very fine, and I was especially impressed by her rendering of *The High Tide on the Lincolnshire Coast*, a Victorian poem by Jean Ingelow. Her success with this made me realise why she had been so greatly in demand at parties in the Nineties, when she would recite (no doubt for an enormous fee) 'Butterflies all White – Butterflies all Black', in competition with Sarah Bernhardt, who was also a fashionable diseuse at the smart houses in those days whenever she acted in London. The two stars became great cronies, and on one occasion they played *Pelléas and Mélisande* together in French. Mrs Campbell had played Mélisande before with Martin Harvey and Forbes-Robertson, and in her recital she used to give an excerpt from the play (in English naturally), delivering the speeches of both the lovers in two contrasting voices, but this was not a very happy experiment as it seemed to me. The two actresses were fond of exchanging long telegrams with one another. I think Stella was not, as Ellen Terry was, an inspired letter-writer, and her correspondence with Shaw compares very poorly with that of Ellen. But I well remember a small luncheon party which I gave in New York when Mrs Campbell read to us aloud an article she had written on Bernhardt for a theatre magazine. This was charmingly written and immensely moving, and of course drew more 'Terry tears' from me.

She had always been amused to shock people by her behaviour, though she was sometimes rather prudish too, and I took care never to make ambiguous jokes when I was with her. My mother told me that once at a dinner party, when Stella was first married, she made a sensation, as the ladies rose to leave the table, by seizing a handful of cigars as they were being passed to the gentlemen by a servant, and, sticking them boldly in her *décolletage* one by one, announced gaily, 'Poor Pat can't afford cigars.'

Her witticisms have become a legend. Of Noël Coward's dialogue, 'His characters talk like typewriting.' Of a leading lady she was acting with, 'Her eyes are so far apart that you want to take a taxi from one to the other.' 'Tell Mr Alexander (who was playing Tanqueray) I never laugh at him while we are on the stage together. I always wait till I get home.' Of Shaw, 'One day he will eat a beefsteak, and then God help us poor women.' But Alexander Woollcott's famous remark after her Hollywood film débâcle a few years before she died, 'She is like a sinking ship firing on her rescuers,' was sadly to the point. She became impossibly difficult, insulted managers who made her offers, appeared in one or two absurdly bad plays, and made them worse by clowning in the serious scenes and assuming a tragic manner in the light ones. When she was appearing in a light comedy of Ivor Novello's in New York, for instance, she insisted on interpolating a speech from *Electra* in the middle of a most unsuitable context. But she never lost her sense of style or her regal bearing, and the deep voice, so often imitated, retained its thrilling range and power. James Agate still talked of 'the questing sweep of her throat' and her feet and ankles were slim and elegant to the last.

I read one of the lessons at her Memorial Service in 1941, on the morning following a first night at the Old Vic at which I had essayed King Lear. Coming out of the Church I heard someone say, 'It was an exciting occasion at the Old Vic last night,' and the answer, 'Yes, until the curtain went up,' was, I felt, one that Stella's shade would have surely relished. She might so easily have delivered it herself.

Review of Mrs Pat *biography by Margot Peters* Published by the Bodley Head

When I first met Mrs Patrick Campbell in the Twenties, at a lunch party at the Metropole Hotel in Brighton, her days of great success were long over. I had heard, of course, many of the legendary tales about her, but I stupidly failed to realise that by this time she was beset by chronic financial difficulties and personal squabbles, and was forced to tour, playing on seaside piers and anywhere else in the provinces and outskirts of London in which she could manage to obtain an engagement, at a poor salary, in her once-famous roles Paula Tanqueray, Hedda Gabler. She was now too old and fat for these, though still able, when she chose, to act with something of her former fire and power.

The paradoxical glamour of her personality and her defiant humour fascinated me immediately, and I was greatly flattered when she seemed to take a fancy to me and to express an interest in my own ambitious career.

I had found her autobiography, when it was first published in 1922, sadly disappointing, full of gushing tributes from titled admirers, poets and painters, but failing to convey anything of her own unique distinction. Alan Dent's account of her, written in 1961, was, to me, equally unsatisfactory. He had, I believe, never seen her act, and relied largely on the memories of James Agate (to whom Dent was secretary), who admired her very much. The result was untidy and only sporadically interesting.

I myself only saw her on the stage about half-a-dozen times, and acted with her only once (Agate described her Mrs Alving as being 'like the Lord Mayor's Coach with nothing in it'). I even attempted to direct her on one occasion, in a play which she sadly abandoned after a few weeks' rehearsal. But the brilliant biography by Mrs Peters has been researched with exemplary care and accuracy. The famous *bons mots* nearly always witty, sometimes cruel and personal, but usually devastatingly apt are quoted with appropriate relish. There is a wealth of material, never before made public, to enthrall the reader: the love affair with Forbes-Robertson (unfortunately no letters exist between them); the two broken marriages to Patrick Campbell and George Cornwallis-West; the fantastic popular acclaim, in both England and America, in the first years of this century, following the sensational Nineties' success of Mrs Tanqueray; the slogging tours and special matinées; the money squandered, generously as well as self-indulgently.

Then comes the slow but inevitable decline, largely, alas, of her own making. She became, as the American critic Alexander Woollcott remarked, 'a sinking ship, firing on her rescuers'. She could not cure herself of her deliberately contemptuous attitude towards her audiences as well as to managers and fellow-players. In her private life came the tragic wartime death of her beloved spoilt son and quarrels with his widow and her long-suffering daughter. Her acting career was to end with the wretched fiasco of her experiences in Hollywood. Her final days of exile and illness are infinitely sad.

Best of all, perhaps, are the chapters dealing with the abortive love affair with Shaw, who carefully guarded her infatuated letters until his wife's death, and which Mrs Campbell bargained so desperately to sell for publication in their last years. His baffling experiences with her in *Pygmalion*, and subsequent refusal to allow her, in several of his later plays, to create the parts which she herself had inspired (Hesione in *Heartbreak House*, the Serpent in *Back to Methuselah*), her pleas for money, and their mutual disillusionment – all this makes fascinating reading. Amidst such wealth of detail, there is a sentence which one would be glad to have elucidated even further. 'Duse had played Mrs Tanqueray's suicide – in front of the audience – and still felt it would be worthless to play it in any other way!' Could Duse have actually produced a phial and expired in a scene which Pinero never wrote? The opportunity offered of such a striking solo curtain would no doubt have appealed to Mrs Campbell. She obviously resented (when I acted with her in Ibsen's *Ghosts*) that Oswald has the final words.

Mrs Peters perceptively sums up Mrs Campbell's whole life and career when she writes:

> A strong sense of the absurd saved her from taking it all too seriously. 'My eyes are nothing in particular,' she would remark of her most admired feature. 'God gave me bootbuttons, but I invented the dreamy eyelid and that makes all the difference.'

Lady Tree

Lady Tree, *née* Maud Holt, had been a medical student and a Greek scholar before she became a successful actress. In her early photographs she appears pretty and slight, but when I first saw her on the stage, and later when I came to meet her, she had become somewhat eccentric-looking, wearing strikingly coloured flowing robes and fantastic hats, with scarves and veils draped about her throat and shoulders. She was supposed to have been a most moving Ophelia, when her husband, Sir Herbert Beerbohm Tree, played Hamlet. In his fair wig and beard Max Beerbohm is said to have remarked that he looked like a German Professor, and described his performance as being 'funny without being vulgar', though Max was always too much of a gentleman to attack his half-brother in his official notices in the *Saturday Review*.

Invited to see a play one evening by some enthusiastic friends, Max was somewhat dismayed to be ushered into a box at His Majesty's to see a performance of *Hamlet*. During the evening his hosts looked round to find his chair unoccupied, but soon found him curled up on a pile of overcoats in the passage, dozing. He woke and murmured apologetically, 'I am so sorry. I always enjoy Herbert's Hamlet this way.'

Sir Herbert was brilliant and eccentric too. He emulated a number of his contemporaries in siring several offspring besides those already presented him by his wife. Lady Tree, playing hostess, was once heard to remark, 'Ah, Herbert, late again? Another confinement in Putney?' And one night, returning late from a party to find Sir Herbert supping *tête à tête* with Esmé Percy, an extremely handsome young actor in his company, she peeped in at the door and murmured, 'The port's on the sideboard, Herbert, and remember it's adultery just the same.'

Many years later she was acting in *The Mask of Virtue*, a comedy in an eighteenth-century setting adapted from the French, in which Vivien Leigh made her first success in London. At the dress rehearsal Lady Tree, gazing hopefully across the empty stalls, called to the director, 'Mr A., it seems a little dark on the stage in this scene. Could you oblige us with a little more light? I think you may not have realised that my comedic effects in this play are almost wholly grimacial.'

At a charity matinée in which I once appeared with her she surveyed her script at rehearsals through an enormous magnifying glass. I was told that she would bring *The Times* crossword puzzle into the wings with her and proceed to solve it during her waits, uttering strange syllabic gasps and grunts to find the word of the exact length and shape she needed. Once in a modern comedy, *Indoor Fireworks*, she seemed to have threaded a lace scarf from one side of her head to the other, passing it through her large red wig and finally tying it under her chin like a bonnet, achieving a very strange result. One day I was lunching in a Soho restaurant, before playing a matinée, and saw her arrive at a neighbouring table with her daughter Viola. Not expecting her to remember me I bowed respectfully in passing them as I rose to go. Halfway down the street I heard my name called after me in dulcet tones, and, looking back, saw Lady Tree standing in the doorway of the restaurant, waving her scarf at me in belated greeting like Isolde or some Arthurian heroine of romance.

When she lay dying in hospital, her lawyer came to see her to help her to put her affairs in order. When he had gone away, her daughter asked her if his visit had not too greatly tired her. 'Not at all,' said Lady Tree, 'he was just teaching me my death duties.'

Dame Lilian Braithwaite

I knew Dame Lilian Braithwaite very well, and also had the delight of working with her very often. Since her early days as a successful *ingénue*, she had acted in every kind of play – farce, melodrama, Shakespeare – and was already a well-known leading lady in a number of West End plays at the time of the First World War. She was considered at that time to be a somewhat sentimental actress of sympathetic parts. But when she made an astonishing success as the vapid manhunting society mother in Noël Coward's *The Vortex* in 1924, critics and public were full of praise for her courage in daring to play with such honesty and conviction. From this new success she continued from one triumph to another both in light comedies and dramatic plays. Her witty timing, which she used to perfection both on and off the stage, gave a delicious edge to what seemed at first a deceptively innocent air of conventional Edwardian charm. Her kindness was unfailing, but the subtlety of the pause she would give to cap a critical remark could be delightfully pungent and occasionally devastating. 'B. told me that she is off to do a play in New York tomorrow . . . but I don't think it can be a very big part as she is going on a very small boat.' 'Of course I'm very fond of G . . . but I know what people mean.' I was with her once at a matinée. One of the leading actresses appearing in the play was known to be distinctly plain, but in a romantic-looking photograph displayed in the programme she appeared as a raving beauty. Lilian glanced at the picture, murmured, 'Fancy!' and quickly turned the page. She was a beautiful woman, always looking cool and elegant both on and off the stage, and she managed her cooing voice and precise diction with impeccable skill. She could drawl in an affected part or dominate in a dramatic scene with unexpected power. I used to watch her, fascinated, as she waited to make her first entrance in *The Vortex*, standing behind the closed door at which she was to appear, bracing herself with deep breaths, like an athlete preparing for a race, before she opened it.

She was a worthy opponent for some of her witty contemporaries, and could even challenge Mrs Campbell and Marie Tempest on their own ground, if either of them tried to patronise her, as they sometimes did. Lunching at the Ivy Restaurant one day with her daughter, a very unattractive man appeared in the doorway. The *maître d'hôtel* enquired politely, 'You want a table, sir? For two?' 'No,' replied the man, 'I'm quite alone.' Lilian was heard to mutter, 'I'm not surprised.'

Her enthusiasm and gallantry never failed her. In the Second War she went on organising concerts and entertainments for ENSA as well as appearing herself with unfailing professionalism and punctuality in the theatre in several long and arduous runs. Returning late one night after acting in *Arsenic and Old Lace*, she took refuge in the ground floor cloakroom during a big air-raid lasting for many hours. Asked the next morning if she was not exhausted by the experience she replied smilingly, 'Certainly not. We were fifty pounds up last night.' To a young actress who rashly remarked, 'Oh, I am so sorry you were in front this afternoon. I always feel I must save myself for the evening performance,' Lilian only shook her head, 'I didn't think you saved anything,' she said. And at a magnificent party to celebrate a long run she pointed to her dress with the remark 'C. has given me a dear little diamond brooch . . . can you see it?'

Actresses seemed in my youth to achieve astonishing changes in their figures in order to suit the fashions of the time. Lilian Braithwaite, a wasp-waisted slim *ingénue* in her early photographs, looked almost ample when I first saw her, during the First War, as the heroine's mother in a play at the Haymarket, *General Post*, with Norman McKinnel, Madge Titheradge, and George Tully. But ten years later she was as slim as a reed in the tubular frocks, short skirts, and shingled hair of the dancing mother in *The Vortex*. Even Ellen Terry, graceful and elegant until the end of the last century, appears matronly and almost stout in the photographs of her in *Captain Brassbound's Conversion* in 1906, though she too became extremely slender in her old age. Yet these were the days before dieting and beauty parlours. Marie Tempest was always plump and Yvonne Arnaud increasingly so as time went on. Lilian could not resist saying of her, 'It's still the dear little face we all loved so in *By Candle Light* (Pause) – but there's another face round it.'

The three actresses in this chapter might have perhaps been ideally cast as the three Queens in *Alice in Wonderland* – their dialogue precisely to the point, their wit as characteristically individual as their delightful and original personalities. Their witticisms would certainly have provided remarkable copy for anyone lucky enough to overhear what they had to say to one another behind the scenes.

Chapter 27

Some Non-Acting Actors

Sir Charles Hawtrey, Allan Aynesworth,
Gerald du Maurier, Ronald Squire, A. E. Matthews

Smart drawing-room comedy has always been staple fare in the
London theatre, and Max Beerbohm, in one of his theatre notices
of the early 1900s, writes mockingly of the absurdly over-
tailored 'mimes' (as he always called the actors) with their
impeccable trouserings with knife-edged creases and their over-
polished hats and boots. But there were a number of fine players
of that generation who could carry off their contemporary
clothes with a more natural air.

Gerald du Maurier, for instance, used to wear old suits on the
stage that were beautifully cut, but had obviously hung in his
wardrobe for years. How fascinating he was, to men as well as
women, although he was not at all conventionally handsome. He
could slouch and lounge and flick his leading lady behind one ear
as he played a love-scene, never seeming to raise his voice or
force an emotion, yet he could be infinitely touching too without
being in the least sentimental. His drunken painter, Dearth, in
Dear Brutus, was a masterpiece of understatement, acted with a
mixture of infinite charm and regretful pathos. He could be
flippant in light comedy or casually efficient in plays like *Raffles*
and *Bulldog Drummond*. His technique was inimitably resourceful,
though so well concealed. In one of his late successes, *Interference*,
he held the audience enthralled while he examined a murdered
man's body in a long scene lasting several silent minutes, and

once, when he played a walk-on valet at a charity matinée he managed to make an effective moment as he took the overcoat from the shoulders of one of the principal characters.

Charles Hawtrey and Allan Aynesworth belonged to the same naturalistic school as du Maurier, and, after their deaths Ronald Squire and A. E. Matthews continued the same kind of tradition on similar lines though they never achieved quite so much success.

Hawtrey and Aynesworth were both portly and well fed, looking more like business men than actors. They wore dark suits for formal occasions, their tweeds or riding breeches for the country were unobtrusively well cut, and their coats were roomy with big flapped pockets. They wore fancy waistcoats, gold watch-chains, and smart boots, and everything they did on the stage was perfect, so perfect that they did not seem to be acting at all. But of course they never experimented far from their own brilliant but limited range. One could never imagine them playing in Ibsen, Chekhov, Shakespeare, Sheridan, or Congreve. They might simply have strolled in for an hour or two for a little exercise as a change from sitting in their clubs. In a period when other actors took hours making-up their faces, whether as juveniles or heavily disguised character-men, their faces looked more natural than anyone else's on the stage. And yet I believe they might have been equally distinguished if they had ventured into more ambitious fields.

At the end of his career, when he was past eighty, Aynesworth played Lord Conyngham in the opening scene of Laurence Housman's *Victoria Regina*, and, partnered by my aunt, Mabel Terry-Lewis, whose distinction of bearing and diction were equal to his own, acted with a period style that put the rest of the cast to shame. And I remember meeting him once on the stone stairs at the back of the Coliseum where there was a gala matinée of *Drake*, dressed improbably as the Archbishop of Canterbury. In his robes and mitre, he looked magnificently authentic and not in the least ridiculous. But his dignified, witty approach to contemporary characters fitted his manner and personality to perfection and there were always new light comedies, however trivial, with parts in them to suit him. He was as solemnly humorous as the butler in Milne's *The Dover Road*, one thumb tucked slyly into a waistcoat pocket, as in playing the lovable monster Lord Porteous in Maugham's *The Circle*, fulminating as he lost his temper and his false teeth over the bridge table. How delightful he must have been when he created Algy in *The Importance of Being Earnest*. He had just the right kind of urbane flippancy, so hard to achieve for the young actors of today, especially in the second act – the Piccadilly dandy Bunburying in the country.

Sir George Alexander, of course, created the part of John Worthing in the original production. I have been told, however, that Wilde first intended the play for Hawtrey, and took it round to the theatre where he was acting at the time demanding a sum down immediately. Hawtrey, usually as hard-up and extravagant as Wilde himself, sent round to the box-office asking them to advance the money, but this they refused to do, on which Wilde went off to the St James's Theatre round the corner and sold the play to Alexander. Hawtrey had created the part of Lord Goring in Wilde's *An Ideal Husband* at the Haymarket some years before, and I have always been deeply shocked to read how he and Charles Brookfield – who played Goring's valet in the same production – had rounded up a number of the more sordid witnesses who appeared for Queensberry in the famous libel action. The two men gave a supper party together to celebrate Wilde's sentence in 1895, when, of course, the enormously successful first production of *The Importance* had to be so suddenly taken off.

Whether Hawtrey (as well as Brookfield) had always hated Wilde is not on record, but he would certainly have been ideal casting for the part of Worthing. No one could tell a lie on the stage with more superb conviction, and his scene of mourning for his lost brother would have been the very kind of thing he always did best. I was lucky enough to see him in a number of plays, *The Naughty Wife* with Gladys Cooper, a revival of Maugham's *Jack*

Straw, with Lottie Venne (a tiny, brilliant farceuse whom I also adored), and in *Ambrose Applejohn's Adventure* by Walter Hackett, in which he was enormously funny, wearing an eighteenth-century pirate costume (in some kind of dream or fantasy scene) and using comic oaths, swaggering about without the slightest appearance of knowing how absurd he was. In Maugham's First War light comedy, *Home and Beauty*, he played the husband of the feather-headed young wife (Gladys Cooper) who, imagining him killed in battle, has rashly married again. Hawtrey entered in a clumsy reach-me-down suit which was immediately funny on his large figure, and discovering a baby in the nurse's arms, suddenly realised what had happened in his absence and brought down the curtain (and the house) with the line, 'Hell, said the Duchess!' And I can see him now trying to cook a rationed meal on the kitchen range with the help of the second husband, exquisitely polite in his exchanges with the spinsterish professional co-respondent whom he has called in to arrange a belated divorce – Jean Cadell at her most acidly respectable.

A great gambler and *bon viveur* in private life, Hawtrey achieved the same airy effect of enjoyment and leisure when he acted, passing off an embarrassing situation, eating a stage meal, or galvanising undistinguished dialogue. In his perfor-mances, as with Aynesworth's, stylishness and ease were ap-parent in everything he did. Entrances, exits, and stage crosses never seemed planned or theatrical, they simply seemed to happen. Diction, phrasing, and timing had been studied, prac-tised, and then concealed, so that dialogue appeared to be completely spontaneous. Both players were solid British gentle-men, Londoners to their finger-tips. The moment they appeared on the stage one sank back comfortably in one's seat. The silk would never be creased, the wheels would revolve with infallible precision. What masters of their craft they were, and how perfectly they executed it!

Ronald Squire had often understudied Hawtrey and followed his methods to great effect. He used a very subtle throw-away technique, with his own particular distinction of personality and deadpan comedy timing. In *By Candle Light*, Lonsdale's *The Last of Mrs Cheyney*, and *On Approval*, he was the aristocratic *flâneur* or the perfect butler to his finger-tips, and in Maugham's *The Breadwinner* his rebellious stockbroker paterfamilias was equally delightful. But he also gave an unexpectedly skilful performance as the Doctor in *A Month in the Country*, with Valerie Taylor and Michael Redgrave, and would I am sure have been equally enchanting as Gaev in *The Cherry Orchard*, which he was rehearsing when the Second War broke out and the production (by Michel St Denis) had to be abandoned.

I once flew with him to Hollywood in 1952 when I was to act Cassius for MGM in *Julius Caesar*, and he was to play a supporting part in a film with Olivia de Havilland and Richard Burton at another studio. I was much embarrassed to find that, while he was greeted with scant ceremony, the red carpet was rolled out for me. I was delighted, however, to hear that, after two days' shooting, the crew working with him had become immediately aware of his unique talents and distinction, and treated him as an important star, though he always loved to pretend, as did many others of the du Maurier school, that the theatre was only a chore to be endured as a means of making money as opposed to the more pleasurable diversions of golf, the race course or the club.

A. E. Matthews outlived the other four players by several years, and was still appearing, both in film studios and in the theatre, when he was past ninety. As a young man he had been an attractive juvenile, playing in *Peter's Mother* with Marion Terry and in *Alice Sit By The Fire* with Ellen, and in America he created Aynesworth's part of Algy in *The Importance of Being Earnest*. I first saw him, during the First War, as the leading man in the famous *Peg O' My Heart*, Laurette Taylor's great success written by her husband J. Hartley Manners. She herself had left the cast after a few months, and Mary O'Farrell — afterwards famous as a radio actress — had now taken over the part of Peg, entering with a shaggy dog in her arms and a cardboard box for luggage. My eldest brother was in love with her at the time and took me in the pit one night to see the play. As Matthews entered he whispered,

'That is the oldest juvenile in London' (a remark which I remembered somewhat ruefully a few years ago when I was probably the oldest Joseph Surface on record). In later life, Matthews looked like a grumpy bloodhound, with mulberry cheeks and pale watery eyes. He appeared, both on and off the stage, in an amazing collection of Edwardian clothes, jodhpurs, hacking jackets, tweed suits with check patterns and narrow turned-up trousers, and squashed shapeless hats.

He learned his lines very sketchily (and improvised and gagged brilliantly when he forgot them) but he had a delightful cheeky nonchalance and a solid basis of technique which always made him a delight to watch. I directed him once in a play and we got on together very well at the rehearsals. Meeting him in the street some time afterwards I asked him where he was going. 'To the Garrick Club,' he replied, and then, quick as a flash, seeing by the look in my eye that I was not yet a member of that august fellowship, added, 'I like the lavatories there so much. They have handles at the sides that help you to pull yourself up!' *The Chiltern Hundreds*, in which he acted very late in his career was an enormous success. Matthews dozed one night in his dressing-room and fell off his chair on to the floor where he proceeded to continue his nap unperturbed. The callboy, finding him there, was terrified and rushed to the stage-manager crying, 'Mr Matthews is dead,' but before the understudy could be sent for the actor had woken up and strolled to his entrance as if nothing unusual had happened. Later he summoned the boy to his room and said to him, 'Next time you find me on the floor I suggest you tell them, "I *think* Mr Matthews is dead." '

He created quite a furore in the press when he staged a sit-down strike, with rugs, pillows, and a shooting-stick, outside his house in protest against a hideous new lamp-post that was to be erected there. The last time I saw him, at a supper-party, he arrived late as he was still acting in the theatre. He consumed a large supper, with a quantity of gin and several glasses of wine, and then, apparently perfectly sober, toddled off to appear in a location shot for a film to be taken at some suburban tube station at two o'clock in the morning.

Of these five comedians, Charles Hawtrey was undoubtedly the most brilliant. Both he and du Maurier were also skilled directors, both of men and women, though I think neither of them ever directed a classic play. But they were the undoubted masters of a school that achieved an enormously high standard during the first twenty years of the century, a standard founded, no doubt, on the productions of the Kendals and the Bancrofts before both couples retired (enormously rich and successful) in early middle age.

Hawtrey and du Maurier, despite their many years of prosperity, spent generously and lavishly, and needed to continue working to the end of their lives, unable to afford to leave the stage when they began to tire. The first successes of Noël Coward, in 1924, must have shaken their confidence considerably, much in the same way as my own acting generation was shaken by the new school of Angry Young Men in 1956. Coward himself had begun his stage career with Hawtrey, and always acknowledged gratefully what he learned from him. Du Maurier trained a number of brilliant players who were to gain important positions in the theatre after his death, but he was suspicious of young highbrows, and only became fond of Coward and Charles Laughton when he met them, in his last years, and was won over by their personal charm. I think he seldom cared to see other productions than his own, and was fearful of being displaced, not realising how enormously he was respected and admired by all the young players who were beginning to be successful in the theatre.

Chapter 28

Two Splendid Character Actresses

Ada King and Haidée Wright

Neither of these two players would have made a fortune by their looks, and neither was ever a great popular star in the commercial sense of the word, but both showed immense distinction in any part I ever saw them play.

Ada King

Ada King had created the part of Mrs Jones, the charwoman, in Galsworthy's play, *The Silver Box*, as a member of Miss Horniman's famous company in Manchester, and among her colleagues were Basil Dean (as stage manager as well as actor), Sybil Thorndike, and Lewis Casson. When I was on tour there in the 1940s I happened to notice a delightful photograph still on display in a pub window opposite the Theatre Royal, showing the whole company grouped together, and I thought of asking if I might buy it, but of course when I was in Manchester a year or two later the pub had disappeared for ever and the photograph as well.

Ada King was short and red-faced, with sandy hair, wearing gold-rimmed pince-nez on her large turned-up nose when she was not on the stage. During the early Twenties, Basil Dean engaged her for several of his productions at the St Martin's Theatre under his ReanDean management, and it was in *RUR*, the Robot play by the Czech brothers Capek, that I saw her for the first time. She played a housekeeper, and in one scene she impressed me greatly as she rushed across the stage crying out some Biblical-sounding speech of impending doom, as Leslie Banks, terrifyingly grotesque in a kind of spaceman's uniform and helmet, climbed in through the windows at the back of the stage. I next saw her in a comic part, an old biddy sitting on the steps of her slum house, in a play by Charles McEvoy, *The Likes of 'Er*. In this play she acted with Mary Clare and the young Hermione Baddeley, who made her first big success as a violent cockney child who smashed up the stage at the climax of the play, hurling china in all directions.

Ada King was as effective in costume as in modern dress. Her performance as Roxanne's duenna in Robert Loraine's production of *Cyrano de Bergerac* (presented by Cochran and decorated by Edmund Dulac, whose fairybook illustrations had meant so much to me when I was a boy) was a delicious thumbnail sketch. Wearing a jaunty little hat with a long feather, she might have stepped straight out of an etching by Callot, while in the Thorndike-Casson *Henry the Eighth* at the Old Empire, she was pure Holbein, inimitable as the Old Lady gossiping to Anne Boleyn. Pathos and broad comedy seemed to be equally within her range, and I admired her in *The Way Things Happen* by Clemence Dane at the Ambassador's Theatre, and in Noël Coward's *The Queen Was In The Parlour* at the St Martin's, a Ruritanian melodrama in which Madge Titheradge starred with Herbert Marshall, Lady Tree, and Francis Lister. In one scene Ada King, playing the secretary of the romantic Queen, got an enormous laugh as she tiptoed back into the throne-room she had just left and murmured, 'Oh, my umbrella.'

One day I instantly recognised her as I passed her in the street. She had on her gold pince-nez, and a little furpiece was round her neck, with a sad little fox's mask clasping it together and hanging down on to her chest, like the woman in one of Katherine Mansfield's short stories. I could not resist going up to her and thanking her for the pleasure her acting had always given me, and she seemed gratified but extremely shy. Some months afterwards, when Emlyn Williams and I were going into management to act in and direct together a play he had written, we were at a loss to cast the part of an eccentric Countess, and I suddenly thought of Ada King, who had not appeared on the stage for a considerable time. We wrote to her and sent her the script, asking her to come and see us as soon as she had read it, and she arrived punctually next day at the Queen's Theatre, where we met her in the foyer. She looked much the same as ever, still the pince-nez and the fur necklet and the odd old-fashioned clothes. She sat down with us, saying she was flattered to think she should be remembered by such young men, and that she liked the part we had suggested for her. 'But,' she added firmly, 'my memory is no longer as good as it once was, and I am afraid I could not dream of accepting an engagement nowadays unless I had several weeks beforehand to study and memorise my lines.' Then she gathered up her bag and her umbrella, shook hands with us both, and stepped briskly out into Shaftesbury Avenue. It was a most touching little interview. I never saw her again.

Haidée Wright

Haidée Wright was also in *The Way Things Happen*, and she had, I remember, a scene with Ada King in which, like the Lion and the Unicorn, each appeared to be fighting for the crown. If Ada King emerged the winner on this occasion it may have been either because her lines were better or because she was extremely funny. Also she was more real, or seemed to be so, though she had not the sheer power of Haidée Wright's taut theatrical temperament. A tiny figure – head erect, ramrod back, and flashing eyes – one could hardly conceive of anything less funny than the acting of Haidée Wright. Like Geneviève Ward (whom I once saw in *The Aristocrat* with George Alexander), she knew how to dominate the stage with absolute authority in what my father always described as The Grand Manner.

It was to her that I wrote my first fan letter to an actress when I was still a schoolboy, after seeing her in a revival of *Milestones*. I said in the letter that I had cried my eyes out, and signed it J. Gielgud. I was somewhat saddened to receive a gracious reply addressed to Miss J. Gielgud! The play, by Arnold Bennett and Edward Knoblock, is the drama of a family whose various members appear in the successive episodes at three separate periods in their lives. Haidée Wright was the spinster aunt, thwarted in early life through some passionate romantic attachment which had gone wrong. Half-way through the play she had a dramatic outburst, dressed in a Victorian bonnet and a dress with a bustle, and carrying a tiny folded parasol in the crook of her arm. In the last act she entered leaning on a cane, and later played her final scene crouched in a low chair before the fire, dressed in a long grey satin gown, with a shawl over her shoulders and a lace cap on her white hair.

She was very moving in the tiny part of the Abbess in the Convent scene of *Cyrano* (again in the same company as Ada King, though in this play they did not meet) and soon afterwards I sat in the gallery to watch her first-night triumph as Queen Elizabeth in Clemence Dane's ill-fated and unequal play *Will Shakespeare*. Her stature might have seemed more appropriate to Queen Victoria, but her performance immediately dismissed any such thought from one's mind. She moved with consummate dignity and grace, wearing her fine costumes superbly and delivering her speeches – the best in the play – in thrilling tones. She was to play Elizabeth again in *The Dark Lady of the Sonnets* some years later, and in Shaw's slight but witty sketch she drew a different portrait of the same woman, an admirable contrast of sly vanity and patriotic fervour.

Another great performance of hers, heartbreaking in its tragic intensity, was as the old nurse in Strindberg's *The Father* in which she had to put her master into a straitjacket, coaxing him with familiar words as if he were still a child.

She could make an enormous effect with a single line, as she did in *The Unknown*, a spiritualistic play by Somerset Maugham, which I was not lucky enough to see, when she cried out, 'Who is going to forgive God?' And in an undistinguished melodrama about Edmund Kean at Drury Lane, during a scene in the green room at the theatre, the double doors at the back of the stage were suddenly thrown open and 'Mrs Garrick' was announced. Haidée Wright, in a dark dress and simple bonnet entered, walking with an ebony stick, and moving down to H. A. Saintsbury, who was playing Kean, handed him a case which she was holding in her hand. As she opened it, she said very simply, 'Mr Kean, these are my husband's medals,' and the whole audience sat spellbound and tearful, although the episode was quite unconnected with the rest of the play.

With American audiences she was equally popular. The part of the old actress in *The Royal Family* (founded on the Barrymores by Kauffmann and Hart) was created in New York by Haidée Wright. In London the part was played by Marie Tempest, but I fancy that Haidée Wright's performance must have had a touch of the barnstormer which may have been broader and more colourful. Her voice, with its strange throbbing tremolo, became more mannered in her later years and it was easy to imitate her quavering tones. But I never liked to hear anyone make fun of her, and refused to go to see her in a stupid play, *The Aunt of England*, in which people said that she was beginning to caricature herself. When I came to know her personally I found that she suffered from poor health and a kind of persecution mania, complaining of being bullied by her directors and harassed by financial worries. 'Dear Haidée Wright,' said the witty Lady Tree, 'always so right, and never in her heyday.'

She told me once that her greatest youthful ambition had been to play Juliet, for which of course she never had the looks. In her earliest days in the theatre she had acted a boy's part in Wilson Barrett's famous religious melodrama, *The Sign of the Cross*, and learned to give blood-curdling screams from offstage as she was being tortured, and she was a painted lady of uncertain age in Forbes-Robertson's greatest commercial success, *The Passing of the Third Floor Back*, a wildly sentimental piece in which Christ, thinly concealed under the disguise of a character called 'The

Stranger', arrived to persuade the guests in a Bloomsbury lodging house to abjure their selfish ways.

She was, I suppose, somewhat old-fashioned in her acting by the time I saw her, and I must reluctantly admit that in two modern plays, *The Distaff Side* by John Van Drúten, and a drama adapted from the French called *No Man's Land* (in which she was a peasant mother forced to shoot her own son at the climax of the play) she did seem to be rather too blatantly stagey to be entirely convincing. Why was she never given the opportunity, I wonder, to play Volumnia, Queen Margaret or Hecuba? She would have been magnificent in such roles, for she needed tragedy – and how few tragedians, men or women, have we ever produced in the English theatre! – to display her emotional powers to the full. She had a great spirit in her little body, and the passionate intensity which she could always evoke, even with indifferent material, revealed an iron discipline and technique as striking in the actress as it was emotionally moving to the audience.

Chapter 29

Three Brilliant Eccentrics

Esmé Percy, Ernest Thesiger, and Robert Farquharson

They were all three very unusual in appearance for those days —
dandified, flamboyant, fond of wearing jewellery and unconven-
tional clothes. Thesiger was tall and angular, with a long turned-
up nose of a most unusual shape, Farquharson thickset and
slightly lame, with big pebble spectacles and reddish-gold hair
which appeared to be dyed, a face which looked as if it were
painted (and possibly was) and a congenital stammer which
disappeared when he was acting. Esmé Percy, on the other hand,
was short and plump, with a broken nose and only one eye,
disabilities which must have been horribly painful to his vanity,
but which he had learned to overcome by sheer force of
personality and charm. He lost his eye just before the Second
War, when he was attacked by a Great Dane he was stroking.
The accident upset him terribly and he even contemplated
suicide. But he always adored dogs and kept one with him to
the end, although he had twice been seriously mauled by them.
As a young man he had been a great beauty but I never heard him
bitter at growing old and losing his looks. He even took it in good
part, when, in *The Lady's Not For Burning*, in which he was
inimitably funny as the drunken tinker in the last act, his false eye
fell out on to the stage. We were all too dismayed to move, until
one of the young men in the cast, who was also a doctor,
managed to step forward and surreptitiously hand it back to him.
Meanwhile Esmé was heard to murmur, 'Don't step on it, for

God's sake. They're so expensive!' After this episode, I suggested he might wear a black patch which suited the part very well, and somewhat reluctantly he agreed to do so. His sweetness over the affair was very typical. Sorting out some old letters written to me at various times about my acting, I found several from him which were among the most generous I ever received from a fellow-player.

He delighted in the company of young people, and when we took *The Lady* to America his enthusiasm was enchanting. Though already an elderly man, he would seek out the most interesting places to visit, and get himself elected to several of the best clubs in Washington, Boston, and New York, to which he took me as his guest, and insisted on giving supper parties in Greenwich Village, at which all the youngsters sitting round him were fascinated by his stories and the amusing comments with which he embellished them.

His mother was French, and Esmé used to boast that he had been trained in Sarah Bernhardt's company, and that she had advised him to leave it because he was too much like her. He gave a wonderful lecture about her in which he imitated her voice to perfection.

His own vocal range was extraordinary. Once, during the war, broadcasting with me in a radio version of *Hamlet*, he acted three parts, the Ghost, the Player King, and Osric, using a different pitch and tone of course for each. He played a great deal of Shaw, and revelled in the elaborate speaking of Shavian prose, though he was also a somewhat inaccurate study and the prompter was apt to be a good deal in evidence during his performances. I saw him in *The Shewing-up of Blanco Posnet*, and as Dubedat in *The Doctor's Dilemma* with Gwen Ffrangcon Davies.

At the end of the First World War when he ran a theatre in Cologne for the British troops, he persuaded Mrs Patrick Campbell to come out and appear with him in *Pygmalion*, when she proceeded to behave in her usual unpredictable fashion. Throughout the first act she kept muttering to Higgins, 'Oh, do get on. Get on. You're so slow.' In the second, as he tried to follow her instructions, she whispered, 'Now you're gabbling, you know. You're much too fast.' And in the third, while he tremblingly awaited the final onslaught, she gazed down sadly at his suede shoes (considered a very unmanly fashion in those far-off days), and remarked, shaking her head sadly as she turned to him with her back towards the audience. 'Oh you're quite wrong. He's not that kind of man at all.'

Ernest Thesiger

Ernest Thesiger too, was a splendid Shavian actor. His famous performance as the Dauphin in the original production of *Saint Joan*, with Sybil Thorndike, was definitive – an astonishing mixture of Gothic fantasy, brilliant comedy and underlying pathos. He later made successes in two other Shaw plays, *Geneva* – in which he wore an eyeglass and looked like Austen Chamberlain – and as Charles the Second in *In Good King Charles's Golden Days*, just before the Second War. During the Twenties, his ghillie in Barrie's *Mary Rose* failed to convince me, though he boasted of having taken long walks to Battersea Park with a real Scottish peasant whom he had hired to teach him the correct accent. But I thought he should never play anything but upper-class characters, though perhaps he might have been amusing as Malvolio, since he could appear very overweening when he chose. He was often waspish and sometimes malicious (though less so as he grew older) but he was also very courageous. He had joined up as a private soldier in the First War, refusing to take a commission, and was very popular with the other men, who were greatly impressed to see him sitting in a trench among them, busily engaged in doing needlework. His hands were badly scarred by shrapnel wounds, but he managed them admirably on the stage and was very proud of his hobbies, painting and petit-point. He was fond of collecting antiques and bibelots. These he would exhibit on a shelf in his dressing-room and would sometimes sell them to members of the company or give them as presents to his friends. He loved hobnobbing with

Royalty, and liked to mention that Queen Mary and Princess Marie-Louise often showed a gracious interest in his work. He was thrifty about money and loved to sharpen his wit on that of his many witty contemporaries. He led the Men's Dress Reform League at one time, and championed shorts and more comfortable leisure clothes, swathing his neck in scarves fastened with jewelled pins long before they began to become a fashion. Somebody once asked him, 'What do you say when you meet Nijinsky?' 'Oh,' replied Earnest gravely, 'say? You don't say anything. You just give him a pearl.' It was said that he always wore a string of very good pearls round his own neck, and never took it off for fear that the loss of the warmth of his skin might spoil their quality. One night at the beginning of 1940 there was an air-raid warning at Oxford, where he happened to be acting in a new play, and was staying at the Randolph Hotel. All the guests were ordered to go down to the basement shelter. Ernest created somewhat of a sensation, vividly dressed in Russian high-necked pyjamas and a spectacular dressing-gown, and sat bolt upright in a corner with his spectacles on his nose and a piece of embroidery in his hands. After a while the assembled company began to doze and he knew he was no longer attracting such conspicuous interest. Suddenly he clutched his throat and cried, 'My God! My pearls! No, no, it's all right. I've got them on.'

He played the first Witch for me in *Macbeth* during 1942, and was very effective and uncanny in the part. He had always a brilliant talent for female impersonation. One of the best scenes in Noël Coward's first big Cochran Revue, *On With The Dance*, was a boarding house sketch in which Thesiger and Douglas Byng, as two old harridans, undressed as they made ready for bed. And I once saw him give an impersonation of Violet Vanbrugh, whose striking looks he managed to caricature most cleverly.

The last time he appeared in London we were together in an unsuccessful play, and I met him one day in the street shortly before we began rehearsing and said how glad I was that he had promised to undertake the part. 'I think it is a splendid play,' I said. 'Don't you?' 'I'm afraid I don't,' Earnest murmured darkly and went his way. I didn't dare to ask him why, in that case, he had agreed to accept the engagement, but during the short run he acted with his usual distinction and received quite an ovation from the audience at his entrance on the first night. But he was tiring fast, and I used to feel sad as I passed his open dressing-room door to see him lying on the sofa half asleep between his scenes. He was an extraordinary and rather touching character, an actor of unique imagination, with a most beautiful perfection of speech and period style.

Robert Farquharson

Robert Farquharson's real name was Robin de la Condamine, and he was reputed to be a rich amateur with a background of Italian nobility. He acted with Tree at His Majesty's and I was surprised to find his name, along with those of Granville-Barker and Courtenay Thorpe, in the cast list of the copyright performance of *Caesar and Cleopatra* given by Mrs Patrick Campbell in 1899, showing that he must have been touring with her at that time in some other play. I had often heard when I was a young man of his huge personal success as Herod in Wilde's *Salome*, given for a private performance, so when he came behind the scenes with a mutual friend after my extremely immature performance of Romeo to Gwen Ffrangcon Davies's Juliet (I was then only nineteen years old) I was extremely flattered to hear him say, 'You have taught me something about the part of Romeo I never knew before!' Unfortunately I boasted of the supposed compliment to the same mutual friend a few days later, and was shattered to be told, 'Robin said it was the first time he had ever realised that Romeo could be played as Juliet.'

It took a good many years for me to recover from this snub, and I was always slightly in awe of Farquharson whenever I happened to meet him. Once, standing in a crowded bus, he called out to me, peering through the heads and shoulders of the other passengers, 'I'm just off to see my d-d-darling d-d-dentist!' Though his acting was vivid and original, I always found it slightly out of key with the rest of the productions in which he played. In *Such Men Are Dangerous*, an adaptation by Ashley Dukes of a German play, he appeared as the mad Emperor Paul the First. I had acted in New York in the same play – then called *The Patriot* (with Lyn Harding, Leslie Faber and Madge Titheradge in the other leading parts) and it had failed completely and closed after only a few performances. But in London, given, as I thought, a much inferior production, with Isobel Elsom and Matheson Lang as the other two stars, the play achieved a considerable run. But Farquharson and Lang were reputed not to get on well together and I seemed to be aware of their disharmony, so that their performances, though individually effective enough, failed to satisfy me. Still, Farquharson was always much in demand for highly-coloured characters, and Lewis Casson and Sybil Thorndike engaged him to play Iachimo in their production of *Cymbeline* and also Count Cenci in Shelley's tragedy, which they were adventurous enough to present for special matinées.

In the early Thirties he appeared as Cardinal Wolsey, with Flora Robson as Queen Katharine and Charles Laughton as Henry the Eighth, under Tyrone Guthrie's direction, at Sadler's Wells and the Old Vic. In 1968, when I was acting the part of Wolsey myself at the Old Vic (with Edith Evans as Katharine and Harry Andrews as the King). I was walking along the Kings Road, Chelsea one fine morning when I suddenly saw Farquharson perilously riding a bicycle among the heavy traffic. I waved to him rather timidly and was greatly surprised when he lightly vaulted off the bicycle and wheeled it on to the pavement. 'How are you, J-J-Jack?' he cried (no one had called me Jack since I first went on the stage in 1921). 'All right,' I answered, rather self-consciously. 'You know I'm trying to play your part in *Henry the Eighth*.' 'Oh yes,' he said, 'I know. We both made the s-s-same mistake. We ought to have padded ourselves and made ourselves look enormously f-f-fat. When I played it the whole production was geared to show off s-s-some film actor or other,[1] and, when I came on, the director lowered all the lights and wheeled an enormous s-s-s-sideboard on to the stage which extinguished me entirely.' So saying he guided his bicycle off the pavement, sprang into the saddle, and, in his green tweed suit and brown boots, disappeared among the tangle of cars and buses and was lost to me for ever.

1 Charles Laughton

Chapter 30

Two Exquisite Comediennes

Dame Marie Tempest and Yvonne Arnaud

During the Twenties and Thirties there were perhaps half a dozen famous names prominently displayed in lights over the entrances of the theatres, though the plays might often prove to be of considerably less distinction than the players who adorned them. The fashionable little comedies of those days would often begin at half past eight or a quarter to nine, and, with two intervals, enlivened by a small and scratchy orchestra sawing away in the recesses of a tiny pit covered with imitation palm-leaves, the final curtain would often fall well before eleven o'clock. But the public seldom seemed to resent such scanty fare, especially when the names of Marie Tempest or Yvonne Arnaud twinkled in lights above the title of the play.

Both actresses were short and a little plump, but they were fascinating performers and played with inimitable inventiveness and style. With a wink here, a nod there, a giggle or a pout, absurd displays of temper or tears among the teacups, an expressive use of a tiny handkerchief, they could provoke or stifle laughter, point a line or repair a moment or two of emotional stress. Experts in phrasing and timing (both were trained musicians) they would take the stage like Millamant, 'sails spread, with a shoal of fools for tenders', the one with her short brisk steps and bristling with authority, the other bustling about with endearing liveliness and humour.

Dame Marie Tempest

My first two meetings with Marie Tempest were somewhat intimidating occasions. At a smart lunch party at which I had been introduced to her for the first time, she suddenly announced that the strap which held her shoes had become undone and I was dispatched to the host's bedroom to find a button-hook. Kneeling clumsily beneath the tablecloth I dug the implement fiercely into the curve of her instep and emerged covered with confusion. One afternoon, a few days later, as I was going round to see a member of her company, she suddenly appeared, veiled and cloaked, at the stage-door, impatient to get home for the evening rest which was such an important item in her inflexible routine. Hoping she might remember me, I crushed her tiny fingers brutally in what I hoped was a manly handshake, and thought I heard her mutter fiercely 'Blast you!' (though such an expression from such august lips seemed wildly improbable) as she plunged into her waiting car and was driven away.

When she created the part of the actress Judith Bliss in Noël Coward's *Hay Fever* in 1925 she immediately regained the enormous popularity which was to continue during the rest of her career. Her prestige had been somewhat in eclipse after she returned to London in 1922 from a world tour and, failing for several seasons to find a suitable vehicle for her talents, she was even forced to play some secondary parts. But she took these reverses in her stride and was soon rewarded with the play she needed. The young playgoers who saw her in *Hay Fever* for the first time marvelled at her grace and composure, her wit and technical skill, while her old admirers continued to praise her beautiful diction and phrasing (she had been trained as a singer by Garcia, and triumphed as a star in light opera during her early years), and to delight in the unfailing distinction with which she walked the stage or sat erect, with her tiny elegantly shod feet crossed in front of her, wearing beautifully cut clothes and (as Noël Coward used to say) one of her crisp little hats.

She was in Edwardian travelling dress when I saw her first,

acting in a revival of *Alice Sit By The Fire* — a sentimental Barrie play which hardly suited her better than it had suited Ellen Terry, for whom it was originally written — and on her first entrance she appeared in a hat which seemed to consist of an entire pheasant, with the beak standing guard above her turned-up nose. The audience applauded vigorously, and she came forward from the open doorway and smiled and bowed her acknowledgements to left and right before beginning her performance. This was the practice of all the great stars of that period — Mrs Patrick Campbell, Irene Vanbrugh, Marion Terry, Julia Neilson — though today we should certainly think such behaviour very odd. On the first night of one of Milne's light comedies the director had even thoughtfully provided a large tray (set out on a sideboard with several vases of artificial flowers) for Irene Vanbrugh to carry round the stage, putting them down on various tables, in order to cover the tremendous applause which greeted her first entrance.

Marie Tempest was very fond of clothes, and wore them to perfection. The short skirts of the Twenties suited her extremely well, and she used to wear pearl stud earrings, one black and one pink, if I remember rightly, and her hair was discreetly tinted to reddish gold. She was meticulous in the care of her stage dresses, always wore a light white cloak over her costume in passing from her dressing-room to the stage, and insisted that all the other ladies in the cast should do the same. Once made up and dressed, she never sat down in her dressing-room but stood on a white drugget, and so her dresses were always fresh and seldom had to be replaced during a long run. It was said that the new shoes ordered to go with each dress were sent straight to her own house, and she would bring old ones to wear in the play that were more comfortable. On one occasion a rather emotional young actress, who had been deservedly chidden for unpunctuality and carelessness during a performance, flung herself at Marie Tempest's feet to beg her pardon, but Dame Marie cut her short with a toss of her head and the brusque command, 'Get up! Get up! Have you no respect for your management's clothes?'

She was a martinet, severe and didactic even to her friends, and a demon of discipline in the theatre. But her bark was worse than her bite. Her marriage to Graham Browne was an ideal partnership, and they had already lived devotedly together for many years before they were able to be married. Browne was a good actor – better sometimes than he was given credit for, as he always stood back to give the limelight to his wife – and a charming, modest man. He died during the run of a play in which they were, as usual, acting together. On the morning of the funeral Marie Tempest ordered her car and came downstairs in a summer frock, having first made sure that all the flowers and wreaths which filled the hall should be cleared away. She spent the morning rehearsing with her husband's understudy and appeared as usual at the evening performance, disregarding the inevitable criticisms of those who were unkind enough to accuse her of indifference and thought she should have closed the theatre.

She never appeared in the classics, though Sheridan and Congreve would surely have suited her stylishness to perfection. My father always compared her favourably with Rejane and Mrs Kendal (both of whom he admired enormously, though I never saw either of them on the stage myself) but both of these actresses had been equally accomplished mistresses of pathos as well as comedy. Much as I revelled in Marie Tempest's comic gifts, I always found her less convincing in the few dramatic scenes I saw her play. However, those who were lucky enough to remember a stage version of *Vanity Fair*, in which she made a big dramatic success as Becky Sharp, maintained that it was the fault of the playwrights that she was not provided with better opportunities to show the more serious possibilities of which she was capable. Her acting in two fine death scenes, both in the Kauffman and Hart *Theatre Royal*, in which she appeared with Madge Titheradge and Laurence Olivier, and in *Little Catherine*, a Russian melodrama from the French of Alfred Savoir which ran for a very few weeks and was only remembered for her fine performance in it, showed her to great advantage in contrast to her usual run of frivolous parts. But in *The First Mrs Fraser*, by St John Ervine, I overheard a rival actress sitting near me murmuring (with some fairness), 'Oh, I can't be very pleased with Mary for that,' as the curtain fell on an emotional scene.

Her Stage Jubilee took place at Drury Lane Theatre in 1937, and I had the honour of being chosen to recite some verses introducing a great pageant of players marshalled by Tyrone Guthrie in her honour. Royalty was in a box, and Marie Tempest was carried on in a big gold chair, wearing a soft pink chiffon dress which floated round her as she made her faltering (but expert) little speech of thanks, curtseying first to the Queen and then to the audience, with her usual consummate grace. Then, after the curtain had finally fallen, she turned and bowed to us all, and, frail, tiny, but still immensely dignified, walked away to her dressing-room.

She continued acting for five years more with undiminished energy, both in London and on tour. She moved to a new flat and decorated her rooms, continued to buy bibelots, dinner services, presents, and to regulate her household with minute attention. From her dressing-room she would send for members of her company and lecture them individually, questioning them about their health, their love-affairs, and their behaviour generally, in private life as well as on the stage, and giving practical orders and advice. She was interested in every detail – in their diets, doctors, and dentists and the workings of their insides as well as in their acting.

I was with her when she created her last new role, the grandmother in Dodie Smith's *Dear Octopus*, produced on the eve of Munich. She behaved impeccably at rehearsals, though we were all a little afraid of her at first, but the young director, Glen Byam Shaw, handled her with perfect tact, and she listened to him obediently. She had some difficulty in learning her lines, and we were convinced that, except for her own part, she had never even read the play. 'Are those some of my children?' she would inquire doubtfully, as another of the large assembly of characters came forward to greet her. One day she sent us all away while she took a lesson to learn 'The Kerry Dances', two verses of which she was to sing in the nursery scene. When we returned some hours later she had mastered it with apparent ease, and sang it enchantingly at the cottage piano, her voice still sweet and true. In the last act I liked to watch her in the scene when she was folding napkins for a dinner party in the shape of water-lilies. She was supposed to have drunk a cocktail and was a little tipsy, throwing one of the napkins into the air and catching it just in time with a wicked chuckle.

We became great friends during the run. I would be invited every evening to go to her dressing-room during one of my waits. There, with the white drugget on the floor and the patience cards laid out (she always played patience every night when she arrived at the theatre) I would be given French bread and butter and a cup of coffee, served by her dresser-companion with impressive ceremony.

When we were in Newcastle to try out the play, Marie Tempest insisted on coming down every morning in the hotel, always beautifully dressed. Sometimes she wore a big shady straw hat with a gardenia decorating the brim, and she always turned back her white gloves over the wrists as she ate her lunch. Sometimes we would go for a short drive together before her afternoon rest, and it was amusing to watch her choosing a cock-lobster ('not a hen,' she stipulated firmly) after she had climbed in her high heels over a steep step into the little white-washed cottage where the woman who was selling the lobsters had her shop. The creatures were scuttling about all over the stone floor, but Marie Tempest went on calmly chattering to her and seemed to understand what she was saying, despite her very thick Northumbrian accent.

When the war broke out, *Dear Octopus* closed in London. Her Regent's Park flat was bombed, and she moved for a few weeks to Great Fosters, the hotel near Windsor, where I also happened to be staying for a few nights while I was making a film at Teddington. Here I would encounter her among the other residents, walking impatiently to and fro in the Great Hall during an air raid, impeccable as ever in a suit of blue slacks, and as a particularly loud explosion shook the walls I heard her remark to her companion, 'Quelle vie de dog!' (A rival actress was once heard to remark, 'Do you think Mary speaks what they call working French?')

My contract in *Dear Octopus* had expired and I left the play which had resumed its run after the blitz, but she continued acting in it for many months. Not long afterwards she was taken ill. I went to call on her with books and flowers, but after ten minutes' nervous conversation she caught me surreptitiously looking at my watch. 'It was sweet of you to come, my dear,' she said drily, 'but you think me rather an old bore really, don't you?' I felt deeply ashamed, for I loved and admired her very much. But a few days later, in October 1942, she was dead.

Yvonne Arnaud

Yvonne Arnaud, like Marie Tempest, was a brilliant musician. She had been something of a prodigy as a child pianist, playing in public with big orchestras abroad. She then achieved great success on the stage in London, where she sang and danced in *The Girl in the Taxi*. This I never saw, but I well remember the coloured poster which advertised it – a man and a girl getting into a cab from opposite sides, 'Mine I think! Mine I believe!' 'Ours I hope!' She was delightful as Mrs Pepys in James Bernard Fagan's play, *And So To Bed*, after she had been leading lady in the splendid Aldwych farces with Ralph Lynn, Tom Walls, and Mary Brough. In the first of these, *Tons of Money*, she scored with a wonderfully funny gag-line at every crisis, 'Aubrey, I've got an idea,' delivered in her inimitable broken English. In *By Candle Light*, an adaptation from the Viennese, she was a perfect foil for Leslie Faber and Ronald Squire, but this success was sadly interrupted by Faber's sudden and untimely death.

When I first acted in New York, in 1928, she was playing next door with the English company of *And So To Bed*, and Emlyn Williams, then a young man of twenty-two, was in the cast.

Emlyn and I would go off to speak-easies (knocking at the gratings of little doors and fearing we should be blinded by bath-tub gin) and Yvonne Arnaud was enchantingly kind to me whenever I was lucky enough to meet her.

Fifteen years later, during the Second War, when she had starred in a number of very slight comedies and carried most of them to success on her supremely capable shoulders, I remembered her performance as Mrs Pepys, and persuaded her to appear as Mrs Frail in a revival that I was planning of Congreve's *Love for Love*. There was some trouble over her costumes, for she could not wear the correctly tight corsets of the period as she had a weak chest and caught bronchitis and bad colds very easily. But she compromised with bones sewn into her bodices, and when, at the dress parade, she stepped on to the stage at the Opera House, Manchester (where we opened the play), spreading her fan and smoothing out her ample skirts, and remarked with a sly wink, 'Not so bad, do you think, for an old girl!' I was her devoted slave.

She would not sleep in London during air-raids but would send her dresser out to shop for her, rushing off to Waterloo as soon as the play was over laden with bags and parcels, and riding triumphantly in the guard's van of a train to reach her country house, coaxing smiles and friendly help from everyone on the way.

When she was ill for several weeks and unable to appear, the play suffered dreadfully without her. We all loved the way she shared our scenes with us, and the skill she could use to cover weaknesses if she was acting with a less accomplished performer than herself.

Her technique was as unfailing as her instinct. One might have supposed that the elaborate verbiage of Congreve would have proved something of a problem for her, with her French accent, after a lifetime of speaking modern colloquial dialogue, but she used her breathing and timing as cunningly as ever and rose to the challenge like a bird. She was the only leading actress I have ever known who looked forward to a first night with happy anticipation and really seemed to enjoy every single moment of it. She should of course have played in some of the Molière comedies and the farces of Feydeau. Best of all, what fun it would have been if one had ever been able to see her acting in a play with Marie Tempest!

Chapter 31

Three Remarkable Character Actors

Leslie Faber, Sir Cedric Hardwicke, Charles Laughton

Leslie Faber

Leslie Faber was a tall, distinguished-looking man with pale blue eyes and a long upper lip. His fair hair, worn rather long and streaked with grey when I knew him, was brushed in wings round either side of his head. His clothes were dark and conventional. Only his hats, worn at a jaunty angle, had curly brims[1] and betrayed the actor. He somewhat resembled the well-known portraits of George Washington, as the American critics were quick to notice when he went to act in New York. He was of Danish extraction, and a photograph of him still hangs in the Theatre Museum at the Fredericksburg Castle in Copenhagen. He was the first West End star to take notice of me and encourage my early efforts as an actor, and apart from that I was to grow deeply fond of him as a friend.

He was extremely successful in disguising himself and evolving clever make-ups. As a mysterious Count in a play called *In The Night* he peered from underneath a large top hat and was enveloped in a huge overcoat with a fur collar. As the Scottish police doctor (who turned out to be the criminal when they finally solved the mystery) in Edgar Wallace's *The Ringer*, he had a square bowler, a red nose, baggy trousers and shabby boots,

1 Though not as curly as the hats worn by Allan Aynesworth, which were always strikingly individual.

and sucked endless cigarettes, holding them, between puffs, in curled mittened fingers. But it was in *Jane Clegg*, a gloomy kitchen-sink drama by St John Ervine, that his acting first made a great impression on me, though I remember little of the play itself. His part was that of a drunken idle husband, nagging and bullying his long-suffering wife (Sybil Thorndike) and his crotchety old mother-in-law (Clare Greet, a fine old actress who had created Shaw's Rummy Mitchens in *Major Barbara* and the charwoman in *Outward Bound*). But he was splendid too in straight parts, and I greatly admired his performances in various melodramas – *Havoc, The Outsider, White Cargo, The Sign on the Door*, and Maugham's *The Letter*, in all of which he acted with power, sensitivity, and taste. But his greatest success proved ironically to be his last. He went into management with Ronald Squire, and they presented together a delightful comedy, *By Candle Light*, in which Leslie Faber as the Baron and Squire as his valet acted the two leading parts, with Yvonne Arnaud, at her enchanting best, as a *soubrette* maid. But Faber was working too hard, filming during the day as well as acting in the theatre every night, and he caught pneumonia after a week-end cruise on a boat he had just bought to celebrate the success of the play, and died after only a short illness.

He had always longed to succeed in romantic parts, but there was something austere in his personality which stood in his way. He could convey sensuality but not great warmth. His natural hauteur must have been effective when he played Jason to Sybil Thorndike's Medea, but apparently he failed when he played Shakespeare's Richard the Second for some special Sunday night performance. He must have invited me to watch a rehearsal, for I have a vivid recollection of him sitting in a big chair, dressed in a dark business suit, with a Homburg hat tilted over one eye for a crown, and an incongruous sceptre held in the crook of his arm, but I never saw him play the part, though he told me afterwards that he had failed to please himself in it. I found in him, as in many fine actors, a strange mixture of vanity, confidence, and self-dissatisfaction. He could be extremely generous, and was always enchantingly kind both to me and my brother Val (who was understudying and walking-on in *The Ringer* when he first met him) but he could also be narrow-minded, bitter and suspicious, and I think he felt he had never achieved the position to which his talents should have entitled him.

He wore period costume with ease, and was a fine Macduff in a very bad production of *Macbeth* in which the American star, James Hackett, appeared with Mrs Patrick Campbell. He would, I am sure, have been an ideal Joseph Surface, but I do not think he ever played the part. He was also a most talented director, and I was lucky enough to work under him on two occasions for special performances in the early Twenties. I was already secretly cherishing an ambition to direct a play myself, and watched with admiration the way in which Faber handled the authors and players under his control, making tactful but important adjustments in the texts, and illuminating the action by the way in which he arranged the entrances and exits and the disposition of the characters.

In the second of these Sunday productions he acted the leading part himself as well as directing the play, a romantic costume melodrama called *Huntersmoon* (adapted I think from the Danish) in which my second cousin, Phyllis Neilson-Terry, who had given me my first professional engagement in 1921, played the heroine, and I was cast as her cowardly husband. Faber's part was a kind of Sydney Carton character, secretly in love with the heroine for whom he sacrificed his life in the last act. He was modest enough to ask me what I thought of his performance, and I ventured to say that I thought he should take the stage more boldly and sweep the audience off their feet in the manner of my great-uncle Fred Terry, Phyllis's father. But he smiled sadly and said he only wished he could act like that.

In 1928 he went, with Lyn Harding and Madge Titheradge, to New York, to appear for Gilbert Miller in a German play, *The Patriot*, translated and adapted by Ashley Dukes. A young actor playing the Tsarevitch proved inadequate and Faber cabled suggesting me as a substitute. I sailed immediately and arrived in time for the dress-rehearsal, having learnt my short but effective part on board ship. But New York would have none of the play and we sadly returned to London after only ten days' run.

In the following year, Faber invited me to go with him to see the English production of the same play, re-named *Such Men Are Dangerous*, with Matheson Lang in the leading part. We both felt the later version to be inferior to the one in which we had appeared in America, but Lang was a great favourite in London, and achieved considerable personal success. He was a fine actor too, less subtle, to my mind, than Leslie, but with greater sex-appeal.

When Faber died, the obituary notices gave a long list of his successful appearances and praised his fine career, but I always felt that his somewhat cynical manner covered an unhappy personal life and a deep sense of disappointment even with the work he loved so well.

Sir Cedric Hardwicke

Cedric Hardwicke was not unlike Faber in some respects — the long upper lip and slightly sardonic reserve. He was somewhat forbidding in straight parts, but could be very endearing when he was able to disguise his appearance and create odd characters quite unlike himself. He was superb as Churdles Ash in *The Farmer's Wife* and in *Yellow Sands*, two Eden Philpotts comedies in which he scored enormous personal successes, and he was always good in Shaw — as the He-Ancient in *Back to Methuselah*, as Caesar (with Gwen Ffrangcon Davies as Cleopatra), as Shotover in *Heartbreak House* and Magnus in *The Apple Cart* with Edith Evans. He was the Gravedigger in the first modern-dress Shakespearean production, with Colin Keith-Johnson as the Prince (it was christened 'Hamlet in Plus Fours'), and of course I was greatly impressed by his performance as the hateful incestuous Father in *The Barretts of Wimpole Street*, again opposite Gwen Ffrangcon Davies. His manner in this part was very subtly sinister, the mouth drawn down at the edges in a hypocritical sneer, with pious looks to Heaven as he made Henrietta swear on the Bible or forced Elizabeth to drink the mug of porter, and the pouting of his sensual lips as he ordered the dog to be destroyed.[1]

His voice was rather dry and thick, but he used it with admirable effect in dialect and light comedy, though I think he did not have the range for tragic parts. A season with the Old Vic Company at the New Theatre, when he played Gaev to Edith Evans's Madame Ranevsky in *The Cherry Orchard*, and also Sir Toby Belch, with great success, was spoilt for him by an ill-fated production in which he was persuaded to appear as Faustus in Marlowe's tragedy. He had a long and distinguished career in films, both in England and California, but in his last years he seemed to lose heart and to break little fresh ground either in the cinema or the theatre.

We worked together only once, in Laurence Olivier's film of *Richard the Third*, and Ralph Richardson, one of his oldest and dearest friends, was also in the cast as Buckingham. Cedric Hardwicke seemed terribly depressed during our days together in the studio, and we all tried to cheer him up. 'I'm too old for this Shakespeare business,' he would say. I asked him what he was planning to do next, 'Oh,' he said, 'I have to go back to California to play Moses in *The Ten Commandments* and Louis the Eleventh in a musical of *If I were King*.' 'Good parts?' I asked. 'Oh Heaven knows,' said Hardwicke gloomily, 'my agent reads the scripts for me. I would never agree to do them if I had to choose them for myself.'

In his last success in the theatre he played, in New York, a Japanese gentleman in a light comedy, *The Majority of One*, starring with a well-known Jewish comedienne, Gertrude Berg. I was acting at a theatre nearby in *Much Ado About Nothing* with Margaret Leighton, and we would both dine with Cedric between performances on matinée days at Sardis, where he seemed happy to be with us and chattered delightfully on all sorts

---

1 I attempted the same role in a film remake of the play in 1958, and felt I was able to do little justice to the part.

of topics. But we both felt that he was lonely and only the shadow of his former self. Like Faber, he had unhappy marriages and lost most of the money he had made in his most successful years. He spent his last months living alone in a hotel and died quite soon afterwards. He always seemed to be vaguely surprised at having received his knighthood and the high esteem in which he was held in his profession. I always loved Hardwicke's own story of being knighted by George the Fifth, who was deaf, and the King, prompted by a whisper from his equerry, saying, 'Rise, Sir Samuel Pickwick.' I should have liked to have known him better and perhaps been able to show him more sympathy and encouragement at a time when he must have needed them so badly.

Charles Laughton

Cedric Hardwicke and Leslie Faber were both, I think, well aware of their physical and vocal limitations. Charles Laughton, who, despite a brilliantly versatile career, was more successful (first in the theatre and afterwards on the screen) than either of the other two, never achieved a real triumph in the parts he most longed to play. At the Old Vic he acted Macbeth with little success, insisted on choosing the part of Prospero rather than Caliban, in which he should have been superb, and never tackled Falstaff, a character for which in many ways he would surely have been ideally suited. Although he triumphed in Korda's film, *The Private Life of Henry the Eighth*, he made no great impact when he appeared as Shakespeare's Henry at Sadler's Wells and the Vic under Tyrone Guthrie, though his magnificent Angelo in *Measure for Measure*, and his Lopakhin in *The Cherry Orchard* during the same season, were unforgettably fine performances. His film creation of Captain Bligh in *Mutiny on the Bounty* was to bring him world-wide recognition[1], but his return to the theatre was less successful when, after a long absence, he appeared in Brecht's

1 He also played Moulton-Barrett in *The Barretts of Wimpole Street* with great success in the first film version of the play with Norma Shearer and Frederic March.

discovered in minor role

Galileo and as Undershaft in Shaw's *Major Barbara* (under Orson Welles's direction) in New York, and came back to appear at Stratford as Bottom and King Lear, and in London in a play called *Party*, when he was theatrical godfather to the young Albert Finney. He had become something of a legend in California, where he trained pupils, gave readings from the Bible and the classics, and took part in a famous reading of the 'Don Juan in Hell' scene from Shaw's *Man and Superman* with Cedric Hardwicke, Charles Boyer, and Agnes Moorehead. He was already ill before he returned to Los Angeles, where he died not long afterwards – in 1962.

In the early Twenties, when he suddenly burst on London, his talent and versatility had taken the town by storm. He arrived from Yorkshire with a scholarship to the RADA, where Alice Gachet, a very perceptive teacher, coached him in some scenes in French, and at once became convinced of his great potential talent. Soon afterwards he was engaged for a part in Molnar's *Liliom* with Fay Compton, but the play failed completely. (It was the second version to be done in London, and equally unsuccessful on both occasions, though in New York the Theatre Guild had one of its first successes with it, starring Joseph Schildkraut and Eva le Gallienne, and later the musical version *Carousel* was to be enormously popular.) At the Duke of York's Theatre in London it was directed by Komisarjevsky, who, with his usual perversity, undertook the production, although he thoroughly disapproved of the casting of Fay Compton and Ivor Novello in leading parts. Charles Laughton, however, in a minor role (the apache friend of the hero) scored an immediate personal triumph, and shortly afterwards was to be seen, again under Komisarjevsky's direction, at the Barnes Theatre, as Solyony, the sinister officer with the scent-bottle in *The Three Sisters*, and as Epihodov in *The Cherry Orchard*. He was soon in demand in the West End where he acted in a series of plays of many different kinds. He appeared as the beaming detective Poirot in Agatha Christie's *Alibi*, and gave a sensational melodramatic performance as a Chicago gangster (derived from Al Capone) in Edgar Wallace's *On The Spot*, and a fascinating study of a seedy murderer in *Payment Deferred* which he later repeated on the screen.

Laughton, as I knew him in those early days, was an amiable mixture of boyish gaiety, moodiness, and charm. When he was first married to Elsa Lanchester they had a tree-house in the country, where they used to spend weekends, and in London they lived in a charming flat in Gordon Square. I remember going to a party there. The big sitting-room had double doors, decorated with paintings of animals by the designer John Armstrong. Round the walls were low open bookshelves, lit from underneath, while on the glass shelves which ran along the top of them were specimen vases, filled with sprigs of blossom and single branches of foliage, which they had brought back from the country and arranged with exquisite taste.

I never knew Laughton very well. His acting did not rely on mimicry and I was greatly struck with the way in which, in spite of his own extraordinary individuality, he always seemed able to sink himself completely in a new part and find new colours and different ranges of voice for the characters he played. His old senator with the Southern accent in the film *Advise and Consent*, made very late in his career, was marvellously detailed and convincing.

His personality was as flexible as his appearance. He could be boyishly attractive or decadently sinister, with a menacing quality that might have made him a fine interpreter of Pinter. When he was cast as Worthing in *The Importance of Being Earnest* in his Old Vic Season, Tyrone Guthrie thought him so unpleasant that he took the part away from him and persuaded him to play Dr Chasuble, the oily rector, instead. But I always admired his courage in revealing the sensual side of his nature with such honesty and power. In the part of Angelo he trod the stage like an evil bat, with the billowing silk sleeves of his black gown flapping round him as he prowled up and down the stage, and he had immense drive, with a strong vein of poetic imagination which gave his performances colour and excitement. One might say, perhaps, that whereas Faber and Hardwicke were highly skilled

dyed-in-the-wool professionals, Laughton was an inspired amateur. The first two men were perfectionists, calculating their
acting to a nicety, and both struck me as being basically modest
men, dry, witty, cynical. Laughton was more of an exhibitionist.
His monsters were vicious with a kind of childlike *naiveté*
fascinating in its contradictions. In *Macbeth* he made a sensation
only in the Banquet Scene when confronted with the Ghost of
Banquo, while in *King Lear* his scene on Dover Cliff made the
greatest impression. He could not find and sustain the progression necessary to achieve either of these great parts to the full.
How often stage and screen, dividing the loyalties of talented
actors, have played havoc with their sense of direction and
crippled their potentialities in consequence.

Chapter 32

A Brilliant Leading Lady

Gertrude Lawrence

Theatre audiences (and women especially), are apt to waste a great deal of time speculating on the ages of the actresses they have come to see. At the opening of a new revue at Manchester, for instance, I once sat behind two ladies who wrangled over the possible ages of Beatrice Lillie and Madge Elliott all through the interval, as well as whispering continually during the performance on the same absorbing topic. But Gertrude Lawrence was such a mercurial creature that the question of her age never occurred to one when she was acting, and when she died at the peak of her career in September 1952, her public and fellow players on both sides of the Atlantic were equally shocked, and the lights outside the theatres both on Broadway and in London were lowered to pay tribute to her memory.

I was never lucky enough to act with her, but once when we were both appearing in New York (she with Noël Coward in *Tonight at 8.30* and I in *Hamlet*), we were asked to take part in a great Midnight Charity Ball at the Astor Hotel. Gertrude Lawrence, as 'Day', was led into the ballroom on a large white horse. It was a very broad-beamed animal and she gave one look at it and remarked, 'A few inches wider and I shan't be able to make the matinée tomorrow.' As 'Night', I bestrode an equally imposing black steed. Our costumes had been specially designed by James Reynolds, a distinguished theatre-artist of the day, and I wore a helmet with long plumes and imposing-looking boots, though I only discovered at the last moment that they had thin paper soles, making it very difficult for me to mount and dismount with reasonable dignity. We were conducted on horseback all round the room, glancing somewhat apprehensively at the slippery floor, and were greeted with polite applause. Our mounts were then led away, and we took our places on two thrones facing each other, where we sat gazing at the back of Gipsy Rose Lee as she performed an elegant striptease, while the Honourable Thelma Furness, as the 'Sun', wearing a golden crown with large spiky rays attached to it, surveyed the scene from above us on another throne. Once the ceremony was over however we were completely forgotten by everyone, and we found ourselves standing rather forlornly together at the bar, drinking gin and tonics with our dressers and glad to slip away immediately afterwards.

Noël Coward has always said that Gertrude Lawrence's instinct was so incredibly quick and true that she ought to be sent home after the first reading of a new play and not be allowed to reappear until the first performance. She was always full of mischief, and incredibly versatile and unpredictable, even in private life. She was declared bankrupt while she was trying out a play in Manchester, and her financial affairs were usually in disorder, but this did not deter her from gaily ordering her flat to be redecorated or commissioning a new Rolls-Royce to be specially built for her, though quite forgetting to pay some small outstanding laundry bill.

She had beautiful jewels and was excessively generous. Edward Molyneux had given her *carte blanche* on condition that he provided her with her entire wardrobe, yet she could not resist sneaking off and buying dresses from other houses. She was apt to assume a different role on different days – the great Star, the Mother figure, the Cockney guttersnipe (she was Eliza Doolittle in Shaw's play in New York, and I would have given much to have seen her play it) or the industrious, approachable actress – all presented with equal skill and charm.

Her greatest fault (according to Coward who had many rows

with her about it) was to embroider her performance after a few weeks with improvisations and funny business which sometimes spoiled the clean line of her otherwise brilliant readings. She had a seemingly effortless technique. Her features were irregular, with a strange blob of a nose, but she had beautiful eyes and hands, wore clothes like a dream, and danced with exquisite grace. Although her voice was never very good (she wobbled if she had to sustain a high note and was frequently out of tune) she had learned to use it with beguiling charm.

In 'Fallen Babies', a sketch in Charlot's Revue (produced at the same time as Coward's play *Fallen Angels*) she and Beatrice Lillie were wheeled on to the stage in a huge double pram, with large rubber teats in their mouths. I think they drank cocktails too and chattered together in racy terms. I have two other favourite memories of her in Coward's first revue *London Calling* – one a monologue (which she played sitting up in a large bed, talking on the telephone to various friends in different voices) in which she was supposed to be a chorus-girl called Poppy Baker – the other, 'Parisian Pierrot', a song which she made nostalgically romantic, lying on a sofa of coloured cushions wearing black pyjamas. In another revue she was a slinky Chinese girl singing 'Limehouse Blues'. She could be fashionable, pathetic or broadly comic in successive scenes, changing from one mood to another without the slightest appearance of effort. Her forgetful hostess in Coward's *Hands Across The Sea* was hilariously funny, but she was equally brilliant half-an-hour later as the slatternly wife in *Fumed Oak*, eating a disgusting-looking bloater and picking the fish bones from between her teeth.

It was in revue and musical comedy that she had her greatest triumphs, though she also carried some rather indifferent straight comedies to success, and acted once in a serious drama of John Van Druten's *Behold We Live*, in which she starred with Gerald du Maurier. She appeared in a number of films (*Rembrandt* with Charles Laughton was one of them) but she was, I imagine, not easy to photograph and the medium did not greatly suit her. I always wondered whether she might not have been fascinating as

Lady Teazle or as Beatrice, but she never ventured further than
Shaw in the classic field. I once spent an afternoon trying to
persuade her to play Sophy Fullgarney in a revival of Pinero's *The
Gay Lord Quex* but though she seemed interested I do not think she
ever found time to read the play. But I am happy to think I saw
her in *The King and I* in New York only a few months before her
death, waltzing enchantingly round the stage with Yul Brynner in
her billowing white satin crinoline. She was a fascinating enigmatic creature, and the gramophone records she left behind,
especially the famous scene with Coward in *Private Lives* and
another in which she sings some of her best songs, remain to
evoke something of her personality for the present generation as
well as for those of us who had the joy of seeing her on the stage.

Chapter 33

Two Forceful Actors

Robert Loraine and Claude Rains

Robert Loraine

Loraine was a powerful, expressive actor, broadshouldered and possessed of a noble presence and a deep resonant voice. I thought his Cyrano perfection, and was greatly moved by his performance of Strindberg's *The Father* at the Everyman Theatre in the Twenties. I had also seen him as the young Australian soldier in Barrie's *Mary Rose* with Fay Compton at the Haymarket, and as Mirabell, to the definitive Millamant of Edith Evans, in *The Way of the World* when Nigel Playfair presented it at the Lyric, Hammersmith, but thought him a little heavy-handed for young romantic parts.

Shaw, who had saved him from drowning once when they were on a bathing expedition together, was always fond of him, and he was a splendid Bluntschli in *Arms and The Man* (in a revival charmingly designed by Hugo Rumbold) and had achieved great success as John Tanner in *Man and Superman* both in England and America. I gather from various hints in letters that Shaw would have liked him to create the part of Higgins in the first production of *Pygmalion*, but that Mrs Campbell firmly put her foot down. From my own slight personal experience of his behaviour and a considerable knowledge of her, I can well imagine that they would have been uneasy partners.

In 1927 I was asked to appear as Cassio to Loraine's Othello, for a Sunday night and Monday matinée, by the Fellowship of Players, with Ernest Thesiger as Roderigo, Ion Swinley as Iago, Gertrude Elliott (Lady Forbes-Robertson, Sir Johnston's widow) as Emilia, and Elissa Landi as Desdemona. Nobody was paid, of course, but actors and actresses would gladly play for the Sunday Societies in those days as a change from long runs, or in the hope of strengthening their technique and reputations if they were out of work.

James Whale (who directed the original *Journey's End* for the Stage Society and was to win fame as a film director in Hollywood not long afterwards) was in charge of the rehearsals. He was an old friend of mine from my days in J. B. Fagan's repertory theatre at Oxford. Every morning we would begin to rehearse without Othello, but some twenty minutes later Loraine, in a mackintosh and bowler hat, would breeze into the theatre and, regardless of us all, proceed to deliver the speech to the Senate from the centre of the stage, forcing our little group to abandon our efforts and huddle bashfully in the wings.

He listened to no one, least of all to the director, but made an exception in the case of Lady Forbes-Robertson, for whose advice he would occasionally ask. She brought along her husband's prompt-book, and Loraine, finding the epilepsy scene had been cut by the great man in his production, decided immediately that he would not play it either. Elissa Landi tried to protest at his violence as he strangled her in the final scene, but he quickly silenced her with a pillow, remarking firmly, 'You mind your own business, my dear young lady, and I'll mind mine.'

At the dress-rehearsal he kept us all waiting for nearly an hour while he indulged in a violent tantrum over his wig and costume, and later sent strict instructions to us all to quit the stage after the first company curtain at the end of the play so that he might take a call alone. At the actual performance he shooed us off like chickens and drew himself up in his robes to acknowledge his reception. I could not help smiling, as I stood in the wings, to see that Swinley (always the most enchantingly modest of men both on and off the stage) had braved the lightning by refusing to budge, and as the curtain had already gone up, Loraine could only blink at him furiously and pretend that he was only too delighted to share the honours with him after all.

The temperament of Othello may have been partly to blame on this occasion for such autocratic behaviour, though I think he was always a man of violent feeling. Edith Evans, however, told me that she greatly enjoyed acting with him in *The Way of the World* (they were together in another play, *Tiger Cats*, a sensational melodrama of no great account), and said he had once given her an excellent piece of advice. Beside the little Hammersmith theatre was a narrow alley, and the ragamuffins of the neighbourhood, who had nothing better to do, would knock with sticks and boots on the iron shutter of the scene dock, rattling and banging while the performance was going on and ruining the concentration of the actors. Loraine, however, turned to Edith Evans and remarked, 'If something in the theatre is troublesome, and can possibly be put right, it is perfectly legitimate to make a fuss. Otherwise you had best ignore it and get on with your work.'

But he could hardly have been able to ignore the situation when, on the first night of his revival of *Cyrano* in London, the stage-hands, resenting his rude treatment of them at the dress rehearsals, deliberately omitted to fasten the cleats holding up the stage tree under which Cyrano has to sit in the final scene, and the poor actor was forced to hold up the sagging piece of scenery with his back and finish the play as best he could.

Claude Rains

He had been callboy at His Majesty's Theatre under Tree, but by the time I first met him in the Twenties he was already much in demand as a successful character actor. He lacked inches and wore lifts in his shoes to increase his height. Stocky but handsome, with broad shoulders and a mop of thick brown hair which he brushed over one eye, he wore beautifully cut double-breasted suits, starched shirts with pointed collars with big cuffs, and wide satin ties. He had piercing dark eyes and a beautiful throaty voice, though he had, like Marlene Dietrich, some trouble with the letter 'R'. Extremely attractive to women, he was divorced several times, and once appeared (as Falkland in *The Rivals*) with Beatrix Thomson, to whom he was then married, in a cast that included two of his former wives. Needless to say, all the girls in my class at the Royal Academy of Dramatic Art, where he was one of the best and most popular teachers, were hopelessly in love with him.

I found him enormously helpful and encouraging to work with and was always trying to copy him in my first years as an actor, until I decided to imitate Noël Coward instead. As I understudied them both at different times, I suppose this was only to be expected. Rains, as Dubedat in *The Doctor's Dilemma*, was just the romantic boyish figure that I hoped to be, whether in his blue painter's smock sketching the doctors, or in the death scene, when he was wheeled on to the stage wrapped in a purple dressing-jacket with a rug over his knees, and his hands, made-up very white, hanging down over the arms of his chair.

He acted another artist, a sculptor this time, dying of morphine addiction, in a melodrama *Daniel* adapted from the French of Louis Verneuil. The part had been originally written for Sarah Bernhardt, who was seen in it during her last season in London. Though her leg had been amputated and she was over seventy, she contrived to give a remarkable effect of youth, and even masculinity, as she lay dying on a studio couch covered with rugs.

In the English version, Rains was extremely effective (Edith Evans, playing a silly mother in a white wig, who was always taking pills in the first act, was also in the cast), and a year or two later I was actually engaged myself to appear in the same character in an adaptation of the story for the cinema. This was my first silent film, with Isobel Elsom, Henry Vibart, and Mary Rorke, and it was shot at Teddington in very hot weather. I tried to emote with suitable abandon, encouraged by music played 'live' on a violin and piano in the film studio and a director who urged me on to absurdly melodramatic heights. In 1921 Nigel Playfair engaged me for my first London appearance in *The Insect Play* by the brothers Capek. He was to direct it at the Regent Theatre, King's Cross (later a cinema but now pulled down), and of course I was thrilled to be engaged for a professional appearance while I was still in my last term as a student at the Academy. Claude Rains led the cast, acting three different parts with his usual versatility, and when the play failed after only a few weeks, Playfair kept me on to appear in John Drinkwater's *Robert E. Lee*. In this play I was to be Lee's aide-de-camp – a very small part in which I had to follow Felix Aylmer about the stage, gazing through my fieldglasses at a good many rows of empty seats through several weeks of a hot summer, and tripping over my sabre in a long military overcoat. I also understudied Rains, who was playing the juvenile lead in the play, and took over from him for a few performances, gaining some confidence from the ordeal, though I imagine I was merely giving a tentative copy of the way I thought he played the part.

But though he won praise from the critics for several years in plays of many different kinds, Rains never achieved a big star position in London. He finally left England to follow a long and distinguished career on Broadway and afterwards in Hollywood, where his first success was, somewhat ironically, as The Invisible Man. 'I can't eat my notices,' he once said to me rather sadly, just before he went away. He acted with striking virtuosity and the London stage suffered a great loss when he deserted it for ever.

Chapter 34

Remarkable Hostesses

Lady Colefax and Lady Cunard

I doubt if either of these two ladies would have been pleased to see their names bracketed together during their lifetime, for they were rivals in similar fields. Although they visited each other's houses and knew a great number of the same people, they were not at all similar in character. Some of their guests may have been inclined to be malicious at their expense, but few refused their invitations. Both of them collected lions, political, literary, and theatrical. Both had beautiful houses, and great taste in arranging their rooms, were experts at mixing the various celebrities they entertained, and adept at sparking off lively conversation.

Lady Colefax

It was said that Sibyl Colefax had founded her career as a successful hostess by inviting H. G. Wells and Bernard Shaw (on postcards) separately, declaring that each was eager to make the acquaintance of the other. At any rate she soon achieved a great reputation as a party-giver. She lived for many years at Argyll House, Chelsea, next door to another of her social rivals, Mrs Somerset Maugham, herself an energetic and talented hostess, destined in later years to compete with Lady Colefax as a professional decorator.

The panelled rooms at Argyll House were deliciously scented, and all the latest books – novels, biographies, and poetry – were heaped on a big low table in the drawing-room. There were always beautiful flowers, and the food and drink were perfect without the least display of ostentation. Lady Colefax was a small woman, though not as small as Lady Cunard, who resembled a brilliant canary, with curiously chiselled pale blue eyes. Both ladies were restless and indefatigable. Lady Colefax would think nothing of spending a week-end in the Isle of Wight, driving from Southampton next morning to lunch in Essex, before returning to London to give a party in the evening of the same day. Her car was always full of new books and stationery, so that she could keep abreast of her reading, or scrawl letters and postcards to her friends, both in England and America, in her almost illegible handwriting.

When she first invited me to supper at Argyll House I was naturally impressed to meet so many well-known people, most of whom I had only known before from their photographs in the newspapers. Gertrude Lawrence was to be an important guest on this occasion, but she was very late in arriving, and we sat down to supper without her. At last she was announced, and appeared in the doorway, looking as glamorous as she did on the stage. As she greeted Lady Colefax, she glanced round the supper table, and, seeing a young man seated on my left, sank to the ground in a deep curtsey, thinking him to be the Duke of Kent. Unfortunately he turned out to be a columnist from the *Daily Express*, but neither Lady Colefax or Miss Lawrence turned a hair. I only went once or twice to Argyll House, as Lady Colefax could no longer afford to live there, and she moved to Lord North Street, Westminster, just before the War, to a much smaller but equally charming house, and opened her decorating business in Brook Street with John Fowler as her partner. However she still continued to entertain with undiminished enthusiasm all through the war and for some years afterwards, when I grew to know her more intimately and became extremely fond of her. During the long painful illness which finally led to her death she stubbornly refused to give up her love of parties, and I found myself one day lunching in her dining room with a group of ten people, though she herself lay ill upstairs, and we were each of us asked to spend a few minutes with her before we left the house. She was faithfully looked after to the end by the two maids who had been with her for many years and ministered to her and to her guests with unfailing tact and sweetness. Only a few weeks before she died I had met her, walking with a stick and sadly bowed, in the beautiful White Garden at Sissinghurst Castle where she was staying with Harold Nicolson and his wife, Vita Sackville-West. We sat down to a big schoolroom tea before we left, with buns and cake and bread and butter – Nicolson (wearing a big straw hat with the brim turned down all round) at one end of the table, and his wife, in boots and breeches, presiding at the other with a large brown teapot in her hand.

Lady Cunard

Her real christian name was Maud, but she disliked it and was always known as Emerald, though I never heard people call her so to her face. She was American, but soon became an important figure in London, though she had hunted in Leicestershire when she first came to live in England with her rich husband, Bache Cunard. Her two most intimate and famous friends were George Moore and Sir Thomas Beecham. She was extremely intelligent, amusing, and elegant, as well as being forthright and eagerly inquisitive. She liked to refer to homosexuals as 'popinjays', and delighted to fling challenging remarks at her guests on every kind of topic as she sat at the head of her table. She had spent large sums of money as a patroness of opera and ballet seasons at Covent Garden and Drury Lane before the First War, and one always met musicians and dancers, as well as writers and politicians, at her parties. Until the Second War she lived in a large house in Grosvenor Square, but I only went there once or twice. She sold the house and went back to America, returning in 1944, when she established herself in a suite at the Dorchester Hotel, where she continued to live until her death, surrounded by her own beautiful impressionist pictures, books, and furniture. During this period I dined with her there a number of times, and often took her to the theatre, of which she was passionately fond, when I was not working myself. We would go by taxi through the blackout to the Chantecler Theatre near Gloucester Road, where Peter Brook was directing his first productions in London of Cocteau's *Infernal Machine* and Ibsen's *John Gabriel Borkman*, and I once spent an evening with her sitting on a very hard uncomfortable pew at a church off Regent Street, watching a semi-professional performance of *Everyman*. She slept very little and read voraciously, Greek and Latin classics and poetry as well as contemporary books. She was always punctual and had beautiful manners. Her coquetry had something of the eighteenth century about it, and she entered or left a room with a brisk authority that reminded me of Marie Tempest.

I cherish one of her best remarks, an example of what we used to refer to, in a vanishing age of class distinction, as 'tumbril talk'. It was at one of her supper-parties at the Dorchester. The waiter looked rather sulky at being kept up late, though it was only about half past nine. Lady Cunard had been, as usual, to the theatre, and had invited nine or ten people to join her afterwards. It was the time of the V-2s, which everybody pretended to ignore, though it was impossible not to notice their whining as they went over. It was remarkable how audiences (and actors too) refused to allow the noise to interfere with performances in the theatres. As we sat down Lady Cunard gave a glance round the table and called the Head waiter to her side. 'Where is the butter?' she demanded. 'Butter, my lady,' said the man. 'I'm afraid there is no butter.' 'No butter?' said Lady Cunard. 'One must have butter. What is the Merchant Navy doing?' At that moment a V-2 exploded on the other side of the park with a hideous crash, but Lady Cunard did not even appear to have heard it.

I should like to have been able to write something of two other distinguished patronesses of the Arts, but I can only claim a very slight acquaintance with either of them. After the First World

War, my eldest brother Lewis went back to Magdalen College, Oxford, invalided from the army. One of his greatest friends, from their earlier Eton days, was Aldous Huxley, whose successful novel *Crome Yellow* made such a great sensation when it was first published. One of the principal characters in this book was drawn from Lady Ottoline Morrell, who then lived at a house called Garsington, near Oxford, which my brother told me he had visited with Huxley. There Lady Ottoline held court with an imposing number of writers, painters, and poets whom she delighted to encourage. She also drove about the country in a yellow phaeton. In 1930 I was acting at Sadler's Wells in a repertoire of Shakespeare plays. Lilian Baylis had only just reopened the restored theatre, where we played alternate weeks with the Old Vic in Waterloo Road, but business at the Wells was very disappointing. A tall, distinguished, but eccentric-looking lady was always conspicuous at our Saturday matinées. One could hardly fail to notice her long nose and strange horselike face, and the large brown velvet hat that she wore, like a chocolate soufflé, as she sat conspicuously among the many rows of empty seats. One day I was flattered to receive a charming note from her inviting me to tea at her house in Gower Street. With some trepidation I accepted, and found several fascinating celebrities, including Lowes Dickinson and H. G. Wells. Lady Ottoline's house, with a fine portrait of her on the staircase by Augustus John, was as individual as her strange clothes and aristocratic bearing, and that single occasion on which I was her guest made a great impression on me.

Lady Oxford was another eccentric figure whom I met on one or two occasions. I had first noticed her at a private view of the Royal Academy Summer Exhibition, to which I used to be taken by my Father when I was quite a small boy. She was then still Mrs Asquith, whose outspoken and somewhat scandalous memoirs had created a furore. As I watched her rushing about the galleries, in a feathered hat, with her hooked nose and raucous voice, I thought she resembled some maliciously hovering raven. During the Second War she lived at the Savoy Hotel, where I would pass her sitting rather disconsolately in the Grill Room, and she came to a party one night at the Apollo Theatre to celebrate the success of one of Terence Rattigan's war plays, *Flare Path*, which had been directed by her son Anthony. Here I found her in a deserted corner of the bar (where the party was being held) hunched in a low basket chair, mournfully chattering of Henry Irving. But my favourite story (told me by Frederick Ashton) is of her standing defiantly in the hall at the reception given for some smart society wedding, muttering to the guests as they arrived, 'Don't go upstairs. The bride's hideous.'

Chapter 35

Music-Halls

I was never a great one for music-halls. I much preferred going to plays, and I never cared for animal acts, conjurors, ventriloquists, or clowns. Even the great Grock failed to amuse me, because he was always pretending to play the piano and never did. This trick with a musical instrument has never failed to irritate me, even with such brilliant virtuoso performers as Jack Benny and Victor Borge.

In the Twenties the 'Halls' were beginning to go downhill. The Tivoli closed in 1914, to be later re-built as a cinema. Already the Alhambra and the Empire, their famous promenades abolished, alternated variety bills with seasons of revue, ballet, and occasional straight plays and musical comedies. But the Chelsea Palace, the Palladium, The New Oxford, the Kilburn Empire, the Canterbury, and the Metropolitan in Edgware Road, still presented many of the great music-hall stars with a supporting programme of individual turns. The Hippodromes and Empires in the big provincial cities began to lose their audiences, and American bands and American star performers were hastily engaged to try to revive their popularity, as Danny Kaye and Judy Garland were to do so successfully twenty years later.

However I became a great follower of Paul Whiteman and his Band, and greatly admired Nora Bayes and Sophie Tucker when they first appeared in London. I would sometimes follow them from the Palladium to the Empire to see them twice in a single night, these double appearances being quite a usual tradition of

the music-hall from the old days. Though I was rather snobbish
and superior in my attitude, and inclined to scoff at the highbrow
critics, who wrote such clever articles maintaining that the great
variety stars were far finer artists than straight actors, I feel very
grateful now for the opportunities I had of enjoying many of the
most accomplished music-hall performers of the time.

I first saw Harry Tate (with Violet Loraine) in a London
Hippodrome revue, *Business as Usual*. The scene was the garden
of his house, 'The Nest, Tooting Bec', and I think 'Fortifying the
Home' was the name of the sketch. Later at the Coliseum, in
'Fishing', he gave a madly surrealist performance (involving the
idiotic fat son who always featured with him as well as a very old
man) and the sketch ended with a lot of property fish, of every
shape and size, whizzing about in the air on twanging fishing rods
as the curtain fell. Will Hay, with his recalcitrant schoolboy
class, was another favourite of mine, and the Boganny Brothers,
who did a riotous sketch involving pie-throwing. There were
usually some ambitious musical interludes in the respectable
Coliseum programmes, Mark Hambourg playing Liszt, and a
turn entitled 'Pattman and his Gigantic Organ', a title which
much appealed to my schoolboy sense of humour. 'Olga, Elga,
and Eli Hudson' used to give an extremely elegant presentation,
appearing in full evening dress in the smartest drawing-room
interior which the Coliseum could provide, with polar bear skin
rugs, brocaded sofas, and tasselled lampshades. In these imposing
surroundings they obliged by playing various instruments and
singing popular ballads.

George Robey was often to be seen in revues and pantomimes, but his solo turn at a music-hall was on the whole more
satisfactory, since he had the stage to himself and there was no
need for him to pretend to defer to a partner or to try to disguise
his unique personality with wigs, make-up, and characterisations.
Of course he had invented his own individual get-up – the
collarless long frock-coat, the big boots, and huge circular
painted eyebrows. Will Fyffe and G. S. Melvin, on the other
hand, excelled at mimicry and strange transformations of ap-

pearance, and I was never sure whether I would recognise them from one number to the next.

There were few funny women. Beatrice Lillie and Cicely Courtneidge had only just begun to appear as great clowns in the revues which were becoming so popular, and Gracie Fields was touring in a revue *Mr Tower of London* with her first husband, Archie Pitt, and had not yet taken the West End by storm. But there were a few clever women mimics – Marie Dainton, for instance, and later Elizabeth Pollock and Florence Desmond, rivalled the brilliant mimics Nelson Keys and Robert Hale. The Houston sisters were a fairly broad comedy act (boy and girl) but were also rather dainty. Once I was actually on the bill with them myself at the Coliseum, where there was often one sketch or scene from the straight theatre in the programme. I had been acting as Romeo to Gwen Ffrangcon Davies's Juliet at the Regent Theatre, King's Cross, and Oswald Stoll suddenly offered us quite a large salary to perform the Balcony Scene for two weeks at the Coliseum after the Regent run had ended. Preceding us in the bill was Teddy Brown, a giant who must have weighed at least twenty stone and played the xylophone with great dexterity. As the revolving stage began to turn in order to allow our setting (an elaborate old-fashioned painted Italian garden) to be wheeled into place, the house was still loudly demanding an encore from Teddy Brown. This, needless to say, did little to increase our confidence, and I was straining every muscle in my upturned neck as I yearned towards the balcony, where Juliet, her red Botticelli wig clashing unhappily with the painted pink marble canvas balustrade on which she leaned, murmured, 'Romeo, Romeo, Wherefore art thou Romeo?' We were neither of us very sorry when the curtain fell ten minutes later to very mild applause, though of course we laboured (twice nightly) to become gradually more accustomed to the acoustics of the enormous theatre – no microphones of course in those days – and we felt we had begun to be a little more relaxed by the end of the second week of our engagement. One of the stagehands even took the trouble to tell me at the last performance that in his opinion we had much improved.

It was rather lonely in my big dressing-room behind the scenes, but I used to enjoy standing in the wings to watch the other turns. One man, a German who appeared under the name of Robbins, gave a fascinating performance without speaking a single word. He made strange noises, whispering, humming, and squeaking to himself, changing his costume all the while in front of the audience. He was dressed in layers of strange garments which he kept changing one by one – waistcoats, gloves, braces, trousers, belts. Everything he wore seemed to melt away and turn into something else. And of course from the side I could enjoy watching the way he concealed the garments he had discarded and managed the trick strings and fastenings which he manipulated so cleverly. It must have been a tremendous business sorting everything out and dressing up again in the right order for the next performance. I made friends in those weeks with Billie and Renée Houston, whose turn used to follow our Balcony Scene, and the audience would roar as Billie greeted her sister in her strong Scots accent with, 'A thousand times good night.'

I was in front at the Coliseum more often than at any other Variety House, and saw many great stage players there in scenes and sketches, as well as a large number of variety stars such as Vesta Tilley, Albert Chevalier, and Little Tich. Seymour Hicks, Violet or Irene Vanbrugh would sometimes be at the top of the bill, to say nothing of Sarah Bernhardt ('Between tigers, not!' Bernhardt is said to have cabled to Stoll when he first approached her), and Ellen Terry best of all. Bernhardt, an old woman with one leg amputated, lay, half-covered with a cloak, at the foot of a tree as a wounded poilu in a patriotic one-act play, but I quite believed in her youthfulness and thrilled to the tones of the famous *voix d'or*, even though she was reciting words that I could not understand. And Ellen Terry, as Portia in the Trial scene, and as Mistress Page in some excerpts from the *Merry Wives*, enchanted me to the exclusion of everything else in the programme.

The turns at the Coliseum were always clearly announced by

large illuminated numbers which were shown in frames at either side of the proscenium. These numbers, though in strict order on the printed programmes, were apt to vary at different performances. The star turn was supposed always to appear just after the interval, but when Gwen and I gave our first performance we found we had been shifted to an earlier less important place. Only after a day or two did we discover that it was customary to send five pounds to the stage manager if we wished to hold the top position in which we were billed. During the one long interval the enormous act drop would be lowered, and when I was in front I delighted in spotting the celebrities painted in a great procession on it by Byam Shaw. I found I remembered the details of the curtain very well when I found the original painting for it in a bar at the Coliseum only the other day – Ellen Terry as Beatrice kissing a mittened hand, Bernhardt as L'Aiglon, Tree as Cardinal Wolsey, John Hare, the Vanbrughs, and at least fifty other stage celebrities and opera stars of the period as well.

I only went once to the Kilburn Empire, where I was lucky enough to see Marie Lloyd shortly before she died. She wore a smart Empire dress for her first appearance, with a high diamond-topped ebony stick and some kind of elaborate head-dress with aigrettes, and sang, 'If you show the boys just a little bit, it's the little bit the boys admire,' following this with her famous charwoman number about 'The old cock linnet'. With birdcage in hand, she sank on to a park bench with very wide slats, remarking, 'Oh dear, I'm nipped in the bud.'

I never went to the Empire in Leicester Square in the days when the famous promenade permitted the 'Pretty Ladies' (as Arnold Bennett called them) to circulate and ply for custom. But after the 1914 war I often went there to enjoy all kinds of different attractions. The Astaires – Fred and Adèle – in *Lady Be Good*; George Graves and Ethel Levey in *Watch Your Step*, the first revue I ever saw ('You've been eating peas – you're rattling' he said as he put his arm round her waist). In more serious contrast was the Casson-Thorndike production of Shakespeare's *Henry the Eighth* (in which I was surprised to see each character come before the curtain to take a call – Buckingham, Wolsey, Katharine – just after they had each played a death-scene) and a spectacular failure, *Arlequin*, with Godfrey Tearle, a romantic-fantasy with an elaborate Venetian setting.

The Alhambra, too, with its twin domes and imitation Moorish architecture ornamenting Leicester Square, had a chequered career from the time of its two great First Wartime revues, *The Bing Boys* and *The Bing Boys on Broadway*. Beatrice Lillie – in top hat and tails – made one of her first successes in London there in a revue, *5064 Gerrard*, and much later, just before the theatre was pulled down (to be rebuilt as the Odeon Cinema) a Shakespeare season was given there by Stanley Bell, including *Henry V* and *The Merchant of Venice*. But the Diaghilev seasons from 1919 till the early Twenties were the great events for me. My father took me to see *Boutique Fantasque* which had just been produced, with Massine and Lydia Lopokova and Karsavina still dancing with the company, while *Carnaval* and *Prince Igor* made up the rest of the programme. Later the company moved to the Coliseum where they would give one ballet at each variety performance, and there I fell madly in love with Tchernicheva, who appeared as the Swan Princess in *Children's Tale*, and *Thamar* with its towering scenery. I would play truant from school (Westminster), and Arnold Haskell and I would climb to the Coliseum gallery, both of us still in our top hats (rubbed to an effect of wet sealskin by constant use), and jam pot collars, to see *Petrushka, Les Matelots* with Lifar, *Le Train Bleu* with Dolin, and of course *Les Sylphides*. *The Good-Humoured Ladies* and *Les Biches, Cléopâtre* and *Schéhérazade*, thrilled me in another Ballet Season at the Princes Theatre (now the Shaftesbury) given with orchestral interludes by Arthur Bliss and Stravinsky.

In 1921 came the great all star revival of *The Sleeping Princess* at the Alhambra, and I was present on the opening night, entranced by the splendours of the Bakst décor and brilliant cast – Olga Spessiva as Aurora, Pierre Vladimiroff as the Prince, Idzikowsky, Woizikowsky, Sokolova, Tchernicheva, and Lopokova. But various disasters occurred to spoil the evening's complete success. The magic wood refused to grow, and Lopokova as the Lilac Fairy kept dancing to and fro along the front of the stage waving her wand, while ominous creakings and crackings almost drowned the orchestra. Pieces of wood emerged from the trap only to break off or keel over after they had risen only a few inches from the floor, and the curtain had to be lowered to cover the confusion, while in the final scene one of the dancers fell on her back during a *pas de deux*.

I went to see the ballet many times during its short run. In the end it lost a great deal of money, and Diaghilev was forced to take the company abroad and leave most of the scenery and dresses behind to cover some of his debt to Stoll, though he did manage to salvage the décor of the last act which he used for many years afterwards in *Aurora's Wedding*. The principals in the original Alhambra production varied on different nights, and I saw three other Auroras — Lopokova, Egorova, and Trefilova. Maria D'Albaicin, a beautiful Spaniard, was carried on in a sedan chair (ivory picked out with blue and green) to dance a slow solo variation with castanets, but *The Three Ivans* and *The Blue Bird* were perhaps the most popular items in the final Wedding scene. The King and Queen presided, though they did not dance, sitting on their thrones in tremendous grandeur, surrounded by negro attendants in magnificent Bakst uniforms. Years afterwards I was lucky enough to meet Stravinsky and his wife in New York, and recognised Mrs Stravinsky, to her great delight, as that impressive lady on the throne whose beauty I could never forget.

Chapter 36

Down to Earth

It is impossible, of course, to award points to an actor or an actress as one might to a horse or a dog, a runner or a cricketer – so many marks for technical ability, so many for timing, characterisation, emotional power. The subtleties of the actor's craft are almost impossible to dissect in general terms, and any attempts to examine them in detail, except with the experienced pen of a perceptive professional writer, are apt to prove tedious and unsatisfactory to the average reader. Had I not become an actor myself, I should never have wanted to spoil my enjoyment of the theatre as a member of the audience by speculating on who should receive the final credit for an outstanding performance – author, actor, or director.

In recent years it has sometimes been suggested that rehearsals of a new play should be open to students, members of the audience, and even to the dramatic critics. I believe I speak for most of my colleagues in thinking that such a procedure would be an intolerable intrusion on the privacy of our work. Already we are bound to complete our experiments by a fixed deadline, hoping to be prepared in time, but the first performance we give in public is often greatly inferior, as we ourselves well know, to the result we can achieve after playing before an audience for several weeks. Hence the modern custom of try-outs, sometimes for more than a month, before we venture to appear in London.

In my young days first nights in the West End were apt to be extremely ragged. The prompter's voice was often much in evidence, and lighting, scene changes, and stage management were apt to go astray. This atmosphere of uncertainty, though the audience might accept it as part of the excitement of launching a new production, must have played more than usual havoc with the nerves of the players, especially in the case of the star of the company who was frequently the manager and director as well.

One evening last summer I was invited to give a talk about the theatre to a group of American students who were on a visit to London, and when, at the end, I asked for questions, a young man with a beard jumped up and demanded in rather threatening tones, 'What, in your opinion, is a star?' I circumvented him with a fairly non-committal answer, remembering too late that, when Ralph Richardson and I had been interviewed on television in America by David Frost, he had asked the same question, and Ralph had swiftly countered him by answering firmly, 'Ethel Merman'.

Was I deceived as a schoolboy into thinking that every actor or actress whose name appeared in big type was a blazing genius? Though I was lucky enough to see three great actresses, Bernhardt, Duse, and Ellen Terry, the aura of devotion which surrounded them, even in their decline, impressed me so greatly that I could not possibly, at that early age, attempt to compare their qualities or discriminate between their respective talents. I could only marvel at their staying-power and the mystique which still clung to them to the very end of their long careers. In my youth I was a wonderfully appreciative member of the audience — less so, alas, today. Though of course I imagined myself to be highly critical I suppose I was easily taken in by claptrap. But I do remember saying once, 'I wish I could have a photograph of Edith Evans. I can never recognise her when she comes on to the stage. She always looks exactly like the part she is playing.' I suppose this was really the greatest compliment I could have paid her. Of course I developed my own personal likes and dislikes and was prepared to voice them in no uncertain terms, and I did begin to realise, even when I was quite young, the difficulty that must beset a critic if he finds the mannerisms of some popular player particularly irritating or unattractive.

What is it that makes the so-called 'star'? Energy, an athletic voice, a well-graced manner, certainty of execution, some unusually fascinating originality of temperament? Vitality, certainly, and the ability to convey an impression of beauty or ugliness as the part demands, as well, as authority and a sense of style.

The actor's loyalty to the playwright has certainly grown steadily during my time. In the early years of the century, Vedrenne and Barker had laboured to create good ensemble companies, and to accustom the public to appreciate them, rather than the bravura vehicles of the Victorian and Edwardian theatre, but their ventures were considered highbrow and were not really popular with the general public. Barker's Shakespeare productions at the Savoy between 1912–1914 were considered stunty and *avant-garde*, and even Shaw's plays (except for *Pygmalion* and *Arms And The Man*) appealed to a very limited audience for many years after they were written. I saw a number of them for the first time when they were given for short seasons after the Great War at the tiny Everyman Theatre in Hampstead, with splendid casts – Nicholas Hannen, Claude Rains, Edith Evans, and many other distinguished players. But *Saint Joan* was surely the first of Shaw's plays to be a big popular success.

The old-fashioned theatre manners died hard – the divisions of class in the audience, evening dress in stalls and boxes, latecomers banging down their seats, booing from the gallery if the patrons were disappointed, incidental music, receptions for the leading players, and curtain calls after every act. (Even up to 1933 this custom still prevailed and we took several bows after each act of *Richard of Bordeaux*.) Some of the artificial excitement generated by all this sense of occasion was, of course, undoubtedly genuine, and helped to make a visit to the theatre a treat for young people and a privileged hobby for the older enthusiasts, who looked upon it as a regular social event at which they were sure to meet their friends, and could discuss the play with them in the intervals, and at each other's dinner-parties in the weeks that followed.

Now of course everything is changed. Men sit in the stalls in their shirt-sleeves with their arms round the necks of their companions. They take off their shoes and put their feet up on the ledges of the boxes. But radio and television have made audiences, on the whole, more intelligently curious and better informed than they used to be, and they tend to be far more punctual as well as more attentive. If they are inclined to read newspapers while they are waiting for the play to start, their behaviour may be justified by the fact that there is now no overture to arouse their expectation, with the lights half-lowered and the footlights glowing, and the curtain is often already up when they come into the theatre. This is one of the strange new obsessions of modern directors that I have never been able to bring myself to like, though of course it is impossible to avoid it on an open stage, but in a proscenium theatre I find it a greatly disenchanting beginning to the evening.

Plays used to be clearly differentiated, and people knew just the kind of thing they wished to see, as well as the actual theatre where they were most likely to find it. Nowadays the agents and coach-parties direct their mass of patrons to a 'good show', promising either wholesome family fun or a few less savoury dishes for the stag-line. Melodrama is scarce, since it can be more richly effective in the cinema, but thrillers still seem to have their old appeal. The serious theatre, with its three main centres, The National, The Royal Shakespeare at the Aldwych, and the English Stage Company at the Court, supply rich and varied programmes, both classical and contemporary, and so do the smaller experimental houses in various parts of London. Television creates new stars. Some of them may have struggled without conspicuous success for many years in the theatre, now to be suddenly taken to the hearts of an enormous audience who might never otherwise have noticed them. The danger of this sudden success is, of course, in over-exposure, a danger equally great in the world of films and pop singing.

In the old days, the great music-hall comedians lived on the same material for their whole lives. Even if they had new songs written for them over the years, the tunes and lyrics were derived much in the same style as the old ones in which they had made their first successes. But television, radio, and piped music tend to exhaust every successful tune in a very few weeks for a larger audience than was ever imagined before, and the resulting competition has created a new world of agents and teams of gag-writers, with frenzied efforts to find new kinds of presentation, often of an abstract and surrealistic kind, which can quickly exhaust their ephemeral popularity.

How often in the past has the theatre been said to be in its last throes, yet it obstinately continues to survive. The changes that have transformed it in all its branches, especially in the last twenty years, have been violent and sudden, and it is often difficult for one to appreciate and understand them as one grows older. But I believe that there are as many great personalities today as there were in the theatre fifty years ago, and that on the whole they are considerably more generous and less selfish people than many of their predecessors used to be.

But the star of today has a very difficult task in trying to maintain some mystery, and yet to behave naturally and with some sort of modesty at the same time. The tape-recorder and the television camera can take his voice, his manner, and his face into millions of homes, while candid cameras and newshounds dog his private life when he is off the stage. But there is no doubt that the public still loves to worship actors and actresses whose personalities are strikingly original, sympathetic, or unusual, and the young adore their stage idols as well as their musical film favourites and pop singers, just as we all did in our own early theatre-going days so many years ago.

Chronological Table
of Parts and Productions

1921

Nov	Old Vic	*Henry V*	Herald

1922

Mar	Old Vic	*Peer Gynt*	Walk on
Mar	Old Vic	*King Lear*	Walk on
Apr	Old Vic	*Wat Tyler*	Walk on
Sept	Tour	*The Wheel*	Lieut. Manners, A.S.M. and understudy

1923

May	Regent	*The Insect Play*	White Butterfly
June	Regent	*Robert E. Lee*	Aide de Camp, understudy
Dec	Comedy	*Charley's Aunt*	Charley

1924

Jan	Oxford Playhouse	*Captain Brassbound's Conversion*	Johnson
Jan	Oxford Playhouse	*Love for Love*	Valentine
Feb	Oxford Playhouse	*Mr Pim Passes By*	Brian Strange
Feb	Oxford Playhouse	*She Stoops to Conquer*	Young Marlow
Feb	Oxford Playhouse	*Monna Vanna*	Prinzevalle
Feb	RADA Theatre	*Romeo and Juliet*	Paris
May	Regent	*Romeo and Juliet*	Romeo
Oct	RADA Players	*The Return Half*	John Sherry
Oct	Oxford Playhouse	*Candida*	Marchbanks
Oct	Oxford Playhouse	*Deirdre of the Sorrows*	Naisi
Nov	Oxford Playhouse	*A Collection will be Made*	Paul Roget
Nov	Oxford Playhouse	*Everybody's Husband*	A Domino

Nov	Oxford Playhouse	*The Cradle Song*	Antonio
Nov	Oxford Playhouse	*John Gabriel Borkman*	Erhart
Nov	Oxford Playhouse	*His Widow's Husband*	Zurita
Dec	Oxford Playhouse	*Madame Pepita*	Augusto
Dec	Film	*Who is the Man?*	Daniel

1925

Jan	Oxford Playhouse	*A Collection will be Made*	Paul Roget
Jan	Oxford Playhouse	*Smith*	Algernon
Jan	Oxford Playhouse	*The Cherry Orchard*	Trofimov
Feb	Royalty	*The Vortex*	Understudy
Mar	Comedy	*The Vortex*	Understudy; 16 and 17 Mar & 21 Apr Nicky Lancaster
Apr	RADA Players (special perf.)	*The Nature of the Evidence*	The lover
May	The Little	*The Vortex*	Understudy
May	Aldwych (special perf.)	*The Orphan*	Castalio
May	Lyric, Hammersmith	*The Cherry Orchard*	Trofimov
May	Royalty	*The Cherry Orchard*	Trofimov
June	The Little	*The Vortex*	Nicky Lancaster
Aug	Oxford Playhouse	*The Lady from the Sea*	A Stranger
Aug	Oxford Playhouse	*The Man with a Flower in his Mouth*	Title Part
Sept	Apollo (special perf.)	*Two Gentlemen of Verona*	Valentine
Oct	The Little	*The Seagull*	Konstantin
Oct	New, Oxford (special perf.)	*Dr Faustus*	Good Angel
Dec	Prince's (special perf.)	*L'Ecole des Cocottes*	Robert
Dec	The Little	*Gloriana*	Sir John Harington

1926

Jan	Savoy (matinées)	*The Tempest*	Ferdinand
Jan	RADA Players (special perf.)	*Sons and Fathers*	Richard Southern
Feb	Barnes Theatre	*Three Sisters*	Tuzenbach
Feb	Barnes Theatre	*Katerina*	Georg
June	Court	*Hamlet*	Rosencrantz
July	Garrick (special perf.)	*The Lady of the Camellias*	Armand
July	Court (300 Club)	*Confession*	Wilfred Marlay
Oct	New	*The Constant Nymph*	Lewis Dodd

1927

Apr	Apollo (special perf.)	*Othello*	Cassio
June	Strand (special perf.)	*The Great God Brown*	Dion Anthony
Aug	Tour	*The Constant Nymph*	Lewis Dodd

1928

Jan	Majestic, New York	*The Patriot*	The Tsarevich
Mar	Wyndham's (matinées)	*Ghosts*	Oswald
Apr	Arts	*Ghosts*	Oswald
June	Arts (matinées)	*Prejudice*	Jacob Slovak
June	Globe	*Holding out the Apple*	Dr Gerald Marlowe
Aug	Shaftesbury	*The Skull*	Captain Allenby
Oct	Court	*The Lady from Alfaqueque*	Felipe Rivas
Oct	Court	*Fortunato*	Alberto
Nov	Strand	*Out of the Sea*	John Martin

1929

Jan	Arts	*The Seagull*	Konstantin
Feb	Little	*Red Dust*	Fedor
	Film	*The Clue of the New Pin*	
Mar	Prince of Wales (special perf.)	*Hunter's Moon*	Paul de Tressailles
Apr	Palace (special perf.)	*Shall We Show the Ladies?*	Captain Jennings
Apr	Garrick	*The Lady with the Lamp*	Henry Tremayne
June	Arts	*Red Sunday*	Bronstein (Trotsky)
Sept	Old Vic	*Romeo and Juliet*	Romeo
Oct	Old Vic	*Merchant of Venice*	Antonio
Oct	Old Vic	*The Imaginary Invalid*	Cléante
Nov	Old Vic	*Richard II*	Richard II
Dec	Old Vic	*A Midsummer Night's Dream*	Oberon
Dec	Prince of Wales (special perf.)	*Duaumont: or the Return of the Soldier Ulysses*	Prologue

1930

Jan	Old Vic	*Julius Caesar*	Mark Antony
Feb	Old Vic	*As You Like It*	Orlando
Feb	Old Vic	*Androcles and the Lion*	The Emperor
Mar	Old Vic	*Macbeth*	Macbeth
Apr	Old Vic	*The Man with the Flower in his Mouth*	Title Part
Apr	Old Vic	*Hamlet*	Hamlet
June	Queen's	*Hamlet*	Hamlet
July	Lyric, Hammersmith	*Importance of Being Earnest*	John Worthing
Sept	Old Vic	*Henry IV, Part I*	Hotspur
Oct	Old Vic	*The Tempest*	Prospero
Oct	Old Vic	*The Jealous Wife*	Lord Trinket
Nov	Old Vic	*Antony and Cleopatra*	Antony

1931

Jan	Sadler's Wells	*Twelfth Night*	Malvolio
Feb	Old Vic	*Arms and the Man*	Sergius
Mar	Old Vic	*Much Ado about Nothing*	Benedick
Apr	Old Vic	*King Lear*	Lear
May	His Majesty's	*The Good Companions*	Inigo Jollifant
Nov	Arts (special perf.)	*Musical Chairs*	Joseph Schindler

1932

Feb	OUDS.	*Romeo and Juliet*	Director
Apr	Criterion	*Musical Chairs*	Joseph Schindler
May	Film	*Insult*	
June	Arts (special perf.)	*Richard of Bordeaux*	Richard (and director)
Sept	St Martin's	*Strange Orchestra*	Director
Oct	Film	*The Good Companions*	Inigo Jollifant
Dec	Old Vic	*Merchant of Venice*	Director

1933

Feb	New	*Richard of Bordeaux*	Richard (and director)
Sept	Wyndham's	*Sheppey*	Director

1934

Jan	Shaftesbury	*Spring, 1600*	Director
Apr	Tour	*Richard of Bordeaux*	
June	New	*Queen of Scots*	Director
July	Wyndham's	*The Maitlands*	Roger Maitland
Nov	New	*Hamlet*	Hamlet (and director)

1935

Apr	New	*The Old Ladies*	Director
Apr	Tour	*Hamlet*	
July	New	*Noah*	Noah
Oct	New	*Romeo and Juliet*	Mercutio (and director)
Nov	Film	*The Secret Agent*	
Nov	New	*Romeo and Juliet*	Romeo

1936

Feb	OUDS.	*Richard II*	Director
Apr	Tour	*Romeo and Juliet*	
May	New	*The Seagull*	Trigorin
Sept	Alexandra, Toronto	*Hamlet*	Hamlet
Oct	St James's, New York	*Hamlet*	Hamlet

1937

Feb	Tour	*Hamlet*	Hamlet
Apr	Tour	*He was Born Gay*	Mason, Producer
May	Queen's	*He was Born Gay*	Mason, Producer

Sept	Queen's	*Richard II*	Richard II (and director)
Nov	Queen's	*The School for Scandal*	Joseph Surface

1938

Jan	Queen's	*Three Sisters*	Vershinin
Apr	Queen's	*Merchant of Venice*	Shylock (and director)
May	Ambassador's	*Spring Meeting*	Director
Aug	Tour	*Dear Octopus*	Nicholas
Sept	Queen's	*Dear Octopus*	Nicholas

1939

Jan	Globe	*Importance of Being Earnest*	John Worthing (and director)
Apr	Globe (special perf.)	*Scandal in Assyria*	Director
May	Globe	*Rhondda Roundabout*	Director
June	Lyceum	*Hamlet*	Hamlet (and director)
July	Elsinore	*Hamlet*	Hamlet (and director)
Aug	Globe	*Importance of Being Earnest*	John Worthing (and director)
Sept	Tour	*Importance of Being Earnest*	John Worthing (and director)

1940

Jan	Globe	*Importance of Being Earnest*	John Worthing (and director)
Mar	Haymarket	*The Beggar's Opera*	Director
Apr	Old Vic	*King Lear*	Lear
May	Old Vic	*The Tempest*	Prospero
July	ENSA and Tour	*Fumed Oak*	Henry Crow
		Hard Luck Story	Old Actor
		Hands across the Sea	Peter Gilpin
Oct	Film	*The Prime Minister*	Disraeli

1941

Jan	Globe	*Dear Brutus*	Dearth (and director)
May	Tour	*Dear Brutus*	Dearth (and director)
Nov	Apollo	*Ducks and Drakes*	Director

1942

Jan	Tour	*Macbeth*	Macbeth (and director)
July	Piccadilly	*Macbeth*	
Oct	Phoenix	*Importance of Being Earnest*	John Worthing (and director)
Dec	Gibraltar	ENSA Tour	

1943

Jan	Haymarket	*Doctor's Dilemma*	Louis Dubedat

Mar	Tour	*Love for Love*	Valentine (and director)
Apr	Phoenix and Haymarket	*Love for Love*	Valentine (and director)
Oct	Westminster	*Landslide*	Director

1944

Jan	Apollo	*Cradle Song*	Director
May	Lyric	*Crisis in Heaven*	Director
June	Phoenix	*Last of Summer*	Director
July	Tour	*Hamlet*	Hamlet
Aug	Tour	*Love for Love*	Valentine (and director)
Sept	Tour	*The Circle*	Arnold Champion-Cheney
Oct	Haymarket	Repertoire Season (*Hamlet, Love for Love, The Circle*)	

1945

Jan	Haymarket	*A Midsummer Night's Dream*	Oberon
Apr	Haymarket	*Duchess of Malfi*	Ferdinand
Aug	Haymarket	*Lady Windermere's Fan*	Director
Oct	ENSA Tour of Far East	*Hamlet*	Hamlet (and director)
		Blithe Spirit	Charles

1946

Apr	Haymarket	*Importance of Being Earnest*	John Worthing (and director)
May	Tour	*Crime and Punishment*	Raskolnikoff
June	New and Globe	*Crime and Punishment*	Raskolnikòff

1947

Jan	Tour of Canada and US	*Importance of Being Earnest*	John Worthing (and director)
Mar	Royale Theatre, New York	*Importance of Being Earnest*	John Worthing (and director)
May	Tour of US	*Love for Love*	Valentine (and director)
Oct	National Theatre, N.Y.	*Medea*	Jason (and director)
Dec	National Theatre, N.Y.	*Crime and Punishment*	Raskolnikoff

1948

July	Haymarket	*The Glass Menagerie*	Director
Aug	Edinburgh Festival	*Medea*	Director
Sept	Globe	*Medea*	Director

Nov	Globe	*Return of the Prodigal*	Eustace
1949			
Feb	Haymarket	*The Heiress*	Director
Mar	Tour	*The Lady's not for Burning*	Thomas Mendip (and director)
Apr	Stratford	*Much Ado about Nothing*	Director
May	Globe	*The Lady's not for Burning*	Thomas Mendip (and director)
Sept	Apollo	*Treasure Hunt*	Director
1950			
Jan	Lyric, Hammersmith	*The Boy with a Cart Shall We Join the Ladies?*	Director
Mar	Stratford	*Measure for Measure*	Angelo
May	Stratford	*Julius Caesar*	Cassius
June	Stratford	*Much Ado about Nothing*	Benedick (and director)
July	Stratford	*King Lear*	Lear
1951			
Jan	Royale, N.Y.	*The Lady's not for Burning*	Thomas Mendip (and director)
June	Brighton	*The Winter's Tale*	Leontes
Aug	Edinburgh Festival	*The Winter's Tale*	Leontes
Sept	Phoenix	*The Winter's Tale*	Leontes
1952			
Jan	Phoenix	*Much Ado about Nothing*	Benedick (and director)
	Stratford	*Macbeth*	Director
Aug	Film	*Julius Caesar*	Cassius
Dec	Lyric, Hammersmith	*Richard II*	Director
1953			
Feb	Lyric, Hammersmith	*The Way of the World*	Mirabell (and director)
May	Lyric, Hammersmith	*Venice Preserv'd*	Jaffier (and director)
July	Bulawayo	*Richard II*	Richard II (and director)
Oct	Tour	*Richard II*	Richard II (and director)
Oct	Tour	*A Day by the Sea*	Julian Anson
Nov	Haymarket	*A Day by the Sea*	Julian Anson
Dec	Brighton	*Charley's Aunt*	Director
1954			
Feb	New	*Charley's Aunt*	Director
May	Lyric, Hammersmith	*The Cherry Orchard*	Director

1955

Apr	Stratford	*Twelfth Night*	Director
June	Brighton	*King Lear*	Lear
June	European Tour	*King Lear*	Lear
July	Palace	*Much Ado about Nothing*	Benedick (and director)
July	Palace	*King Lear*	Lear
Aug	Film	*Round the World in Eighty Days*	Foster
Sept	European Tour	*King Lear and Much Ado*	
Dec	Film	*Richard III*	Clarence

1956

Apr	Haymarket	*The Chalk Garden*	Director
	Film	*The Barretts of Wimpole Street*	Mr Barrett
Sept	Tour	*Nude with Violin*	Sebastian (and director)
Nov	Globe	*Nude with Violin*	Sebastian (and co-director)
	Film	*St Joan*	Warwick

1957

June	Covent Garden	*The Trojans*	Director
Aug	Stratford	*The Tempest*	Prospero
Sept	Edinburgh Festival	*The Ages of Man*	
Sept	Tour	*The Ages of Man*	
Dec	Drury Lane	*The Tempest*	Prospero

1958

Jan	Brighton	*The Potting Shed*	James Callifer
Feb	Globe	*The Potting Shed*	James Callifer
Apr	Globe	*Variation on a Theme*	Director
May	Old Vic	*Henry VIII*	Wolsey
June	Cambridge	*Five Finger Exercise*	Director
Sept	Tour of Canada and US	*The Ages of Man*	
Dec	46th Street Theatre, N.Y.	*The Ages of Man*	

1959

Mar	TV	*A Day by the Sea*	Julian Anson
Apr	TV	*The Browning Version*	Andrew Crocker Harris
May	Tour	*The Complaisant Lover*	Director
June	Globe	*The Complaisant Lover*	
July	Queen's	*The Ages of Man*	
Sept	US Tour	*Much Ado about*	Director

Dec	Music Box, New York	*Five Finger Exercise*	Director

1960

Sept	Phoenix	*The Last Joke*	Prince Ferdinand Cavanati

1961

Feb	Covent Garden	*A Midsummer Night's Dream*	Director
Mar	ANTA Theatre, New York	*Big Fish, Little Fish*	Director
June	Globe	*Dazzling Prospect*	Director
Oct	Stratford	*Othello*	Othello
Dec	Aldwych	*The Cherry Orchard*	Gaev

1962

Apr	Haymarket	*The School for Scandal*	Director
Oct	Haymarket	*The School for Scandal*	Joseph Surface (and director)
Dec	Majestic, New York	*The School for Scandal*	Joseph Surface (and director)

1963

Jan	Majestic, New York	*The Ages of Man*	
June	Tour	*The Ides of March*	Caesar (and co-director)
Aug	Haymarket	*The Ides of March*	Caesar (and co-director)
Aug	TV	*The Rehearsal*	The Count
Sept	Film	*Becket*	Louis VII

1964

Apr	Lunt-Fontanne, New York	*Hamlet*	Director
May	World Tour	*The Ages of Man*	
Aug	Film	*The Loved One*	Sir Francis Hinsley
Oct	Film	*Chimes at Midnight*	Henry IV
Dec	Billy Rose, New York	*Tiny Alice*	Julian

1965

Aug	Tour	*Ivanov*	Ivanov (and director)
Sept	Phoenix	*Ivanov*	Ivanov (and director)

1966

Mar	US Tour	*Ivanov*	Ivanov (and director)
May	Shubert Theatre, N.Y.	*Ivanov*	Ivanov (and director)
July	US TV	*The Love Song of Barney Kempinski*	
Aug	TV	*Alice in Wonderland*	Mock Turtle
Aug	TV	*The Mayfly and the Frog*	Gabriel Kantara

1967

Jan	US Tour	*The Ages of Man*	
Feb	Film	*Assignment to Kill*	
Mar	TV	*From Chekhov with Love*	Chekhov
Apr	Film	*Mr Sebastian*	Head of British Intelligence
Apr	Film	*The Charge of the Light Brigade*	Lord Raglan
Oct	Tour	*Half Way Up The Tree*	Director
Nov	Queen's	*Half Way Up The Tree*	Director
Nov	Old Vic (NT)	*Tartuffe*	Orgon

1968

Jan	Film	*The Shoes of the Fisherman*	The Pope
Feb	TV	*St Joan*	Inquisitor
Mar	Old Vic (NT)	*Oedipus*	Oedipus
Apr	Film	*Oh! What a Lovely War*	Count Berchtold
Aug	Coliseum	*Don Giovanni*	Director
Oct	Apollo	*40 Years On*	Headmaster

1969

Apr	TV	*In Good King Charles's Golden Days*	King Charles
Apr	TV	*Conversation at Night*	The Writer
June	Film	*Julius Caesar*	Caesar
Oct	Film	*Eagle in a Cage*	Lord Sissal

1970

Jan	Lyric	*The Battle of Shrivings*	Sir Gideon Petrie
Apr	TV	*Hassan*	The Caliph
May	TV	*Hamlet*	Ghost
June	Royal Court	*Home*	Harry
Nov	Morosco, New York	*Home*	Harry

1971

| July | Chichester | *Caesar and Cleopatra* | Caesar |

1972

Mar	Royal Court	*Veterans*	Sir Geoffrey Kendle
Mar	Film	*Lost Horizon*	Chang
Aug	Queen's	*Private Lives*	Director

1973

July	Albery	*The Constant Wife*	Director
Sept	Film	*Eleven Harrowhouse*	Meecham
Oct	TV	*Edward VII*	Disraeli

1974

Jan	Film	*Gold*	Farrell
Mar	Old Vic (NT)	*The Tempest*	Prospero
Apr	Film	*Murder on the Orient Express*	Beddoes
July	Film	*The Life of Galileo*	Cardinal
Aug	Royal Court	*Bingo*	Shakespeare
Sept	US	*Private Lives*	Director
Nov	Royal, York	*Paradise Lost*	Milton
Dec	US	*The Constant Wife*	Director

1975

June	Albery	*The Gay Lord Quex*	Director
July	Old Vic (NT)	*No Man's Land*	Spooner
Oct	Film	*Aces High*	Headmaster

1976

Jan	Film	*Caesar and Cleopatra*	Caesar
Apr	National Theatre (Lyttelton)	*No Man's Land*	Spooner
Apr	Film	*Joseph Andrews*	Doctor
May	Film	*Providence*	Clive
July	Film	*A Portrait of the Artist as a Young Man*	Preacher
Aug	Film	*Caligula*	Nerva
Nov	Longacre, New York	*No Man's Land*	Spooner

1977

Mar	National Theatre (Oliver)	*Julius Caesar*	Caesar
Apr	National Theatre (Olivier)	*Volpone*	Sir Politic Would-Be
Nov	TV	*No Man's Land*	Spooner
Nov	National Theatre (Cottesloe)	*Half-Life*	Sir Noel Cunliffe
Dec	BBC Radio	*Romeo and Juliet*	Chorus

1978

Jan	TV	*Richard II*	John of Gaunt
Feb	TV	*The Cherry Orchard*	Gaev
Mar	Duke of York's	*Half-Life*	Sir Noel Cunliffe
June	Film	*Les Misérables*	Valjean's father
Sept	TV	*The Dame of Sark*	Butler
Sept	Records	*The Ages of Man*	

1979

May	Film	*The Conductor*	Title role
May	Film	*Omar Mukhtar*	Sheikh
June	Film	*The Human Factor*	Brigadier Tomlinson

Sept	Film	*The Elephant Man*	Carr Gomm
Oct	TV	*The Parson's Pleasure*	Clergyman
Dec	Film	*Sphinx*	Abdu

1980

Feb	TV	*Brideshead Revisited*	Edward Ryder
	Film	*The Formula*	Dr Esau
Apr	Film	*Chariots of Fire*	Master of Trinity
May	Film	*Priest of Love*	Herbert G. Muskett
June	Film	*Arthur*	Hobson
Sept	TV	*Seven Dials Mystery*	Marquis of Caterham

1981

Jan	Film	*Wagner*	Counsellor to King Ludwig
Apr	Film	*Marco Polo*	Doge
July	TV	*The Critic*	Lord Burleigh
Oct	Film	*Hunchback of Notre Dame*	Torturer
Nov	Film	*Inside the Third Reich*	Speer's Father

1982

Mar	Film	*Buddenbrooks*	Narrator
July	Film	*The Wicked Lady*	Hogarth
July	Film	*The Vatican Pimpernel*	Pope Pacelli
Aug	Film	*Invitation to a Wedding*	Texan Evangelist
Nov	Film	*Scandalous*	Uncle Willie

1983

Apr	TV	*The Master of Ballantrae*	Lord Dumsdeer
Sept	Film	*The Shooting Party*	Cardew
	TV	*Six Centuries of Verse*	

1984	Film	*Leave All Fair*	John Middleton Murry
	Film	*Plenty*	Leonard Darwin
	TV	*Romance on the Orient Express*	Charles Woodward

1986	TV	*War and Remembrance*	Aaron Jastrow
	BBC Radio	*Gordon the Escapist*	
	TV	*Quartermain's Terms*	Eddie Loomis
	TV	*The Canterville Ghost*	Sir Simon du Canterville
	Film	*The Whistle Blower*	Sir Adrian Chapple
	Film	*Barbablú Barbablú*	
	TV	*Quartermaine's Terms*	Eddie

1988	Apollo	*The Best of Friends*	Sir Sydney Cockerell
	TV	*Man for All Seasons*	Cardinal Wolsey

	Film	*Arthur 2: On the Rocks*	Hobson
	Film	*Appointment with Death*	Colonel Carbury
1989	TV	*Dante: The Infernal Cantos I–VIII*	Virgil
	TV	*Getting it Right*	Sir Gordon Munday
	TV	*War and Remembrance*	Aaron Jastrow
	TV	*Summer's Lease*	Haverford Downs
1990	Film	*Strike it Rich*	Herbert Dreuther
1991	TV	*Walk through Prospero's Library*	Prospero
	TV	*The Strauss Dynasty*	Dreschler
	Film	*Prospero's Books*	Prospero
1992	Film	*Swan Song*	Svetlovidov
	Film	*Shining Through*	Konrad Friedrichs/ Sunflower
1994	TV	*Scarlett*	Pierre Robillard
1995	Film	*First Knight*	Oswald
	Film	*Haunted*	Doctor Doyle
1996	TV	*Gulliver's Travels*	Professor of Sunlight
	Film	*Dragonheart*	Voice of King Arthur
	Film	*Looking for Richard*	Himself
	Film	*Shine*	Cecil Parkes
	Film	*The Leopard Son*	Voice of the narrator
	Film	*Portrait of a Lady*	Mr Touchett
	Film	*Hamlet (long version)*	Priam
1997	TV	*A Dance to the Music of Time*	St John Clarke
1998	Film	*The Tichborne Claimant*	Cockburn
	TV	*Merlin*	King Constant
	Film	*Quest for Camelot*	Voice of Merlin
	Film	*Elizabeth*	Pope Paul IV

Index